SECRETS

SISSELA BOK

SECRETS

On the Ethics of Concealment and Revelation

PANTHEON BOOKS

New York

Library of Congress Cataloging in Publication Data
Bok, Sissela.
Secrets: on the ethics of concealment and revelation.
Includes index.
1. Secrecy--Moral and ethical aspects.
I. Title.
BJ1429.5.B64 1983   177   82-47891
ISBN 0-394-51581-1

Since the copyright page cannot accommodate all permissions
acknowledgments, they appear on the following pages.

Book design by Camilla Filancia
Manufactured in the United States of America
First Edition

PERMISSIONS ACKNOWLEDGMENTS

Grateful acknowledgment is made to the following for permission to reprint previously published material:

American Association for the Advancement of Science: Excerpt from "The Human Study of Human Beings" by Margaret Mead, from *Science*, vol. 133 (January 20, 1961). Copyright © 1961 by the American Association for the Advancement of Science. Reprinted by permission of the American Association for the Advancement of Science.

American Bar Association: For permission to adapt material from "The Sound of Professional Suicide" by Louis Clark, from *Barrister Magazine*, vol. 5, (Summer 1978), published by the Young Lawyers Division of the American Bar Association. Copyright © 1978 by the American Bar Association. Reprinted by permission of the American Bar Association.

American Psychiatric Association: Excerpt from article "Denial and Affirmation in Illness and Health" by Arnold R. Beisser, from *The American Journal of Psychiatry*, vol. 136, no. 8 (1979). Copyright © 1979 by the American Psychiatric Association.

Doubleday & Company, Inc.: "Willie Fryer," adapted from excerpt from *Children's Secrets* by Thomas J. Cottle. Copyright © 1980 by Thomas J. Cottle. Reprinted by permission of Doubleday & Company, Inc.

Harcourt Brace Jovanovich, Inc., and A. M. Heath & Company Ltd.: Excerpts from *Nineteen Eighty-Four* by George Orwell. Reprinted by permission of Harcourt Brace Jovanovich, Inc., A. M. Heath & Company Ltd., the estate of the late Sonia Brownell Orwell, and Martin Secker & Warburg Ltd.

Harvard Business Review: Excerpt from "Trade Secrets: What Price Loyalty?" by Michael S. Baram, from *Harvard Business Review* (November/December 1968). Copyright © 1968 by the President and Fellows of Harvard College, all rights reserved. Reprinted by permission of the *Harvard Business Review*.

Harvard University Press: Excerpt from *The Homeric Hymns and Homerica* by Hesiod, trans. Hugh G. Evelyn-White, 1914. Reprinted by permission of Harvard University Press, and the Loeb Classical Library, and the translator. Also, excerpt from *Robert Oppenheimer: Letters and Recollections*, eds. Alice Kimball Smith and Charles Weiner (1980).

Houghton Mifflin Company: Excerpt from *An Anthropologist at Work*, ed. Margaret Mead. Copyright © 1959 by Margaret Mead. Reprinted by permission of Houghton Mifflin Company.

The Journal Press: Excerpt from "The Facts of Observation in Psychoanalysis" by

For My Parents

Contents

ACKNOWLEDGMENTS

I want to thank all those whose interest, conversation, and criticism were of such help to me as I worked on this book, and especially those who were kind enough to comment on all or part of the manuscript: Rosemary Chalk, Alva Mydral, Robert Nozick, Emma Rothschild, Richard Sacks, Elizabeth Tillinghast, Ruth Weinreb, and Lloyd Weinreb. I am also grateful to Elizabeth Tillinghast for assisting me with research, and to Nuala Dalton for expert help in preparing the manuscript.

My warm thanks go to André Schiffrin, James Peck, Jeanne Morton, and the staff at Pantheon for the support, the skillful and patient editing, and the help I received over the years of completing this work. Finally, I thank my family—Hilary, Victoria, Tomas, and Derek—for their encouragement and understanding, and for the invaluable help they gave me, ranging from photography and proofreading to most spirited and challenging comments on successive drafts.

Introduction

We are all, in a sense, experts on secrecy. From earliest childhood we feel its mystery and attraction. We know both the power it confers and the burden it imposes. We learn how it can delight, give breathing-space, and protect. But we come to understand its dangers, too: how it is used to oppress and exclude; what can befall those who come too close to secrets they were not meant to share; and the price of betrayal.

We know the feel of secrecy, then—and yet the moral questions it raises puzzle and elude us. How far should one go in protecting one's secrets? Should one conceal all that friends and colleagues confide? When may a promise of secrecy be broken? Are there times when it *must* be breached? Under what circumstances is it wrong to gossip about the secrets of others, or to pry into them? Is secrecy corrupting when it permits the unchecked exercise of power? And do probing and secrecy raise different problems or pose greater risks when practiced by groups or entire governments?

In taking up these questions, I continue the exploration of concrete moral issues begun in my book *Lying*. Here, as in that book, I discuss the choices of how to act and how to shape one's conduct in private and public life. The central themes of the two books—lying and secrecy—intertwine and overlap. Lies are part of the arsenal used to guard and to invade secrecy; and secrecy allows lies to go undiscovered and to build up.

Lying and secrecy differ, however, in one important respect. Whereas I take lying to be *prima facie* wrong, with a negative presumption against it from the outset, secrecy need not be. Whereas every lie stands in need of justification, all secrets do not. Secrecy may accompany the most innocent as well as the most lethal acts; it is needed for human survival, yet it enhances every form of abuse. The same is true of efforts to uncover or invade secrets.

In setting out to explore the ethics of secrecy, I have wanted to come as close as possible to the concrete contexts in which people experience secrecy. What is it like to have secrets and to confront those of others—in childhood, in family life, at work, with friends and strangers, in religious and political activities? What do people feel justified in concealing or revealing, prying into or leaving untouched? Any inquiry into the ethics of secrecy must consider the conflicts that we all experience in making such choices: between keeping secrets and revealing them; between wanting to penetrate the secrets of others and to leave them undisturbed; and between responding to what they reveal to us and ignoring or even denying it. These conflicts are rooted in the most basic experience of what it means to live as one human being among others, needing both to hide and to share, both to seek out and to beware of the unknown.

The ethics of secrecy concerns our reflection and choice in grappling with these conflicts. Within the larger field of ethics, it plays an oddly unexplored role. It is not merely a subcategory of ethics more generally, but mirrors it, bringing parts of it into sharper focus and illuminating some of its most secluded recesses. The study of how one learns to deal with secrecy sheds light on the paths to becoming more aware of one's self among others, and thus of the possibility of moral choice.

Not only does the ethics of secrecy mirror and shed light on much of ethics; in ways that seem paradoxical, secrecy both protects and thwarts moral perception, reasoning, and choice. Secret practices protect the liberty of some while impairing that of others. They guard intimacy and creativity, yet tend to spread and to invite abuse. Secrecy can enhance a sense of brotherhood, loyalty, and equality among insiders while kindling discrimination against outsiders. And in situations of moral conflict, secrecy often collides with a crucial requirement for justifying a choice: that the moral principles supporting it be capable of open statement and defense.

I have sought out personal reports of the experience of secrecy, and drawn on the traditions in philosophy, religion, and law that have analyzed and shaped it. I have also benefited from recent work on secrecy in the social sciences. Yet I have often found the different approaches isolated, not only from one another, but from much actual experience of secrecy.

The same isolation and lack of scope constrain professional debates over secrecy and openness. Those, for example, who discuss the role of investigative journalists searching out corruption rarely take up the probing by social scientists or industrial spies, much less small-town gossip or encounter groups. In the same way, lawyers may discuss the propriety of FBI undercover operations, business managers consider whether to require job applicants not to reveal trade secrets, psychiatrists debate whether or not to disclose a patient's threats of violence against family members or political figures. But all too often such debates remain partial and narrowly professional, permitting biases to go unexamined; or if they are conducted in public, it is strictly for purposes of advocacy. As a result, the underlying issues of concealment and revelation and probing are too often ignored, and moral problems get short shrift.

Powerful new techniques of storing and of probing secrets increase the need for careful debate. From the miniature cameras that can be hidden in a pen to the invisible wire-tapping devices and electronic mechanisms for overhearing conversations at a great distance, from the "truth serums" and mind-altering drugs to the methods of securing and invading computerized information banks, new means beckon to anyone who would abuse either openness or secrecy.

Entire new professions are now being trained to use these methods for probing or concealing secrets. Government surveillance and information-gathering has reached unprecedented dimensions throughout the world; so have infiltration by social scientists for scholarly or commercial purposes, undercover journalism in search of exposés, investigation by private agents and underworld sources, and industrial surveillance and espionage. These practices invite imitation and retaliation, and thus in turn generate a need for still more effective and more secret prying.

The new techniques and the changes they make possible join with the long-standing personal and professional conflicts over secrecy to raise practical moral problems for us all. Yet these problems are often postponed or explained away or dismissed altogether; or else they are accorded stereotyped, almost ritual responses—invoking, as if to ward off further inquiry, important but poorly articulated rationales such as "the right to privacy," "national security," "the freedom of inquiry," or "the public's right to know."

Why such defenses against examining the ethics of secrecy and openness? And why are these defenses so often couched in the moral language of rights and obligations? To seek answers to these questions is as much my aim as to study the moral problems of secrecy in their own right. In pursuing my inquiry into the ethics of secrecy I have therefore also had to trace the paths of secrecy in ethics—the uses of moral reflection to ward off, dismiss, obscure, and conceal.

In thus exploring secrecy and openness, I have come up against what human beings care most to protect and to probe: the exalted, the dangerous, the shameful; the sources of power and creation; the fragile and the intimate. Such an inquiry must of necessity be incomplete. I hope, nevertheless, that it will help to shed light on the crucial moral issues that secrecy and openness raise in every life, and invite the debate that these issues now require more urgently than ever.

SECRETS

Chapter I

Approaches to Secrecy

The Gift of Pandora

Hesiod recounts how Zeus hid fire from men, and tells of his anger when he learned that Prometheus had carried it off in secret for the use of mortals, hidden in a hollow stalk. Zeus used corresponding stealth in his revenge. He planned to create and send forth Pandora, the first woman, as beautiful as she was false; and to send with her a jar concealing all the miseries that would, if allowed to escape, forever afflict mankind. Laughing aloud, he asked Hephaestus to

make haste and mix earth with water and put in it the voice and strength of human kind, and fashion a sweet, lovely maiden-shape, like to the immortal goddesses in face; and Athene to teach her needlework and the weaving of the varied web; and golden Aphrodite to shed grace upon her head and cruel longing and cares that weary the limbs. And he charged Hermes, the slayer of Argus, to put in her a shameless mind and a deceitful nature. . . . And he called this woman Pandora, because all they who dwelt on Olympus gave each a gift, a plague to men who eat bread.

And when he had finished the sheer, hopeless snare, the Father sent glorious Argus-slayer, the swift messenger of the gods, to take it to Epimetheus as a gift. And . . . he took the gift, and afterwards, when the evil thing was already his, he understood. For ere this the tribes of men lived on earth remote and free from ills and hard toil and heavy sicknesses which bring the Fates upon men; for in misery men grow old quickly. But the woman took off the great lid of the jar with her hands and scattered all these and her thought caused sorrow and mischief to men. Only Hope remained there in an unbreakable home within under the rim of the great jar, and did not fly out at the door. . . . But the rest, countless plagues, wander amongst men; for earth is full of evils and the sea is full.[1]

Secrets stolen and offered as gifts, arousing longing, fear, and anger, bringing benefit or misery—the myth of Pandora's box unfolds interweaving layers of secrecy and revelation. It is one of the many tales of calamities befalling those who uncover what is concealed and thereby release dangerous forces that should have been left in darkness and silence.*

Other myths tell of secrets that are destructive only so long as they *remain* concealed. Not until someone penetrates them can their evil power be defeated. Learning the name of a monster, or guessing its riddle, ends the spell it casts. The myth of the riddle of the winged Sphinx that terrorized the inhabitants of Thebes concerns such a secret. The Sphinx asked a riddle of passers-by, and tore to pieces and devoured those who could not give the right answer. When Oedipus heard of the city's plight, he climbed up to the cliff on which the Sphinx perched, and offered to solve her riddle. She asked him what creature it is that, having but one voice, is first four-footed, then two-footed, and at last three-footed. Oedipus answered, "You have spoken of man, who creeps on all four in infancy, then walks on two feet, and leans on a staff in old age, as a third foot." Enraged that he had solved her riddle, the Sphinx threw herself from the cliff and perished.[2]

The question whether to leave evil secrets alone or try to defeat them by draining them of their destructive power recurs in many of the therapeutic and investigative practices that I shall discuss in this book. A separate question concerns secrets not in themselves linked with evil, but necessary, rather, to preserve something precious—love, friendship, even life itself—and sometimes endowed with the power to transform those who approach. Thus tales of initiation into mysteries recount how those who follow the prescribed steps of cleansing and devotion are

---

*In later versions of the tale of Pandora's box, the good was enclosed with the evil; when the lid was raised, all that was good scattered and was lost to mankind, while what was evil remained to plague men. There are several versions, too, of what happened to Hope: whether it was kept in the jar, as Hesiod relates, or flew out; and if it flew out, whether it helped men or merely deceived them into thinking their fate bearable, in order to keep them from committing suicide.

granted access to illumination, whereas those who approach the mystery by wrongful means are changed, corrupted, even destroyed.[3]

The Faust-legend warns of what can befall those who lose all caution in approaching forbidden secrets. Charlatan, magician, seeker after cures for every disease, Faust probed all the secrets of nature. He desired to know how to ride the clouds, change metals into gold, stave off death, and even create new life—a homunculus—and thus attain the innermost core of knowledge. In exchange for twenty-four years of access to such knowledge and power, he surrendered his soul to Lucifer. Marlowe portrays his ensuing corruption and ruin in *Doctor Faustus*; at the end, the chorus comments:

> *Faustus is gone: regard his hellish fall,*
> *Whose fiendful fortune may exhort the wise*
> *Only to wonder at unlawful things,*
> *Whose deepness doth entice such forward wits*
> *To practice more than heavenly power permits.*[4]

Awareness of the allure and the dangers of secrecy that these and so many other stories convey is central to human experience of what is hidden and set apart. Rooted in encounters with the powerful, the sacred, and the forbidden, this experience goes far deeper than the partaking of any one secret.[5] Efforts to guard secrets, probe them, or share them often aim for this deeper and more pervasive experience. If we do not take this into account in considering particular forms of concealment, such as clandestine scientific research, underground political groups, or long-buried family mysteries, then we shall but skim the surface; and the secrets, once revealed, will seem paltry and out of proportion to all that went into guarding them. Similar care is needed in approaching and defining the concept of secrecy itself.

Defining Secrecy

a. Secrecy as Intentional Concealment

A path, a riddle, a jewel, an oath—anything can be secret so long as it is kept intentionally hidden, set apart in the mind of its keeper as requiring concealment. It may be shared with no one, or confided on condition that it go no farther; at times it may be known to all but one or two from whom it is kept. To keep a secret from someone, then, is to block information about it or evidence of it from reaching that person, and to do so intentionally: to prevent him from learning it, and thus from possessing it, making use of it, or revealing it.* The word "secrecy" refers to the resulting concealment. It also denotes the methods used to conceal, such as codes or disguises or camouflage, and the practices of concealment, as in trade secrecy or professional confidentiality.

Accordingly I shall take concealment, or hiding, to be the defining trait of secrecy. It presupposes separation, a setting apart of the secret from the non-secret, and of keepers of a secret from those excluded. The Latin *secretum* carries this meaning of something hidden, set apart.[6] It derives from *secernere*, which originally meant to sift apart, to separate as with a sieve. It bespeaks discernment, the ability to make distinctions, to sort out and draw lines: a capacity that underlies not only secrecy but all thinking, all intention and choice.[7] The separation between insider and outsider is inherent in secrecy; and to think something secret is already to envisage potential conflict between what insiders conceal and outsiders want to inspect or lay bare.

Several other strands have joined with this defining trait to form our concept of secrecy. Although they are not always present in every secret or every practice of secrecy, the concepts of sacredness, intimacy, privacy, silence, prohibition, furtiveness, and deception influence the way we think about secrecy. They intertwine and sometimes conflict, yet they come together in our experience of secrecy and give it depth.

Both their diversity and their coming together are reflected in the evolution of the words for "secret" in many languages. At first, different strands or aspects were stressed in different languages; yet over time the words in each language took on the added meaning of the other strands, and came to perform the intricate function required by the experience of what is secret.

One such aspect is that of the sacred, the uncanny, and the mysterious. It is conveyed by words such as *arcanum*, another Latin word for "secret." [8] The sacred and the secret have been linked from earliest times. Both elicit feelings of what Rudolph Otto called the "numinous consciousness" that combines the daunting and the fascinating, dread and allure.[9] Both are defined as being set apart and seen as needing protection. And the sense of violation that intrusion into certain secrets arouses is also evoked by intrusions into the sacred.

Intimacy and privacy represent another aspect of secrecy: one expressed

---

*There are, of course, many other reasons why information or evidence may not reach a person, quite apart from intentional secrecy. Unintended distortions or blockages may occur either at the source, en route, or at the receiving end of any communication.

in the German word *heimlich*.[10] At first, *heimlich* meant that which pertains to the home, the hearth, and the intimate; later, it took on the added meaning of something kept from the view of strangers and finally also of all that is secret. The private constitutes, along with the sacred, that portion of human experience for which secrecy is regarded as most indispensable. In secularized Western societies, privacy has come to seem for some the only legitimate form of secrecy; consequently, the two are sometimes mistakenly seen as identical.

Still another aspect of secrecy—that of silence, the first defense of secrets—is conveyed by the Greek word *arretos*. At first, it meant the unspoken; later it came to mean also the unspeakable, the ineffable, and the prohibited, sometimes also the abominable and the shameful, and then the secret in all its shadings.

Stealth and furtiveness are linked to secrecy through words such as the Church Slavic *tanjinu*. And the Swedish *lönn* connects secrecy not only to such stealth but also to lying, denial, and every form of deceit. The link between secrecy and deceit is so strong in the minds of some that they mistakenly take all secrecy (especially when protected by silence) to be deceptive. In so doing, they confuse secrecy with what is undoubtedly a common means for preserving it. To confuse secrecy and deception is easy, since all deception does involve keeping something secret— namely, that about which one wishes to deceive others. But while all deception requires secrecy, all secrecy is not meant to deceive. Consider the many forms of secrecy in which there need be no aim to mislead: that which may accompany human intimacy, for instance, or protect voters in casting their ballot.

While the hidden is part of the meaning of all these words for "secret," the different shadings of each one—whether of something sacred, intimate, private, unspoken, silent, prohibited, shameful, stealthy, or deceitful— come together in our understanding of the meanings of the secret and of secrecy. We cannot encompass all these meanings in a single definition; for while they form a family of related meanings, they are not always present together in any one instance of secrecy. For the same reasons, it would be a mistake to define secrecy in terms of only one or two of these meanings, or to view it too narrowly by assuming from the outset an evaluative stance either for or against secrets in general. Yet many have taken such a position.

b. A Neutral Definition

Too exclusive an emphasis on the links between the secret and the sacred can lead one to see all secrecy as inherently valuable, and all harm from it as stemming from the errors and lack of caution of those it injures. And those who think primarily of the links between secrecy and privacy or intimacy, and of secrets as personal confidences, have regarded them as something one has a duty to conceal. Thus the French *Encyclopédie* of 1765 stated, in the first of two entries under "secret":

It is everything that we have confided to someone, or that someone has confided to us, with the intention that it not be revealed. . . . If one must not tell one's own secret imprudently, still less must one reveal that of another; for that is perfidy, or at least an inexcusable fault.[11]

Negative views of secrecy are even more common. Why should you conceal something, many ask, if you are not afraid to have it known? The aspects of secrecy that have to do with stealth and furtiveness, lying and denial, predominate in such a view. Woodrow Wilson's experience in political life, for example, led him to claim that "secrecy means impropriety."[12] He echoed a long tradition of protest against government secrecy, holding it incompatible with democracy.

Many social scientists and psychotherapists have similarly assumed that secrets are in themselves discreditable: that what people conceal is what they regard as shameful or undesirable. A striking illustration is found in a survey in which researchers asked students to reveal, anonymously, what secret they would be least willing to share with the group. On finding that a number of students had specified highly positive secrets, the investigators placed such responses in the category they had labeled "non-secrets."[13]

The view that secrets are by nature discreditable and negative is understandable, given the fear that so many secrets have inspired. The fear of conspiracies, of revenge, and of the irreversible consequences of opening Pandora's box nourishes this view, as does awareness of the corruption that secrecy can breed. Thus Jung wrote that the keeping of secrets acts like a psychic poison, alienating their possessor from the community.[14] Like other poisons, he wrote, it may be beneficial in small doses, but its destructive power is otherwise great.

The notion of the secret as a form of poison or infection has long antecedents. Ellenberger traces the concept of what he calls the "pathogenic secret" back to primitive healers, and to magnetists and hypnotists who worked at drawing painful and intolerable secrets into the open.[15] Origen, in the third century A.D., described the goal of confession in just such terms:

There were evil thoughts in men, and they were revealed for this reason, that being brought into the open they might be destroyed, slain, and put to death, and cease to be. . . . For while these thoughts were hidden and not brought into the open they could not be utterly done to death.[16]

The concern with evil secrets arouses conflicting responses: the desire to leave them undisturbed and so avoid the suffering they might release, or on the contrary, to bring them into the open and drain them of their destructive power. The latter aim—the very reverse of leaving Pandora's box sealed—is often expressed in terms of healing and sunlight and fresh air being brought to secrets that would otherwise fester and infect. Both aims have their place, whether in religious or therapeutic practices, or yet in politics or in criminal investigations. But to allow them to influence the definition of what is secret risks casting a pall on *all* that is kept secret, including much that stands in no need of being done to death.

We must retain a neutral definition of secrecy, therefore, rather than one that assumes from the outset that secrets are guilty or threatening, or on the contrary, awesome and worthy of respect. A degree of concealment or openness accompanies all that human beings do or say. We must determine what is and is not discreditable by examining particular practices of secrecy, rather than by assuming an initial evaluative stance.

The Secret and the Unknown

Samuel Johnson listed three subentries under the noun "secret" in his *Dictionary*:

> 1. Something studiously hidden
> 2. A thing unknown; something not yet discovered
> 3. Privacy, secrecy; invisible or undiscovered state.[17]

The first entry singles out what I have called the defining trait of secrecy: intentional concealment. Should the second and third also be part of the definition? Many have thought so. The unknown and the private are obviously closely linked to secrecy. In considering the ethics of secrecy, does it matter whether or not we take them to form part of the definition?

"A thing unknown; something not yet discovered"—Johnson's words recall deeply rooted perceptions of secrecy and of its elusiveness for outsiders. In thinking about secrecy, one cannot always know what is and is not intentionally kept hidden. Certain religious traditions hold that all that we do not know is kept from our view on purpose. References to the secrets of the human body or of the cell or of the universe echo these uncertainties and beliefs.

Some have included still more than the unknown in their definition of the secret: all that people forget, repress, and ignore. All such definitions tantalize: they hint at powers intending to keep us in the dark. A hidden intention may be at play—most paradoxical of all when it is taken to be our own intention to forget and to keep knowledge at arm's length.

Any inquiry into the ethics of secrecy must take such views seriously. They remind us of the persistent concern about whether outside powers or forces within us keep us in the dark. But all assumptions about hidden intentions and secrets kept from oneself must be examined and questioned, rather than presupposed in the very definition of secrecy. The relationship between what is unknown and what is kept secret must not be settled at the definitional stage.

Some things we believe we know; many we are conscious of not knowing; and in between are countless shadings of belief, vacillation, and guesswork. The concept of what is secret is central in each of these domains. What we believe we know or belong to defines the area in which we move with greater assurance; and within that area, what we keep secret requires our most intense and often most active attention. Similarly, amidst the vastness of all that we are conscious of not knowing, or of trying to ascertain, we experience as secret the spaces from which we feel shut out.

Secrecy and Privacy

> *His mind of man, a secret makes*
> *I meet him with a start*
> *He carries a circumference*
> *In which I have no part*
> EMILY DICKINSON

It is equally important to keep the distinction between secrecy and privacy from being engulfed at the definitional stage.[18] The two are closely linked, and their relationship is central to the questions I shall raise throughout this book. In order to maintain the distinction, however, it is important first to ask how they are related and wherein they differ. Having defined secrecy as intentional concealment, I obviously cannot take it as identical with privacy. I shall define privacy as the condition of being protected from unwanted access by others—either physical access, personal information, or attention. Claims to privacy are claims to control access to what one takes—however grandiosely—to be one's personal domain. Through such claims, and the counterclaims they often generate, people try to reinforce or expand this control.[19]

Privacy and secrecy overlap whenever the efforts at such control rely on hiding. But privacy need not hide; and secrecy hides far more than what is private. A private garden need not be a secret garden; a private life is rarely a secret life. Conversely, secret diplomacy rarely concerns what is private, any more than do arrangements for a surprise party or for choosing prize winners.[20]

Why then are privacy and secrecy so often equated? In part, this is so because privacy is such a central part of what secrecy protects that it can easily be seen as the whole. People claim privacy for differing amounts of what they are and do and own; if need be, they seek the added protection of secrecy. In each case, their purpose is to become less vulnerable, more in control.

In these efforts at control, how do individuals protect privacy? They guard, first of all, against others coming too near by protecting what has come to be called personal space and territoriality.[21] To be sure, the boundaries of this space are differently envisaged according to culture and personality and imagination; but recent work in the social sciences shows that most individuals do conceive of certain near-physical boundaries enclosing their bodies, some of the space immediately surrounding them, and at times certain objects and living beings, animal or human. Some people also sense boundaries around their names, their thoughts, their inventions, and what they have created.[22] Particularly close to some is that into which they have put work—a garden or a farm built up from scratch, a work of art, or a painstakingly assembled collection. Many look at their children in this way—a proprietary attitude likely to conflict with their children's own sense of privacy.

A similar range has been demonstrated for many species of animals with reference to territoriality and spacing. The "flight distance" is the distance at which an animal will flee from an intruder of another species: around five hundred yards for an antelope, six feet for a wall lizard. With respect to their own species, many animals, given a chance, will space themselves at some distance from one another, whether on telephone wires, in flying formations, or when sleeping.[23]

Spacing and territoriality occur in varying degrees across a wide range of species, including our own. But the developed sense of privacy common to human societies concerns not only physical access but also information about personal matters and attention to them or to one's person. Thus many would feel their privacy invaded if personal medical information about them were published in the local newspaper, or if they knew that their movements were under constant surveillance by satellite, quite apart from physical nearness and territoriality. Therefore, while it is helpful to find similarities in other species, excessive reliance on such analogies can lead to a stunted interpretation of the complex role of human efforts at privacy.

Human beings find the most ingenious ways to protect their privacy, even under conditions of near-constant physical proximity to others. In many cultures, even minimal control over physical access can be hard to come by in the midst of communal and family life. Some villages have huts with walls so thin that sounds can easily be heard through them; others have no walls at all separating couples, or families. Many ways are then devised to create privacy. Villagers may set up private abodes outside the village to which they go for days or even months when they want to be alone or with just one or two others. Many cultures have developed strict rules of etiquette, along with means of dissimulation and hypocrisy that allow certain private matters to remain unknown or go unobserved. In such ways, it is possible to exercise some control over one's openness to others even in the midst of communal life or crowds.

An arresting example of how such control can be maintained is provided by the Tuareg men of North Africa who wear blue veils and long robes of indigo cotton, so that little of them shows except their hands, their feet, and the area around their eyes. The veil is worn at home as well as outside, even when eating or smoking. Some wear it even when asleep. It is raised to cover the face most completely in the presence of highly placed persons or family members granted special respect, such as in-laws. One observer noted that the veil protects ceremonial reserve and allows a "symbolic withdrawal from a threatening situation."

The veil, though providing neither isolation nor anonymity, bestows facelessness and the idiom of privacy upon its wearer and allows him to stand somewhat aloof from the perils of social interaction while remaining a part of it.[24]

Erving Goffman has described the efforts to diminish and erode privacy in "total institutions" such as prisons:

On the outside, the individual can hold objects of self-feeling—such as his body, his immediate actions, his thoughts, and some of his possessions—clear of contact with alienating and contaminating things. But in total institutions these territories of the self are violated; the boundary that the individual places between his being and the environment is invaded and the embodiment of self profaned.[25]

Heads may be shaved, property and clothing removed, letters read by censors. Even in the most carefully supervised institutions, however, inmates often find a way, often through deception and secrecy, to preserve at least a modicum of privacy. One study describes children's efforts to seek privacy in a psychiatric ward where staff control was nearly continuous.[26] Sleeping, eating, bathroom visits, all were regimented in such a way that doors could not be closed and solitude was impossible. The result, according to the authors, was that the children resorted to ingenious forms of misbehavior in the hope of being put in the isolation room from time to time. In so doing, they were no different from most other human beings in their desire to avoid ceaseless observation.[27] Where ordinary forms of withdrawal are forbidden, circuitous or disguised methods take their place, even for persons who have nothing to hide of a discrediting or guilty nature.

When do secrecy and privacy most clearly overlap? They do so most immediately in the private lives of individuals, where secrecy guards against unwanted access by others—against their coming too near, learning too much, observing too closely. Secrecy guards, then, the central aspects of identity, and if necessary, also plans and property. It serves as an additional shield in case the protection of privacy should fail or be broken down. Thus you may assume that no one will read your diary; but you can also hide it, or write it in code, as did William Blake, or lock it up. Secret codes, bank accounts, and retreats, secret thoughts never voiced aloud, personal objects hidden against intruders: all testify to the felt need for additional protection.

Similarly, groups can create a joint space within which they keep secrets, surrounded by an aura of mystery. Perhaps the most complete overlap of privacy and secrecy in groups is that exemplified in certain secret societies. The members of some of these societies undergo such experiences that their own sense of privacy blends with an enlarged private space of the group. The societies then have identities and boundaries of their own. They come into being like living organisms, vulnerable; they undergo growth and transformation, and eventually pass away.

It is harder to say whether privacy and secrecy overlap in practices of large-scale collective secrecy, such as trade or military secrecy. Claims of privacy are often made for such practices, and the metaphors of personal space are stretched to apply to them. To be sure, such practices are automatically private in one sense so long as they are not public. But the use of the language of privacy, with its metaphors of personal space, spheres, sanctuaries, and boundaries, to personalize collective enterprises should not go unchallenged. Such usage can be as sentimental as the excessive resort by poets to the "pathetic fallacy" (in which personal feelings such as grief or cruelty are ascribed to nature) and can then distort our understanding of the role of these enterprises.[28]

The obsessive, conflict-ridden invocation of privacy in Western society has increased the occasions for such expanded uses of the metaphors of privacy;[29] so has the corresponding formalization of the professional practices of secrecy and openness. At times the shield of privacy is held up to protect abuses, such as corporate tax fraud or legislative corruption, that are in no manner personal.

While secrecy often guards what is private, therefore, it need not do so, and it has many uses outside the private sphere. To see all secrecy as privacy is as limiting as to assume that it is invariably deceptive or that it conceals primarily what is discreditable. We must retain the definition of secrecy as intentional concealment, and resist the pressure to force the concept into a narrower definitional mold by insisting that privacy, deceit, or shame always accompanies it. But at the same time we must strive to keep in mind these aspects of our underlying experience of secrecy, along with the others I have mentioned—the sacred, the silent, the forbidden, and the stealthy.

Without such a neutral and nonlimiting definition, it will be difficult to frame the moral questions about secrecy. If we regard secrecy as inherently deceptive or as concealing primarily what is discreditable, we shall be using loaded concepts before we even look at the practices that require us to make a choice; in this way we shall only confuse or deflect the moral questions that they raise. It is almost as if the effort to define *secrecy* reflected the conflicting desires that approaching many an actual *secret* arouses: the cautious concern to leave it carefully sealed, or on the contrary, the determination to open it up, cut it down to size, see only one of its aspects, hasten to solve its riddle.

Secrecy and Moral Choice

"Tell me your secrets."
I say not a word, for this is under my control.
"But I will fetter you."
What is that you say, man? Fetter me?
My legs you will fetter, but my deliberate
choice not even Zeus has the power to overcome.
                    EPICTETUS, *Discourses*

A Thought-Experiment

Imagine four different societies: two of them familiar from religious and mythological thinking, the other two closer to science fiction. To the extent that each reflects aspects of our own world, it will arouse the ambivalence and unease characteristic of conflicts over secrecy.

—In the first of the four imaginary societies, you and I cannot keep anything secret; but others, or at least someone, perhaps a deity, can. We are transparent to them, either because we are incapable of concealment or because they have means of penetrating all our defenses.

—In the second society, all is reversed. You and I can pierce all secrets. A magic ring and a coat of invisibility give us access to these secrets, unbeknownst to those on whom we focus our attention.

—In the third society, no one can keep secrets from anyone who desires to know them. Plans, actions, fears, and hopes are all transparent. Surprise and concealment are out of the question.

—In the fourth society, finally, everyone can keep secrets impenetrable at will. All can conceal innocuous as well as lethal plans, the noblest as well as the most shameful acts, and hatreds and conspiracies as much as generosity and self-sacrifice. Faces reveal nothing out of turn; secret codes remain unbroken.

Abstract, for now, from possible supernatural influences that might render these societies either more or less benign, and consider how it would be to live in each one. Would these societies not all turn out to be less desirable than our own, with all its conflicts over secrecy and openness, all its unpredictability and imperfection? Despite its inadequate protection of personal liberties, its difficulties in preserving either the secrecy or the openness on which human beings thrive, and its many abuses, our own world nevertheless differs from each of the four above in ways for which we must be grateful.

It is precisely those elements of our own experience which bring us closest to one or another of the four that are most troubling. Thus the first society—in which you and I can keep no secrets—might appeal to saints who seek to live with few shelters, few secrets, and to the publicity-hungry who want the spotlight for theirs. But life for most of us would be too exposed, too vulnerable, without a measure of secrecy. We might wish for the transparency of this imagined world at chosen moments, with close friends; but we are also aware of its resemblance to the experience of persons subjected to the modern methods of interrogation, surveillance, and thought-control now employed in so many countries. Even Epictetus, quoted at the beginning of this chapter as saying that his secrets are under his control—that his feet might be fettered but never his deliberate choice—would have to use all his strength to resist these techniques, and still could not count on being able to hold out.

The second world, in which you and I can penetrate all secrets, echoes the perennial desire to satisfy all one's curiosity by moving unseen among others while learning their most closely held secrets. Yet as we reflect on the power that would be ours in this second world, we might hesitate to accept it. We would have to recognize not only its intrusiveness but its dangers to us, the unseen intruders and manipulators. The experience of this imagined society is brought closer for those who employ the new techniques of surveillance and of surreptitious probing— the one-way mirrors, the electronic eavesdropping, the elaborate undercover investigations. That even many who avail themselves of such techniques are uneasy about them is clear from the debates over their use among social scientists or reporters or police agents.

Some might argue that these new techniques of probing, along with refined versions of very old ones, are becoming so common that we are approaching, rather, the third imaginary society, in which no one can keep secrets from anyone intent on knowing them. Thus one intelligence analyst has recently claimed that there "is no privacy from a well-financed, technically adept person or agency determined to gain personal information about an individual, group, or country." [1] One may wish to dispute his estimate, or argue that the expense of the efforts he has in mind is so great that most people would be safe from such intense probing. But what would the world be like if methods making secrecy impossible were generally available?

Might there be benefits in such universal transparency, as long as all could avail themselves of it? It would not only rule out secrecy but the very possibility of deceit and hypocrisy. Would such a state of openness among human beings not be nobler than the concealment we live with, and all the dissimulation it makes possible? Openness and sincerity, after all, are qualities we prize. As Meister Eckhart said, we call him a good man who reveals himself to others and, in so doing, is of use to them. [2]

On reflection, even those most in favor of openness among human beings might nevertheless reject the loss of all secrecy; or else advocate it only for certain exceptional persons who choose it for themselves and are able to tolerate it. Advocates of *universal* transparency have usually envisioned it for some future society free of the conflicts and contradictions of our own. Thus Sartre held that "transparency must substitute itself at all times for secrecy," but that this will be possible only when material want has been suppressed. At such a time, he argued, the relationship between men will no longer be antagonistic:

I can imagine rather easily the day when two men will have no more secrets from one another because they will keep secrets from no one, since the subjective life, just as much as the objective life, will be totally offered, given. [3]

Yet the desire for such mutual transparency, even when relegated to a future, idealized world, should give pause. We must consider the drawbacks of too much information as well as those of being kept in the dark. And we must take into account our responses to all that we might learn about one another in such a world. Would we be able to cope with not only the quantity but also the impact upon us of the information thus within reach? And if secrecy were no longer possible, would brute force turn out to be the only means of self-defense and of gaining the upper hand? It is not inconceivable that the end result of a shift to the third imagined society would be chaos.

Aspects of the fourth society, finally, might develop precisely in response to the felt threat from increased transparency. They are foreshadowed in the governmental and commercial use of the "unbreakable codes" that cryptographers are currently designing, and in mechanisms to foil electronic eavesdropping. If such methods became available to everyone, and were capable of protecting all that people might wish to hide, how would our lives change? It is not certain that society as we now know it could survive such changes, for it depends in part on the possibility of predicting and forestalling or preparing for danger. Given a state in which no one could penetrate the secrets of others, nor know what harm they threatened, would those with the most far-reaching plans for aggression or crime win out? Or would so many fear such plans, and try to forestall them with violence of their own, that all would end in one great pre-emptive conflagration?

We contemplate these four imaginary societies with uneasiness. As I turn, in later chapters, to such practices as confession, psychotherapy, gossip, trade secrecy, cryptography, and undercover policing, I hope to show that our ambivalence toward them partakes of the same uneasiness. Is this response justified? If so, for what reasons? And what distinctions may we then wish to draw between forms of keeping, probing, and revealing secrets?

The Need for Secrecy

Secrecy is as indispensable to human beings as fire, and as greatly feared. Both enhance and protect life, yet both can stifle, lay waste, spread out of all control. Both may be used to guard intimacy or to invade it, to nurture or to consume. And each can be turned against itself; barriers of secrecy are set up to guard against secret plots and surreptitious prying, just as fire is used to fight fire.

We must keep in mind this conflicted, ambivalent experience of secrecy as we study it in its many guises, and seek standards for dealing with it. But because secrecy is so often negatively defined and viewed as primarily immature, guilty, conspiratorial, or downright pathological, I shall first discuss the need for the protection it affords.

Consider how, in George Orwell's *Nineteen Eighty-four*, Winston Smith tried to preserve one last expression of independence from the Thought-police. He had decided to begin a diary, even though he knew he thereby risked death or at least twenty-five years in a forced-labor camp. He placed himself in an alcove in his living room where the telescreen could not see him, and began to write. When he found himself writing DOWN WITH BIG BROTHER over and over, he panicked and was tempted to give up.

He did not do so, however, because he knew that it was useless. Whether he wrote DOWN WITH BIG BROTHER, or whether he refrained from writing it, made no difference. Whether he went on with the diary, or whether he did not go on with it, made no difference. The Thought-police would get him just the same. He had committed—would still have committed, even if he had not set pen to paper—the essential crime that contained all others in itself. Thoughtcrime, they called it. Thoughtcrime was not a thing that could be concealed forever. You might dodge successfully for a while, even for years, but sooner or later they were bound to get to you.[4]

Subjected to near-complete surveillance, Winston Smith was willing to risk death rather than to forgo the chance to set down his thoughts in secret. To the extent that he retained some secrecy for his views, he had a chance to elude the Thought-police. Though aware that "sooner or later they were bound to get to you," he did not know that he was under surreptitious observation even as he prepared to write—that his most secret undertaking was itself secretly spied upon.

Conflicts over secrecy—between state and citizen, as in this case, or parent and child, or in journalism or business or law—are conflicts over power: the power that comes through controlling the flow of information.[5] To be able to hold back some information about oneself or to channel it and thus influence how one is seen by others gives power; so does the capacity to penetrate similar defenses and strategies when used by others. True, power requires not only knowledge but the capacity to put knowledge to use; but without the knowledge, there is no chance to exercise power. To have no capacity for secrecy is to be out of control over how others see one; it leaves one open to coercion. To have no insight into what others conceal is to lack power as well. Those who are unable or unwilling ever to look beneath the surface, to question motives, to doubt what is spoken, are condemned to live their lives in ignorance, just as those who are unable to keep secrets of their own must live theirs defenseless.

Control over secrecy provides a safety valve for individuals in the midst of communal life—some influence over transactions between the world of personal experience and the world shared with others. With no control over such exchanges, human beings would be unable to exercise choice about their lives. To restrain some secrets and to allow others freer play; to keep some hidden and to let others be known; to offer knowledge to some but not to all comers; to give and receive confidences and to guess at far more: these efforts at control permeate all human contact.

Those who lose all control over these relations cannot flourish in either the personal or the shared world, nor retain their sanity. If experience in the shared world becomes too overwhelming, the sense of identity suffers. Psychosis has been described as the breaking down of the delineation between the self and the outside world: the person going mad "flows out onto the world as through a broken dam." [6] Conversely, experience limited to the inside world stunts the individual: at best it may lead to the aching self-exploration evoked by Nietzsche: "I am solitude become man.—That no word ever reached me forced me to reach myself." [7]

In seeking some control over secrecy and openness, and the power it makes possible, human beings attempt to guard and to promote not only their autonomy but ultimately their sanity and survival itself. The claims in defense of this control, however, are not always articulated. Some take them to be so self-evident as to need no articulation; others subsume them under more general arguments about liberty or privacy. But it is important for the purposes of considering the ethics of secrecy to set forth these claims. Otherwise it will not be possible to ask, in particular cases, to what extent they should apply and what restraints they might require. Nor will it be possible to study the extrapolations made from them in support of collective practices of secrecy.

The claims in defense of some control over secrecy and openness invoke four different, though in practice inseparable, elements of human autonomy: identity, plans, action, and property. They concern protection of what we are, what we intend, what we do, and what we own.

The first of these claims holds that some control over secrecy and openness is needed in order to protect identity: the sense of what we identify ourselves as, through, and with. Such control may be needed to guard solitude, privacy, intimacy, and friendship. It protects vulnerable beliefs or feelings, inwardness, and the sense of being set apart: of having or belonging to regions not fully penetrable to scrutiny, including those of memory and dream; of being someone who is more, has become more, has more possibilities for the future than can ever meet the eyes of observers. Secrecy guards, therefore, not merely isolated secrets about the self but access to the underlying experience *of* secrecy.

Human beings can be subjected to every scrutiny, and reveal much about themselves; but they can never be entirely understood, simultaneously exposed from every perspective, completely transparent either to themselves or to other persons. They are not only unique but unfathomable.* The experience of such uniqueness and depth underlies self-respect and what social theorists have called the sense of "the sacredness of the self." [8] This sense also draws on group, familial, and societal experience of intimacy and sacredness, and may attach to individual as well as to collective identity. The growing stress in the last centuries on human dignity and on rights such as the right to privacy echoes it in secular and individualized language.

Without perceiving some sacredness in human identity, individuals are out of touch with the depth they might feel in themselves and respond to in others. Given such a sense, however, certain intrusions are felt as violations—a few even as desecrations. It is in order to guard against such encroachments that we recoil from those who would tap our telephones, read our letters, bug our rooms: no matter how little we have to hide, no matter how benevolent their intentions, we take such intrusions to be demeaning.

Not only does control over secrecy and openness preserve central aspects of identity; it also guards their *changes*, their growth or decay, their progress or backsliding, their sharing and transformation of every kind.† Here as elsewhere, while secrecy can be destructive, some of it

---

*Many have written about individuals as worlds, universes, or networks, unfathomable in practice if not in principle. And the death of an individual has been likened to the burning down of a great library or to a universe going extinct, as the inwardness and focus and connections of a life are lost, along with the sense of what William Blake called "the holiness of minute particulars."

†Identities and boundaries may themselves be transformed by the revelation or the penetration of certain secrets. And revealing, penetrating, and guarding secrets, in turn, often make use of transformations:

—Some ways of revealing secrets require a transformation, such as an initiation, on the part of those who are to share the secret. Their oath of secrecy, too, transforms their obligations. Their identity may undergo a metamorphosis of growth or destruction.
—Some secrets are transformed so as to be more easily guarded, through codes, miniaturization, or oracular sayings that only initiates will understand.
—Certain transformations allow the penetration of secrets. Becoming a "fly on the wall," or wearing the invisibility ring of myth or folk tale; all kinds of disguise; the bugging of rooms and electronic surveillance from afar: these changes allow probing of secrets otherwise carefully guarded.

is indispensable in human lives. Birth, sexual intimacy, death, mourning, experiences of conversion or of efforts to transcend the purely personal are often surrounded by special protections, and with rituals that combine secrecy and openness in set proportions.

Consider, for example, the role of secrecy, probing, and revelation with respect to pregnancy. In most cultures its workings have been thought mysterious, miraculous, at times terrifying. Like other experiences in which human boundaries are uncertain or shifting, pregnancy often increases vulnerability and the need for secrecy. Merely conjectured at first and pondered in secret by women, then perhaps revealed to a few, it is destined to unfold and to become known to many more. It is a period of heightened inwardness, awe, and joy for many women, giving them a sense of mattering in part because they have such a secret to keep or to reveal. At times these feelings are overwhelmed by fear and anxiety—concerning the future of the baby, perhaps, or of the pregnant mother herself once her condition becomes known.

A work that illuminates such conflicts over secrecy in pregnancy is *The Confessions of Lady Nijō*, written in fourteenth-century Japan.[9] When still a child, Lady Nijō was forced to become the concubine of a retired emperor. She had several babies not fathered by him. Her book tells of the stratagems required each time to conceal her pregnant state, and to give birth in secret to a baby she could never hope to rear but had to turn over to others; it recounts her despair over this fate, her fear lest the emperor should learn she was the mother of a baby not his own, and her repeated attempts to escape her life at court to travel and write poetry as a Buddhist nun. Like Lady Nijō, women in many other cultures have had to conceal their condition, fearful that it be noticed, and afraid of the gossip, the loss of face if they were unmarried, perhaps the dismissal from work once concealment was no longer possible.*

The second and third claims to control over secrecy presuppose the first. Given the need to guard identity, they invoke, in addition, the need for such control in order to protect certain plans and actions.

Choice is future-oriented, and never fully expressed in present action.

---

*Even when a pregnancy is acknowledged, and after the expected baby is born, uncertainty and secrecy may persist regarding the identity of one or both of the parents. Strindberg, in *The Father*, has conveyed the anguish of a husband who suspects that he might not be the true father of his daughter. His brain "grinding at the empty thoughts until it burns out," he goes over and over in his mind all that he knows about reproduction, arguing that no man is ever fully certain of the paternity of his children. Women alone, he believes, are able to "know absolutely." "A man has no children—it is only women who bear children," he concludes, "and that is why the future may be theirs, when we die without offspring!" [10]

It requires what is most distinctive about human reasoning: intention—the capacity to envisage and to compare future possibilities, to make estimates, sometimes to take indirect routes to a goal or to wait. What is fragile, unpopular, perhaps threatened, such as Winston Smith's plan to express his views freely in his diary, seeks additional layers of secrecy. To the extent that it is possible to strip people of their capacity for secrecy about their intentions and their actions, their lives become more transparent and predictable; they can then the more easily be subjected to pressure and defeated.

Secrecy for plans is needed, not only to protect their formulation but also to develop them, perhaps to change them, at times to execute them, even to give them up. Imagine, for example, the pointlessness of the game of chess without secrecy on the part of the players. Secrecy guards projects that require creativity and prolonged work: the tentative and the fragile, unfinished tasks, probes and bargaining of all kinds. An elopement or a peace initiative may be foiled if prematurely suspected; a symphony, a scientific experiment, or an invention falters if exposed too soon. In speaking of creativity, Carlyle stressed the need for silence and secrecy, calling them "the element in which great things fashion themselves together." [11]

Joint undertakings as well as personal ones may require secrecy for the sharing and working out of certain plans and for cooperative action. Lack of secrecy would, for instance, thwart many negotiations, in which all plans cannot easily be revealed from the outset. Once projects are safely under way, however, large portions of secrecy are often given up voluntarily, or dispelled with a flourish. Surprises are sprung and jokes explained. The result of the jury trial can be announced, the statue unveiled, the secretly negotiated treaty submitted for ratification, the desire to marry proclaimed. Here again, what is at issue is not secrecy alone, but rather the control over secrecy and openness. Many projects need both gestation and emergence, both confinement and publicity. Still others, such as certain fantasies and daydreams and hopes, may be too ephemeral or intimate, at times too discreditable, ever to see the light of day.

Secrecy about plans and their execution, therefore, allows unpredictability and surprise. These are often feared; yet without them human existence would not only be unfree but also monotonous and stifling. Secrecy heightens the value of relevations; it is essential for arousing suspense, whether through stories told, surprises prepared, or waiting times imposed. It can lend the joy of concentration and solemnity to the smallest matters. Secrecy may also lower intensity and provide relief, so that when a revelation is finally made—as after the death of those most intimately connected with events described in an author's private diaries—the anguish of exposure is lessened. In all these ways, secrecy is the carrier of texture and variety. Without it, and without the suspense and wit and unexpectedness it allows, communication would be oppressively dull—lifeless in its own right.

The fourth claim to control over secrecy concerns property. At its root, it is closely linked to identity, in that people take some secrets, such as hidden love letters, to *belong* to them more than to others, to be *proper to* them.[12] We link such secrets with our identity, and resist intrusions into them. But the claim to own secrets about oneself is often far-fetched. Thus the school-bus driver who has a severe heart condition cannot rightfully claim to *own* this medical information, even though it concerns him intimately. Even when outsiders have less need to share the information than in such a case, the question who owns a secret may be hard to answer. Should one include only those "about whom" it is a secret, those who claim a right to decide whether or not to disclose it, or all who know it?

In addition to such questions of owning secrets, secrecy is invoked to protect what one owns. We take for granted the legitimacy of hiding silver from burglars and personal documents from snoopers and busybodies. Here, too, the link to identity is close, as is that to plans and their execution. For had we no belongings whatsoever, our identity and our capacity to plan would themselves be threatened, and in turn survival itself. As H. L. A. Hart points out, life depends on the respect for at least "some minimal form of the institution of property (though not necessarily individual property) and the distinctive kind of rule which requires respect for it."[13] At the most basic level, if crops are to be grown, land must be secure from indiscriminate entry, and food must be safe from being taken by others.

The four claims to control over secrecy and openness to protect identity, plans, action, and property are not always persuasive. They may be stretched much too far, or abused in many ways. No matter how often these claims fail to convince, however, I shall assume that they do hold for certain fundamental human needs. Some capacity for keeping secrets and for choosing when to reveal them, and some access to the underlying experience of secrecy and depth, are indispensable for an enduring sense of identity, for the ability to plan and to act, and for essential belongings. With no control over secrecy and openness, human beings could not remain either sane or free.

The Dangers of Secrecy

Against every claim to secrecy stands, however, the awareness of its dangers. It is the experience of these dangers that has led so many to view secrecy negatively, and that underlies statements such as that by Lord Acton, that "everything secret degenerates." [14] Such categorical dismissals are too sweeping, but they do point to the harm that secrets can do both to those who keep them and to those from whom they are kept—harm that often thwarts and debilitates the very needs for which I have argued that control over secrecy is indispensable.

Secrecy can harm those who make use of it in several ways. It can debilitate judgment, first of all, whenever it shuts out criticism and feedback, leading people to become mired down in stereotyped, unexamined, often erroneous beliefs and ways of thinking. Neither their perception of a problem nor their reasoning about it then receives the benefit of challenge and exposure. Scientists working under conditions of intense secrecy have testified to its stifling effect on their judgment and creativity. And those who have written about their undercover work as journalists, police agents, and spies, or about living incognito for political reasons, have described similar effects of prolonged concealment on their capacity to plan and to choose, at times on their sense of identity.

Secrecy can affect character and moral choice in similar ways. It allows people to maintain façades that conceal traits such as callousness or vindictiveness—traits which can, in the absense of criticism or challenge from without, prove debilitating. And guilty or deeply embarrassing secrets can corrode from within before outsiders have a chance to respond or to be of help. This deterioration from within is the danger Acton referred to in his statement, and is at the root of the common view that secrecy, like other exercises of power, can corrupt.

These risks of secrecy multiply because of its tendency to spread. Aware of the importance of exercising control over secrecy and openness, people seek more control whenever they can, and rarely give up portions of it voluntarily. In imitation and in self-protection, others then seek more as well. The control shifts in the direction of secrecy whenever there is negligence or abuse to cover up; as a result, as Weber pointed out, bureaucracies and other organizations surround themselves with ever greater secrecy to the extent that circumstances permit.

As secrecy debilitates character and judgment, it can also lower resistance to the irrational and the pathological. It then poses great difficulties for individuals whose controls go awry. We know all the stifling rigidity that hampers those who become obsessed with secrecy. For them, secrecy no longer serves sanity and free choice. It shuts off the safety valve between the inner and the shared worlds. We know, too, the pathologies of prying into the private spheres of others, and of losing all protection for one's own: voyeurism and the corresponding hunger for self-exposure that destroy the capacity to discriminate and to choose.

The danger of secrecy, however, obviously goes far beyond risks to those who *keep* secrets. If they alone were at risk, we would have fewer reasons to try to learn about, and sometimes interfere with, their secret practices. Our attitude changes radically as soon as we suspect that these practices also hurt others. And because secrecy can debilitate judgment and choice, spread, and become obsessive, it often affects others even when it is not intended to. This helps explain why, in the absence of clear criteria for when secrecy is and is not injurious, many people have chosen to regard all secrecy as potentially harmful.

When the freedom of choice that secrecy gives one person limits or destroys that of others, it affects not only his own claims to respect for identity, plans, action, and property, but theirs. The power of such secrecy can be immense. Because it bypasses inspection and eludes interference, secrecy is central to the planning of every form of injury to human beings. It cloaks the execution of these plans and wipes out all traces afterward. It enters into all prying and intrusion that cannot be carried out openly. While not all that is secret is meant to deceive— as jury deliberations, for instance, are not—all deceit does rely on keeping something secret. And while not all secrets are discreditable, all that is discreditable and all wrongdoing seek out secrecy (unless they can be carried out openly without interference, as when they are pursued by coercive means).

Such secrecy can hamper the exercise of rational choice at every step: by preventing people from adequately understanding a threatening situation, from seeing the relevant alternatives clearly, from assessing the consequences of each, and from arriving at preferences with respect to them. Those who have been hurt in such a way by the secrecy of others may in turn seek greater control over secrecy, and thus in turn experience its impairment of choice, its tendency to spread, its capacity to corrupt and to invite abuse.

Moral Considerations

Given both the legitimacy of some control over secrecy and openness, and the dangers this control carries for all involved, there can be no presumption either for or against secrecy in general. Secrecy differs in this respect from lying, promise-breaking, violence, and other practices for which the burden of proof rests on those who would defend them. Conversely, secrecy differs from truthfulness, friendship, and other practices carrying a favorable presumption.

The resulting challenge for ethical inquiry into the aims and methods of secrecy is great. Not only must we reject definitions of secrecy that invite approval or disapproval; we cannot even begin with a moral presumption in either direction. This is not to say, however, that there can be none for particular practices, nor that these practices are usually morally neutral. But it means that it is especially important to look at them separately, and to examine the moral arguments made for and against each one.

In studying these moral arguments, I shall rely on two presumptions that flow from the needs and dangers of secrecy that I have set forth. The first is one of *equality*. Whatever control over secrecy and openness we conclude is legitimate for some individuals should, in the absence of special considerations, be legitimate for all. If we look back at the four imaginary societies as illustrations, I can see no reason why some individuals should lack all such control, as in the first and second societies, and not others: no reason why, as in the first society, only you and I should be unable to keep anything secret or, as in the second, be able to penetrate all secrets. No just society would, if it had the choice, allocate controls so unequally. This is not to say that some people might not be granted limited powers for certain of those purposes under constraints that minimize the risks—in journalism, for instance, or government; but they would have to advance reasons sufficient to overcome the initial presumption favoring equality. On the basis of this presumption, I reject both the first and the second of the imaginary societies, and any others that come close to them even in part.

My second presumption is in favor of *partial individual control* over the degree of secrecy or openness about personal matters—those most indisputably in the private realm. (I shall leave for later consideration the question of large-scale collective control over secrecy and openness regarding personal matters, as well as individual *or* collective control over less personal matters, such as professional, business, or government secrets.) Without a premise supporting a measure of individual control over personal matters, it would be impossible to preserve the indispensable respect for identity, plans, action, and belongings that all of us need and should legitimately be able to claim.

Such individual control should extend, moreover, to what people choose to share with one another about themselves—in families, for example, or with friends and colleagues. Without the intimacy that such sharing makes possible, human relationships would be impossible, and identity and plans would themselves suffer. For these reasons, I reject also the third imaginary society, in which all is openness, and where people have no choice between such openness and secrecy, even in personal and intimate matters.

At the same time, however, it is important to avoid any presumption in favor of *full* control over such matters for individuals. Such full control is not necessary for the needs that I have discussed, and would aggravate the dangers. It would force us to disregard the legitimate claims of those persons who might be injured, betrayed, or ignored as a result of secrets inappropriately kept or revealed. I must therefore also reject the fourth imaginary society, in which all have such control and can exercise it at will.

Given these two presumptions, in favor of equal control over secrecy and openness among all individuals, and in favor of partial individual control over personal matters, exercised singly or shared with other individuals, I shall go on to ask: *What considerations override these presumptions?* This will require us to look at the reasons advanced in favor of unusual secrecy, probing, or revelation by some, and to ask when even the partial control exercised by an individual in personal matters must be overridden. It will also require us to examine the role of loyalty and promises in counteracting such reasons to override personal control; and the crucial difference it makes if it is one's own secret or that of another that one wonders whether to reveal.

In approaching such questions about the ethics of secrecy, I hope to show how they mirror and shed light on aspects of ethics more generally. But these questions also create special difficulties; for no matter what moral principles one takes to be important in moral reasoning, they have a near-paradoxical relationship with secrecy. Thus secrecy both promotes and endangers what we think beneficial, even necessary for survival. It may prevent harm, but it follows maleficence like a shadow. Every misdeed cloaks itself in secrecy unless accompanied by such power that it can be performed openly. And while secrecy may heighten a sense of equality and brotherhood among persons sharing the secret, it can fuel gross intolerance and hatred toward outsiders. At the heart of secrecy lies discrimination of some form, since its essence is sifting, setting apart, drawing lines. Secrecy, moreover, preserves liberty, yet this very liberty allows the invasion of that of others.

Coming to Experience Secrecy and Openness

The Self Among Others

How do children come to experience secrets and secrecy, given that newborns neither keep nor recognize secrets? How does this experience affect the ability to cope with the conflicts of secrecy and openness? And what is the relationship between responses to such conflicts and those to moral choice more generally?

The ability to deal with secrecy is rooted in the child's growing consciousness of identity, and of being able to act, to intervene, to alter, to resist if need be. At first, infants are one with what surrounds them. They do not feel separate from those who care for them, nor do they express any self-awareness when confronted, for example, with a mirror. They come to know themselves through experience with others. Out of the early symbiosis comes the realization of separateness, of an identity, with boundaries in space and continuity in time. Infants learn that they can have an effect on self and others. Individuality becomes delineated, as do the social bonds that sustain it. Only then can there be a possibility of wanting to shield and to hide. Only then can the wonder arise about what others might be hiding and about all that is secret and mysterious.

To hide and seek: how much experience must be gained before this seemingly simple game can be played. One-year-olds do not know that an object persists after they cease looking at it. Simple hiding games amaze them over and over again. They learn about absence and presence, and master shifts in perspective and focus. They come to know beginnings and duration and endings. In gaining such knowledge, playing with it, and testing it in so many ways, children learn to look at themselves as both subjects and objects—as perceiver and perceived, as agent and the one who is acted upon—and thus to guess at how others see them.

Not until children develop some rudimentary understanding of separateness—their own or that of their group—and of lasting identity, can they experience secrecy. And not until reciprocity and perspective and the sense of an enduring private realm are possible can they do much about their own secrets or those of others.

In all cultures, children then come face to face with prohibitions about large clusters of experience, concerning, for instance, sexual life or religion or death. They are asked not to have anything to do with what is thus forbidden, and not to inquire into it or talk about it. Cultures differ in their attitudes toward any one form of secrecy. Thus sexual relations among the unmarried are freely acknowledged in one, while branded as the most shameful of secrets in another. And Ruth Benedict has described the differences between two cultures with respect to whether rivalry is open or concealed.[1] The inhabitants of Dobu Island, off the southern shore of New Guinea, put a premium on treachery, and resort to magic, deceit, and secret poisoning to defeat rivals. The successful man is he who has cheated another of his place. Among the Kwakiutl on the northwest coast of America, on the other hand, all conflicts are aboveboard and arrogant, conducted in the full glare of publicity. The object of all Kwakiutl enterprise, according to Benedict, is to show oneself superior to one's rivals, in as open and uninhibited a way as possible.

Cultures differ not only with respect to the kinds of matters kept secret but also in the degrees of secrecy that characterize them. Thus Elizabeth Brandt has described the intricate and wide-ranging systems of secrecy in the Taos Pueblo culture and compared it with other societies that place less formal stress on keeping secrets.[2] Among modern states, the differences are no less striking, from the point of view of their reliance on, say, administrative secrecy and secret police.

We have much to learn from such comparisons. But it would be wrong to imagine that there are societies in which the conflicts between secrecy and openness do not arise, or to see culture as so formative that we ignore individual variation in coping and failing to cope with openness and secrecy within any one society. Granted that what is secret in one culture may be freely approached in another, and that some societies appear to be more secretive than others. But there are sharp differences in experience and response among members of even the most rigidly secretive group. As Mary Douglas has pointed out, cultural anthropologists who assume that the human personality settles into a hard mold after infancy have fallen victim to a theoretical stance that is helpless in the face of change.[3]

Too rigid as well are those views of child development that take children to be incapable of keeping secrets until they reach a particular age or cognitive stage. Piaget, for instance, saw young children as "unable to keep a single thought secret."

Apart from thinking by images or autistic symbols which cannot be directly communicated, the child, up to an age, as yet undetermined but probably somewhere about seven, is incapable of keeping to himself the thoughts which enter his head. He says everything. He has no verbal continence.[4]

Piaget based these judgments on observations of children playing near one another. He saw children as encapsulated in an egocentric mode of thinking and as incapable of assuming the point of view of others. As a result, he argued, they speak to themselves, not to others. Unable to conceive of themselves as watched by others, they have no capacity for secrecy.

Recent studies have shown, however, that Piaget may have underestimated the complexity of early childhood experience and the gradual nature of the development of different ways of seeing and understanding. As early as a few weeks after birth, infants distinguish the category of people from the category of things.[5] They quickly learn to follow the gaze of their caretakers and others around them. Games of hiding are incomprehensible if one does not assume some capacity to consider the point of view of others. Most four-year-olds can not only participate in such games but even advise another child on where to go in a test situation where it is important to hide from a number of policemen, and where intersecting walls provide different hiding-places.[6]

Such studies go counter to Piaget's claim that small children are unable to assume the point of view of others, the claim meant to support the argument that children are incapable of secrecy. While we may benefit from Piaget's subtle analysis of what goes into the developing experience of self and others, and thus of secrecy, we need not be bound by his view of this experience as locked into invariant cognitive stages, any more than we need accept rigid cultural molds for it.

Nor, finally, need we assume that the growing capacity to experience secrecy must be localized in some hypothetical compartment of the self, or tied to some particular childhood conflict, any more than to a developmental stage. Yet the effort to find some unique explanation for secrecy has led many to suggest such links. Thus Freud linked attitudes toward secrecy and early sexuality. Alfred Gross went so far as to ask "whether there is not in our subconscious a complete identity between the secret on the one hand, and the bodily excretions (respectively the organs of secretion) on the other." And Selma Fraiberg has interpreted all concern with secret treasures—in literature as in life—as reflecting masturbatory and incestuous daydreams.[7]

Such speculations are doubtless occasionally to the point. Childhood sexual development is one aspect of learning about the self and about relations with others. But to see an identity between secrets and bodily excretions or masturbatory or incestuous daydreams short-circuits efforts to understand the complexity of secrecy. Not through any one aspect of experience, but throughout the growing consciousness of self and others, do individuals come to learn about secrecy. And the consciousness of others is not merely external but precisely an awareness that they, too, are capable of concealment, of hidden intentions, and of curiosity about one's own secrets. The entire self takes part in this growth, and expresses itself through it.

Confronting Secrets from the Outside

Myths and fairy tales convey the experience of confronting what is secret. Silent forests that frighten and yet allure; sealed caves entrusted to the charge of spirits; beckoning sirens whose promises of delight cause sailors to perish; realms of the dead where to look backward is to be turned to stone: all bear witness to the spell secrets cast and to their dangers.

As *outsiders* to secrets, children project their groping view of the unknown against the background of such tales. Only gradually do they begin to distinguish the secret from the rest of what they do not know. All that is unknown can both attract and inspire caution, but the secret does so most intensely, for hiding invites probes, and boundaries and prohibitions incite to transgression.[8] Yet special traps and revenges may lie in wait for those who violate secrets.

The fear that some secrets inspire is of the harm they can do, or of being hurt or changed through them in ways one cannot control. To acquire any new knowledge is to be changed; but the change from learning secrets is less predictable, less in the power of the learner. The fear of secret knowledge, then, may be a fear of what learning it will entail—of being drawn into a guilty secret, perhaps, entangled in its protection, or polluted through mere contact with it.

The change, moreover, may be irreversible. One cannot at will unlearn a secret, no matter how unpalatable or dangerous it turns out to be. It is hard enough to forget anything on purpose,[9] but to forget a secret on purpose is even harder. The very effort to do so singles out what one wants to erase from memory. To be sure, one forgets some secrets, but one can never choose to do so.

Respect is the other strong motive for leaving secrets alone. It protects not merely the self, as in the fear of secrets, but also the secret itself and its owners or guardians. Certain objects, persons, or institutions inspire respect that partakes of awe—a response to what is set apart, alien, perhaps sacred, and seeming to possess a power that calls for restraint even as it generates among certain outsiders a desire to be included and to be made a participant. Such awe is what Calvin called for in castigating Christians for their curiosity about God's secrets, and especially about the mysteries of predestination, the fate foreordained by God's will for each human life. This curiosity, he warned, is dangerous:

Let them remember that when they inquire into predestination they are penetrating the sacred precincts of divine wisdom. If anyone with a carefree assurance breaks into this place, he will not succeed in satisfying his curiosity and he will enter a labyrinth from which he can find no exit. For it is not right for man unrestrainedly to search out things that the Lord has willed to be hid in Himself, and to unfold from eternity itself the sublimest wisdom, which He would have us revere but not understand that through this also He should fill us with wonder.[10]

Apuleius tells in his *Metamorphoses* of what befell a young man in antiquity who lacked the proper restraint and awe with respect to the supernatural.[11] Lucius, desirous of adventure and with "an irresistible impulse to study magic," had come to Thessaly, known as the center of sorcery and magic. Having fallen in love with a beautiful slave-girl, he learned from her that her mistress was a sorceress who could transform herself into different animal shapes. He begged to be allowed to witness such a session in secret, and saw the sorceress change herself into an owl. Immediately, he longed to do the same, so that he could try flying. He begged the girl to let him try the magic ointment that the sorceress had used; but when he applied it, he found to his horror that he had turned into a donkey instead—and that he had no means of reversing this transformation.

The story then recounts the suffering and humiliations Lucius had to endure and the obstacles he had to overcome before he could regain his human shape. It ends by telling how he sought initiation into the mysteries of the goddess Isis, this time taking care not to exceed the prescribed boundaries, and how he succeeded in journeying to the gates of death and returning to a new, enlightened existence.

Outsiders to secrets recognize the tension between fear and awe on the one hand and fascination on the other. The desire to learn, to know, to quench one's curiosity determines the attitude toward many secrets, not only on the part of those with most at stake but on the part of all who gossip and wonder. Other powerful motives behind the attraction of secrets are the desire to gain control, to feel superior to those not in possession of the secrets, and the longing for the sheer enjoyment and intimacy that learning secrets can bring. These motives nourish the desire to be an insider rather than an outsider to the secret, to be accepted as an intimate or an initiate, and to cross forbidden boundaries.

Leon Trotsky conveys this desire in his autobiography, describing his feelings as a seventeen-year-old in Tsarist Russia in 1896, on the threshold of secret revolutionary activities:

In the intellectual circles in which I moved, nobody did any actual revolutionary work. We realized that between our endless tea-table discussions and revolutionary organization there was a vast gulf. We knew that any contacts with workers demanded secret, highly "conspiratory" methods. And we pronounced the word solemnly with a reverence that was almost mystic. We had no doubt that in the end we would go from the discussions at the tea-table to "conspiratia"; but nobody was definite as to how and when the change would take place.[12]

The same desires draw us to seek to understand the inwardness and essence of other human beings—bearers of sacredness, mysterious to outsiders as to themselves. To live locked into oneself is to feel ignorant, limited, at times barely alive at all. We assume that certain others are different. Through seeking to learn their secrets, we hope to share their intensity and aliveness. In *To the Lighthouse*, Virginia Woolf expresses the desire to erase the personal boundaries that both protect and imprison, and to be included within those of another:

She imagined how in the chambers of the mind and heart of the woman who was, physically, touching her, were stood, like the treasures in the temples of kings, tablets bearing sacred inscriptions, which if one could spell them out, would teach one everything, but they would never be offered openly, never made public. What art was there, known to love as cunning, by which one person pressed through into those secret chambers? What device for becoming, like waters poured into one jar, inextricably the same, one with the object one adored? [13]

The sense of the mysterious and the unfathomable in human beings bespeaks the recognition that no one can be known in entirety, neither from within nor from without. Some aspects will remain forever in the dark; others will be glimpsed briefly, and with all the distortions that we know, only to sink out of sight as attention moves elsewhere or is forced aside.

Not only are we, as outsiders, aware of the conflict between attraction and resistance to certain secrets of others; we are equally torn between acknowledgment and avoidance of what they do not keep secret at all. Stanley Cavell has analyzed the strains and complexities of this additional conflict in *The Claim of Reason*. He has traced the sources of both skepticism and tragedy to the avoidance and the failures of imagination of human beings face to face with one another:

Imagination is called for, faced with the other, when I have to take the facts in, realize what is going on, make the behavior real for myself, make a connection.

If it makes sense to speak of seeing human beings as human beings, then it makes sense to imagine that a human being may lack the capacity to see human beings as human beings. It would make sense to ask whether someone may be soul-blind. [14]

Cavell's work illuminates the difficulties, the temptations, the indulgences of this conflict. But in his insistence on its exceptional importance, he seems at times to intimate that there may be neither mystery nor unavoidable secrecy about human inwardness—that nothing need remain hidden. It is as if, in order to focus on the varieties of acknowledgment and avoidance of what is there to be understood in human beings, he had to downplay, indeed avoid, the outsider's conflict with respect to secrecy:

It is true of a great deal of what goes on in me, that normally if it is to be known I must tell it, or give expression to it. But for nothing in me is this absolutely true. Whatever in me I have to conceal I may betray exactly by the way in which I conceal it. . . . There are those who know how to read such concealments. [15]

A similar claim is often made by social researchers or military experts: that any one secret, no matter how carefully concealed, can be betrayed or penetrated. Such a claim can neither be proved nor disproved, but it is highly improbable. And even if it were shown to hold for any one secret, the step from such a conclusion regarding a particular secret to one for secrets in general would be unwarranted. No matter how many secrets those who know how to read concealments manage to ferret out, and no matter how many additional secrets people unwittingly betray, still more would always remain.

Secrecy will never be reducible to any one set of secrets, any more than to one stage of human development or figurative compartment of the self. Efforts to downplay the role of secrecy echo the illusory longing for full transparency among human beings that Sartre and so many others have voiced—often in its own right a form of resistance to the difficulties of knowing human beings, including oneself. The outsider's tension with respect to experienced secrecy generates the desire to cut it down to size, confine it, preferably dispel it altogether. But this tension need not force us into such a posture. It is our perverse lot that as outsiders—whether to others or to ourselves—we not only feel the tension between attraction and resistance to what we believe secret, or that between acknowledgment and avoidance of what is no secret at all, but we are also similarly conflicted even when it comes to *remaining aware* of these tensions simultaneously. We are at constant risk of slipping into simplifying moods. We deny and rationalize even in trying to take these forms of experience into account.

Having Secrets

As *insiders* to secrets, we experience a related set of tensions: between concealing and revealing, and between pressing upon others what is no secret at all and refraining therefrom. These tensions invite the clues and the taunts, the half-measures and the mysterious smiles, that may in turn increase the conflict felt by outsiders between wanting to unmask and to respect the secret.

All human relationships partake of such revealing in the midst of restraint, of hinting, at the very moment of disclosure, that yet further secrets remain to be unveiled. Georg Simmel described this tension that lends such intensity to many secrets, creating a sense of being alive to every touch, every challenge:

The secret contains a tension that is dissolved in the moment of its revelation. . . . It is surrounded by the possibility and temptation of betrayal; and the external danger of being discovered is interwoven with the internal danger, which is like the fascination of an abyss, of giving oneself away.[16]

The control over secrecy and openness functions, I have suggested, as a safety valve that allows partial control over privacy and human contact. It is not possible to conceal and to fence off without sensing the corresponding possibility of revelation. The desire to share one's secret, to confide, to unburden, to reach out for greater intimacy, often conflicts with the desire to keep the secret to oneself and to draw protection or power from its preservation—at times in obedience to the forces of resistance that bespeak the risk of "betraying oneself."

Carl Gustav Jung gives an example of the significance for him of a secret he kept as a child. He describes "a little manikin" that he carved at age ten, making for it a small bed and a woolen coat in his pencil case, adding "a smooth oblong blackish stone from the Rhine," and hiding the whole in the attic:

No one could discover my secret and destroy it. I felt safe, and the tormenting sense of being at odds with myself was gone. . . . This possession of a secret had a very powerful formative influence on my character; I consider it the essential fact of my boyhood.[17]

Other childhood secrets can have an equally powerful hold: secret treasures or hiding places, unspoken fears, suspicions too terrible to voice. Consider the experience of children who grow up believing in one identity, one lineage and set of parents, only to stumble upon the secret that they have been adopted; or that of children who know that they have been adopted, but are told that the identity of their biological parents must remain secret. They live with a secret that concerns their very identity, but cannot reach to its center, nor understand why it should be kept from them.[18] Many children—perhaps the majority—similarly wonder at some point in childhood whether they are truly the children of those who call themselves their parents, or whether some mistake or planned exchange at birth brought them where they are. It is natural to wonder thus; to ask just how one relates to a family that may seem alien in outlook and feeling; and in so doing, to delineate oneself in contrast.

A child's discovery that he alone knows something secret can come as a relief and a great joy. In *Father and Son*, Edmund Gosse describes the bliss of making such a discovery at the age of six. He suddenly realized that his father, who had seemed up to then hardly distinguishable from God, and at any rate quite as all-knowing, actually did not know that it was he, Edmund, who had unwittingly broken the lead pipe that was to bring water to a small fountain being built in the garden:

There was a secret in this world and it belonged to me and to a somebody who lived in the same body with me. There were two of us, and we could talk with one another. . . . It was in this dual form that the sense of my individuality now suddenly descended upon me.[19]

To realize that one has the power to remain silent is linked to the understanding that one can exert some control over events—that one need not be entirely transparent, entirely predictable or, as Gosse pointed out, at the mercy of parents who have seemed all-seeing and all-powerful. Later on, secure in this knowledge, children may learn to cope with the question of personal responsibility without needing to conceal mistakes. But this learning only comes through repeated experience with secrets kept and revealed.

Through the sharing of secrets with others, children also learn about loyalty and betrayal. Sometimes they discover that the very sharing of a secret can be meant to injure and to split allegiances. Consider, for example, the story told by Willie Fryer. When he was fifteen years old, his mother told him she was planning to leave his father. She asked Willie and his two sisters to help keep her plans secret from their father, explaining that she did not wish to worry him just while he was finishing a big project at work. Willie described his feelings:

I'll tell you how I felt then, especially when she said, "You want to tell me anything?" and all I could say was "Not really. Maybe I'll think of something." I felt like all the clocks in the world stopped and time went back to the beginning. All of us had to start all over again. It was like a new me.

The next time the clock stops and starts all over again is six months later. Now both my parents come to me one night. They're both so straightfaced they look like they're going to ask me for the toothpaste. My father by now knows everything. The bomb went off and nothing. No one heard a noise. If it hit him no one could have guessed by the way he was looking at us.

I was actually relieved. She waited so long she had me believing she wouldn't go through with it. But now I didn't have to keep the secret anymore.

You want to hear the kicker? They take one secret off the agenda for us, now they got another one. This time it's my father who is breaking the big news. We shouldn't breathe a word of this to anyone. It was the right word for him to use, too, because I couldn't breathe anymore at all. For his business and reputation, and her business and reputation, divorce wouldn't look good. So there we were, pledged to secrecy all over again. And there was the clock stopping and starting again. I was beginning to feel like a car bumping along a dirt road without any gas.

As you can see, I'm not doing all that well with my parents, but I've got to be among the world's top secret keepers. I didn't tell a soul; I led my life like a good little boy, and let myself choke on the whole scene. The secrets were still going strong in the Fryer home. If the split bothered anybody at 18 Willow Road, nobody could have told. My parents arranged to go to certain important social events together, the whole works, just to let people think they were together. No one at their jobs knew, and the people they work with are the biggest gossips I've ever met. The fact is, the greatest family project the Fryers ever undertook was the keeping of that secret.

That's my story. I still feel strangled to death, like I can't get air, and like every time I turn around I hear clocks stopping and starting and stopping and starting. . . . Talk about people you live with, or used to live with, or are *supposed* to live with, being strangers. I don't know who they are, *what* they are. The big secret is the charade. The all-night, all-day drama playing over at Willow Road.[20]

Stifled by the secrecy imposed upon him by his parents, Willie felt he was losing his sense of who he was and who they were. When his mother asked for his loyalty in keeping her secret from his father, Willie felt he was an accomplice in what he saw as her betrayal. The more loyally he protected the secret, the more his sense of being capable of loyalty was undermined. And when both parents asked him to help disguise the breakup of the family by deceiving the outside world, they undermined his integrity further. "The secrets took it all out of me. I told nothing in exchange for giving up every feeling I've had."

Few can resist the request for a "promise not to tell," least of all when a family member makes such a plea. But an important part of learning how to deal with secrecy is coming to recognize the aggressive intent behind some such requests: the desire to split loyalties, to burden, and to injure. Compare another kind of secret Willie might have been asked to keep from his father: a surprise birthday celebration. Keeping such a secret would have required no betrayal of his father's interest, no breach of faith. While all shared secrets set some individuals apart from others, many are meant to surprise and to delight, not to split loyalties. Adolescence is a period when learning to distinguish between requests for secrecy becomes possible, yet is too often thwarted. It is a time of seeking intimacy, of wondering who one is, of testing the bonds of loyalty and of promise. Sometimes, as in the case of Willie Fryer, a promise of secrecy that should never have been either requested or made is kept at immense personal cost.

Keepers of secrets can experience the powerful, the forbidden, and the sacred with the same awareness that outsiders have of such secrets as both endangered by and dangerous for those who come too near or who expose them. This experience underlies what I shall call the *esoteric rationale* for protecting what is held sacred and the secrets that partake of it. Invoked far beyond the boundaries of the strictly religious, this rationale inheres in the sense of sacredness that people can have with respect to themselves, their families, their professions, their nations. It serves an indispensable function in protecting these, but it can also deflect moral inquiry through the incentives it offers people to remain in a childish relationship to secrecy and power. They may then see too many secrets as manifestations of some power that must be obeyed, rather than as matters that require the assumption of responsibility and the exercise of judgment.

In sum, the conflicts between insider and outsider about control over secrecy and openness arise in every form of human encounter. And within each perspective, the same tensions are felt: for outsiders, between seeking to probe secrets and refraining therefrom, and between accepting and avoiding what is revealed; and for insiders, between keeping secrets and divulging them, and between seeking to overcome the restraint of outsiders with respect to what is in no way a secret, and acquiescing.

Discretion and Moral Judgment

Through experiencing the tensions of insider and outsider with respect to secrets, children confront immense possibilities for insight and choice. To conceal what is the case and to communicate what is not: these powers serve secrecy and openness, and thereby in turn influence all moral choice.

Choice about secrecy, like all other, can be used for good or for ill. The capacity to perceive such choice, and to judge one's freedom to act upon it, is gained in childhood and developed in adolescence. But this freedom may be haunted by a desire to return to symbiosis, complete intimacy, and freedom from personal responsibility. Similarly, the knowledge of how much lies hidden, out of sight or understanding, may be haunted by a desire to return to the center of power and to a sense of omniscience—a desire to possess all knowledge at once, illuminated, with no dark corners or mysteries.

To mature is in part to realize that while complete intimacy and omniscience and power cannot be had, self-transcendence, growth, and closeness to others are nevertheless within one's reach. It is to experience isolation and wonder, and to live with the partial and the unknown; to learn to shift focus and perspective so that new aspects appear while others fall into the penumbra, mysterious, perhaps kept secret. It is to come to terms, therefore, with hiding and with seeking, and to see their powers for equilibrium, freedom, and delight while remaining aware of their risks.

Those who come to terms thus with hiding and with seeking share a characteristic that I shall call discretion. At its best, discretion is the intuitive ability to discern what is and is not intrusive and injurious, and to use this discernment in responding to the conflicts everyone experiences as insider and outsider. It is an acquired capacity to navigate in and between the worlds of personal and shared experience, coping with the moral questions about what is fair or unfair, truthful or deceptive, helpful or harmful. Inconceivable without an awareness of the boundaries surrounding people, discretion requires a sense for when to hold back in order not to bruise, and for when to reach out. The word "tact" conveys the physical sense of touching that these boundaries evoke.

Such a use of the term "discretion" corresponds to some of its meanings, those closest to discernment and to judgment. It is related to but far from identical with the conventional use of the word "discretion" to connote good manners and a concern for appearances; and to the sense of that word which connotes power, as in judicial or parental exercises of discretion: the sense in which a government official has discretion over certain decisions, and parents over how they bring up their children, so long as they are not known to transgress minimal standards of treatment. I shall use the word "discretion" to connote the capacity to exercise judgment about secrecy.[21]

Some have developed a finely calibrated intuitive sense of discretion in this strong sense.[22] But the learning process is never completed, since every new understanding of another person can set in motion slight changes of response. A question that is overly familiar or bruising when asked by a stranger may be welcomed from a friend. What is surrounded by secrecy in one culture is openly revealed in others. And what some take to be intensely personal, others spill forth at every opportunity.

It takes both experience and sensitivity to accept and communicate personal information discreetly: not to overwhelm with sudden bursts of revelation, the intensity of which may be "shy-making" and can rarely be kept up, nor to be so restrained when sharing is called for that the opportunity passes and interest fades. Consider children just learning to form friendships, and seeing them break, over and over again. Today's best friend turns into tomorrow's bitter enemy whose secrets are divulged with relish. Each time, the newfound solidarity excludes outsiders as rigidly as before.

Such an inability to cope with conflicts of secrecy and openness connotes indiscretion. The indiscreet overstep boundaries in both directions—often without discerning them. They have little respect for autonomy, either that of others or their own, and their promises of

silence are as quickly given as they are forgotten. They blunder thought-
lessly across private regions. At best, they are merely clumsy; but they
may easily wound, and as easily be wounded, since they lack discernment
for what requires shelter and the self-control to provide it.

Many are compulsive disclosers of intimacies. They may gossip about
personal affairs and reveal the confidences of former friends or spouses
to every new acquaintance. What happens to them is instructive. They
find themselves increasingly isolated and less and less trusted. Studies
have shown that whereas self-disclosure usually invites reciprocation,
so that people match openness with openness, this breaks down if one
of the interlocutors is felt not to be selective.[23]

To "spill" too many secrets is to be like a sieve that lets too much
through. Some have lost—and others never learned—the sense for how
to select and make distinctions in what they say and to whom they
speak. Their instant familiarity all too often breeds but instant contempt.
Conversely, others are equally incapacitated in that they are like sieves
that let nothing through of substance, even when communication is
needed. They are just as undiscriminating, just as unable to achieve
lasting intimacy and friendship, and thus to give and receive confidences.

The ability to maintain control over secrecy and openness has often
been discussed in the context of *silence*: the virtue that Plutarch called
"profound and awesome," and that many classical thinkers thought
indispensable to practical wisdom.[24] Only those capable of silence exhibited
the self-control making them worthy of trust, according to these thinkers;
the garrulous betrayed their unreliability at every turn.

This view of silence as a virtue fundamental to practical wisdom has
always been tempered by the recognition that it also has negative aspects:
in particular, that it can pose barriers to understanding and intimacy,
that it can be deceptive, and that it can conceal suffering, guilt, and
wrongdoing. In our century, a shift has taken place to a dominant
emphasis on these negative aspects of silence. Such a one-sided view of
silence, and of secrecy in general, has been especially common in some
psychotherapeutic traditions, leading practitioners to offer advice that
encourages indiscriminate self-revelation. Thus one psychologist characterized people who withhold information as either "hermits, prudes,
paranoids, or rascals." The overriding question, he said, is "how to
maintain an atmosphere of trust and confidence which will enable us
to talk about personal affairs as freely as we talk about automobiles; to
share experience as we share the weather."[25]

The same encouragement of effusive openness about personal matters
is offered in many of the encounter groups that have flourished in the

last decades. These groups have brought together individuals, often strangers, to talk freely about themselves and about their feelings. Through sensory stimulation, movement, dance, and talk, leaders have encouraged such self-disclosure. The goal has been to foster a freer interaction between participants by breaking down ordinary barriers of distance and reticence, and thus to bring group members closer to one another and make them more capable of trust, affection, and joy in their lives.[26]

When guided with discernment, such groups can undoubtedly help members overcome fear, and experience the relief of exploring shared problems. But the dangers of such practices should not be underestimated. Human barriers are often frail. Participants urged to accept group norms for self-revelation or physical closeness to strangers have experienced acute anxiety; and at times intense group hostility has come to focus on certain group members. Some participants have suffered nervous collapses, and a few attempted suicide. The authors of a large-scale study of encounter groups estimate that over 9 percent of those who attended a series of encounter-group meetings underwent significant psychological injury.[27]

Someone who has suffered such injury has been hurt by pressures for openness just as much as Willie Fryer was hurt by his mother's urging him to keep her plans for divorce secret from his father. Each lacked sufficient control over secrecy and openness; for each, overpowering outside pressures undercut discretion. Each would have benefited from an ability to evaluate what was asked of them, to judge when claims to group or family loyalty are legitimate or on the contrary manipulative or excessive, and to decide when promises of secrecy or revelation should be accepted or refused, kept or broken. This ability, which I have called discretion, therefore calls for the judgment to pick and choose among incoming messages and possible outgoing ones; and thus in turn for sensitivity to certain forms of manipulative rhetoric and advocacy, whether in family or group settings or in such large-scale practices as advertising or campaign bombast.

But discretion concerning secrecy and openness is often both limited and biased. When people are sensitive only to the needs of some— adults, perhaps, or their peers, or those belonging to a certain social class or religious faith—they see no need to be discreet with respect to all others. They may make light of those they think immature, beneath them, outside their social circle, or otherwise insignificant. What a child confides in deepest secrecy may then be laughed at around the party table. The most intimate details of the private lives of the retarded or the mentally ill may be the subject of gossip by their caretakers. And as shown by societies such as Victorian England or slave-owning America, elaborate rules of discretion and good manners toward some may go hand in hand with neglect and brutal mistreatment of others.

Discretion can also be incomplete and debilitating when it is not seen as reciprocal: either when it is believed to be due to oneself but not necessary toward others, or when it leads one to be overly deferent to others while ignoring the need for self-respect. Discretion, finally, can become so distorted that it calls for silence and a failure to inquire no matter what the nature of the secrets one shares. The discreet butler in a wealthy Mafia household or the receptionist in a substandard home for the aged may have learned to hear no evil and see none. Such a contracted form of discretion reflects an equally contracted sense of personal responsibility and of what is due other human beings.

The experience of secrecy and of the perspectives of insider and outsider to secrets mirrors a central aspect of moral relations between self and others more generally. Learning to handle secrecy with discretion blends with and reflects moral development. In each, one must come to see oneself and others as capable of moral choice and as owed respect. And at the root of each lies the capacity for sifting apart and for discernment that is indispensable for all thinking, all choice.

This relationship between the experience of secrecy and that of moral choice, and between discretion and moral judgment, is nevertheless not one of parallelism or point-by-point correspondence. Though we can hardly learn about discretion without learning about moral judgment, nor lack the first without lacking the second, there is obviously more to moral choice than questions of secrecy. But because experience with secrecy tests human relationships as little else does, it may shed light on aspects of moral choice otherwise easily overlooked. To illustrate the influence that intense and pervasive secrecy can have on moral development, I turn next to secret societies.

Secret Societies

Groups Sworn to Secrecy

Few human activities convey the allure and the dangers of secrecy as vividly as do the secret societies that have sprung up in so many parts of the world.[1] From primitive times to our own, these secret groups have served the desires for intimacy, enjoyment, knowledge, and power, sometimes to cruel excess. Some have furthered purposes of bigotry and greed; others have worked as hard for enlightenment and tolerance. Can anything be said to unite groups so different as the twelfth-century Assassins who terrorized the Near East and the "speculative" branch of the Freemasons in eighteenth-century France, in which members such as Diderot battled ignorance and fanaticism? Or the contemporary Ku Klux Klan and the Pythagorean Brotherhood in the sixth century B.C., whose members prepared themselves through asceticism and research to receive secret wisdom? Or yet the Skoptsi, also known as Castrators, in eighteenth-century Russia, who believed that castration was a first step to receiving secret powers over others, even the power to perform miracles, and the Italian Carbonari, dedicated to religious and political liberation?

What unites them is not any one purpose or belief. It is, rather, secrecy itself: secrecy of purpose, belief, methods, often membership. These are kept hidden from outsiders and only by gradual steps revealed to insiders, with further secrets always beckoning, still to be penetrated. In this way the secret societies hold out the possibility of exclusive access to the forbidden roots of secrecy, and promise the brotherhood and community feeling that many lack in their everyday life. Few experiences of secrecy are more intense, or give insiders so stark a sense of separation from outsiders.*

For this reason secret societies offer an unusually sharp, almost foreshortened perspective on the effects of secrecy on moral choice. They show how secrecy can both protect and injure human identity through efforts to transcend and to mold it, and how creativity and reasoning and moral concern can thrive or deteriorate as a result.

Repressive states provide especially fertile ground for secret societies. At times, the authorities employ such societies as tools to carry out anonymous acts of intimidation or reprisal. Thus the Spanish Garduñas, who claimed a God-given right to kill for the greater glory of religion, carried out clandestine crimes for the Holy Inquisition in the sixteenth century. Calling themselves the Holy Warriors, they looted and burned the houses of heretics, abducting women and killing for a fee.

More common still, under a repressive regime, are secret organizations and conspiracies that work against its oppression. For the downtrodden in feudal societies such as nineteenth-century Russia or China, the secret societies offered a new identity instead of anonymity, a community for perhaps the first time in their lives, and the possibility of working toward personal and social transformation.[2] Deprived of any chance to speak out about their condition or to alter it, members often saw the secret society as offering an opportunity to take part in a group in which they would be given a name, have belongings to protect, and be able to speak forbidden thoughts freely. They could thus not only gain meaning for their own lives but take part in something beyond themselves of absorbing importance. They mattered both as persons having such an

---

*Practices of secrecy are important in the initiation rites of primitive societies, and were so in the mysteries of antiquity and in the medieval guilds and brotherhoods. The groups emphasized in this chapter, however, were explicitly created as secret societies, often by a single individual. Unlike the institutionalized secret practices of guilds and primitive initiation rites, these societies often led a precarious existence at the margins of the larger community. In addition, certain contemporary secret societies touch members but marginally. I shall concentrate in this chapter on those that require a conversion to new beliefs and to a new way of life.

affiliation and as partaking of its identity. The same conditions of anonymity, exploitation, and hopelessness have created fertile conditions for secret societies among peoples suffering from foreign domination. Thus Ireland, nineteenth-century Italy, and many Mediterranean countries have known an uncommon number of such groups; other states, few or none.

Founders and leaders of many secret societies have aimed to produce both personal and social transformation, whether in opposition to the larger society or as a tool of the regime in power. They may have wanted to improve upon trivialized or corrupt religious practices, or else to supplant them altogether. It is no coincidence that the Freemasons and so many other secret societies came to prominence in Europe during the Enlightenment period. Many hoped that the overthrow of a regime they regarded as unjust would only be the preliminary to a society of justice and brotherhood.

States with an openly authoritarian structure in religious and political life and a strong hierarchical class or caste structure are especially likely to give rise to secret societies.[3] In China, for example, secret societies were used by each side in the struggle that brought Mao to power. The 1911 Chinese revolution was greatly aided by secret societies, and Sun Yat-sen was himself the member of one such society. The Chinese Communists decided as early as 1926 that they ought to work with one secret society, called the Red Spears. The executive committee of the Comintern argued that the Red Spears, though directed by reactionaries, were "objectively revolutionary" in character by reason of their mass nature.[4]

Whether formed in imitation of or in opposition to coercion and hierarchy, secret societies often turn out to impose these even more rigidly on their members, in new guise. In part, this may be because they have no experience of anything different—much as religious groups that have suffered persecution are too often the first to persecute in turn, once they are free to do so. In part it may result from the need for hierarchy and strict obedience in order to preserve secrecy, and from the resultant recourse to small cells and structures of strict authority by a governing elite known to only a few of the members.

At times the governments most tolerant of the right to join associations and to speak freely inspire the growth of secret societies through their very tolerance. Whenever individuals entertain a conspiracy theory regarding a particular racial or religious or political group, or perhaps about a profession such as banking, or even another secret society, they may regard the state's tolerance of this group as misguided. If the state does not repress the group they find dangerous, and if they know they cannot themselves try to do so openly without legal repercussions, they may seek to carry out their aims by secret means.

Still others have political or commercial aims they know they cannot carry out lawfully, and so they, in turn, are drawn to the secrecy that such societies make possible. Indeed, because secret societies stress silence and loyalty, and because they possess a ready-made set of members willing to take risks for one another, criminal groups often see them as tempting targets for infiltration. In this way, smugglers and opium traders took over many a secret society in nineteenth-century China, just as political and financial plotters were alleged, in the 1981 scandal that rocked Italy, to have taken over Freemason lodges.

Even persons with the most idealistic aims may argue that the political tolerance of the democracy in which they live is but a cover for pervasive exploitation, and that the only way to overthrow the government is through secret action by a self-constituted elite. Here again, secret societies offer networks for pursuing such goals. Finally, the government itself, no matter how democratically installed, may wish to carry out activities at home or abroad that it cannot avow; and the organizations it sets up for such purposes often come to function much like secret societies.

Many secret societies, however, have no such ulterior aims. They are rewarding and inspiring to insiders while harmless to outsiders. They may offer the pleasure of secret rites, challenging ordeals, and a group identity few other organizations can muster. Without any of the dangers of other secret societies, such groups can then help members develop their ability to cope with secrecy and openness. Through vivid experiences with the tensions of both insiders and outsiders, individuals can come to recognize the values and the excesses of each, and to weigh methods of dealing with them.

Adolescents, in particular, often join such secret groups. In trying to sort out what belongs to the world of self and to that of others, and in probing their own identities, they are especially open to the allure of secret societies. They may long, too, for hierarchy and for clear lines of authority, and relish the chance to prove themselves in accepted rites of passage. They may see around them no inspiring models of adulthood, or else find models too numerous and conflicting, especially at a time, as in adolescence, when ambiguity and confusion are hard to sustain. They are then more open to appeals from groups that seem to offer structure and ritual, dramatic signs of passing from one stage to another, and a chance at self-change and self-transcendence.[5] Initiation into such a society serves as proof that they count. It marks their acceptance into a community of those who *can* keep secrets, and who have important secrets to keep.

The secret society can, under such circumstances, serve purposes of growth, with respect not only to secrecy but to the double life in public and private worlds. Like play, it offers the freedom to trust and to be creative, and the excitement of transcending ordinary limitations.[6]

It is when play deteriorates that even such seemingly innocuous secret societies present serious drawbacks. The lines between play and reality may become erased, so that members, under the cloak of secrecy, take action against outsiders in a manner for which they would otherwise be held accountable. Or else the playing goes on too long, and overage adolescents repeat and repeat again what they should long since have left behind, making the secret activities a surrogate for forms of human contact and exhilaration they cannot find elsewhere.

For Jung, secret societies were an intermediate stage on the way to assuming personal responsibility in leading one's life. In this, he took them to resemble many other groups and ideologies by means of which people reach out for a collective identity. Simply to look at secret societies as traps, he argued, would be to underestimate the needs they serve. He saw them as "crutches for the lame, shields for the timid, beds for the lazy, nurseries for the irresponsible," but pointed out that they are also "a home port for the shipwrecked, the bosom of a family for orphans, a land of promise for disillusioned vagrants and weary pilgrims." [7]

Jung's words help answer the questions that must surely be uppermost when one reads about some of the most brutal and oppressive secret societies: How does someone come to join such a group? How do people turn into the cowed or corrupted initiates used to carry out the plans of leaders in whom they have been brought to have blind faith? All may recognize the need for human fellowship and the allure of secrecy without therefore wishing to take the risks such societies present; what Jung points to is the sense of desperation, of having nothing left to lose, out of which some such allegiances are formed.

Even those who have much more to lose sometimes look at such organizations as groups through which they can achieve stature and identity more easily than in the world at large. Through secrecy they seek access to an esoteric tradition and to clear standards for good and evil, friend and enemy. To facilitate adherence, moreover, such a society rarely allows those who are being wooed to join to see its shadier sides from the outset. Novices are drawn in by talk of furthering brotherhood and peace, or of the ideals of a particular religious sect. Once they make a commitment to a group, they are less quick to criticize it, especially as still further mysteries are held before them as inducements to joining. And gradually, when novices are deemed ready to absorb more information without criticism and in complete secrecy, they are exposed to tasks and methods they would earlier have questioned.

Still others actively seek out questionable activities and personal danger. As Karl Menninger has pointed out, it is hard to interpret the extraordinary spread of societies like the Russian Skoptsi, or "Castrators," except as evidence of a desire for self-punishment.[8] And some seek out such danger assuming that it is there to be overcome and that they are strong enough to do so. Aching to test themselves, they seek self-transformation through ordeal.

Many members of the most brutal societies, finally, might well not have joined had they not been tricked or seduced into doing so, and might well have left were it not for the threats leveled against anyone showing such disloyalty. If they have taken part in an act they fear to have known, the group has an additional hold over them. The differences between groups in their methods of recruiting members are evident in, and accentuated by, their methods of initiation.

Initiation

Initiation rites serve group purposes of transforming individuals from indifferent outsiders to completely loyal insiders. For individuals, the rites promise access to innermost secrecy, prestige, self-transcendence, and enlightenment. The work of initiation can be carried out in a single period of time or proceed by stages that are sometimes spread out over years. It may mark the initiate's personality permanently, depending on its duration and intensity and on his malleability. Outward attraction and force and inner drive and lack of resistance together determine the extent of the change and its power to rearrange and to transform allegiances, boundaries, and identities. In weighing such rites, I shall concentrate on those aiming at a thorough reorientation.

It is remarkable to see how similar certain elements of the rites are from one secret society to another, no matter how different their garb or how exotic or ordinary their symbols and secret signs. They often combine the same devices to impair judgment, disorient, and weaken resistance: silence and chanting at set intervals, darkness alternating with or succeeded by light, deprivation of food and sleep, inducement of trance, isolation from daily life, and solitude alternating with heady or oppressive group activities. These techniques alter the would-be member's sensory and cultural environment, and exclude all persons who might question the aims of the secret society. Toward the end of the initiation period, the novice's disorientation is often heightened through ordeals and dangers and the sudden and illuminating appearance of priests or superiors. The illumination is experienced as a rebirth, and the old identity is seen as discarded.

The following is a description of an unusually elaborate and dramatic initiation ceremony used by the Magis in India:

The candidate for initiation was prepared by numerous lustrations with fire, water, and honey. The number of probations he had to pass through was very great, and ended with a fast of fifty days' continuance. These trials had to be endured in a subterranean cave, where he was condemned to perpetual silence and total solitude. This novitiate in some instances was attended with fatal effects; in some others the candidate became partially or wholly deranged; those who surmounted the trials were eligible to the highest honours. Following the novitiate came the actual initiation rite, which took place underground in a cave. The candidate was led through gloomy mazes, by dangerous cliffs and drops, into a den full of howling, ravenous wild beasts (some of them initiates in costume) which seldom let him off unhurt, through raging thunderstorms (again, simulated by the initiates underground) by a priest who thrust a living serpent into his bosom, and into a cavern where he beheld in every appalling form "the torments of the wicked in Hades."

Only after this long journey did he arrive at the Sacellum, or Holy of Holies, which was brilliantly illuminated, and which sparkled with gold and precious stones. A splendid sun and starry system moved in accordance with delicious music. The archimagus sat in the east on a throne of burnished gold, crowned with a rich diadem decorated with myrtle-boughs, and habited in a tunic of bright cerulean hue; round him were assembled the praesules and dispensers of the mysteries. By these the novice was received with congratulations, and after he had entered into the usual engagements for keeping secret the rites of Zoroaster, the sacred words were entrusted to him.[9]

Another secret society, the Chinese Boxers, or Righteous Harmony Fists, had worked against foreign domination of China from their inception in the late nineteenth century. Their attack on the foreign legations in Peiping in 1900 during the Boxer Rebellion brought them to the world's attention. They were initiated in "darkness alternating with light, in the depths of temples to the accompaniment of fasting and invocation."[10] They were taught to repeat incantations (designed in part to render them invulnerable to Western weapons), given drugs of many kinds, and induced to participate in complicated gestures of dancelike boxing.

Onlookers, seeing such violence, reacted with terror, not least when told that the exercises were but practice for the hunting down and killing of foreigners.

A number of secret societies seek transformations as profound, though they have no "total immersion" rites of initiation. Instead, they proceed by degrees in a process that may take years, or be entirely out of reach for those not deemed ready. The German Illuminati of the eighteenth century had thirteen degrees, ranging from Preparation and Novice to Magus and Rex, in the course of which increasingly antireligious and anti-authoritarian purposes were revealed, and the killing of princes and priests recommended along with the infiltration and takeover of educational and religious institutions and above all of the press.

At the beginning of such a stepwise initiation, some relatively insignificant secrets are conveyed, with the promise that deeper and more powerful ones will follow once the novice demonstrates loyalty. The assault on judgment here is less direct than through the sensory and cultural deprivations and pressures mentioned earlier, but it can be just as powerful. Those aspiring to membership are asked to set aside ordinary prudence and moral judgment for the sake of the secrets to be revealed and to keep silent about the process they are undergoing, as in the following explanation of the vow of secrecy among the Rosicrucians:

He who speaks of his experiences to other than his personal Master-Teacher, is either very weak or foolish, or is a sham. . . . The true student does not speak of the work he is engaged in nor of his experiences, or the degree of his development, to other than his Master.[11]

It is important to distinguish other forms of teaching from such initiation while recognizing all the intermediate forms: to see the difference between helping someone to learn in a manner that is open to scrutiny and criticism, and the gradual unveiling of secrets as part of a procedure intended to change personality. Those who use the initiatory technique undercut the capacity for criticism by relying on mystification and by promising answers to all questions "in due course of time." The more a secret society requires initiates to take on faith, the more likely it is also to shroud its origins—often quite recent—in ancient mysteries, now unverifiable but endowed with the weight of tradition. And as novices invest time, effort, and often belongings in the secret society, it becomes ever harder for them to envisage the possibility that it may all have been a mistake. Indeed, studies indicate that the more severe the initiation which individuals undergo, the more attractive they find the group.[12] No matter how tedious or suspect its practices in the eyes of outsiders—and presumably in the pre-initiation perception of many a novice as well—they automatically appear more valuable after a difficult initiation.

This phenomenon is surely one that novices and others considering whether or not to join should take into account. If they could have such information in advance, and know, too, that the initiation might involve deceit and psychological pressure and force of the kind I have discussed, most of them would judge the process differently—especially if they could compare all the groups resorting to such means. Many would then, I believe, choose not to take part. If the group leaders should then argue that some would nevertheless wish to undergo the process, no matter how coercive, the answer must be that in that case there is no reason for not telling them about the group's methods and its aims in advance. Methods that use deceit and coercion to achieve personality change are unacceptable from a moral point of view because they override legitimate personal autonomy—the more so when they weaken this autonomy for the future by producing obedient, uncritical, and malleable group members. The very secrecy that accompanies such recruitment of converts must be seen as protecting, from novices as well as from outsiders, not only the felt sacredness and integrity of what is to be revealed but also methods that can ill afford to be exposed to the light of day.

Apart from such concealment, what difference does secrecy make to processes of initiation? After all, initiation occurs under many circumstances, not all of them secret.[13] Likewise the techniques of depriving novices of food and sleep, isolating them, and putting them through ordeals and group pressure are common to many forms of initiatory experience, whether secret or not. Consider, for example, the practice of "Husquenaughing" that John Lawson, in his *History of North Carolina* (1714), described as common in certain Indian tribes:

You must know, that most commonly, once a Year, at farthest once in two Years, these People take up so many of their young Men, as they think are able to undergo it and Husquenaugh them, which is to make them obedient and respective to their Superiors, and, (as they say) is the same to them as it is to us to send our Children to School, to be taught good Breeding and Letters. This House of Correction is a large, strong Cabin, made on purpose for the Reception of the young Men and Boys, that have not passed this Graduation already; and it is always at Christmas that they husquenaugh their Youth, which is by bringing them into this House and keeping them dark all the time, where they more than half starve them. Besides, they give them Pellitory Bark, and several intoxicating plants, that make them go raving mad as ever were any People in the World; and you may hear them make the most dismal and hellish Cries and Howlings that ever human Creatures expressed; all which continues about five or six Weeks, and the little Meat they eat, is the nastiest loathsome stuff, and mixt with all manner of Filth it is possible to get. After the Time is expired, they are brought out of the Cabin, which never is in the Town, but always a distance off, and guarded by a Jayler or two, who watch by Turns. Now when they first come out, they are as poor as ever any Creatures were: for you must know that several die under this diabolical Purgation. Moreover, they either really are, or pretend to be dumb, and do not speak for several Days; I think twenty or thirty, and look so ghastly, and are so changed, that it is next to an impossibility to know them again, although you was never so well acquainted with them before.[14]

Where indoctrination or coercive initiation cannot be carried out openly, secrecy prevents intervention by outsiders, as well as massive resistance by would-be initiates. In such communities, secrecy makes the practices both more attractive, because so mysterious, and more impervious to outside criticism. But is it not the coercion, the disorientation, and the assault on judgment, when they occur, that are objectionable, regardless of the secrecy that shrouds them?

Certainly, these are the disturbing elements in initiation, whether secret or not. And conversely, a number of such rites, secret or non-secret, are quite devoid of coercive elements. Secrecy therefore need not in itself be a negative factor. Rather, when it seals groups against outsiders, and when it takes over entire lives rather than merely guards particular secrets, it creates hothouse conditions that intensify and speed up certain aspects of both growth and decay. On the one hand, it shapes a strong sense of identity and creativity, nourishes the desire to surpass past achievements and give direction to life, and encourages rare intimacy and loyalty; on the other hand, it increases all the risks to participants that I discussed in Chapter II. The lack of criticism and feedback from outsiders can skew the judgment of initiates, so that they become mired in rigid, stereotyped attitudes, unable to grow and change out of what might otherwise merely have been an experimental stage in their development. The control acquired by the leaders can work to the detriment of initiates; and because of the all-enveloping secrecy, they may have less resistance to irrational and pathological states. In the long run, secrecy may help focus the emotion directed toward scapegoats and enemies, and end by brutalizing members and rendering them incapable of independent judgment.

Secrecy is dangerous and debilitating when it draws initiates into malevolent or unjust practices, such as violence directed against religious or racial groups. I shall assume a presumption against secrecy in such cases, as in two additional sets of circumstances. First, processes of initiation that rely on great amounts of secrecy, even without recourse to coercion and forms of manipulation, create special risks of overwhelming members and of reducing their ability to deal with secrecy and openness. A person, a group, or a government agency dominated by secrecy, enveloped in it, runs special risks. And all who have dealings with such groups then have legitimate cause for concern.

Second, individuals differ in the degree to which they are open, even gullible at times, to being drawn into initiation and in the end victimized. Though Diderot, for example, was willing to work with a group of Freemasons in eighteenth-century France, one can hardly imagine him undergoing the Magi initiation described on page 51, except possibly out of sheer curiosity. But to others, such secrecy could prove much more harmful. Therefore, I suggest that we consider a presumption against secret practices whenever they draw in initiates too young, too suggestible, or too inexperienced to be able to respond to them with an awareness of the risks involved. Those who have not worked out personal standards of discretion will be ill-equipped to deal with the difficult questions of loyalty, promise-keeping, and possible harm to self and others that certain initiations raise.

Because secret societies can create hothouse conditions of secrecy that intensify and accelerate change, they deserve close study. We still know far too little about how these conditions affect judgment and autonomy; and even less about how individuals differ in their responses. Yet it is hard to think of knowledge which would be more valuable for anyone considering whether or not to join such a society, or to enter a career requiring clandestine or undercover work. Such knowledge would be equally valuable to groups wishing to reform existing practices of secret initiation.

The fear of secrecy when it conceals injustice, becomes too enveloping, or draws in persons too inexperienced explains why outsiders have traditionally been so suspicious of secret societies, even the most innocuous ones. The secrecy makes it difficult, if not impossible, to judge these societies, and inevitably sets in motion gossip and rumors concerning what the societies do and speculation about excesses in their midst. Such suspicion is reflected in the following remarks made about American college fraternities in the last century:

A good man ought to have nothing in outward conduct or acts to conceal. It is the nature of sin to seek concealment and darkness, and every thing seeking concealment looks suspicious.

It is dangerous for young men, it is dangerous for men of *any age*, to associate together and hide themselves from public responsibility, under the cover of secret articles and promises.

In a despotic country, secret associations may be a necessary, though lamentable resort of those who aim at revolution, or as in the case of the medieval secret tribunal aim to execute justice denied by grim colossal tyranny. . . .

But what object can a society honestly propose to itself in a free country, which may not be reached without secrets and watchwords and mysterious grips as well as with them? The secrecy is in itself naturally odious, and inevitably productive of suspicion. . . . [15]

Blind Obedience

*By learning to suffer injustice in silence one becomes unjust in
turn; and blind obedience fosters slaves or tyrants.*
AUGUST STRINDBERG

In spite of the many innocuous or inspiring examples of secret societies, the suspicion they arouse is understandable. Too often they have been instruments for oppression. The fear is that such societies, by depriving members of autonomy, thereby injure them and cause them to lead thwarted lives; and that, reduced to such a state, the members may the more easily be used as tools for injuring others.

The loss of autonomy that can result from a thoroughgoing initiation is also a loss of identity and of personal judgment. However fervently initiates extol their newfound humility and self-abnegation, outsiders view them as exploited to the extent that they forswear independent judgment and promise blind obedience.

Such allegiance is differently judged whenever it is freely chosen and can be freely revoked. Some secret societies have no interest in retaining doubters. Others—often precisely those whose practices can least afford publicity—insist on permanent and irreversible adherence. A great many oaths testify to the importance placed on lifelong allegiance and voice gruesome threats of retaliation against those who are false to their oaths. Thus the Italian Carbonari, a secret society dedicated to resisting the rule imposed by Austria after the fall of Napoleon in 1815, required selected members to swear the following oath:

I, a free citizen of Ausonia, swear before the Grand Master of the Universe, and the Grand Elect Good Cousin, to devote my whole life to the triumph of the principles of liberty, equality, and progress, which are the soul of all the secret and public acts of Carbonarism. I promise that, if it be impossible to restore the reign of liberty without a struggle, I will fight to the death. I consent, should I prove false to my oath, to be slain by my Good Cousins Grand Elects; to be fastened to the cross in a lodge, naked, crowned with thorns; to have my belly torn open, the entrails and heart taken out and scattered to the winds.[16]

The Spanish Garduñas swore to obey their Grand Master absolutely and blindly. The German Illuminati swore to obey their Director and, in a more "advanced" stage, to work under the orders of their masters without doubt or question. They promised not to use their critical faculties in any matter connected with their instruction. The oaths of many secret societies are indeed remarkably similar, including a pledge of complete and permanent allegiance, an acceptance of gruesome punishment for anyone who reneges or reveals the group's secrets, the relinquishing of ties to family and friends outside the society, and thorough obedience to superiors in the society.

Should the loss of autonomy come close to being complete, little chance for discretion or free choice will remain. It is then no longer the individual who has personal boundaries, an identity, a life to protect; it is the group itself. Nor does the member thus submissive recoil before assaults on the persons, even the lives, of others. When the capacity for moral choice fails, the respect for the freedom of others fails as well. They may then be perceived primarily as members of groups—political or religious—or of races to be fought. Not uncommonly, the foremost target is another secret society. The African Master Builders, who flourished in France and in Germany in the nineteenth century, modeled their structure on that of the Freemasons—the very brotherhood they meant to eradicate.

Few have expressed the absolute self-surrender that certain secret societies aim for more vividly than Nechaev and Bakunin in the *Revolutionary Catechism*.* Written in 1869, secretly published in encoded Latin letters, and brought into Tsarist Russia, it was first made public at a trial of Nechaev's followers. It reads in part:

The revolutionary is a lost man; he has no interests of his own, no cause of his own, no feelings, no habits, no belongings; he does not even have a name. Everything in him is absorbed by a single, exclusive interest, a single thought, a single passion—the revolution.

In the very depths of his being, not just in words but in deed, he has broken

---

*This aim is hard to fulfill, however. Even in clandestine groups united against outsiders, or perhaps especially in such groups, insiders clash. The minutest differences over doctrine take on vast proportions; accusations of treason to the cause proliferate.

every tie with the civil order, with the educated world and all laws, conventions and generally accepted conditions, and with the ethics of this world. He will be an implacable enemy of this world, and if he continues to live in it, that will only be so as to destroy it the more effectively. . . . For him, everything that allows the triumph of the revolution is moral, and everything that stands in its way is immoral.[17]

Nowhere is the link between belief and action so direct as when the loss of personal judgment and of the capacity to deliberate freely removes all restraints on what human beings may do to one another. It is to this link that a remark attributed to Voltaire points: "Those who can make you believe absurdities can make you commit atrocities."

Were these activities out in the open, criticism and social action might call into question the practices of secret societies. But here, their secrecy guards them against such open inspection and thus prevents the feedback and correction that might have helped the initiates as well as affected the group's decision. Secrecy, here, encourages closed minds and prevents open debate, once again going against the purposes that secrecy at its best can serve, and once again demonstrating its dangers, not only to self but to others. Both the capacity to deal with secrecy and moral judgment more generally are then injured; and the distortions of the first reflect and shed light on aspects of the second.

The forces of bias and rationalization play a central role in such warping of judgment by placing obstacles in the way of discernment and reasoning. We may also ask whether they do not hinder our very thinking *about* secrecy and moral choice, perhaps to the point of hampering any further exploration of the ethics of secrecy. For do these forces not represent secrecy and deception turned against the self? Are we not often both insider and outsider to the same secrets? Do we not keep secrets from ourselves, deceive ourselves, even lie to ourselves? If so, how can we even begin to sort out the problems of moral choice and of responsibility with respect to secrecy?

Chapter V

Secrecy and Self-Deception

Misleading Oneself

Petrarch kept by his bedside a book he called his *Secret, or The Soul's Conflict with Passion*, which he intended for his personal use alone. It reveals a remarkable self-analysis. With the Lady Truth listening in silence, Petrarch conducts three dialogues with Saint Augustine, the thinker whom he admired above all others. Early in the first dialogue, Saint Augustine warns Petrarch against self-deception, "the most deadly thing in life." When Petrarch asks to know more, Augustine answers:

O race of mortal men, this it is above all makes me astonished and fearful for you, when I behold you, of your own free will, clinging to your miseries; pretending that you do not know the peril hanging over your heads, and if one brings it under your very eyes, you try to thrust it from your sight and put it far off.[1]

What was it about which human beings were so insistent on deluding themselves? What was the peril they refused to see, though it was hanging over their heads?

Sin and death, and above all the likelihood of suffering eternally after death: these were the perils of which Petrarch's Saint Augustine warned.

In the face of this danger, nothing would suffice but to give up all other interests, all passions for the life of this world—for love and for studies and politics, in Petrarch's own case—and to devote all thought to the care of one's soul by contemplating one's sinfulness and the nearness of death.

Before and after Petrarch, a great many thinkers have similarly warned of the corrosive and perversely self-destructive nature of such avoidance of the truth, of the lies we tell ourselves, and of the secrets we keep from ourselves. But they have seen far different truths—equally obvious in their own minds—as the ones we so obstinately reject through self-deception. In our time, Marx and Freud have signaled, as false consciousness and defense mechanisms, the clinging to illusion that stands in the way of becoming free. Only through unmasking, demystification, above all interpretation, can we break through the web of illusion and become aware of our role in perpetuating it.[2]

Some have claimed that we would not only become more free through the dispelling of self-deceit, but also more capable of acting morally and of leading nobler lives. Echoing Plato, they have argued that if only we could discern what is right and what is true, we would surely choose it. Others have held, more pessimistically, that self-deception may be our only shield against knowledge that would otherwise cripple us—that without what Ibsen called our "life-lies" we could not survive.

Whatever the role they assign to self-deception, most have taken its presence for granted. To see the self as deceiving itself has seemed the only way to explain what might otherwise be incomprehensible: a person's failure to acknowledge what is too obvious to miss. How, if not through such intentional misleading of self, can someone fail to notice that his work leads nowhere, that he lives beyond his means, that his marriage is a farce? How else can so many patients listen to a doctor's explanation of their life-threatening disease, respond as if they understood, yet know nothing about it a few hours later?

Postulating such self-inflicted ignorance helps point to the biases and weaknesses besetting perception and testifies to the perennial effort to understand human failures that would otherwise seem inexplicable.[3] And it is secrecy that lies at the center of such self-deception: the secrecy that is part of all deception. In deceiving ourselves, according to such a view, we keep secret from ourselves the truth we cannot face.*

---

*True, the view of the self keeping secrets from itself is not identical to that of its deceiving itself or lying to itself. These can no more be equated than can keeping secrets, deceiving, and lying in their own right. For our purposes, however, of asking whether such views are possible in the first place, and what implications they hold for moral

As helpful as such a view may be, it is also a troubling one. For exactly how can one be both insider and outsider thus, keeping secrets from oneself, even lying to oneself? How can one simultaneously know and ignore the same thing, hide it and remain in the dark about it?* The paradoxical nature of such a view also seems to undercut reasoned choice *about* secrecy. If there is a deceiving and a deceived part in any one individual, then should one part only (and if so, which?) be considered responsible for choices made in such a state of self-deception? Which part is it that can exercise discretion or any other form of moral judgment? And how can we know that it is not deceiving itself in so doing? If we cannot, finally, then how can we even begin to sort out the moral problems of choice and responsibility?

On all counts, the view of the self keeping secrets from itself seems paradoxical. In this, it is not merely problematic, as are so many concepts concerning relations *between* people when used instead with respect to the self: duties to oneself, for example, or promises to oneself. These do not have the element of paradox inherent in the notion of keeping secrets from oneself. For while we can envision so construing duties and promises that they apply, in somewhat different form, to oneself as well as to others, it is much harder to envision just how one goes about keeping a secret from oneself—being at once included and shut out.

The most sustained effort to overcome this seeming paradox has been that of psychoanalysis. Its view of human defense mechanisms is surely much more complex than the standard versions of self-deception. Freud's therapy was based on the assumption that people repress much of what they seem not to know, or to have forgotten, and that this material is capable of being retrieved. Heinz Hartmann argued that "a great part of psychoanalysis can be described as a theory of self-deceptions and of misjudgments of the external world." [4] And a number of psychiatrists have described all unconscious material as secrets kept from the self by the self. [5] They have categorized as secret all that they could infer a person to have forgotten or repressed, relying on Freud's partitioning

---

choice, they need not be dealt with one at a time; especially as all self-deception must involve keeping something secret from oneself.

*Without the simultaneity, the claim loses its paradoxical character, but also much of its explanatory value with respect to what is so unaccountable about human ignorance of the seemingly self-evident. No one doubts that we can hide things and then forget where they are (though hiding them *in order* to forget is less likely to succeed); or that we can set our watches late or play other tricks on ourselves in order to achieve a change in behavior.

of the psyche, and on his imagery of strata, resistances, censors, and conflicting forces ranging back and forth across regions of differing accessibility.

The very profusion of metaphors that Freud brought in to convey such a picture of internal, self-imposed secrecy or deceit has not escaped criticism. Sartre, among others, has derided the idea of the unconscious keeping secrets from the conscious; he has argued that Freud needed to postulate a process complete with "censor, conceived of as a line of demarcation, with customs, passport division, currency control, etc.," in order to re-establish within the self the duality of deceiver and deceived.[6] Freud, he argued, has merely interposed these barriers in order to overcome the paradox, and must then in turn overcome the duality itself through recourse to a "magic unity."

Having criticized Freud's attempt to overcome the contradiction inherent in attributing self-deception and concealment from self, Sartre proceeded to set forth an even more improbable theory of self-deception as "bad faith." It is the denial that consciousness directs toward itself, and results from the fear of facing the abyss of one's own freedom. Sartre did nothing to overcome the paradox inherent in such bad faith; instead he underlined it by claiming, "I must know, as deceiver, the truth that is masked from me as deceived. . . . Better still, I have to know this truth very precisely in order to hide it from myself the more carefully." [7]

"Bad faith," for Sartre, carried a stronger overtone of blame than "self-deception." Because it is something one intends and is aware of, one is morally responsible for being in such a state, and for what one does or avoids as a result. But the concept also reflects Sartre's ambivalence toward moral reasoning. He intended throughout his life to set forth a complete moral theory, announcing such a project repeatedly, only to postpone it and finally to abandon it altogether. His extraordinarily subtle understanding of human motives may have flourished best in the absence of such a theory, and indeed might well have undermined it. Yet he also had a judgmental, often moralizing attitude toward those persons and groups he opposed. The concept of bad faith combined fluidity and blame in such a way as to allow him to assign moral responsibility without indicating just how he had arrived at his conclusions.

Not only did Sartre not offer criteria for determining when bad faith is and is not present; he never explained how he could retain the paradox of lying to oneself without contradiction. Rather than weakening the paradox, as Freud had, and introducing some distance between deceiver and deceived by means of the unconscious and of the processes of censorship, Sartre merely blurred it. He attributed to bad faith a mysterious quality of "evanescence" and described it as oscillating in perpetuity between good faith and cynicism. Many, he argued, live in a continuous state of bad faith with intermittent and sudden awakenings in either direction.[8]

Freud, on the other hand, remained profoundly concerned throughout his career to overcome the paradox. He was still struggling to do so in the last article he wrote, which he had to leave unfinished. In this article, Freud postulated that the ego of a person in analysis must, when young, "have behaved in a remarkable manner" under the influence of "a powerful trauma." The child must have been tormented both by the desire to satisfy a strong instinct and by fear of the dangers that might ensue through doing so. The response is a split whereby the child both satisfies the instinct symbolically and rejects any knowledge concerning the matter:

The two contrary reactions to the conflict persist as the centre-point of a split in the ego. The whole process seems so strange to us because we take for granted the synthetic nature of the workings of the ego. But we are clearly at fault in this. The synthetic function of the ego, though it is of such extraordinary importance, is subject to particular conditions and is liable to a whole series of disturbances.[9]

By means of the split ego, Freud thought to do away with the paradox while allowing that the process did seem strange. Others have argued, in a similar vein, that a split self or even several selves are at work in self-deception to guard against anxiety-producing knowledge.[10]

Yet on closer inspection the contradiction remains. The view of the split ego or self is but another metaphor—and an even more personalized one—for the mind in conflict. No more than the image of the self keeping secrets from itself or the unconscious from the conscious can it explain the complex defense mechanisms to which human beings resort, nor avert the paradox of both knowing and not knowing the same thing at the same time, both keeping a secret and ignoring it.

Neither such mutually secretive parts of the ego or the self, nor even the deception by a split ego or self, can be shown to be either present or absent in any one person. As a result, someone presumed to be lying to himself—about incestuous fantasies, for example, or hatred too painful to confront—has no convincing way to deny the fact. Every effort at refuting the notion can arguably be seen as further proof of resistance, and of the force with which one part of the self is suppressing the secret truth. Anyone can then impute such "secrets" to anyone else, and point to a disavowal as further proof of their existence. A glance at the psychiatric literature will yield innumerable examples of such reasoning. A person's secrets, in such an extended view, may then turn out to encompass not only all that he knowingly conceals but also what he has forgotten or never noticed, and even all that he is imagined to be keeping from consciousness or from part of his ego.

The concept of "self-deception," and those of "split self," "bad faith," "false consciousness," and "defense mechanisms" are nevertheless compelling metaphors. They point to internal conflicts and self-imposed defeats that we all recognize as debilitating. These metaphors are surely not empty ones: they remind us of all that stands in the way of perceiving and thinking. We cannot easily do without these metaphors; the danger comes when we begin to take them for *explanations*. As metaphors, they help us to see the paradoxes of human failure to perceive and react; as explanations of how the paradoxes are overcome, they short-circuit understanding and become misleading in their own right—one more way in which we avoid trying to understand the complexity that underlies our experience of paradox. They function then as what I. A. Richards called "premature ultimates," bringing inquiry to an end too suddenly.[11]

At such times, these concepts blur the distinction between intentional concealment and ignorance; between lies and all the other ways in which one can influence perception and action; and between deceiving and being deceived. As a result, they permit some people to impute clear-cut intention, directness, and simplicity to the intricate processes of coping with information, while at the same time allowing others to dismiss the questions of responsibility and intention altogether. Each of the two responses obstructs the effort to sort out just what part individuals do play in what we take for self-deception. Before considering how to try to avoid these oversimplified responses, it is worthwhile to look at the difficulties each can give rise to in practice.

Attributing Self-Deception

Because self-deception and secrecy from self point to self-inflicted and often harmful ignorance, they invite moral concern: judgments about responsibility, efforts to weigh the degree of harm imposed by such ignorance, and questions of how to help reverse it. If the false belief is judged harmless and even pleasurable, as may be the case with the benevolent light in which most of us see our minor foibles, few would consider interfering. But clearly there are times when people are dangerously wrong about themselves. The anorexic girl close to starving to death who thinks that she looks fat in the mirror, and the alcoholic who denies having a drinking problem, are both in need of help; yet the help cannot consist merely in interference, but must somehow bring about a recognition on their part of their need and the role they play in not perceiving it accurately.

Judgments about when and how to try to help people one takes to be in self-inflicted danger depend on the nature and the seriousness of the danger, as well as on how rational one thinks they are. To attribute self-deception to people is to regard them as less than rational concerning the danger one takes them to be in, and makes intervention, by contrast, seem more legitimate. But this is itself dangerous because of the difficulties of establishing that there is self-deception in the first place. Some feel as certain that anyone who does not believe in their deity, their version of the inevitable march of history, or their views of the human psyche deceives himself as they might feel about the self-deception of the anorexic and the alcoholic. Frequently, the more improbable their own views, the stronger is their need to see the world as divided up into those who perceive the self-evident and those who persist in deluding themselves.

Aiding the victims of such imputed self-deception can be hard to resist for true believers and enthusiasts of every persuasion. If they come to believe that all who do not share their own views are not only wrong but actually know they are wrong in one part of their selves that keeps the other in the dark, they can assume that it is an act of altruism to help the victimized, deceived part see through the secrecy and the self-deception. What could be more legitimate than helping to bring about a change that one takes the self-deceived person's more rational self to desire?

Zealots can draw on their imputing self-deception to nonbelievers in yet another way, to nourish any tendency they might have to a conspiracy theory. If they see the self—their own and that of others—as a battleground for a conspiracy, they may then argue that anyone who disagrees with them thereby offers proof that his mind has been taken over by the forces they are striving to combat. It is not long before they come to see the most disparate events not only as connected but as *intended* to connect. There are no accidents, they persuade themselves; nothing is too trivial or improbable to count as evidence of such intent.

Indeed, calling something trivial or far-fetched counts, for holders of such theories, as further evidence of its significance. And denying what they see as self-evident is still more conclusive proof. How well we recognize the tone in which the eminent sixteenth-century philosopher and jurist Jean Bodin denounced those who scoffed at the belief in the existence of witches. Their protestations of disbelief, he declared, showed that they were most likely witches themselves.[12] He wrote of the pact that "confessed" witches—among them several judges and a doctor of theology—said they had signed with Satan. It obliged them to ridicule all talk of witchcraft as superstitious invention and contrary to reason. They persuaded many naïve persons, Bodin insisted, whose arrogance and self-deception was such that they would dismiss as impossible even the actions of witches that were right before their eyes.

By itself, the scope for abuse is of course no argument against a theory that postulates self-deception. But the frequent lack of criteria for attributing self-deception or its absence represents a problem for any such theory and increases the likelihood that it will be misapplied.

Another way to misapply such a theory is to invoke it to explain away guilt. In this way, the populations in Nazi Germany and elsewhere who claim to have been ignorant of concentration camps in their vicinity deny what was too obvious to be in any sense a secret. Ignorance, even though self-imposed, is put forward as an excuse. Admitting the knowledge, on the other hand, would call for a response—of approval and collaboration, or toleration, or outright rejection. In the last case, a choice of stance would be required: whether or not to voice one's rejection, or act to put it into effect, and at what personal risk.

The Plea of Self-Imposed Ignorance

If we agree with Kant that "ought implies can" and that no one should therefore be held morally responsible for failing to do what he cannot do, then we must hold, further, that no one can be blamed for failing to do what he did not know needed doing. A paraplegic cannot be blamed for not trying to rescue a drowning child, nor can a swimmer asleep on the beach. Both capacity to act and knowledge that acting is required must be present for there to be moral obligation, and responsibility for its breach.

At times, even pleas of ignorance do not suffice to acquit one of responsibility. If one has the obligation to remain alert to signs of danger— say, as a lifeguard on the beach—then the fact that one failed to do so gives no excuse. And even without having it as one's job to be aware of danger to others, there are many times when one would feel at fault for not perceiving it. Between full responsibility to know and none at all the gradations are numerous; and it is with respect to making such determinations that the issues of self-deception enter in. How does self-imposed ignorance resemble or differ from other forms of ignorance? Does its self-inflicted aspect add or remove responsibility? In what ways are the strategies of avoidance by those who claim ignorance of avoidable cruelty and suffering like being asleep while children drown?

Albert Speer has explored his responsibility for the Nazi atrocities and its relation to ignorance and delusion in his book *Inside the Third Reich*.[13] As a member of Hitler's government and of his innermost circle of advisers, Speer had much more direct responsibility for the government's actions than he would have had purely as a citizen. He details the elaborate forms of avoidance and of rationalization whereby he maintained his self-respect at the time.

Speer not only knew about the persecution of Jews and the slave-labor practices and the concentration camps; first as Hitler's principal architect and later as minister of armament, he took an active part in the design of the munitions factories, fully aware of the inhumane treatment of the prisoners who worked there. Yet he talked himself into believing that his work was strictly that of an architect and administrator, and that it was not his role to agonize over "political" matters.

In this way Speer refused to confront the atrocities in an other than abstract way. The day after the Kristallnacht in November 1938, driving by the smoking remnants of Berlin's synagogue, he remembers being disturbed, not by the destruction and all it stood for, but by the disorder and messiness that disturbed his architect's sense of design. And later in his career, his friend Karl Hanke warned him not to visit Auschwitz. Rather than ask why, he purposely did not follow up this line of inquiry with anyone.

I did not query him, I did not query Himmler, I did not query Hitler, I did not speak with personal friends. I did not investigate—for I did not want to know what was happening there. . . . from fear of discovering something which might have made me turn away from my course, I had closed my eyes. This deliberate blindness outweighs whatever good I may have done or tried to do in the last period of the war. Those activities shrink to nothing in the face of it. Because I failed at that time, I still feel, to this day, responsible for Auschwitz in a wholly personal way.[14]

As Speer rightly recognized, he was not in a position to deny responsibility. His failure to seek out the information about Auschwitz and to respond to all the evidence right before his eyes was inexcusable. Considering all that he already knew, any residual ignorance on his part of such matters, whether incurred through self-deception or not, was beside the point.[15]

It would certainly be excessive, on the other hand, to stretch the notion of moral responsibility so far as to cover all that individuals ignore or fail to notice, or all the situations in which we perceive some rationalization or other strategy of avoidance.[16] We are obviously not responsible for much that we do not know, or do not know that we should look into; the less so if we have no duty in the first place to respond to the situation of which we are ignorant—either because we have no power to change it, or because it lies outside our reach. At other times, we do acknowledge responsibility, but only partially, as when we should have noticed, but didn't, that a friend was becoming severely depressed, or that a family member brought home far more money than he was being paid at work.

In many such cases where ignorance and avoidance of knowledge blend, the lines are hard to draw. We are especially likely to deceive ourselves, as Bishop Butler pointed out, precisely where the lines of responsibility are blurred.[17]

Whoever will consider the whole commerce of human life, will see that a great part, perhaps the greatest part, of the intercourse amongst mankind, cannot be reduced to fixed determinate rules. Yet in these cases there is a right and a wrong: a merciful, a liberal, a kind and compassionate behavior, which surely is our duty; and an unmerciful contracted spirit, an hard and oppressive course of behavior, which is most certainly immoral and vicious. But who can define precisely, wherein that contracted spirit and hard usage of others consist, as murder and theft may be defined? There is not a word in our language which expresses more detestable wickedness than *oppression*: yet the nature of this vice cannot be so exactly stated, nor the bounds of it so determinately marked, as that we shall be able to say in all instances, where rigid right and justice ends, and oppression begins. In these cases there is great latitude left, for everyone to determine for, and consequently to deceive himself.[17]

Ignorance, Error, Bias, and Avoidance

If the doors of perception were cleansed, everything
would appear to man as it is, infinite.
For man has closed himself up, till he sees all things
thro' the narrow chinks of his cavern.

WILLIAM BLAKE,
The Marriage of Heaven and Hell

How might we disentangle the factors that are lumped together in the notion of keeping secrets from oneself, or deceiving oneself? And how sort out the destructive forms these factors take from much-needed self-protection?

Consider all the possible knowledge that an individual might acquire: with all the openness and acuity in the world, he could acquire only a minute portion of this knowledge, even in principle. Every direction chosen forecloses innumerable others. And even out of the limited amount of knowledge available to him in theory, he could respond, as a practical matter, only to a fraction. Thousands of sensory impressions reach the average individual per second, according to some estimates:[18] the vast majority of these are dealt with—adapted to or rejected—at the simplest organic levels. Had we no such protection from all the information that bombards us, we would be exposed to far more than we could cope with: it would be like having no skin. At such an organic level, it makes no sense to speak of secrecy and deception toward the self.

A related form of rejecting knowledge is what is known as "psychic numbing." It comes much closer to what is often called self-deception, yet it can be a reflex response to overwhelming pain or fear. Recall an intensely painful experience, and notice that it is impossible to recapture the sheer physical sense of that pain. In the same way, the initial impact of suffering may wear off with repeated exposure, leaving us incapable of responding to what at first aroused sharp reactions. This numbing can be dangerous when it lowers resistance to avoidable injuries; but without the capacity for some such self-protection we might be condemned to relive endlessly our most unbearable memories or fears.

Of the remaining messages that reach the individual, each may be more or less accurate, complete, diffused, hard to decipher, intertwined with or in conflict with other messages, and deflected or impaired en route. Add, now, his own characteristics as a recipient: his deafness, or fatigue, his difficulties of memory and of understanding; his habits, biases, hopes, and fears. He starts out, in sum, with information already severely winnowed out, incomplete, erroneous, twisted, confused, and conflicting. To label as secrecy from self all the resulting ignorance and error is to try to lend purposiveness to much that is haphazard and accidental in human responses. By attributing to individuals powers to keep such knowledge at bay, one internalizes the ancient belief in all-knowing powers that keep secret from human beings all that they do not know.

Other processes come closer to achieving self-imposed ignorance. Compartmentalization allows us to avoid responding to situations that would otherwise require us to make a choice. Beliefs or messages may be kept separate, never confronted with one another, and thus never seen to be contradictory. We may postpone following through with a troublesome lead, or succeed in not spelling out exactly what it will mean to take a certain action.[19] And rationalization helps us to incorporate and to disarm threatening information.

Of all the responses that seem clearly self-deceptive to many, denial is most striking. Doctors find, for example, that among seriously ill patients who learn that death is near, at least 20 percent have no memory after a few days of having received such news. Faced with intolerable anxiety, they have blocked out the information.[20] In such responses, there are aspects of secrecy, but not the concealment that is the core of secrecy, nor the deception of self that many imagine. Rather, the responses of denial are linked with the element of separation, of setting aside and sifting apart that is present in all secrecy, and also with that of the unspoken and the unspeakable.

Sometimes the setting aside is quite conscious and in no way secret to the self, as in much procrastination. The same is true of conscious refusals to spend much time worrying about possible but unlikely dangers about which one can do nothing, such as the chance of being struck by lightning. Such dismissals of concern are often eminently reasonable, as are similar means by which people compensate for misfortune and handicaps. One psychiatrist, Arnold Beisser, has written of the way physicians may misinterpret as denial of illness what he regards, rather, as affirming attitudes that contribute to health. He has used his own experience of severe physical handicap to show how the focus can shift between degrees of awareness of one's condition:

I am actively engaged in my profession and, when doing so, am absorbed with the tasks at hand. I am frequently asked such questions as, "How do you bear spending your life in a wheelchair?" On such occasions I am aware that my attention is redirected from what I am doing in an affirmative way to what I am unable to do in accordance with the standards implied by the question. Thus when what I cannot do becomes foreground, I am aware that I am disabled; while I am working or carrying out my social or family activities, my disability becomes background and my competence and health are foreground.[21]

Most of us shift focus in similar ways, without thinking of the changes as evidence of denial. We should be no hastier in attributing denial to others at those times when we realize that they do not, any more than ourselves, maintain a constant and acute awareness of the full extent and variety of their problems.

There are nevertheless times when we might all agree that denial is present: times when someone seems to block information completely, about the death of a family member, for example, or the diagnosis of cancer. For some, such blockage is a temporary reflex only, allowing them time to regroup their forces and to begin to take it all in. For others, it is permanent.

It is when the combined forms of avoidance no longer merely filter but block needed information, when they are no longer temporary but permanent, and when they prevent people from doing something about a danger which could be averted or alleviated, that they do the greatest disservice. Far from protecting individuals, avoidance then leaves them defenseless against threats they could otherwise have tried to combat. To block out knowledge of the symptoms of a disease that is curable in its early stages is a common form of such avoidance. On a collective scale, the inability to think about the growing likelihood of a nuclear devastation exhibits it at its most irrational. For whereas all the forms of avoidance can be protective of self when they avert attention from an unlikely danger, or one about which nothing can be done, they have the opposite effect whenever there is something one could do if one responded in time.

Without a doubt, the various forms of avoidance and rejection I have mentioned do point to striking responses to threatening or unusable information. However supportive they may be on occasion, their cumulative burden is great. True, we could not survive if bombarded ceaselessly by information of a useless, threatening, or unduly burdening nature.[22] But we struggle along with such thick layers of bias and rationalization, compartmentalization and denial, that our choices suffer immeasurably.

In answer to the question raised earlier, whether the concept of secrecy from oneself might not undercut all efforts to pursue the ethics of secrecy or indeed any questions of moral choice and reponsibility, I would therefore argue that such a concept can, but need not, undercut these efforts. It can blur moral inquiry and permit moral reflection to run in comfortable, well-worn circles. But when the processes of avoidance that it points to are studied more closely, we find that they undercut some, but far from all, questions of responsibility; and that even as they reveal the extent of our present ignorance about the interactions of organic and other obstacles to perception, they underline the need for moral inquiry, not its impossibility. Given the role of these processes, the ways in which they skew or shut out knowledge, and the resulting ignorance, error, and uncertainty, what is the role of moral deliberation?

While such deliberation can counteract these forces, it can undoubtedly never dissolve them; and so one of its most important tasks must be to remain mindful of them and to devise means of reducing their sway, but also to watch how they are imputed: to whom, on what grounds, and with what power to bring about changes. Consider once again, from this point of view, Petrarch's *Secret*, containing the dialogues between Saint Augustine and himself. In response to Saint Augustine's exhortations that he recognize his self-delusion and set aside his passionate interest in the world and in his studies so as to contemplate sin, death, and the life to come, Petrarch agonized and demurred. To the very end, he refused to obey his mentor fully.

Indeed I owe you a great debt of gratitude . . . for you have cleansed my darkened sight and scattered the thick clouds of error in which I was involved. And how shall I express my thankfulness to Her also, the Spirit of Truth? And now, as She and you have your dwelling-place in heaven, and I must still abide on earth, and, as you see, am greatly perplexed and troubled, not knowing for how long this must be, I implore you, do not forsake me. . . . I will be true to myself, so far as in me lies. . . . I am not ignorant that, as you said a few minutes before, it would be much safer to attend only to the care of my soul. . . . But I have not the strength to resist that old bent for study altogether.[23]

We who are the beneficiaries of Petrarch's "old bent for study" cannot but cheer his independent spirit. Many others have faltered when pressed to acknowledge self-deception of a particular kind and to accept the world-view urged upon them. Consider in this light the generations of women who have been told that their drive toward self-expression and independence stemmed from a lack of feminine modesty or of piety, or more recently, from sexual envy of men. At such times, imputations of self-deception have reinforced the pressure on women to conform to whatever stereotype of femininity prevailed. Whatever the current dogma, countless men and women have been similarly persuaded that their efforts to think for themselves revealed the sin of pride, the error of ideological deviation, or some grievous failure of psychological insight.

Efforts to understand the nature of self-deception and its links to hypocrisy pervade the two practices of talking over human lives to which I turn next: confession and gossip. Both represent efforts at moral deliberation, weighing conduct, and setting standards. As Georg Simmel noted, while secrecy sets barriers between men, it also offers "the seductive temptation to break through the barriers by gossip and confession."[24] This temptation, he added, accompanies the psychic life of the secret like an overtone.

Confessions

The Act of Confessing

Practices of confession have provided, throughout the centuries, a setting for some of the most intimate and highly charged confrontations between insider and outsider. They have set in motion powerful tensions between concealment and revelation, and intricate strategies of pointing to and away from the self. Meant to reduce deceit and self-deception, they have led to intense probing of secrets, leaving, at times, little room for discretion; but they have also helped to heal and to reconcile. In studying the ethical issues of confession, we have an opportunity to see at close hand the ingenuity, the range, and the pitfalls of what human beings have thought to do for and to one another as well as themselves.*

In considering various practices of confession in religious, political, and therapeutic contexts, I shall ask what moral considerations arise

---

*These practices can be looked at as distinct—though with many intermediate and overlapping cases—from other forms of confiding considered in this book, such as the informal exchanges of personal, even intimate information among friends, much of the information given to doctors and other professionals, and the confessions and revelations directed to the police. And literary confessions, though briefly mentioned here, raise so many separate issues that I have decided to discuss them in a later book.

for those who take part in such practices—those who receive or extract confessions, as well as those who offer or submit to them. Within each of these perspectives, I shall trace three clusters of moral distinctions: between openness and concealment (and the related shadings of intimacy, silence, shame, and deceit), between freedom and coercion, and between revealing one's own secrets and those of others.

Consider, as an example of the first set of distinctions, Rousseau's *Confessions*: an extraordinary blend of laying bare, disguise, concealment, and invention, of flaunting the self in public while yet nourishing a sense of mystery. From the outset, Rousseau staked a double claim to uniqueness. Not only was he "other," set apart, unlike any other in existence; in revealing himself as fully and as intimately as he planned to, he also took himself to be the only person who would be thus explored.

I want to show to my fellow men a man in all the truth of nature: and this man will be myself.

Myself alone. I feel my heart and I know men. I am not made like any of those whom I have seen; I dare believe that I am not made like anyone in existence. If I am not worth more, at least I am other.[1]

The intention to confess may invite such exaltation. It awakens fascination, in return, among outsiders, but also caution, doubt, at times recoil. Camus explored both points of view in *The Fall*, through the monologue of Clamence, the self-proclaimed "judge-penitent." Clamence, a past master at every nuance of confession, tells his listener that he has reached the point of liking to read only confessions. But he has found that authors of confessions write above all in order not to confess, so as to say nothing of what they know. And he warns: "When they pretend to begin their avowals, be on your guard, it is time to put makeup on the corpse." [2]

For an example of the second set of moral distinctions, having to do with the degree of freedom and manipulation in confessions, let us take the report of a group of Jesuits traveling among the Algonquin Indians in 1653, in the territory called Nouvelle France.[3] They recount how the Indians tell of a land where the cold in winter is so intense that all that is spoken freezes into ice. When the spring comes, the frozen words melt, and all that has been said during the winter can be heard "as if in a single moment." However that may be, wrote the Jesuits, the fact is that when spring comes, the Indians gather for a joint confession on the banks of a river, and all the evil that has been done in the great woods during the winter is disclosed. The Jesuits felt it necessary to add that these confessions took place "without torture or exaction." Their very disclaimer serves to remind readers of the role that torture has played, and still plays in large parts of the world, in extracting personal revelations.

I shall consider the third set of distinctions, finally—between revealing one's own secrets and those of others— in the contexts of psychotherapy and of self-disclosure to the public, and in later discussions of gossip, betrayal, and whistleblowing.

To confess something to someone is to avow what one has not previously disclosed to that person about oneself—often something one regrets, or wishes one could regret. It can take place informally between friends, acquaintances, even strangers, or more formally in an institutional, often ritualized setting. The latter promises more expert help than ordinary forms of confiding, and at times access to the sacred;* but it carries greater dangers as well.[4]

In the Christian tradition, what is avowed in confession is a sin: what Aquinas defined as a word, act, or desire that is against the eternal law.[5] But many confessions, religious as well as secular, are meant to disclose something more than a trivial assortment of peripheral personal facts: something intimate and central to one's life, such as religious or political deviation, or a dissolute or obsession-ridden life. They reveal a lack of harmony with accepted standards, and an effort to restore that harmony, often by making restitution or accepting a penance or submitting to a ritual of purification.†

Many confessions are, as a result, dramatic. They are often meant to shock and trouble listeners, while at the same time bringing them closer, by arousing sympathy and by stressing the distance traveled from a life now disavowed. Thus Saint Augustine, John Bunyan, and Leo Tolstoy, so different in other respects, all reveal having stolen, indulged in sinful pleasures, and doubted or denied God's existence.[6]

By contrast, certain statements concerning the self are meant to protect and to purify the speaker precisely by *denying* all guilt. I know of no earlier efforts to do so than the declarations of innocence sometimes called "negative confessions" painted on the walls of Egyptian tombs

---

*Criminal confession, by contrast, though it can serve such purposes of help to the confessant, has as its major function the achievement of justice and the protection of the community. In many societies, both therapeutic and religious confessional practices have nevertheless at times been used to acquire evidence for criminal prosecution.

†The accepted standards need not, however, be those accepted by the majority; they may be standards that the confessant accepts but has been afraid to declare openly, such as those of a persecuted religious group. The sin, therefore, may not always lie in what has been hidden, but rather in the hiding itself.

and sarcophagi in the third millennium B.C. Through these declarations, pleaders hoped to protect themselves against accusations after their death that might influence their fate as the god Osiris weighed their hearts in his scales and pronounced judgment upon their lives. Their testimony certifies that they have *not* lied, cheated, stolen, committed adultery, killed, or sinned in other ways. Thus one statement reads in part:

Grant ye that I may come before you, for I have not committed sin, I have done no act of deceit, I have done no evil thing, and I have not borne [false] witness; therefore let nothing [evil] be done to me. I have lived upon truth, I have fed upon truth, I have performed the ordinances of men, and the things which gratify the gods. I have propitiated the god by doing his will, I have given bread to the hungry man and water to him that was athirst, and apparel to the naked man, and ferried him that had no boat.[7]

People confess only to previously concealed matters over which it is (or has been) possible, at least in principle, to exert some control, or for which they acknowledge at least shared responsibility. Thus they may confess to incest or to child abuse, but not to having unwittingly transmitted polio; they may confess to religious backsliding, but not to loss of memory. But they also seek support against forces they may regard as too strong to combat alone—addiction, perhaps, or weakness of will, or supernatural powers of evil. By confessing, they often hope to align themselves with communal or sacred forces that will help in this battle. Because they accept responsibility and seek such assistance, they are in a position to offer some assurance of efforts to change: efforts great enough to affect their entire way of life, perhaps also to allow them to transcend their old selves and attain forgiveness or salvation in a future life. The change may be from deviance to normalcy, from wrong to right, from ignorance about the self to insight.

In this way, confession may serve as a means for transforming one's life. It may bring new insight and a chance to re-create oneself. This cannot easily be achieved through introspection alone. To seek out a confessor is, then, to look for someone who can share one's burdens, interpret one's revelations, and show the path to release. Confessing may be a call for intervention and for help in reaching through to the layers of secrecy sensed in oneself or in the authority one confronts. Thus Dietrich Bonhoeffer sees confession as a breakthrough to fellowship and community. By making manifest "all that is secret and hidden," confession brings the sin into the light.[8]

Confession strengthens resolve for many, and thus serves as an added control for those who are not certain that they will be capable of keeping the temptations of their past lives subdued. They see their lives as a battleground between great forces, and the confessor as an ally in the battle. Naming the temptations and the hostile forces may give strength to resist them. So long as these forces are nameless, they remain blurred and shadowy. Once named, they are forced into the light, compelled to take on an identity. Perhaps they may then be "done to death," as Origen put it when describing the need to bring sins into the open:

For if we do this and reveal our sins not only to God but also to those who can heal our wounds and sins, our wickedness will be wiped out by him who says "I will wipe out your wickedness like a cloud." [9]

Healing and wiping out wickedness: these functions of confession may bring out a difference with respect to whether or not some punishment should follow the confession. When the function of the confession is primarily one of healing, penance is less frequent. Bringing the "pathogenic secret" into the open is then considered therapeutic in itself. Neither penance nor further expiatory suffering is thought necessary. But the closer the practice of confession comes to the exercise of justice— whether secular or religious—the stronger is the role of penance within it. The sinner may be thought to have offended against God, against the community, and against himself in such a way that healing is not possible without penance. [10]

The nature of the healing and the punishment is, however, often differently interpreted by outsiders to the tradition. Depending on the methods used and the aims for which self-revelation is sought, outsiders to the tradition at times see as brainwashing what participants take for healing and reconciliation. They may see those methods as tyrannical that participants view as necessary and beneficial.

Innumerable spiritual traditions have employed practices of confession, from Buddhism to African rites, from Oriental mystery religions to Judaism and Hinduism. But it is the Christian tradition that has been most torn by disputes over its role. Should confession occur only once after baptism, as Tertullian insisted, or more often, perhaps even after each new lapse? [11] Should it concern only serious sins or every possible kind of misstep? Should revelations be public, before the whole community, or secret?* If secret, should they be directed solely to God, or must they be made to a priest? Are repentance and confession sufficient, or must

---

*Among the Early Christians, public confession was used for the disclosure of serious sins, and the ensuing penance was public as well. From the eighth century on, the

the sinner also do penance? And what are the links between penitence, penance, expiation, and guilt?

In 1215, the Lateran IV Council decreed that "all the faithful, of both sexes, when they have arrived at the age of discretion, are to confess all their sins at least once a year to their own priest." [12] This stress on *all* sins was a departure from the earlier practice of including in one's confession a statement asking forgiveness also for possible forgotten sins. Confession was by then firmly established as part of the Holy Sacrament of Penance. And anxiety about what to include had risen. Depictions of the sufferings that awaited sinners after death had grown ever more specific. Many lived in terror of omitting some sins that were hard to pin down. For instance, "consenting to pleasure" merely in one's thoughts (*consensus in delectationem*) was a sin which, unless confessed, could lead a person to lose his soul for eternity, according to Aquinas.[13] But just what is an instance of such a sin? Consenting to pleasure in thinking about sinful sexual intimacy or other mortal sins? Even fleetingly? How could one recognize such sins of thought or be sure to remember them each time, even if it were possible to specify them in all their variations?

It was no wonder that individuals, faced with the threat of eternal damnation for sins so elusive and so hard to forestall, turned increasingly to their confessors in their concern not to offend God—the more so as they were sure that He already knew each and every one of their sins, so that there could be no refuge in a false or too casual or incomplete confession. Nor was it a wonder that confessors took it upon themselves to probe ever more minutely into transgressions. Probing and revelation of the most secret recesses of the soul fed one another; and the confessors' manuals came to treat at ever greater length ways of overcoming the reticence of confessants and of relieving the resultant obsession with sinfulness, or "scrupulosity," that immobilized so many. The burden they hoped to alleviate through confession had often been imposed by the very authorities who then proffered assistance through confession. Such was the case as the catalogues of sins multiplied in the Middle Ages and later in the Calvinist and Puritan communities, and as accusations of witchcraft brought confessions from hundreds of thousands who were led to feel possessed, or who were tortured until they confessed even the most outlandish acts imputed to them.[14]

---

disclosure was more often made to priests, but the penance might still be public. By the time of the Council of Trent, in 1551, the Church recommended that the confessions, by then numerous and required of all, should be secret, since it would "not be very prudent to enjoin by any human law that offenses, especially secret ones, be divulged by a public confession."

One who was beset with scrupulosity to the point of exasperating his confessors was the young Martin Luther in the Augustinian monastery at Erfurt. His breach with the Roman Church over the issue of the nature of confession and penance split the Christian world. Luther fought the system of indulgences whereby penance in monetary form was required for the forgiveness of sins. He wrote that he was proud to have delivered believers from "the great eternal torture" of the obligation to confess sins to priests, and in general from "the terrible domination of the clergy over the laity." Christ, he argued, "manifestly gave the power of pronouncing forgiveness to anyone who had faith in him." [15] Yet the burden of sinfulness was not thereby lifted, for Luther held that all is sin that is not done in faith; and the boundaries of such sin proved no easier to determine than those of the sins Aquinas had specified. Man's inherent sinfulness could be wiped away by God alone, not through confession or penance in themselves.

The torment regarding guilt and confession in the Reformation and the Counter Reformation, and the ever more precise and exhaustive soul-searching it inspired, resonate in contemporary practices of psychotherapy—above all in psychoanalysis. Like the earlier religious practices, current secular ones focus intensive and detailed probing on the individual's experience present and past, and especially on sexuality in all its stages and manifestations, seeking thereby to alleviate guilt and to bring about a personal transformation. Just as religious confessors have urged those in their charge not to leave out of account a single sin or even a sinful thought, so analysts have stressed the basic rule of analysis: that not a single secret, no matter how seemingly irrelevant, be held back. Without such complete openness, each of the traditions has held, it might not be possible to help revealers overcome their suffering. Without it, the desired freedom and transformation would be out of reach.

Michel Foucault has pointed to the roots of psychoanalysis in the earlier traditions of institutionalized confession, and in the "medicalization" of sexuality—the view that it is "an area of particular psychological fragility." He regards both these developments as peculiarly characteristic of the West. The links he discerns are striking; yet all evidence goes to show that the practice of confession, as well as the view of sexuality as thus problematic, have far more ancient and extensive analogues in world cultures. [16]

Theodor Reik, in *The Compulsion to Confess,* saw a near-universal urge among human beings to bare personal secrets. [17] This urge had found outlets in the past, he argued, through art, social custom, and religion. Now for the first time, he proclaimed, psychoanalysis could channel it rigorously and systematically. Psychoanalysis at last offered a scientific method for eliciting repressed material. Its main concern ought therefore to be to assist the compulsion to confess and to find outlets for the need for penance.

Even Reik might be surprised, a half-century later, at the sheer number of professionals who now see it as their task to facilitate the compulsion to confess. Through analytic techniques of diverse kinds, through group therapies and encounter groups, by means of hypnosis, drug therapy, and brain stimulation, self-disclosure is aided and interpreted. But the therapeutic value of any one of these techniques is far from established; and the need for caution in choosing persons best qualified to listen to personal revelation is increasingly clear.

The caution is well-founded. One cannot trust all who listen to confessions to be either discreet or especially capable of bringing solace or help. In addition, the act of confessing can in itself increase the vulnerability of persons who expose their secrets, especially in institutionalized practices. Studies have shown that when self-revelation flows in one direction only, it increases the authority of the listener while decreasing that of the speaker.[18] In ordinary practices of confiding, the flow of personal information is reciprocal, as the revelations of one person call forth those of another; but in institutionalized practices, there is no such reciprocity. On the contrary, therapists and others who receive personal confidences are often taught to restrain their natural impulse to respond in kind. Thus Freud advised psychoanalysts not to reciprocate patient confidences: "The doctor should be opaque to his patients, and, like a mirror, should show them nothing but what is shown to him." [19]

Caution in looking for someone in whom to confide need not rule out seeking professional help with self-revelation. But it calls for even greater discretion than the personal confiding I have discussed in earlier chapters, primarily because of the added power the institutional role lends to those who receive the confidences. Given that this power has been used over the centuries to the frequent benefit of persons in need of help, but that it has also been exploited to waylay the gullible and to ensure unquestioning allegiance, those who listen to personal revelations and those who convey them have every reason to try to distinguish between beneficial and injurious practices.

The Listener

What responsibilities do those who listen to confessions have? How do they justify their role vis-à-vis confessants, and in the institution they serve? How well-founded do they consider the institution's views of what is guilty or sinful, of the help it can hold forth, and of the dangers of holding back information? To what extent should they, as listeners, try to probe ever more deeply, or on the contrary, leave the amount and kind of disclosure up to the confessant? And if they wish to probe more deeply, what means do they feel justified in using? Does their role in the institution they serve offer special justifications for manipulative probing, finally, or for the use of pressure or deceit?

Too rarely do listeners ask themselves such questions. Least of all do they look critically at the views of guilt and sin they have been taught, and at the interpretations they accordingly place on what is revealed to them. Underlying this failure are two views often taken for granted in an equally uncritical way: that of secrecy as pathogenic, so that whole-hearted and thorough revelation is by definition believed therapeutic; and that of self-deception as an explanatory metaphor that justifies otherwise unwarranted action. I have argued, in earlier chapters, that each of these views is inadequate and can blur moral discernment of what is owed human beings. Certain practices of confession illustrate these shortcomings.

The two views are prominent, first of all, in deflecting questions about the justifications for probing as deeply and as intimately as possible. At times, such probing is entirely warranted. Thus the patient who discloses guilt feelings and disturbances to a psychiatrist, but who does not see their connection to his having left the scene of an automobile accident in which he caused the death of a child, clearly needs help in probing these links and in considering, belatedly, what to do about them. The help that confessors and therapists can offer clearly depends on reaching beneath surface talk to what individuals find it difficult to convey.

Without denying the importance of exploring certain secrets, we must nevertheless still ask whether therapists should not exercise discretion in this respect. Do *all* who come for advice—say, about sleeping disturbances or study problems—require the intimate probing about family and other matters they now often routinely undergo? And should patients be encouraged to relinquish all control over what they say—through techniques of free association, for example?

The view of secrecy as mainly pathogenic makes it easy to ignore such questions. Secrets left hidden will continue to fester, it holds, unless exposed. Patients risk nothing in exposing harmless secrets, and stand to benefit greatly by bringing harmful ones into the open: as a result, they have nothing to lose and much to gain by the fullest possible disclosure. But such an assumption is far from indisputable. I have pointed in earlier chapters to injuries that can stem from indiscriminate self-revelation. They should at the very least be taken into account in weighing how deeply to probe.

In response to such suggestions, therapists point out that they might well agree if only they knew which secrets mattered in achieving a cure and which did not. But looking for a harmful or guilty secret, they argue, is a little like looking for a needle in a haystack. All secrets must therefore be drawn out, just in case they are the right ones, or will lead to them. In addition, proponents of such a view often claim that all probing is legitimate whenever patients have given their consent, and so long as all that is spoken remains confidential.

But tese arguments cannot be made to carry such a weight. Patients and confessants consent to much that is not necessarily in their best interest. And while confidentiality (if respected) guarantees that third parties will not know what has been said, it cannot prevent the harm that may come from saying it in the first place. Many have compared psychological probing to surgery. Thus Anaïs Nin wrote that the pain of living was nothing compared to the pain of the investigation of her first psychoanalysis. Of one meeting with her analyst, she wrote:

He questioned me relentlessly. He feels there is a secret. The theme of flight does not satisfy him. I feel that something in me escapes from his definitions. I dread the scalpel.[20]

Such psychological probing can be as much needed as some surgery; but when it is undertaken without clear need, it is as hard to justify as unnecessary surgery. That patients have consented to the treatment, or that it remains confidential, cannot justify the former any more than the latter.

When the probing for secrets is not only needlessly invasive but also carried out by coercive means, self-deception may be invoked as added justification. Listeners who threaten or otherwise force people to confess may argue that those who protest want, at the same time, to be helped, so that coercing them only *seems* to go counter to their will, no matter how strong their objections; for there is that other, deceived part of their selves that in fact desires help in overriding the protests. It is a voiceless and invisible part, to be sure, but those who impute it can then come to assume a new type of informed consent: the implied informed consent. And this consent is as difficult to disprove as the original imputation of self-deception.

Much thought-reform and indoctrination rely on such a fallacious argument. The stated aim is not only to do what is in the best interests of the persons being coerced into a new frame of mind but to carry out a desire these same persons harbor deep within themselves. But the confessant's later gratefulness cannot give retroactive justification to the methods used, any more than reliance on "implied" informed consent. Some confessants are cowed from the beginning; this does not render mistreating them more legitimate. Others may resist, but declare, after having confessed, that they are grateful for the treatment that led to their new insight. But such gratefulness cannot be taken as evidence that the methods are acceptable; for one of the end results of thorough indoctrination is the docile acceptance of all that has been done to bring about the change to a new way of thinking, and the willingness to use the same methods in turn on still other recalcitrants.

Many whose work it is to listen to personal revelations are, of course, outspokenly opposed to such manipulation. They reject the coercion involved; and they have little faith in the usefulness to individuals of any self-knowledge thus obtained. The encounter between listener and speaker can be extraordinarily helpful, at times illuminating; but it must be conducted with the utmost respect for human dignity.

The Revealer

> *For him who confesses, shams are over and realities have begun;*
> *he has exteriorized his rottenness. . . . One would think that*
> *in more men, the shell of secrecy would have to open, the pent-*
> *in abscess to burst and gain relief, even though the ear that*
> *heard the confession were unworthy.*
>
> WILLIAM JAMES, *The Varieties of Religious Experience*

In all self-revelation, still one other listens and seeks to penetrate the secret regions being explored. This other is the speaker himself. The serious confession is a soul-searching both from within and from without. Some have compared it to an underground journey, fraught with obstacles and dangers, undertaken to explore secrets guarded by disconcerting, sly, at times monstrous forces. In this search the speaker experiences not only the insider's conflict between concealing and revealing but also that of the outsider between probing and desisting—between the chance for self-knowledge and remaining a stranger to oneself.

Such soul-searching can be richly satisfying; and in times of grief or anxiety it is all but indispensable. It offers a chance to work to counteract the rigidity and all the strategies of avoidance that stand in the way of self-knowledge; but it requires discretion and careful judgment on the part of the speaker quite as much as on that of the listener. So long as the speaker has the freedom to decide how much to reveal and when, and the discretion to exercise this freedom, he will be able to pursue the joint exploration without fear of the risks discussed earlier. But he should still consider the degree to which his revelations might burden or manipulate the person to whom he speaks.

Someone who reveals personal and confidential matters may seek to influence listeners in ways that are not necessarily manipulative. The person who unveils a secret gains a measure of control over how others see it. The partially shared secret mystifies and tantalizes; as the revelation continues, the speaker establishes his identity in the eyes of the listeners, coming to matter to them in a new way. He no longer feels blurred and anonymous in their eyes; his life has taken on meaning for them. He is set apart, unique through what he has revealed.

Self-revelation becomes manipulative when the unspoken aim is to secure from others some response they would otherwise restrain: confidences in return, or a bond that can be exploited, or some form of co-optation. Seduction is the aim of much self-disclosure of a manipulative nature. In *Les Liaisons dangereuses,* for instance, the Vicomte de Valmont works on his most recalcitrant and his least suspecting victims alike by seeming to pour forth his heart in the tone most likely to gain access to them, and to elicit from them confidences and intimacy in return. In this way he learns things about them that he can then use to apply pressure on them. And the Marquise de Merteuil, his partner in scheming to seduce and corrupt, confides to him that she regards it as a fundamental precaution to learn the secrets of those she uses for her purposes, saying of one young girl whose "disastrous amour" she has learned about:

She knows, then, that her fate is in my keeping; and if the impossible happens and she defies these considerations, is it not obvious that her past, when it is revealed, not to speak of the punishment she must suffer, will deprive whatever she says of all credibility? [21]

Awareness of the possibilities for such manipulation doubtless contributes to the rules enjoining confessors and psychotherapists not to give in to the natural impulse to reveal personal matters in return for the secrets they are told. But efforts to manipulate a listener through self-disclosure may also result from his own excessive pressure or manipulation. When employees in business firms are encouraged, for example, to speak freely about themselves to company guidance counselors or in joint encounter sessions, they may be placed in an impossible situation, one in which silence or reticence is regarded as "uncooperative" while forthrightness in the company of colleagues or employers may cost them their jobs. To require counseling or encounter-group participation on the part of new employees as some organizations do is to set the stage needlessly either for indiscretion or for manipulation in self-defense.

In psychotherapy, likewise, unwarranted pressure calls forth such responses. I mentioned earlier the pressure that Anaïs Nin felt from her psychoanalyst. When he demanded that she never see certain friends again, she told him—falsely—that she had broken with them. She asked herself, "Could I deceive a professional analyst?" [22] The story of her analysis is one of needless manipulation on her part as well as on that of her analyst. His failures of discretion called forth and in turn probably responded to hers, in a steadily deteriorating relationship.

Efforts to manipulate through self-revelation sometimes overwhelm both speakers and listeners. Consider again the "judge-penitent" in Camus's *The Fall*. His self-imposed penance is to confess his failures over and over to strangers, implicating them in his torment, taunting them, fanning their guilt, in order to master them.

Since one cannot condemn others without thereby judging oneself, it was necessary to oppress oneself in order to have the right to judge others. Since every judge ends some day as penitent, I had to take that road in the opposite direction and take up the trade of penitent in order to finish as judge. [23]

Revealing the Secrets of Others

It is not possible to probe one's life in depth without having to ask whether one should also reveal intimate matters about others. No one lives in complete isolation; and the problems of each person are intertwined with those of family members, friends, adversaries, colleagues, and other individuals. But they usually take no part in the self-exploration; nor have they always given their consent to having their lives raked over. They may even object bitterly—as parents or children of someone in psychoanalysis, for instance—to intimate revelations or to what they see as intrusive speculation about their feelings. The resulting conflict is one that goes far beyond therapeutic or confessional contexts. How *should* we regard the secrets of others? May we reveal them with the same freedom with which we reveal our own? If not, what considerations should we take into account in deciding whether or not to do so?

A stronger case can be made for breaching the secrets of others in a therapeutic context than for doing so in, say, casual gossip. If it is true that we cannot speak meaningfully and in depth about ourselves without at times saying things about others that they would not wish us to say, we could reject such talk only at the cost of also forgoing self-revelation. Yet the need to examine personal experience may be great; and confidentiality—to the extent that it holds—prevents the secrets from spreading, and from embarrassing and discrediting those whose secrets they are.

Even without such a personal need, and even in the absence of confidentiality, denying people the right to decide whether or not to reveal their own personal secrets would interfere in the most fundamental way with their freedom. The same would be true of efforts to censor what they say about personal secrets that involve others, as in revelations about an unhappy childhood or marriage. As I argued in Chapter II, the burden of proof is on those who would override such personal control.

While this control must be protected, it need not be exercised without discretion. Whereas one has only oneself to blame if one is indiscreet about one's personal matters, one has a special responsibility to consider the feelings and claims of others about whom one speaks. They may be highly vulnerable and uneasy at the thought of what is said about them. And it is often unnecessary to draw them into one's revelation. In addition, friends or family members may have revealed highly private matters with every expectation of loyalty—at times even after receiving a promise of silence. These promises should count; if there is still to be a breach of secrecy, it should only be after requesting to be released from the promise, or for overriding reasons, as when the promise was extracted under duress or made in ignorance of factors that would have led to its rejection. Such a breach requires one to think through one's motives with the greatest possible candor. Often, what seems to be an overriding reason to talk to a therapist or confessor about the failings of others is less persuasive than we imagine.

Accusation of self is common in self-disclosure; accusation of others, hardly less so. In the modulations of openness and secrecy, there is great scope for choice about how complete or incomplete to make one's revelations, and how accurate or inaccurate.* As Camus said, a confession

---

* I shall not discuss, in this context, the question whether one can ever know or tell the truth about oneself, but rather the speaker's choices about what he *takes* to be truthful or deceptive, full or partial, correct or erroneous information.

often signals the moment for applying make-up to the corpse; and part of the embellishment may turn on implicating others in one's guilt, or placing it on their shoulders altogether. Add to this the layers of denial and rationalization through which one perceives past experience, and the absence of precisely those others about whom the revelations are made. Surely they have every reason to argue for the exercise of discretion on the part of the self-discloser.

Confidentiality on the part of the confessor or therapist is indispensable as a protection for third parties whose secrets are thus revealed. And it mitigates the problem of possible inaccuracies and mistakes in discussing these secrets. The question of accuracy is especially troubling in political and criminal confessions because of what can befall those implicated; it is less so in therapeutic self-revelation, from the point of view of the consequences for those drawn in, so long as the bond of confidentiality holds.

But accuracy is not all that is at issue; nor do those implicated regard the matter as insignificant so long as the revelations regarding them are held in confidence; nor, finally, do they have reason to trust that professional confidentiality will always be maintained.[24] The questions about what ought to be revealed regarding third parties arise just as much when the revealer has the facts right. Even if what he has to say about others is not so much accusatory as exploring what he takes to be their weaknesses or obsessions or excesses, he should weigh the reasons for and against including them in his disclosures. Family members and former intimates may not be injured by any outward effects of the revelations about their personal affairs, yet still feel intruded upon.

Much depends, moreover, on the nature of what is thought to be deviant and guilty. In those societies, for example, where children are pressed to report on any religious or political dissent in their homes, family members have reason for profound concern, even if the reports go to a school psychologist who professes to honor the obligation of confidentiality.

We must be alert to links between therapeutic and other purposes for encouraging self-revelation, especially when confessants come to act as unwitting informants, or when one of the signs of their progress or of their trustworthiness is said to be their willingness to reveal all about former associates.[25] And we must ask about the effect on discretion and loyalty of encouragement to hold nothing back about others, even when this is done for strictly therapeutic purposes. Consider this passage in an article claiming that the role of psychoanalysis is to remove obstacles to the confession of secrets:

Telling the story of last evening's party, the patient mentioned a certain Mr. X. whom he knows to be a friend of the analyst. The report on the remarks of some of the people present was obviously incomplete and the patient resisted completing it. "As you know," said the analyst, "in psychoanalysis it is one's duty to say things which in ordinary life would be stamped as gossip." Thereupon the patient admitted that he had heard some unfriendly remarks about Mr. X. and that he felt uneasy in his role as gossip. He then repeated the insults against Mr. X., some of which were new to the analyst. This episode is very similar to the removal of obstacles in every-day conversation above discussed. Under the pressure of the fear of appearing a gossip, or of making the analyst cross, a part of the material had become "secret." In reassuring the patient, the analyst removed this obstacle and the confession was forthcoming.[26]

In itself, this incident may seem trivial. But its assumption that "in psychoanalysis it is one's duty to say things which in ordinary life would be stamped as gossip" requires qualification. No patient should be asked to accept such a "duty" without further thought. At times such disclosures may be necessary; often they are harmless. But a patient has every reason to weigh duties of loyalty in deciding what to say about others, as well as respect for their feelings and possible risks to them from indiscriminate disclosures. The need for help with personal problems may require that one override the constraints of loyalty, promises, and respect for privacy, the more so if the listener's guarantee of silence can be trusted.* But the constraints should not be left out of the process of deliberation altogether.

To sum up, institutional practices of self-revelation may bring solace, alleviation of guilt, group acceptance, personal growth, even self-transcendence, but they are also unequaled means for imposing orthodoxy of every kind. Without concern for the moral problems these practices raise, both speakers and listeners risk violating the boundaries that protect the self and human relationships. In such violations, the self-revealer often cooperates; for while pressure and manipulation may be used to make him more tractable, his own yearning for acceptance and forgiveness, sometimes for humiliation, is of equal assistance. Ideological compliance could not prevail for so long in so many societies through coercion alone; it requires the responsiveness that brings some to want to confess even at the price of their freedom, hoping to reach together with their questioners the underlying layers of secrecy that always elude them.

---

* I shall discuss in later chapters other factors that may override these constraints, such as the duty to help someone bent on self-harm or to prevent people from injuring others.

Chapter VII

Gossip

Definitions

*Round the samovar and the hostess the conversation had been
meanwhile vacillating . . . between three inevitable topics: the
latest piece of public news, the theater, and scandal. It, too,
came finally to rest on the last topic, that is, ill-natured gossip. . . .
and the conversation crackled merrily like a burning fagot-stick.*

Tolstoy's group portrait from *Anna Karenina* brings to mind many a
cluster of malicious gossips, delighting in every new morsel of intimate
information about others, the more scandalous the better.[1] So well do
we recognize this temptation, and so often do we see it indulged, that
it is easy to think of all gossip as petty, ill-willed, too often unfounded—
as either trivial and thus demeaning to those whose lives it rakes over,
or else as outright malicious. In either case, gossip seems inherently
questionable from a moral point of view.

Dictionary definitions reinforce the view of gossip as trivial. Thus
the *American Heritage Dictionary* defines it as "trifling, often groundless
rumor, usually of a personal, sensational, or intimate nature; idle talk."[2]

Thinkers who adopt a normative point of view often stress the more negative evaluation of gossip. Aristotle wrote of that tantalizing and yet strangely limited "great-souled man," who "claims much and deserves much," that he is no gossip [*anthropologos*],

for he will not talk either about himself or about another, as he neither wants to receive compliments nor to hear other people run down . . . ; and so he is not given to speaking evil himself, even of his enemies, except when he deliberately intends to give offense.[3]

Thomas Aquinas distinguished "talebearers" from "backbiters": both speak evil of their neighbors, but a talebearer differs from a backbiter "since he intends, not to speak ill as such, but to say anything that may stir one man against another," in order to sever friendship.[4]

Kierkegaard abhorred gossip. He spoke out against its superficiality and its false fellow-feeling. Gossip and chatter, he wrote, "obliterate the vital distinction between what is private and what is public" and thereby trivialize all that is inward and inherently inexpressible. He castigated his own age as one in which the expanding press offered snide and leveling gossip to a garrulous, news-hungry public.[5] Heidegger likewise, in pages echoing those of Kierkegaard, deplored idle talk as "something which anyone can rake up." He held that it perverts genuine efforts at understanding by making people think they already know everything.[6] And in their 1890 article on the right to privacy, Samuel Warren and Louis Brandeis spoke of gossip with similar distaste, assailing in particular its spread in the expanding yellow press: "Gossip is no longer the resource of the idle and vicious but has become a trade which is pursued with industry as well as effrontery."[7]

Cheap, superficial, intrusive, unfounded, even vicious: surely gossip can be all that. Yet to define it in these ways is to overlook the whole network of human exchanges of information, the need to inquire and to learn from the experience of others, and the importance of not taking everything at face value. The desire for such knowledge leads people to go beneath the surface of what is said and shown, and to try to unravel conflicting clues and seemingly false leads. In order to do so, information has to be shared with others, obtained from them, stored in memory for future use, tested and evaluated in discussion, and used at times to encourage, to entertain, or to warn.

Everyone has a special interest in personal information about others. If we knew about people only what they wished to reveal, we would be subjected to ceaseless manipulation; and we would be deprived of the pleasure and suspense that comes from trying to understand them.

Gossip helps to absorb and to evaluate intimations about other lives, as do letters, novels, biography, and chronicles of all kinds. In order to live in both the inner and the shared worlds, the exchange of views about each—in spite of all the difficulties of perception and communication—is indispensable.[8]

Thanks to the illuminating studies of gossip by anthropologists and others—in villages around the world as in offices, working teams, schools, or conventions—we now have a livelier and clearer documentation of the role it actually plays.[9] These studies have disproved the traditional stereotype of women as more garrulous and prone to gossip than men, and have shown how such forms of communication spring up in every group, regardless of sex.[10] By tracing the intricate variations of gossip, these writings have led to a subtler understanding of how it channels, tests, and often reinforces judgments about human nature.

Before considering the moral problems that some forms of gossip clearly raise, we must therefore define it in a less dismissive way than those mentioned at the beginning of this chapter. We shall then be able to ask what makes it more or less problematic from a moral point of view, and weigh more carefully the dangers that Kierkegaard, Heidegger, and others have signaled.

I shall define gossip as informal personal communication about other people who are absent or treated as absent. It is informal, first of all, unlike communication in court proceedings or lectures or hospital records or biographies, in that it lacks formal rules setting forth who may speak and in what manner, and with what limitations from the point of view of accuracy and reliability. It is informal, too, in that it takes place more spontaneously and relies more on humor and guesswork, and in that it is casual with respect to who ends up receiving the information, in spite of the frequent promises not to repeat it that are ritualistically exacted along its path. (In each of these respects, gossip nevertheless has standards as well, though usually unspoken, as all who have tried to take part in gossip and been rebuffed have learned.) And the formal modes of discourse may themselves slip into more or less gossipy variations.

Secrecy is one of the factors that make gossip take the place of more formal communication about persons. Gossip increases whenever information is both scarce and desirable—whenever people want to find out more about others than they are able to. It is rampant, for instance, in speculations about the selection of prize-winners, or the marriage plans of celebrities, or the favors of a capricious boss. Gossip is more likely, too, when formal modes of discourse, though possible, have drawbacks for the participants. Thus hospital and school personnel gossip about their charges rather than entering the information on institutional records. And those who have the power to retaliate should they learn that their personal affairs are discussed are criticized in gossip rather than to their faces.

The seventeenth- and eighteenth-century New England Puritans illustrate in their writings the intensity with which human lives may be raked over, both in personal soul-searching and in talking about the lives of others. They labored with the strongest fears of not being among those who would turn out to be saved in the life to come; but they had no evidence for who was and who was not saved, and recognized no way to influence their fate, believing that it had been decided for them before birth. Might they nevertheless discern traces of such evidence in their own lives and in those of others? Might behavior and demeanor not hold some clues? Speculating about imperceptible yet all-important differences between persons took on an urgency rarely exceeded before or since. Hypocrisy naturally abounded. One of the foremost tasks of thinkers such as Thomas Shepard and Jonathan Edwards became the effort to separate the hypocrites from the sincere, and above all, to discern in self and others what they called the "inner hypocrisy" or self-deception that masked one's sins and doubts even from oneself.[11]

The second element in my definition of gossip is personal communication. The original source of what is said may be hidden or forgotten, but each time, gossip is communicated by one or more persons to others, most often in personal encounters, but also by telephone, by letter, or, in the last few centuries, in the mass media. This personal element, combined with the third—that the information is also *about* persons— makes gossip a prime vehicle for moral evaluation. Part of the universal attraction of gossip is the occasion it affords for comparing oneself with others, usually silently, while seeming to be speaking strictly about someone else. Few activities tempt so much to moralizing, through stereotyped judgments and the head-shaking, seemingly all-knowing distancing of those speaking from those spoken about. The result is hypocrisy—judging the lives of others as one would hardly wish one's own judged. As one student of the anthropology of gossip has said:

If I suggest that gossip and scandal are socially virtuous and valuable, this does not mean that I always approve of them. Indeed, in practice I find that when I am gossiping about my friends as well as my enemies I am deeply conscious of performing a social duty; but that when I hear they gossip viciously about me, I am rightfully filled with righteous indignation.[12]

Because gossip is primarily about persons, it is not identical with the larger category of rumor; there can be rumors of war or rumors of an imminent stock-market collapse, but hardly gossip.[13] And there can be stories, but not gossip, about the foibles and escapades of animals, so long as humans are not part of the plot, or the animals taken to represent individual persons or endowed with human characteristics.

Gossip, finally, is not only about persons but about persons absent, isolated, or excluded, rather than about the participants themselves. The subjects of gossip, while usually physically absent, can also be treated as if they were absent should they be part of the group engaging in gossip. While the conversation is directed past them and around them, they are then its targets, and are meant to overhear it. Least of all can people gossip about themselves, unless they manage to treat themselves as if they were absent, and as subjects of scandal or concern. Though it is hard to gossip about oneself, one can lay oneself open to gossip, or talk about one's doings that include others in such a way as to arouse gossip. Compare, from this point of view, the rumored divorce and the announced one, or the gossip about a young girl's pregnancy and her acknowledgment of it.

These four elements of gossip—that it is (1) informal (2) personal communication (3) about persons who (4) are absent or excluded—are clearly not morally problematic in their own right. Consider the many harmless or supportive uses of gossip: the talk about who might marry, have a baby, move to another town, be in need of work or too ill to ask for help, and the speculations about underlying reasons, possible new developments, and opportunities for advice or help. Some may find such talk uninteresting, even tedious, or too time-consuming, but they can hardly condemn it on moral grounds.

On the other hand, it is equally easy to conceive of occasions when the four elements do present moral problems. The informality and the speculative nature of what is said may be inappropriate, as it would be if gossip were the basis for firing people from their jobs. The communication about other persons may be of a degrading or invasive nature that renders it inappropriate, whether in gossip or in other discourse. And the talk about persons in their absence—behind their backs—is sometimes of such a nature as to require that it either be spoken to their faces or not spoken at all. Pirandello's play *Right You Are! (If You Think So)* shows how irresistibly such gossip can build up among men and women in a small town, and the havoc it can wreak.[14]

For an example of gossip that is offensive on all such grounds, and as a contrast to the many forms of harmless gossip mentioned earlier, consider the alleged leak by an FBI official to a Hollywood columnist about the private life of the actress Jean Seberg. The leak indicated that she had engaged in extramarital relations with a member of the

Black Panther Party, who was said to have fathered her unborn child.[15] It was meant to cast suspicion on her support of black nationalist causes. Reprinted by *Newsweek*, it was disseminated, as intended, throughout the world. Such uses of gossip have not been rare. They injure most directly the person whose reputation they are meant to call in question. But they debilitate as well those who take part in manufacturing and spreading the rumor, and their superiors who are responsible for permitting such a scheme to go ahead; and thus they endanger still others who may be the targets of similar attacks. Such acts, with all their ramifications, overstep all bounds of discretion and of respect for persons. They are especially reprehensible and dangerous when undertaken in secrecy by a government agency in the name of the public's best interest.

In between these extremes of innocuousness and harm lie most forms of gossip: the savoring of salacious rumors, the passing on of unverified suspicions, the churning over seemingly self-inflicted burdens in the lives of acquaintances, and the consequent self-righteousness and frequent hypocrisy of those passing judgment in gossip. No testing ground for the exercise of discretion and indiscretion is more common than such everyday probing and trading of personal matters. Just as all of us play the roles of host and guest at different times, so all of us gossip and are gossiped about. Gossip brings into play intuitive responses to the tensions of insider and outsider, and forces us to choose between concealing and revealing, between inquisitiveness and restraint. Each of us develops some standards, however inarticulate, however often honored in the breach, for amounts and kinds of gossip we relish, tolerate, or reject. Can these standards be made more explicit? If so, how might we weigh them?

Reprehensible Gossip

Why is gossip like a three-prongued tongue? Because it destroys three people: the person who says it, the person who listens to it, and the person about whom it is told.
THE BABYLONIAN TALMUD

Not all gossip, as I have defined it, is injurious or otherwise to be avoided. But when it is, it can harm all who take part in it, as the Babylonian Talmud warned.[16] Out of respect for oneself as much as for others, therefore, it matters to discern such cases. Three categories of gossip should be singled out as especially reprehensible: gossip in breach of confidence, gossip the speaker knows to be false, and unduly invasive gossip.

It is wrong, first of all, to reveal in gossip what one has promised to keep secret. This is why the gossip of doctors at staff meetings and cocktail parties about the intimate revelations of their patients is so inexcusable. True, pledges of confidentiality must at times be broken— to save the life of an adolescent who confides plans of suicide, for example. But such legitimate breaches could hardly be carried out through gossip, because of its lack of discrimination with respect to who ends up hearing it. Such information should, rather, be disclosed only to those who have a particular need to know, and with the utmost respect for the privacy of the individual concerned.

Must we then bar all gossip conveyed in spite of a pledge of silence? And would we then not exclude *most* gossip? After all, few pieces of information are more rapidly disseminated than those preceded by a "promise not to tell." At times such a promise is worthless, a mere empty gesture, and both parties know it; one can hardly call the subsequent repeating of the "secret" a breach of confidence. Sometimes the person who asks for the promise before sharing his bits of gossip may believe it to be more binding than it turns out to be. But, as La Rochefoucauld asked, why should we imagine that others will keep the secret we have ourselves been unable to keep? [17] At still other times, a promise may have been sincere, but should never have been made to begin with. Many promises of secrecy are exacted with the aggressive intent of burdening someone, or of creating a gulf between that individual and others. The best policy is to be quite sparing in one's promises of secrecy about any information, but scrupulous, once having given such a promise, in respecting it.

Second, gossip is unjustifiable whenever those who convey it know that it is false and intend to deceive their listeners (unlike someone who makes it clear that he exaggerates or speaks in jest). Whether they spread false gossip just to tell a good story, or to influence reputations, perhaps even as a weapon—as when newly separated spouses sometimes overstate each other's misdeeds and weaknesses in speaking to friends— they are exceeding the bounds of what they owe to their listeners and to those whose doings they misrepresent. The same is true of the false gossip that can spring up in the competition for favor, as in office politics or in academic backbiting, and of collective strategies for deceit. Thus in the re-election campaign of President Nixon in 1972, some individuals had been assigned the task of spreading false rumors about his opponents. Conspiratorial groups and secret police have employed such methods through the ages. Whatever the reason, there can be no excuse for such dissemination of false gossip.

Might there not be exceptional circumstances that render false gossip excusable?* I argued, in *Lying*, that certain lies might be excusable, such as those that offer the only way to deflect someone bent on violence. But whatever lies one might tell such an assailant, false gossip about third parties would hardly provide the requisite help at such a time of crisis; and if by any chance the assailant could be stalled simply by talking about other persons, there would be no need to use falsehood in so doing.

Are there forms of false gossip that correspond to innocent white lies? Gossip to please someone on his deathbed, for instance, who has always enjoyed hearing about the seedy and salacious doings of his friends, by a wife who can think of nothing truthful that is sufficiently titillating? Should she then invent stories about neighbors or friends, thinking that no harm could come thereof, since her husband would not live to spread the stories further? Such a way out would be demeaning for both, even if it injured no one else: demeaning to the dying man in the unspoken judgment about what would most please him, and in the supposition that lying to him would therefore be acceptable; and demeaning to his wife, as she reflected back on her inability to muster alternative modes of silence and speech at such a time. No matter how well meant, falsehoods about the lives of others bear little resemblance to harmless white lies.

Much of the time, of course, those who convey false gossip do not know it to be false. It may rest on hearsay, or be unverified, or be pure speculation. Often the facts cannot easily *be* verified, or not without serious intrusion. Thus to spread rumors that a person is a secret alcoholic is made more serious because of the difficulty that listeners have in ascertaining the basis of the allegation. At times such gossip cannot be known to be true by the speakers, nor credibly denied by the subjects. This was one reason why the dissemination of the rumor about Jean Seberg's unborn baby was so insidious. She had no way before the baby's birth to demonstrate the falsity of the rumor.

In the third place, gossip may be reprehensible, even if one has given

---

*One could imagine a club dedicated to false gossip, in which members vied with one another for who could tell the most outrageous stories about fellow human beings. So long as all knew the tales were false, and the stories went no farther, the practice would not be a deceptive one, and more allied to storytelling and fiction than to the intentional misleading about the lives of others that is what renders false gossip inexcusable. Such a club, however, would be likely to have but few members; for gossip loses its interest when it is *known* to be false.

no pledge of silence and believes one's information correct, simply because it is unduly invasive. On this ground, too, planting the rumor about Jean Seberg's sexual life and the identity of the father of her unborn child was unjustifiable, regardless of whether the FBI thought the story accurate or not.

Is any gossip, then, unduly invasive whenever it concerns what is private, perhaps stigmatizing, often secret? If so, much of the gossip about the personal lives of neighbors, co-workers, and public figures would have to be judged inexcusable. But such a judgment seems unreasonable. It would dismiss many harmless or unavoidable exchanges about human foibles. To such strictures, the perspective of Mr. Bennett in Jane Austen's *Pride and Prejudice* should give pause: "For what do we live," he asked, "but to make sport for our neighbors and to laugh at them in turn?"[18]

How then might we sort out what is unduly invasive from all the gossip about private and secret lives? To begin with, there is reason to stop to consider whether gossip is thus invasive whenever those whose doings are being discussed claim to feel intruded upon. But these claims must obviously not be taken at face value: they are often claims to ownership of information about oneself. While such claims should give gossipers pause, they are not always legitimate. People cannot be said, for instance, to own aspects of their lives that are clearly evident to others and thus in fact public, such as a nasty temper or a manipulative manner, nor can they reasonably argue that others have no right to discuss them. Least of all can they suppress references to what may be an "open secret," known to all, and half-suspected even by themselves— a topic treated in innumerable comedies about marital infidelity. Similarly, more concealed aspects of their lives may be of legitimate interest to others—their mistreatment of their children, for example, or their past employment record. And the information that government leaders often try to withhold through claims to executive privilege is often such that the public has every right to acquire it. At such times, gossip may be an indispensable channel for public information.

Merely to *say* that gossip about oneself is unduly invasive, therefore, does not make it so. I would argue that additional factors must be present to render gossip unduly invasive: the information must be about matters legitimately considered private; and it must hurt the individuals talked about.* They may be aware of the spreading or of the harm; or else

---

*For this reason, gossip should give pause whenever the speaker believes it may reach someone in a position to injure the person spoken of. If the listener is a judge, for instance, or an executive having the power to make decisions over someone's em-

they may be injured by invasive gossip without ever knowing why—fail to keep their jobs, perhaps, because of rumors about their unspoken political dissent. But the speculations in bars or sewing circles concerning even the most intimate aspects of the married life of public figures is not intrusive so long as it does not reach them or affect their lives in any way. Such talk may diminish the speakers, but does not intrude on the persons spoken about.

While the three categories of reprehensible gossip—gossip in breach of confidence, gossip that is known to be false, and gossip that is clearly invasive—should be avoided, each one has somewhat uncertain boundaries and borderline regions. One cannot always be sure whether one owes someone silence, whether one is conveying false gossip, or whether what is said of an intimate nature about people will find its way back to them or otherwise hurt them. In weighing such questions, discretion is required; and, given the capacity of gossip to spread, it is best to resolve doubts in favor of silence.

Extra caution is needed under certain circumstances, when the temptation to indulge in any of the three forms may be heightened. At such times, the borderline cases carry an even stronger presumption against taking part in gossip. Discretion is then needed more than ever to prevent gossip from blending with one or more of the kinds earlier ruled out. The desire to have an effect, first of all, to impress people, perhaps to deal a blow, easily leads to greater pressure to breach secrecy or exaggerate in gossip or to speak intrusively about others. As soon as a speaker gains in any way from passing on gossip, these pressures arise. Prestige, power, affection, intimacy, even income (as for gossip columnists): such are the gains that gossipers envisage. It cannot be wrong to gain from gossip in its own right, since in one sense most gossip aims at a gain of some sort—if nothing else, in closeness to the listener, or in the status of someone who seems to be "in the know." But the prospect of such gain increases the likelihood that promises will be broken, unverified rumors passed on, privacy invaded. The misfortunes of another may then be used in such a way as to traffic in them. This is in part why

---

ployment, the gossiper must weigh his words with care. Even when the listener is not in an official position, gossip directed to him is problematic if he is given to injurious responses: if he is malicious, slanderous, indiscreet, profiteering, or in any way likely to put the information to inappropriate use. Gossip is problematic, too, if the listener is a poor intermediary: perhaps one who exaggerates gossip in conveying it further, or who is likely to misunderstand it and spread it in false garb, or is unable to discriminate in turn between listeners, so that he conveys the gossip to one who is incompetent or dangerous.

the inside gossip of the former employee or the divorced spouse is more troubling when it is published for financial gain or as revenge.

A desire for gain of a different kind motivates those who take special pleasure in passing on discreditable gossip. Maimonides, like Aquinas and many others, distinguished the talebearer from the person who speaks to denigrate: the scandalmonger, or, as Maimonides expressed it, "the evil tongue." [19] He spoke, too, of "the dust of the evil tongue": the insinuations that sow suspicion without shedding light either on the implied offense or on the evidence concerning it. Before scandalmongers and insinuators are known as such, they can destroy trust among friends or in entire communities; in consequence they have been more distasteful to commentators than all others. And yet, all disparaging or discreditable personal information cannot be avoided. On the contrary, it must sometimes be conveyed, as when the deceitful or the aggressive or, indeed, the indiscreet are pointed out to put newcomers on their guard. Consider, as an illustration of such cautioning remarks, the following exchange in a Mexican village:

Down the path someone spotted a young man named Xun, whose reputation as a drunkard made everyone anxious to be on his way.
 "If you meet him drunk on the path, he has no mercy. He won't listen to what you say, that Xun."
 "He doesn't understand what you say; you're right. If he's just a bit tight when you meet him on the path–puta, 'Let's go, let's go,' he'll say. You will be forced to drink."
 "But doesn't he get angry?"
 "No, no. He'll just say, 'Let's go have a little soft drink.' "
 "He's good-natured."
 "But he doesn't bother to ask if you're in a hurry to get someplace . . ."
 "No, he's good-hearted . . ."
 "If you find yourself in a hurry to get somewhere and you see him coming the best thing to do is hide . . ."
 ". . . or run away."
 And with that, the various men went on about their business. [20]

Trivializing Gossip

Beyond such questions of avoiding reprehensible and harmful gossip lies a larger one: that of the tone gossip can lend to discourse about human lives. It is this tone that Kierkegaard and Heidegger aimed at, in arguing that gossip streamlines and demeans what is spoken. What is utterly private and inward, Kierkegaard held, cannot be expressed; as a result, talking about it must necessarily distort and trivialize. Gossip therefore has a leveling effect, in conveying as shallow and ordinary what is unfathomable. It levels, moreover, by talking of all persons in the same terms, so that even the exceptionally gifted, the dissident, and the artist are brought down to the lowest common denominator. Finally, it erases and levels the differences between the different modes of talking, so that all is glossed over in the same superficial and informal chatter.

According to such a view, the informality with which we talk about the weather or the latest price rises can only trivialize what we say about human beings. And this informality of gossip can combine with the special liberties taken in the absence of those spoken about so as to permit the speaker to indulge in a familiarity disrespectful of their humanity and in turn of his own. It was this reflection that gossip casts on so many who convey it that made George Eliot compare it to smoke from dirty tobacco pipes: "it proves nothing but the bad taste of the smoker." [21]

Gossip can also trivialize and demean when it substitutes personal anecdote for a careful exploration of ideas. Someone incapable of taking up political or literary questions without dwelling endlessly on personalities can do justice neither to the ideas nor to the persons under debate.

Such gossip can be an intoxicating surrogate for genuine efforts to understand. It can be the vehicle for stereotypes—of class, for instance, or race or sex. It turns easily into a habit, and for some a necessity. They may then become unable to think of other human beings in other than trivial ways. If they cannot attribute scope and depth and complexity to others, moreover, it is unlikely that they will perceive these dimensions in themselves. All news may strike them as reducible to certain trite formulas about human behavior; all riddles seem transparent.

Many do not merely gossip but are known *as* gossips. They may serve an important group function; but such a role should cause concern to the individuals thus labeled. It is far more likely to tempt to breaches of confidence, to falsehoods, to invasive gossiping—and thus to a general loss of discernment about reasons to avoid gossip and persons to shield from it. At the extreme of this spectrum is the pathological gossip, whose life revolves around prying into the personal affairs of others and talking about them.

Plutarch wrote of the garrulous that they deny themselves the greatest benefits of silence: hearing and being heard. In their haste to speak, they listen but poorly; others, in turn, pay little heed to their words. [22]

And Heidegger expounded on the strange way in which gossip and all facile discourse, so seemingly open and free-ranging, turns out instead to inhibit understanding: "by its very nature, idle talk is a closing-off, since to go back to the ground of what is talked about is something which it *leaves undone*." [23] Those whose casual talk stops at no boundaries, leaves no secret untouched, may thereby shut themselves off from the understanding they seem to seek. Gossip can be the means whereby they distance themselves from all those about whom they speak with such seeming familiarity, and they may achieve but spurious intimacy with those *with whom* they speak. In this way gossip can deny full meaning and depth to human beings, much like some forms of confession: gossip, through such trivializing and distancing; confession, through molding those who confess and overcoming their independence.

These warnings go to the heart of the meaning of discernment concerning human beings, including oneself, and of its links with the capacity to deal with openness and secrecy. Quite apart from the obvious problems with false or invasive gossip discussed earlier, all gossip can become trivializing in tone, or turn into garrulity.

Yet gossip need not deny meaning and debilitate thus. Those who warn against it often fail to consider its extraordinary variety. They ignore the attention it can bring to human complexity, and are unaware of its role in conveying information without which neither groups nor societies could function.[24] The view of all gossip as trivializing human lives is itself belittling if applied indiscriminately. When Kierkegaard and Heidegger speak out against idle talk, gossip, and chatter, and against "the public" and the "average understanding" taken in by such discourse, they erase differences and deny meaning in their own way.[25] One cannot read their strictures without sensing their need to stand aloof, to maintain distance, to hold common practices vulgar. In these passages, they stereotype social intercourse and deny it depth and diversity, just as much as gossip can deny those of individuals. When moral judgment takes such stereotyped form, it turns into moralizing: one more way in which moral language can be used to avoid a fuller understanding of human beings and of their efforts to make sense of their lives.

Chapter VIII

Secrecy, Power, and Accountability

The Shared Predicament

In the preceding chapters I have examined the nature of secrecy and its significance for moral choice; and considered the role of discretion in deciding whether or not to reveal one's own secrets, what difference it makes if the secrets concern others, and when to refrain from probing the secrets of others. Throughout, I have tried to convey how secrecy can work in opposite directions, so as both to inhibit and to support moral choice.

I now want to turn to large-scale collective practices of secrecy, revelation, and probing. Do these practices—in medicine and industry, for example, or in government and law—reflect the same moral conflicts as those I have examined up to now? Does collective choice about secrecy present special dangers, and is it different when made *in* secrecy? How, finally, do the arguments for and against secrecy apply to such practices?

Throughout, my discussion presupposes a view of the relationship between individual and joint human problems that lies at the heart of much moral inquiry: a view of each human life as of the highest worth, and yet as caught up in a joint existence beset with unpredictable and at times incomprehensible difficulty. Magnificently conveyed in the great confessional works, this view rejects all reductionist accounts of human nature. It assumes human beings to matter, and therefore their conduct and the way they are treated. But it recognizes as well the collective burden of suffering, ignorance, and evil in human lives, a burden that limits and distorts choice so severely as to constitute a dispiriting shared predicament. The severity of this burden has led many to believe that it must have been imposed upon mankind on purpose, perhaps by a power unconcerned with the resultant suffering, or wishing to put humans to a test, or even vengeful. Thus the Pythagorean poet Empedocles described earthly life as a region of adversity through which souls must pass, weighed down by disease, suffering, and toil, impeded by forgetfulness and confusion, and by failures of insight and character.[1]

Without striving for simultaneous awareness of these two aspects of human existence, it is hard to grasp the scope and complexity of moral choice, and thus hard, in turn, to avoid the cynicism that comes with seeing neither of the two aspects, or the shallowness of seeing only one. The cynicism undercuts moral reasoning, and the shallowness results in moralizing: rhetoric about morality that spins in the void because it fails to connect with an essential aspect of human existence. Such a failure to connect is closely related to the forms of avoidance that I have discussed, and serves as a protection against the full force of the double perception, much as squinting guards against strong sunlight.

The joint burden of suffering, ignorance, and evil has gone under many names. Recently, G. J. Warnock has discussed its role as a shared human predicament.[2] Among the factors contributing to its severity, three are central: the difficult and often uncontrollable external conditions of human beings, their inadequate powers of reasoning and judgment, and their problems of character.

The first of these factors is that of the difficult external conditions of human life: the scarcity of so many of the resources needed to satisfy even the most basic human needs for health, nourishment and shelter, work and affection and pleasure; the vast disparity among individuals, so that some have more of these resources than they can ever use, while others have nothing; and the unpredictable assaults on all of the resources and on their distribution by both natural and human forces. Given the severity of these conditions as most encounter them, conflicts over how to alleviate suffering and bring about benefits arise at every step.

Second, when we try to cope with these conflicts posed by suffering, scarcity, and inequality, we are hampered by inadequate powers of reasoning and judgment. Our capacity to perceive and to remember is so limited, and the reliability and predictability of what we learn so uncertain, that we are hindered from the very outset. And our ability to reason, to take the information, such as it is, into account, and to arrive at judgments, is in itself severely limited and subject to bias from all directions. Ignorance, error, and prejudice lead us astray; we compensate through rationalization and at times through denial of the factors we most need to take into account.

The third factor (though by no means separable in practice from the first two) is that of the weaknesses and vices of character that interfere relentlessly with efforts to resolve conflicts and to make reasoned choices. These efforts would benefit from a disposition to sympathetic understanding of what others suffer through and of what they need; benefit also from traits such as fairness and veracity, and from the capacity to cooperate and to carry through good choices once they have been made. But these character traits are limited at best, and often warped.

Together, these failures of character act to increase the burden of suffering and the difficulties of reasoning and judgment that are already so severe. As a result, the conflicts of human needs, interests, and goals are reinforced—not only between individuals and groups but within each person. Working at cross-purposes, these conflicts defy the neat hierarchies that theorists erect and the longings of utopians to overcome discord once and for all.

The rational and the moral aspects of choice are thus deficient from the outset, and the defects of each ceaselessly skew the other.[3] Any effort to bypass one, moreover, is injurious to both. Thus concern for reasoning and judgment alone has led many to crude cost-benefit calculations that ignore the pull of the shared predicament in skewing such calculations, and that omit the question who should do the calculating for whom and why. Likewise concern for moral principles or character alone has all too often led to fanaticism, to a retreat into irrationality (do what is right though the heavens may fall), and to elevating personal bias to the status of moral principle.

Normative inquiry seeks how best to cope with this shared predicament in the light of the respect due human beings. It has taken several paths. Many have sought to grasp the double perception in its entirety through religious thinking. They have probed all that to which the sense of sacredness attaches, often seeing it as concentrated and embodied in ritual and in the divine; they have offered supernatural explanations for the severity of the predicament; and they have tried to mold judgment and character accordingly. Through law and custom, communities have striven to set norms for conduct in response to the conflicts and the harm imposed by the shared predicament. Moral philosophy, finally, addresses the same conflicts; but it also questions the justification for choice, for ways of life, and for goals, including the answers arrived at in religion and in law, as well as the nature of justification itself.

In religion as in law and ethics, reductionist theories have arisen that slight either the worth of each human life or the severity of the shared predicament. To these reductionist views, the ethical questions of secrecy present a special threat: for all reductionism seeks to avert inquiry by cutting down to size, denying depth, papering over contradiction; yet secrecy presupposes precisely scope, depth, and contradiction. Thus secrecy calls forth reductionist approaches as well—the different ways that I have discussed of warding off inquiry by means of definition, metaphor, and theoretical construct. Any effort to counteract simplifying views of secrecy may therefore contribute, as well, to a fuller awareness of moral conflicts more generally.

How do collective practices of secrecy, probing, and revelation influence moral conflicts? Some control over secrecy and openness is needed to ensure respect for the significance and scope of human life, and sometimes for survival itself; yet this control can also be used to undercut this respect. Likewise, such control can help to alleviate the burden of the shared human predicament—but it can also add to the suffering, skew judgment, and allow abuses and deterioration of character. Is it right to assume, as many have, that secrecy is especially dangerous when joined with great power?

Power and Secrecy

Every thing secret degenerates, even the administration of justice; nothing is safe that does not show how it can bear discussion and publicity.

* * *

I cannot accept your canon that we are to judge Pope and King unlike other men with a favorable presumption that they did no wrong. If there is any presumption it is the other way against holders of power, increasing as the power increases. Historic responsibility has to make up for the want of legal responsibility. Power tends to corrupt, and absolute power corrupts absolutely.

LORD ACTON

Lord Acton made these statements on quite separate occasions.[4] Each one, taken separately, goes too far. Every thing secret need not degenerate;

some are needed, on the contrary, for growth and creativity. Nor does power always tend to corrupt. It can be exercised with integrity and even tenderness, as in the caring for most infants. A measure of control over secrecy and openness—and thus of one form of power—is needed in personal life for equilibrium, liberty, even survival. Both secrecy and power are capable of lightening as well as of increasing the burden of the shared predicament.

Taken together and in their full political context, Lord Acton's two statements nevertheless carry a valid warning. When linked, secrecy and political power are dangerous in the extreme. For all individuals, secrecy carries some risk of corruption and of irrationality; if they dispose of greater than ordinary power over others, and if this power is exercised in secret, with no accountability to those whom it affects, the invitation to abuse is great.

The combination of secrecy and political power is not dangerous only when exercised by "Pope and King" and other political authorities. The lawyer who succeeds in making unlawful business deals under the cover of confidentiality presents the same risks; so does the labor union official or political lobbyist who disposes of secret funds for influencing legislators; and so does the journalist who fabricates a lurid exposé and then invokes the principle of confidentiality regarding sources when asked for corroborating evidence. Just as secrecy protects such abuses of power, so it also gives those who employ it successfully *more* power, thus increasing their susceptibility to corruption, and in turn a still greater need for secrecy. In the absence of accountability and safeguards, the presumption against secrecy when it is linked with power is therefore strong.

Less obvious than the risks of active abuse in such circumstances, but cumulatively at least as harmful to society, are the acts of omission that secrecy makes possible—such as the failure of many to carry their part of the collective tax burden whenever they can conceal some of their income. As Kant pointed out, the problem in setting up a state is "to organize a group of rational beings who together require universal laws for their survival, but of whom each separate individual is secretly inclined to exempt himself from them." [5]

The inclination to which Kant refers is usually not meant to harm the community. Many see good reason why they ought to be able to exempt themselves from joint efforts. They may believe they can serve the community better in other ways, or think the efforts not worth making, possibly even destructive—as when tax money goes for public buildings they deem wasteful or military efforts to which they are opposed. Ideally, such reasons should be openly stated and debated, as in tax revolts or draft resistance, so that others can consider them, perhaps act on them, possibly bring about reform, and so that some alternative form of service can be asked of those unwilling to take part in activities they reject. Most often, however, those who exempt themselves from collective efforts do so in secret if they can, without stating their reasons explicitly in public or even to themselves.

Secrecy, when available, is peculiarly likely to increase the temptation not to cooperate with others to reduce shared burdens. Even where joint efforts are of clear benefit to all, as in working to ensure fire protection or a pure water supply, secrecy has such an effect. It is then a test of the strength of people's altruism and sense of public responsibility—much like the imaginary society I described in Chapter II, where anybody could keep secrets at will. Secrecy then removes accountability, and thus the chance of disapproval or sanctions that exempting oneself from shared efforts while enjoying their fruits would otherwise arouse. Such self-exemption is perhaps especially frequent in large, highly mobile societies such as ours, where anonymity is more easily achieved than, say, in small rural communities, and where fewer acknowledge joint obligations unless forced to do so by legislation. How many, if given the chance of complete secrecy regarding taxation, would take advantage of it to give less?

Far from all would do so, to be sure. Many traditions have encouraged the practice of secret benefaction—of acting anonymously to do one's share and to do good beyond what is expected. Thus the Bible enjoins those who give alms to take heed not to do so before the eyes of men; and Maimonides urged anonymous giving as a higher form of giving, especially when neither giver nor recipient knows the other's identity.[6]

Whether through acts or through omission, wrongdoing is nevertheless more likely to result from the combination of secrecy and power that shield the unscrupulous and increase collective burdens, and that tend, as Lord Acton said, to corrupt. What factors increase the likelihood of such developments? If the risk grows when the secret practices spread, does it thereby also increase with the number of persons involved in these practices? Is there something about collective secrecy that renders it more problematic than individual secrecy?

Individual and Collective Secrecy

In itself collective secrecy is not bound to be any more corrupting than that exercised by individuals in positions of power. It is often legitimate, and at times indispensable, as in certain forms of negotiation or in the protection of confidential medical records. Yet such secrecy brings added opportunities for abuse and calls, therefore, for special safeguards.

A crucial difference between the secrets an individual keeps, even confides to another, and those shared within a larger group adds to the risks of collective secrecy. This difference lies in the means required for maintaining shared secrets. Benjamin Franklin's remark "Three may keep a secret if two of them are dead" [7] points up the problem: the incentives and restraints that individuals use in order to keep secrets to themselves are far from sufficient when it comes to a shared secret. Control over shared secrets may require inducements of a different character, and sometimes coercion. The very act of sharing makes betrayal possible.

What bonds will be strong enough to prevent such betrayal—say, among public servants privy to defense secrets? Rewards and initiation procedures, loyalty oaths and censorship, threats and indoctrination may all be tools for collective secrecy; yet all increase the risks that the original purposes of the group will be overwhelmed by the sheer difficulty of maintaining secrecy.*

Whenever secrets are recorded, the problems of keeping them concealed multiply. From then on, the secrets can spread and even be used against the original holders, as was the case with the Watergate tapes and the Pentagon Papers. They can fall into the "wrong" hands; and if they are encoded or disguised so as to be decipherable only by those for whom they are intended, they may in the end be understood by no one. Such has been the fate of much esoteric writing, meant to provide signs of recognition for insiders that will mean nothing to outsiders. Modern bureaucracies have sometimes entangled themselves in extraordinarily cumbersome and self-defeating methods of safeguarding secrets thus recorded: classification of materials, screening processes for those with access to them, barriers to oversight, and retaliation for transgression. But few tasks are as thankless as that of trying to reverse the spread of such measures. Thus the very means of protecting shared secrets can add to the already considerable drawbacks of secrecy linked with power: the chances of corruption, of spreading secrecy, and of impaired rationality.

Not only is collective secrecy therefore more problematic than individual

---

*These methods also increase the likelihood of a felt split between those in the know and all outsiders, and, in turn, of conspiracy theories. More and more can come to seem explicable only as a result of the tension between insiders and outsiders, and increasing numbers of connections between seemingly disparate events are then often postulated.

secrecy; the same is true of collective choice when compared with individual choice, as contemporary theorists have pointed out.[8] Burdened by limitations of judgment and character and by problems inherent in collective decision-making, groups fall far short of making the choices that would be in their best interest; and the larger the group, the greater its shortcomings in this respect. If we superimpose the difficulties of collective secrecy on those of collective choice, it is easy to see why secret collective choices are so likely to exhibit poor judgment.

Poor judgment often manifests itself in faulty assumptions regarding risks. Thus studies indicate that members of groups are at times willing to take larger risks than each member would have taken individually.[9] The "risky shift," as this phenomenon has been called, may help to explain government decisions that seem hasty and unwise in retrospect, such as those leading to the Bay of Pigs invasion in 1961.[10]

Not all group decisions are affected by such a "risky shift." On the contrary, joint decisions about financial investments or dangerous surgery are often more cautious than what any one individual might make on his own. The prospects of future recrimination and adverse publicity all work to ensure restraint with respect to risk. The "risky shift" attends, rather, shared choices made under conditions of decreased individual responsibility.

Secrecy can diminish the sense of personal responsibility for joint decisions and facilitate all forms of skewed or careless judgment, including that exhibited in taking needless risks. It offers participants a shield against outside criticism, and can obscure the possibilities of failure—especially if the decision-makers come to think that the situation resembles a game.

The game analogy to human conflicts is useful as a theoretical exercise, because it allows clarity in setting forth alternatives and strategies; but when taken too literally, it is a major force for psychological distancing and even numbing. When individuals who are in charge of joint decisions of great importance—say, in banking or in diplomacy—come to think of themselves and of their adversaries as players, they view moral considerations differently. They may lose sight of the significance of each human being who will be affected by their choice, and downplay the seriousness of the consequences of their actions—especially of subtle or long-range consequences. They may then come to assume attitudes of playfulness even about the most inhumane choices. "Après nous le déluge" is an attitude that can be maintained with far greater equanimity in secret than in the light of full publicity.

Still another factor adds to the dangers of collective secrecy: the discrimination, at the heart of all secrecy, between insider and outsider, between those set apart and all others. Such discrimination is one thing when it sets an individual apart as unique and protects his privacy. It is quite another thing for a group. The criteria selected for inclusion or exclusion may then lead to discriminatory action toward those excluded—on racial grounds, perhaps, or on sexual, political, or religious ones.

Long-term group practices of secrecy, finally, are especially likely to breed corruption and to spread. Every aspect of the shared predicament influences the secret practice cumulatively over time: in particular the impediments to reasoning and to choice, and the limitations on sympathy and on regard for human beings. The tendency to view the world in terms of insiders and outsiders can then build up a momentum that it would lack if it were short-lived and immediately accountable.

When power is joined to secrecy, therefore, and when the practices are of long duration, the danger of spread and abuse and deterioration increases. The power may be in the hands of individuals, either because of the authority they are known to wield or the unscrupulous means they are prepared to adopt. Or it may be collective power, with secrecy shared among members of a group; or power that is attributed to them because of their group membership.

In all such cases, the presumption shifts. I argued in Chapter II for a presumption in favor of individual control over secrecy and openness regarding personal matters. The burden of proof is on those who would deny them such control. But when those who exercise power of the kinds discussed above claim control over secrecy and openness, it is up to them to show why giving them such control is necessary and what kinds of safeguards they propose.

The reasons for collective secrecy are sometimes overriding, as in certain kinds of administrative and military secrecy; but because of the shift in presumptions, the reasons cannot simply be extrapolated from claims individuals might make. It is fallacious to argue, for instance, from individual privacy to corporate privacy, or from an individual's right to keep personal documents secret to a government's right to classify information as it sees fit.

Even where persuasive reasons for collective practices of secrecy can be stated, accountability is indispensable. The difference it makes is illustrated by the comparison between the practice of secrecy in two types of court proceedings: jury deliberations, and the secret tribunal or Star Chamber trial. Jury members are selected so as to be representative and without evident personal bias in a case. Their task is to arrive at a joint decision about an individual's innocence or guilt. Secrecy for their deliberations protects the members from attempts to influence them, increasing the likelihood of a fair decision; and it allows the resolution of difficult conflicts even when the evidence is ambiguous, generating a degree of confidence in the final result that might otherwise be unattainable.[11] Full publicity to every aspect of the deliberations might cast doubt on the most careful of decisions. The secrecy, moreover, is terminated as soon as a decision has been reached, and the verdict itself is open to public scrutiny and to appeal.

No such safeguards have accompanied the many secret police systems that have plagued humanity. They have permitted secret probes and accusations, secret verdicts and punishments. The secret tribunals of the Holy Vehm, formed in mid-thirteenth-century Westphalia, illustrate the dangers of corruption and abuse when law is carried out in secret by self-appointed avengers answerable only to their own group. These tribunals were instituted as a response to an atmosphere of lawlessness such that no one could expect to live unassailed for long. Their members swore to uphold the Christian faith and the Ten Commandments; and to compel others to observe them by means of secret investigations and trials, followed by execution of those found guilty and confiscation of their property. Many, including persons themselves engaged in crime, found it safest to gain immunity through joining the organization. By the fourteenth century, the Holy Vehm had over 100,000 members. Dispensing rough justice at first, it grew increasingly corrupt. Not until Napoleon invaded Germany was it finally rooted out, and it was referred to again and again with admiration by early Nazi groups.[12]

The secrecy, the handing down from one generation to another of powers over life and death, the incentives for criminals to join in order to escape persecution—all conspired with the original vague mandate to facilitate brutalization of the Holy Vehm. With time, more and more actions were accounted as being against the Ten Commandments or the Christian faith. A 1490 document from Arnsburg lists crimes such as heresy and perjury and falling back from faith into heathen practices, but also the added one of revealing the secrets of the Holy Vehm. To reveal the secrets of the tribunals had itself become a crime against which the tribunals could proceed. Thus their power became self-perpetuating, and correction of their practices even more difficult.

The Holy Vehm may seem an extreme illustration of the joining of secrecy and power to do harm. But analogous groups still operate today, some alone, some under government sponsorship, in different parts of the world. Because they evade accountability, any deterioration or corruption among their members goes unchecked—a lack of control that turns out to be as threatening to members as it is to potential victims. Such groups illustrate Lord Acton's warning against secrecy in the administration of justice, and offer support for his claim that "nothing is safe that does not show how it can bear discussion and publicity."

Publicity

Discussion and publicity about government practices were regarded as indispensable by thinkers such as Acton, Bentham, and Mill.[13] But is there not a contradiction between the appeals for such publicity and the secrecy that remains necessary for each human being and certain group practices as well—the secrecy that offers some freedom from observation and constant accountability? Is it possible to require both publicity and secrecy?

The tension between the two is inevitable. But it can be reduced by stressing the publicity of moral choice *about* secrecy. The moral arguments for any secret practices must be capable of being publicly discussed. They should never themselves require secrecy; nor should the existence of the practices themselves. Thus there should be no secrecy about the moral principles supporting medical confidentiality about what patients reveal to their physicians; but in order to debate these principles, and the limitations upon them in different circumstances, it is not necessary to reveal the secrets of individual patients.

Because I take moral arguments to require such publicity and open discussion, I find that the oddest and perhaps the most corrupting exercise of secrecy is secrecy about one's moral position: esoteric ethics. It is practiced by all groups that have one set of moral principles for public consumption and another for themselves. Esoteric ethics allows groups to follow strictly self-serving and subjective calculations. Conspiratorial groups routinely adopt such a double standard; but its appeal goes far beyond such groups. As Kant pointed out in the passage quoted earlier, most of us are inclined to exempt ourselves secretly from the universal laws we recognize as necessary for human communities.

The double standard has been of special interest to utilitarians. Why not adopt more flexible rules for oneself, some have argued, so long as they remain secret and thus not confusing to others, and so long as they allow secret action to advance human happiness? Even Henry Sidgwick wrote, near the end of his *Methods of Ethics*:

Thus the Utilitarian conclusion, carefully stated, would seem to be this; that the opinion that secrecy may render an action right which would not otherwise be so should itself be kept comparatively secret; and similarly it seems expedient that the doctrine that esoteric morality is expedient should itself be kept esoteric.[14]

The calculations that a utilitarian might make to advance human happiness, Sidgwick argued, are so complex that they would be likely to lead to bad results in the hands of "the vulgar." [15] Such self-exemption, however, is open to the most blatant biases. The very determination of who is to count among "the vulgar" for whom ordinary morality should remain the rule is one that calls out for publicity; so does the thought of what the self-chosen elite might undertake in secret for the good of humanity.

A utilitarian truly concerned for consequences would have to endorse publicity and thus to condemn esoteric ethics categorically, as a minimal requirement to offset some of the worst effects of the shared predicament on moral judgment and character. He would regard secret ethics as a force for skewing choice and thus harming both those who choose in secret and those affected thereby.

In countering the tendency to self-exemption, publicity requires more than mere openness regarding actual practices; the arguments for and against these practices must themselves be submitted to debate. In *Lying* I suggested a three-step procedure for weighing a problematic moral practice such as that of lying to voters and to the seriously ill: first, to ask whether there are alternative courses of action that will achieve the aims one takes to be good without requiring deception; second, to set forth the moral reasons thought to excuse or justify the lie, and the possible counterarguments; and third, as a test of these two steps, to ask how a public of reasonable persons would respond to such arguments.[16]

To deliberate, to reason, to seek to justify in public: these are all ways of stating and of testing views, of talking them over, of making them explicit and thus open to inspection and to criticism.[17] Such openness challenges private biases, errors, and ignorance, and allows the shifting of perspectives crucial to moral choice. Publicity does not eliminate the difficulties of moral choice. But as Mill pointed out, it is invaluable even when it does no more than "compel deliberation and force everyone to determine, before he acts, what he shall say if called to account for his actions." [18]

Such deliberation about moral reasons cannot always *be* public, depending on time and circumstances; but in principle, it must at least be capable thereof. Unlike Mill, philosophers who have stressed publicity have tended to view it, following Kant, as a strictly theoretical exercise—

"an experiment of pure reason." [19] But such experiments are open to all the vicissitudes of private speculation. If moral deliberation is intended from the outset to remain a mere thought-experiment, it allows secrecy to re-enter by the back door of bias and self-serving rationalization.

To be sure, the thought-experiment is an indispensable first effort in evaluating a choice. If taken seriously, it will certainly eliminate some of the more blatant abuses. But if it is not capable of being put to the test—if it remains an "experiment of pure reason"—it bypasses the controls of the test of *actual* publicity: the necessity to articulate one's position carefully, to defend it against unexpected counterarguments, to take opposing points of view into consideration, to reveal the steps of reasoning one has used, and to state openly the principles to which one appeals.

The test of publicity should be capable not only of such open implementation but also of being undertaken before a public that excludes neither those likely to be affected by the decision nor those likely to disagree with it. In choices about secrecy, the public must not exclude outsiders. If, for example, the practice under debate is one of secret trade negotiations, or classified research on chemical warfare, or undercover infiltration of political groups, the principles and arguments to which the practices appeal should be openly debated, not only with those who are in charge of them but without excluding persons who have something at stake in how the debate is resolved.* Similarly, the discussion of the practices of confession and initiation that I have discussed in earlier chapters should not be closed to those who stand to gain or lose through such practices.

While such deliberation should be possible in theory, it is far from always possible in fact. The conditions in many societies do not permit open debate. Under repressive regimes, it requires heroism; even in thoroughly open societies, lack of interest often precludes deliberation, and large or small special-interest groups may resort to harassment of the outspoken to discourage debate.

Another difficulty for public debate of the kind I have urged is that it is never devoid of publicity in another sense of the word: that of "public relations," or presenting the best possible image of a person or

---

*In saying that such debates should not exclude outsiders and dissenters, I obviously do not mean to imply that every such person must be *included*. But it would not be enough to include only token dissenters, sworn to secrecy. These dissenters might be swayed by the majority, or ignored by them, even indulged as the token opposition while being overruled.

organization or event. Publicity of this kind can involve manipulation, secrecy, at times deception and outright lies, such publicity can orchestrate and arrange how something is to appear, and how its problematic aspects are to be concealed. It is therefore in no sense opposed to secrecy, and often makes a mockery of publicity in the sense of public discussion and accountability. Indeed, the motives and actions kept secret or blurred by avalanches of information or by manipulation are often precisely those that go against the public interest.

Bias and hypocrisy blend with genuine efforts at justification in many debates concerning collective practices of secrecy. In discussing these practices, I shall use the term "rationales" in order to underline their double function: as *reasons* that defend practices on grounds of fundamental human needs such as trust and survival, but also as *rationalizations* that shield practices from scrutiny.

The rationales complicate the task of deliberation and publicity by serving, each in its different way, to deflect inquiry. Terms such as "confidentiality" or "national security" or "the public's right to know" are used as code words to create a sense of self-evident legitimacy. They confront the questioner with what seems like a premise fundamental to an entire profession and hint that anyone who ventures to question the premise will have to question, in turn, the justification for the entire professional edifice built upon this foundation.

My aim is precisely to question the premises and to test the supposition that all else is thereby rendered uncertain. Each rationale can be subjected to inquiry, as can the steps leading to the conclusions groups have reached with respect to the secrecy or the probing they wish to justify. The purpose of the remaining chapters is to undertake such a task in a number of different settings. I shall first take up, in the next five chapters, five rationales for large-scale collective secrecy: those of confidentiality, trade secrecy, secrecy for scientific research, administrative secrecy, and military secrecy. In so doing, I shall examine the ways in which these rationales, whether breached or honored, are often misused, invoked in one another's place, expanded beyond all reason or, on the other hand, contracted to near extinction.

In each of the collective practices of secrecy that these rationales support, elaborate systems for guarding the secrets spring up—systems that in turn also render the secrets more vulnerable to betrayal. Together, the practices thus protected create a vast network of collective efforts to achieve control over secrecy and openness that adds to the burden of each element of the shared predicament.

The Limits of Confidentiality

The Professional Secret

Fiercely defended, yet under ever greater stress, the duty of professional confidentiality spans all the issues of control over secrecy and openness discussed in earlier chapters. Individual and collective secrecy combine in its defense. And it is invoked with respect to increasing amounts and kinds of information that are, in turn, due to new forms of record-keeping and collaboration, ever more difficult to keep secret.

Doctors, lawyers, and priests have traditionally recognized the duty of professional secrecy regarding what individuals confide to them: personal matters such as alcoholism or depression, marital difficulties, corporate or political problems, and indeed most concerns that patients or clients want to share with someone, yet keep from all others.[1] Accountants, bankers, social workers, and growing numbers of professionals now invoke a similar duty to guard confidences. As codes of ethics take form in old and new professions, the duty of confidentiality serves in part to reinforce their claim to professional status, and in part to strengthen their capacity to offer help to clients.

Confidential information may be more or less intimate, more or less discrediting, more or less accurate and complete. No matter how false or trivial the substance of what clients or patients convey, they may ask that it be kept confidential, or assume that it will be even in the absence of such a request, taking it for granted that professionals owe them secrecy. Professionals, in turn, must not only receive and respect such confidences; the very nature of the help they can give may depend on their searching for even the most deeply buried knowledge.

All the pressures for and against secrecy noted in earlier chapters are present in such relationships. But the duty of confidentiality is no longer what it was when lawyers or doctors simply kept to themselves the confidences of those who sought their help. How can it be, when office personnel and collaborators and team members must have access to the information as well, and when clients and patients with numerous interdependent needs consult different professionals who must in turn communicate with one another? And how can it be, given the vast increase in information collected, stored, and retrievable that has expanded the opportunities for access by outsiders? How can it be, finally, when employers, school officials, law enforcement agencies, insurance companies, tax inspectors, and credit bureaus all press to see some of this confidential information?

So much confidential information is now being gathered and recorded and requested by so many about so many that confidentiality, though as strenuously invoked as in the past, is turning out to be a weaker reed than ever. Employers, schools, government agencies, and mental health and social service organizations are among the many groups now delving into personal affairs as never before. Those with fewest defenses find their affairs most closely picked over. Schools, for instance, are looking into the home conditions of students with problems, sometimes even requesting psychiatric evaluations of entire families, regardless of objections from health professionals on grounds of confidentiality. And access to public welfare assistance, work training programs, and many forms of employment may depend on the degree to which someone is willing to answer highly personal questions.

At the same time, paradoxically, a growing number of discreditable, often unlawful secrets never even entered into computer banks or medical records have come to burden lawyers, financial advisers, journalists, and many others who take themselves to be professionally bound to silence. Faced with growing demands for both revelation and secrecy, those who have to make decisions about whether or not to uphold confidentiality face numerous difficult moral quandaries. Legislation can sometimes dictate their choice. But the law differs from state to state and from nation to nation, and does not necessarily prescribe what is right from a moral point of view. Even if it did, it could never entirely resolve many of the quandaries that arise, since they often present strong moral arguments on both sides. Consider, for example, the following case:

A forty-seven-year-old engineer has polycystic kidney disease, in his case a genetic disorder, and must have his blood purified by hemodialysis with an artificial kidney machine. Victims of the disease [at the time of his diagnosis] usually die a few years after symptoms appear, often in their forties, though dialysis and transplants can stave off death for as much as ten years.

The patient has two children: a son, eighteen, just starting college, and a daughter, sixteen. Though the parents know that the disease is genetic—that their children may carry it and might transmit it to their own offspring—the son and daughter are kept in the dark. The parents insist the children should not be told because it would frighten them unnecessarily, would inhibit their social life, and would make them feel hopeless about the future. They are firm in saying that the hospital staff should not tell the children; the knowledge, they believe, is privileged and must be kept secret. Yet the hospital staff worries about the children innocently involving their future spouses and victimizing their own children.[2]

It is not difficult to see the conflicting and, in themselves, quite legitimate claims on each side in this case: the parents' insistence on privacy and on the right to decide when to speak to their children about a matter of such importance to the family; and the staff members' concern for the welfare of the children. But the question of whether the parents are wrong to keep the information from the children must be separated from that of what the staff members should do about what they see as harmful secrecy. Should they reject their obligation of confidentiality in this case?

Even those who arrive at clear answers concerning the parents' responsibility may recognize that their views could change if the facts were somewhat different. If they conclude, for example, that the children have a right to be told, they might decide differently if the disease were less severe, if a cure seemed likely to be found shortly, if the chances of the illness striking the children were low, or if the children were much younger. And those who decide that the parents are right to insist on secrecy might similarly come to a different conclusion if the illness were more certain to strike the children, or to afflict them sooner. A few might hold rigidly to one choice or the other no matter what the circumstances, but many would discern cases where the conflicting claims are so nearly equal that choice is difficult. At such times, the additional weight to be placed on confidentiality becomes crucial. Should it matter at all? If so, why? And in what sorts of conflicts should it be rejected?

These questions require us to look more closely at the nature of confidentiality and its powerful hold and to ask what it is that makes so many professionals regard it as the first and most binding of their duties.

Confidentiality refers to the boundaries surrounding shared secrets and to the process of guarding these boundaries. While confidentiality protects much that is not in fact secret, personal secrets lie at its core. The innermost, the vulnerable, often the shameful: these aspects of self-disclosure help explain why one name for professional confidentiality has been "the professional secret." Such secrecy is sometimes mistakenly confused with privacy; yet it can concern many matters in no way private, but that someone wishes to keep from the knowledge of third parties.

Confidentiality must also be distinguished from the testimonial privilege that protects information possessed by spouses or members of the clergy or lawyers against coerced revelations in court. While a great many professional groups invoke confidentiality, the law recognizes the privilege only in limited cases. In some states, only lawyers can invoke it; in others, physicians and clergy can as well; more recently, psychiatrists and other professionals have been added to their number. Who ought and who ought not to be able to guarantee such a privilege is under ceaseless debate. Every newly established professional group seeks the privileges of existing ones. Established ones, on the other hand, work to exclude those whom they take to be encroaching on their territory.

The principle of confidentiality postulates a duty to protect confidences against third parties under certain circumstances. Professionals appeal to such a principle in keeping secrets from all outsiders, and seek to protect even what they would otherwise feel bound to reveal. While few regard the principle as absolute, most see the burden of proof as resting squarely on anyone who claims a reason for overriding it. Why should confidentiality bind thus? And why should it constrain professionals to silence more than, say, close friends?

Justification and Rationale

The justification for confidentiality rests on four premises, three supporting confidentiality in general and the fourth, professional secrecy in particular.

They concern human autonomy regarding personal information, respect for relationships, respect for the bonds and promises that protect shared information, and the benefits of confidentiality to those in need of advice, sanctuary, and aid, and in turn to society.

The first and fundamental premise is that of individual autonomy over personal information. It asks that we respect individuals as capable of having secrets. Without some control over secrecy and openness about themselves, their thoughts and plans, their actions, and in part their property, people could neither maintain privacy nor guard against danger. But of course this control should be only partial. Matters such as contagious disease place individual autonomy in conflict with the rights of others. And a variety of matters cannot easily be concealed. No one can maintain control, for example, over others' seeing that they have a broken leg or a perennially vile temper.[3]

The second premise is closely linked to the first. It presupposes the legitimacy not only of having personal secrets but of sharing them, and assumes respect for relationships among human beings and for intimacy. It is rooted in loyalties that precede the formulation of moral justification and that preserve collective survival for one's tribe, one's kin, one's clan. Building on such a sense of loyalty, the premise holds that it is not only natural but often also right to respect the secrets of intimates and associates, and that human relationships could not survive without such respect.

This premise is fundamental to the marital privilege upheld in American law, according to which one spouse cannot be forced to testify against the other; and to the ancient Chinese legal tradition, so strongly attacked in the Maoist period, that forbade relatives to report on one another's misdeeds and penalized such revelations severely.[4] No more than the first premise, however, does this second one suffice to justify all confidentiality. It can conflict with other duties, so that individuals have to choose, say, between betraying country or friend, parents or children; and it can be undercut by the nature of the secret one is asked to keep.

The third premise holds that a pledge of silence creates an obligation beyond the respect due to persons and to existing relationships. Once we promise someone secrecy, we no longer start from scratch in weighing the moral factors of a situation. They matter differently, once the promise is given, so that full impartiality is no longer called for.

In promising one alienates, as Grotius said, either a thing or some portion of one's freedom of action: "To the former category belong promises to give; to the latter, promises to perform."[5] Promises of secrecy are unusual in both respects. What they promise to give is allegiance; what they promise to perform is some action that will guard the secret—to keep silent, at least, and perhaps to do more. Just what performance is promised, and at what cost it will be carried out, are questions that go to the heart of conflicts over confidentiality.[6] To invoke a promise, therefore, while it is surely to point to a *prima facie* ground of obligation, is not to close the debate over pledges of secrecy. Rather, one must go on to ask whether it was right to make the pledge in the first place, and right to accept it; whether the promise is a binding one, and even if it is, what circumstances might nevertheless justify overriding it.[7]

Individuals vary with respect to the seriousness with which they make a promise and the consequent weight of the reasons they see as sufficient to override it. Consider the CIA agent who takes an oath of secrecy before gaining access to classified information; the White House butler who pledges never to publish confidential memoirs; the relatives who give their word to a dying author never to publish her diaries; the religious initiate who swears on all he holds sacred not to divulge the mysteries he is about to share; the engineer who signs a pledge not to give away company trade secrets as a condition of employment. Some of these individuals take the pledge casually, others in utter seriousness. If the latter still break their pledge, they may argue that they were coerced into making their promise, or that they did not understand how it bound them. Or else they may claim that something is important enough to override their promise—as when the relatives publish the author's diaries after her death for a sum of money they cannot resist, or in the belief that the reading public would be deprived without such documents.

For many, a promise involves their integrity and can create a bond that is closer than kinship, as the ceremonies by which people become blood brothers indicate. The strength of promising is conveyed in such early practices as those in which promisors might offer as a pledge their wife, their child, or a part of their body.[8] And promises of *secrecy* have been invested with special meaning, in part because of the respect for persons and for relationships called for by the first two premises.

Taken together, the three premises give strong *prima facie* reasons to support confidentiality. With certain limitations, I accept each one as binding on those who have accepted information in confidence. But of course there are reasons sufficient to override the force of all these premises, as when secrecy would allow violence to be done to innocent persons, or turn someone into an unwitting accomplice in crime. At such times, autonomy and relationship no longer provide sufficient legitimacy. And the promise of silence should never be given, or if given, can be breached.

It is here that the fourth premise enters in to add strength to the particular pledges of silence given by professionals.[9] This premise assigns weight beyond ordinary loyalty to professional confidentiality, because of its utility to persons and to society. As a result, professionals grant their clients secrecy even when they would otherwise have reason to speak out: thus lawyers feel justified in concealing past crimes of their clients, bankers the suspect provenance of investors' funds, and priests the sins they hear in confession.

According to this premise, individuals benefit from such confidentiality because it allows them to seek help they might otherwise fear to ask for; those most vulnerable or at risk might otherwise not go for help to doctors or lawyers or others trained to provide it. In this way, innocent persons might end up convicted of crimes for lack of competent legal defense, and disease could take a greater toll among those ashamed of the nature of their ailment. Society therefore gains in turn from allowing such professional refuge, the argument holds, in spite of the undoubted risks of not learning about certain dangers to the community; and everyone is better off when professionals can probe for the secrets that will make them more capable of providing the needed help.

The nature of the helpfulness thought to override the importance of revealing some confidences differs from one profession to another. The social worker can offer support, counsel, sometimes therapy; physicians provide means of relieving suffering and of curing disease; lawyers give assistance in self-protection against the state or other individuals. These efforts may conflict, as for army psychiatrists whenever their mission is both to receive the confidences of troubled military personnel and to serve as agents of the state, obligated to report on the condition of their patients. And the help held to justify confidentiality about informants by police and journalists is not directed to individuals in need of relief at all, but rather to society by encouraging disclosures of abuses and crime.

Such claims to individual and social utility touch on the *raison d'être* of the professions themselves; but they are also potentially treacherous. For if it were found that a professional group or subspecialty not only did not help but actually hurt individuals, and increased the social burden of, say, illness or crime, then there would be a strong case for not allowing it to promise professional confidentiality. To question its special reason for being able to promise confidentiality of unusual strength is therefore seen as an attack on its special purposes, and on the power it acquires in being able to give assurances beyond those which non-professionals can offer.

A purely strategic reason for stressing professional confidentiality is that, while needed by clients, it is so easily breached and under such strong pressures to begin with. In schools and in offices, at hospitals and in social gatherings, confidential information may be casually passed around. Other items are conveyed "off the record" or leaked in secret. The prohibition against breaching confidentiality must be especially strong in order to combat the pressures on insiders to do so, especially in view of the ease and frequency with which it is done.

Together with the first three premises for confidentiality, the defense of the fourth helps explain the ritualistic tone in which the duty of preserving secrets is repeatedly set forth in professional oaths and codes of ethics. Still more is needed, however, to explain the sacrosanct nature often ascribed to this duty. The ritualistic nature of confidentiality in certain religious traditions has surely had an effect on its role in law and medicine. A powerful esoteric rationale for secrecy linked the earliest practices of medicine and religion. Thus Henry Sigerist points out that in Mesopotamia medicine, like other sacred knowledge, was kept secret and not divulged to the profane; conversely, many religious texts ended with a warning that "he who does not keep the secret will not remain in health. His days will be shortened." [10]

However strong, these historical links between faith and professional practice give *no* added justification to professional confidentiality. The sacramental nature of religious confession is a matter of faith for believers. It may be respected even in secular law on grounds of religious freedom; but it adds no legitimacy to that of the four premises when it comes to what professionals conceal for clients. [11]

The four premises are not usually separated and evaluated in the context of individual cases or practices. Rather, they blend with the ritualistic nature attributed to confidentiality to support a rigid stance that I shall call the rationale of confidentiality. Not only does this rationale point to links with the most fundamental grounds of autonomy and relationship and trust and help; it also serves as a rationalization that helps deflect ethical inquiry. The very self-evidence that it claims can then expand beyond its legitimate applications. Confidentiality, like all secrecy, can then cover up for and in turn lead to a great deal of error, injury, pathology, and abuse.

When professionals advance confidentiality as a shield, their action is, to be sure, in part intentional and manipulative, but in part it also results from a failure to examine the roots of confidentiality and to spell out the limits of its application. It can lead then to sweeping claims such as that made by the World Medical Association in its 1949 International Code of Medical Ethics: "A doctor shall preserve absolute secrecy on all he knows about his patient because of the confidence entrusted in him." [12]

If such claims go too far, where and how should the lines be drawn? Granting the *prima facie* importance of the principle of confidentiality in the light of the premises which support it, when and for what reasons must it be set aside? I shall consider such limits with respect to the secrets of individual clients, of professionals themselves, and of institutional or corporate clients.

Individual Clients and Their Secrets

Among the most difficult choices for physicians and others are those which arise with respect to confidences by children, mentally incompetent persons, and those who are temporarily not fully capable of guiding their affairs. While some such confidences—as about fears or hopes—can be kept secret without difficulty, others are more troubling. Consider the following case:

Janet M., a thirteen-year-old girl in the seventh grade of a small-town junior high school, comes to the office of a family physician. She has known him from childhood, and he has cared for all the members of her family. She tells him that she is pregnant, and that she has had a lab test performed at an out-of-town clinic. She wants to have an abortion. She is afraid that her family, already burdened by unemployment and illness, would be thrown into a crisis by the news. Her boyfriend, fifteen, would probably be opposed to the abortion. She asks the doctor for help in securing the abortion, and for assurance that he will not reveal her condition to anyone.

Cases such as Janet's are no longer rare. In small towns as in large cities, teen-age pregnancy is on the rise, teen-age abortion commonplace. Many families do provide the guidance and understanding so desperately needed at such times; but when girls request confidentiality, it is often out of fear of their families' reaction. Health professionals should clearly make every effort to help these girls communicate with their families. But sometimes there is no functioning family. Or else family members may have been so brutal or so unable to cope with crisis in the past that it is legitimate to be concerned about the risks in informing them. At times, it is even the case that a member of the girl's own family has abused her sexually. [13]

Health professionals are then caught in a conflict between their traditional obligation of confidentiality and the normal procedure of consulting with a child's parents before an irreversible step is taken. In this conflict, the premises supporting confidentiality are themselves in doubt. Just how autonomous should thirteen-year-olds be with respect to decisions about pregnancy? They are children still, but with an adult's choice to make. And what about even younger girls? In what relation does a physician stand to them, and to their parents, regarding such secrets?

Because the premises of autonomy and of relationship do not necessarily mandate secrecy at such times, deciding whether or not to pledge silence is much harder. Even the professional help that confidentiality allows is then in doubt. Pregnant young girls are in need of advice and assistance more than most others; confidentiality too routinely extended may lock them into an attitude of frightened concealment that can do permanent damage. Health professionals owe it to these patients, therefore, to encourage and help them to communicate with their families or others responsible for their support. But to *mandate*, as some seek to do, consultation with family members, no matter how brutal or psychologically abusive, would be to take a shortsighted view. Not only would it injure those pregnant girls forced into family confrontations; many others would end by not seeking professional help at all, at a time when they need it most.

Childhood and adolescent pregnancies are far from the only conditions that present professionals with conflicts over confidentiality. Venereal disease, drug and alcohol addiction among the young, as well as a great many problems of incompetent and disturbed individuals past childhood, render confidentiality similarly problematic.

Even where there is no question about maturity or competence, professionals worry about the secrecy asked of them when someone confides to them plans that seem self-injurious: to enter into a clearly disastrous business arrangement, or to give all his possessions to an exploitative "guru," or to abandon life-prolonging medical treatment. He may have no intention of hurting anyone else (though relatives and others may in fact be profoundly affected by his choice) and may be fully within his rights in acting as he does. But his judgment may itself be in doubt, depending on how self-destructive the plans are that he is confiding.

Here again, an absolute insistence on confidentiality would be unreasonable. No one would hesitate to reveal the secret of a temporarily deranged person about to do himself irreversible harm. Patients and clients do not have the requisite balance at such a time to justify silence—and thus complicity—regarding their self-destructive acts, the less so as the very revelation of such plans to a professional is often correctly interpreted as a call for help.

If, on the other hand, the act has been carefully thought through, breaches of confidentiality are much less justified, no matter how irrational the project might at first seem to outsiders. Say the person planning to give his money away wants to live the rest of his life as a contemplative, or that the patient planning to abandon medical treatment has decided to cease delaying death in view of his progressively debilitating and painful disease; it is harder to see the basis for a breach of professional confidentiality in such cases,* since it is more difficult to prove that the person's act is necessarily self-destructive from his point of view. Professionals are constantly at risk of assuming too readily that the purposes they take to be overriding and to which they have dedicated their careers—financial prudence, for instance—are necessarily more rational for all others than conflicting aims. This professional bias has to be taken into account in any decision to override confidentiality on grounds of irrationality and self-harm.

Sometimes, however, a patient's insistence on confidentiality can bring quite unintended risks. Because people live longer, and often suffer from multiple chronic diseases, their records have to be accessible to many different health professionals. Their reluctance to have certain facts on their medical records may then be dangerous. One physician has pointed to some of the possible consequences of such concealment:

The man who insists that no record be made of a psychiatric history, or the drugs that would suggest that there is one, and wants no record of his syphilis and penicillin injections and subsequent recovery, is the same man who must face squarely the risk of future syphilitic disease of the nervous system or even lethal penicillin reactions because future medical personnel never followed through in the right manner. They do not even know that the problem existed; they and the patient stumbled blindly into trouble.[14]

At times, the insistence on secrecy can become obsessive, so that confidentiality may come to surround the most trivial matters, even when less secrecy could be useful not only to oneself but to others. Thus many refuse to release information about their blood types or past illnesses, even at the cost of slowing down research that might help other sufferers. Here as always, secrecy can shut out many forms of feedback and assistance and consequently encourage poor judgment.

Do patients have the same claims to confidentiality about personal information when persons from whom it is kept run serious risks? Consider

---

*A number of questions having to do with paternalism arise in these cases. It is important to note, however, that breaching confidence for paternalistic reasons does not necessarily involve interfering with the persons whose confidences are revealed, nor coercing them.

again the family mentioned earlier in which the father wishes to conceal from his children that he suffers from polycystic kidney disease. It is now two years later. The father, much closer to death, has told his two children about the genetic nature of his disease. He was prompted to do so, in part, by his daughter's plans to marry. She, however, fears disclosing to her future husband that the same disease may strike her and affect their children. Now it is her turn to insist on confidentiality, not only from her father but from all others who know the facts, including the health professionals involved.

The dilemma they face is in one sense very old, in another quite new. It resembles all the choices through the ages about whether or not to reveal to intimates and future spouses that someone suffers from incurable venereal disease, sexual problems, a recurring psychiatric condition, or a degenerative disease as yet in its early stages. But it has taken on a new frequency because there is now so much more information, especially of a genetic nature, than even a hundred years ago. The category of problematic and troubling predictions has expanded, raising new conflicts of secrecy for parents, prospective spouses, and many others, and of confidentiality for health professionals. Lacking the genetic information, this family would not have faced the same choice in an earlier period. With increased knowledge of risks, therefore, the collective burden of confidentiality has grown as well.

Does a professional owe confidentiality to clients who reveal plans or acts that endanger others directly? Such a question arises for the lawyer whose client lets slip that he plans a bank robbery, or that he has committed an assault for which an innocent man is standing trial; for the pediatrician who suspects that a mother drugs her children to keep them quiet; and for the psychiatrist whose patient discloses that he is obsessed by jealousy and thoughts of violence to his wife.

The conflicts that psychotherapists face in this respect were brought to public attention by the murder in 1969 of a young woman, Tatiana Tarasoff. The young man who killed her had earlier told his psychotherapist that he wanted to do so. The psychotherapist had alerted the police, who detained the student briefly, then released him after determining that he seemed "rational" and asking him to promise to leave Miss Tarasoff alone. When the police reported the matter back to the director of psychiatry, he asked that the matter be dropped and that the correspondence with the police be destroyed. The student did not return for further treatment, and no effort was made to get in touch with him. Two months later, he went to Miss Tarasoff's home and shot and stabbed her to death. Her parents then brought suit against the university, the campus police, and the therapists for negligence in failing to warn either their daughter or themselves.

The California Supreme Court concluded that the psychotherapists had breached a duty overriding that of confidentiality: the duty to use reasonable care when they determine that a patient presents a serious danger of violence to another, to protect the intended victim against such danger.[15] "The privilege ends," the court held, "when the public peril begins."

The Tarasoff decision troubled psychiatrists. They argued, first, that one cannot know whether a threat uttered by a patient will be put into effect: that it usually is not, and that as a group psychiatrists often overpredict violence, being more often wrong than right. But such an argument does not stand up under scrutiny. Obviously, if a threat of violence is a vain boast only, or a fantasy never to be put into effect, no one is at risk; a psychiatrist who can be sure of the harmlessness of such a threat has no reason to breach confidentiality. But if there is a reasonable chance that it might be put into effect, the psychiatrist's inability to predict accurately is no reason not to consider the danger to the potential victim. It is no consolation to survivors to learn that the victim's risk had been, say, merely one in five, once the threat has been carried out. The potential victims or their family members have every interest in knowing about even such dangers. And they might legitimately argue that speculations about the degree of risk, once it is known to exist at all, should not be left up to the psychotherapist alone.

Psychiatrists have argued, moreover, that the duty to warn potential victims threatens the trust between patient and therapist. They might concede that the first premise supporting confidentiality—the claim to patient autonomy with respect to personal information—no longer holds when that information concerns serious harm to others. Just as no one is granted autonomy when it comes to *doing* violence to others, so there is no reason to concede such autonomy and control for *plans* to do so, once divulged. Having conceded the first premise, however, psychiatrists who oppose the Tarasoff decision stress the remaining three all the more. They argue that the therapeutic relationship and its implicit promise must be inviolate if therapy is to stand a chance.[16] This is especially the case in psychiatry, where probing secrets serves special purposes. If pain and fear and hatred can be brought into the open, healing may take place, so that the patient will have better control over the relations between inner and shared experience. The promise of secrecy, impicit or explicit, allows this process to take place. Many patients have already felt betrayed in ways that left them vulnerable, and the assurance of full loyalty is therefore indispensable. A duty to warn potential clients prevents doctors from offering such assurance. Such a duty, Alan Stone has argued, "will deter both patients and therapists from undertaking treatment, thereby further increasing the risk of violence to which society is exposed." [17]

Two objections arise to this line of argument. The first is empirical. No evidence suggests that therapy will be imperiled if patients know that therapists have the duty to reveal their plans of violence. Even if therapy were thus imperiled, it is not clear that more violence would result. Not only have such contentions not been proved; many doubt that they are even probable. Patients rarely place much trust in confidentiality regarding their most extreme statements anyway, and may even hope that their threats *will* lead to some preventive action. [18]

The second objection is independent of such a weighing of benefit and harm. Even if we were to concede, for the sake of argument, that patients will fare better and society be less burdened by violence if psychotherapists have no duty to reveal threats to potential victims, such a duty might nevertheless still be owed to those who risk their lives without knowing it. It is not right, according to such an objection, to risk one person's life in order to help patients and reduce the violence in society. Tatiana Tarasoff should not have had to run that risk without having consented thereto.

I agree with these objections. Once psychiatrists undertake to receive and even probe for information threatening to others, they can no longer ignore those others, out of concern either for their patients or for society. The *prima facie* premises supporting confidentiality are overridden at such times.

The autonomy we grant individuals over personal secrets, first of all, cannot reasonably be thought to extend to plans of violence against innocent persons; at such times, on the contrary, someone who knows of plans that endanger others owes it to them to counteract those plans, and, if he is not sure he can forestall them, to warn the potential victims. Nor, in the second place, can patients who voice serious threats against innocent persons invoke confidentiality on the basis of their relationship with therapists or anyone else without asking them to be partially complicitous. The third premise, basing confidentiality in part on a promise, is likewise overridden, since in the absence of legitimacy for the first two, it ought to be clearly understood that no one, whether professionally trained or not, should give such a pledge. The benefits invoked in the fourth premise, finally, are not only not demonstrated in these cases; even if they were, they could not override the injustice done to those unwittingly placed at risk.*

Long before psychiatrists worried about these problems, Catholic theologians had studied them with a thoroughness often lacking in contemporary discussions. The distinctions they worked out over the centuries concerning different types of secrets and the obligations of professionals were detailed and well reasoned. Most theologians agreed that certain types of secrets were not binding on professional recipients, foremost among them grave threats against the public good or against innocent third persons.[19]

An example they often described is the following: What should a doctor do if he has a patient who suffers from an incurable and highly contagious venereal disease and who plans to marry without disclosing this fact to his fiancée? According to many theologians, the doctor's obligation of secrecy would then cease: the young man forfeits such consideration through his intent to act in a way that might gravely injure his fiancée. The doctor is therefore free to speak, but with certain limitations: he must reveal only so much of the secret as is necessary to avert the harm, and only to the person threatened, who has a right to this information, rather than to family members, neighbors, or the curious or gossip-hungry at large.

These commentators also discussed a subject that still divides the contemporary debate: should the breach of secrecy to avert grave harm be obligatory, or merely permitted? Should the professional feel free to choose whether or not to warn the endangered person, or acknowledge a duty to do so? It is one thing to say that he no longer owes the client confidentiality; but does he also *owe* the endangered person the information? Do lawyers, for example, owe any information to persons who may be injured by their clients' unlawful tax schemes, plans for extortion, or threats of violence? And if they do recognize some such obligation, how does it weigh against that of confidentiality?

The duty of confidentiality clearly has some weight; as a result, the obligation to warn potential victims is not as great for professionals as it might be for others who happen to hear of the danger. Yet it is a

*Such a conclusion carries with it line-drawing problems: how likely the danger should be before one assumes serious risk; how sure one should be about the identity of the potential victim; how much this individual already knows about the risk; the degree of precautions already in place, etc. But line-drawing problems would occur no matter what the conclusion unless one postulated either no duty to breach confidentiality under any conditions whatsoever, or, on the contrary, no obligation of confidentiality at all.

strong one nevertheless, especially where serious harm is likely to occur. In such cases, the duty to warn ought to be overriding. Professionals should not then be free to promise confidentiality, nor should a client expect to be able to entrust them with such projects, any more than with stolen goods or lethal weapons. [20]

The same is true for confidences regarding past crimes. Here, too, confidentiality counts; but it must be weighed against other aims—of social justice and restitution. It is therefore hard to agree with those lawyers who argue as a matter of course that they owe clients silence about past, unsolved murders; it is equally hard to agree with Swiss bankers claiming that confidentiality suffices to legitimate the secret bank accounts that attract so many depositors enriched through crime, conspiracy, and political exploitation.

Secrecy as a Shield

The greatest burden of secrecy imposed by confidentiality, however, is that of the secrets professionals keep to protect themselves rather than patients and clients. Confidentiality can be used, here as elsewhere, as a shield for activities that could ill afford to see the light of day. An example of how dangerous such shielding can be is afforded by the story of the death in 1976 of Anneliese Michel, a young German student, after ten months of exorcism. [21]

Anneliese Michel had been under periodic medical care since she was sixteen years old. She had been diagnosed as suffering both from recurrent epileptic seizures and from anorexia nervosa. When she was twenty-two, her parents persuaded her to withdraw from university studies. Ernst Alt, the local parish priest, suspected that she might be possessed by devils and that exorcism might cure her. He saw the seizures as evidence of such possession rather than of epilepsy, and decided to consult Germany's leading "satanologist," the eighty-three-year-old Adolf Rodewyk, S.J. Father Rodewyk concluded that the convulsions were trancelike states of possession in which, among other manifestations, a devil calling himself Judas made no secret of his identity.

Father Rodewyk recommended exorcism. The *Rituale Romanum* of 1614, still followed in cases of exorcism, prescribes that a bishop must agree to the procedure before it can be undertaken, and that the person thus treated must be beyond medical help. Father Rodewyk assured Bishop Joseph Stangl of Wurzburg that Anneliese's case was one for exorcists, not for doctors; and the bishop authorized the rites, ordering "strictest secrecy and total discretion."

For ten months, the young woman took part in lengthy sessions with the parish priest and Father Wilhelm Renz, an expert called in for the exorcism. The two prayed with her and tried, by means of holy water, adjurations, and commands, to drive out the devils—by then thought to number at least six and calling themselves, in addition to Judas, by such names as Lucifer, Nero, and Hitler. Anneliese was convinced that she was thus possessed and that the powers of good and of evil were fighting over her soul. She wrote in her diary that the Savior had told her she was a great saint. Fearing that doctors might diagnose her voices and seizures as psychiatric symptoms and send her to a mental hospital, she avoided health professionals. As the months wore on, she grew weaker, eating and drinking next to nothing. During one particularly stormy session of exorcism, she rushed head first against the wall facing her bed, then lay back exhausted. The devils were finally declared to have left. The next morning, she was found dead in her bed.

In April 1978, her parents and the two priests who had conducted the exorcism were brought to trial. They were convicted of negligent homicide for having failed to seek medical help up to the very end. Physicians testified that, even as late as a few days before Anneliese died, her life could have been saved had she had medical attention. The four accused were sentenced to six months imprisonment.

The priests sincerely believed that they were doing their best to save Anneliese Michel. Insofar as they believed Father Rodewyk's attesting to the presence of devils, they could hardly think medical treatment appropriate. But they knew their belief that Anneliese was possessed by devils would be shared by few, and so they conspired with her parents to keep the sessions of exorcism secret to the very end. Two kinds of confidentiality come together here: that between priest and penitent, and that between caretaker and patient. But neither one should have been honored in this case, for while they protect much that is spoken by penitents and by patients, they were never intended to protect all that is done by priests or caretakers in response, least of all when it constitutes treatment of very sick persons by dangerous methods without medical assistance.

The case is an extreme one. Strict adherence to the stipulation in the *Rituale Romanum* of 1614 that someone must be beyond medical help would have required much more careful consultation with physicians before leaping to the conclusion that exorcism was called for. When publicity about the case arose, Catholics and non-Catholics alike were distressed at how the young woman had been treated. What is worth noting, however, is that her need for medical help went unnoticed because of the secrecy in which the exorcism was conducted. The case illustrates, therefore, what can happen in almost any system of advising and helping those in need whenever secrecy shrouds what is done to them. And it raises broader questions about confidentiality: Exactly whose secret should it protect? The patient's or client's alone? Or the professional's? Or all that transpires between them?

In principle, confidentiality should protect only the first. But in practice, it can expand, like all other practices of secrecy, to cover much more. It may even be stretched so far as to include what professionals hide *from* patients, clients, and the public at large.

The sick, the poor, the mentally ill, the aged, and the very young are in a paradoxical situation in this respect. While their right to confidentiality is often breached and their most intimate problems openly bandied about, the poor care they may receive is just as often covered up under the same name of confidentiality. That is the shield held forth to prevent outsiders from finding out about negligence, overcharging, unnecessary surgery, or institutionalization. And far more than individual mistakes and misdeeds are thus covered up, for confidentiality is also the shield that professionals invoke to protect incompetent colleagues and negligence and unexpected accidents in, for instance, hospitals, factories, or entire industries.

The word "confidentiality" has by now become a means of covering up a multitude of questionable and often dangerous practices. When lawyers use it to justify keeping secret their client's plans to construct housing so shoddy as to be life-threatening, or when government officials invoke it in concealing the risks of nuclear weapons, confidentiality no longer serves the purpose for which it was intended; it has become, rather, a means for deflecting legitimate public attention.

Such invocations of confidentiality are facilitated by the ease with which many transpose the confidentiality owed to individuals to the collective level. Consider, for example, the prolonged collaboration between asbestos manufacturers and company physicians to conceal the risks from exposure to asbestos dust. These risks were kept secret from the public, from workers in plants manufacturing asbestos insulation, and even from those workers found in medical checkups to be in the early stages of asbestos-induced disease. When a reporter approached a physician associated with the concealment as consultant for a large manufacturer, the physician turned down his request for an interview on grounds of confidentiality owed as a matter of "the patient's rights," and explained, when the astonished reporter inquired who the "patient" was, that it was the *company*.[22]

Government agencies sometimes request confidentiality, not so much to deflect inquiry as to be able to conduct it in the manner most likely to resolve difficult problems. Thus the United States Center for Disease Control argued, in 1980, that it needed to be able to promise confidentiality to hospitals seeking its help for nosocomial, or hospital-induced, infections. Such infection is a major health risk, conservatively estimated as killing 20,000 persons a year in the United States alone, and contributing to the deaths of over 40,000 others in a substantial manner. When a hospital experiences an outbreak of nosocomial infection, it can call on the expert advice of the Center for Disease Control in order to find the cause of the infection and to reverse its course; but to do so under conditions of publicity is to invite rumor, lawsuits, and patient anxiety, according to those who argued in favor of extending confidentiality to the hospitals.[23] The center saw a need to promise such confidentiality to a hospital in order to help it combat infection, much as a doctor might promise silence to an individual patient with a similar affliction.

The center's request for an exemption from the Freedom of Information Act on such grounds was turned down. No proof had been advanced that the dangers the hospitals feared were realistic. Patients did not appear to be staying away from hospitals that had experienced outbreaks of nosocomial infection; and no suit had been won on the basis of information provided by the center.

The step from patient confidentiality to hospital confidentiality is a large one, but it is often lightly taken in arguments that ignore the differences between the two. The first two premises underlying confidentiality, of autonomy regarding personal information and the respect for intimacy and human bonds, are obviously applicable, if at all, in a different manner when it comes to institutions. And the fourth premise, concerning the benefit to individuals from having somewhere to turn when vulnerable and in need of help, and the indirect benefit to society from allowing professionals to give counsel in strict confidence, must be scrutinized with care whenever the claim is made that it applies to government agencies, law firms, or corporations. We ask of them a much higher degree of accountability.

To be sure, these institutions should be able to invoke confidentiality for legitimate activities such as internal memoranda and personnel files; but it is a different matter altogether to claim confidentiality for plans that endanger others. Such protection attracts all who seek surreptitious assistance with bribery, tax evasion, and similar schemes. And because corporate or consulting law is so lucrative, the power to exercise confidentiality for such secrets then shields not merely the company and the client but the lawyer's own links to, and rewards from, highly questionable practices.

The premises supporting confidentiality are strong, but they cannot support practices of secrecy—whether by individual clients, institutions, or professionals themselves—that undermine and contradict the very respect for persons and for human bonds that confidentiality was meant to protect.

Chapter X

Trade and Corporate Secrecy

Protection Against Betrayal and Theft

*I believe I undertook amongst other things not to disclose any
trade secrets. Well, I am not going to.*
JOSEPH CONRAD, *Heart of Darkness*

The evils exposed in *Heart of Darkness* were indeed no trade secrets,
though they had been kept secret and did concern trade, and though
their disclosure might well have destroyed that trade. Except in an
extended and sinister sense, they were far from the most widely cited
legal definition of trade secret as

any formula, pattern, device, or compilation of information which is used in
one's business and which gives him an opportunity to obtain an advantage over
competitors who do not know or use it.[1]

Trade secrecy is the most frequent claim made by those who want
to protect secrets in business—legitimate secrets as well as many forms
of abuse and exploitation. To call something a trade secret is to invoke
for it the protections due property, in particular that of keeping it hidden
from others. Like property, trade secrets can be bought and sold, stolen

and recaptured, even lost for good if their owner dies without passing them on. But unlike most property, trade secrets can also be betrayed. The great clandestine wars over trade secrecy have been fought with every means of seduction, bribery, and threat precisely in order to induce or prevent betrayal.

For an illustration of the different shadings of openness and secrecy in trade, and their effects on industry in all the senses of that word, consider the evolution in Europe of the intricate art of porcelain-making.[2] Long familiar to the Chinese, the products of this art astonished Europeans as traders began to bring them back from the East in the seventeenth century. The beauty of porcelain and the variety of its uses made many Europeans long to work with it, but they had no process for manufacturing it and knew that the Chinese methods were carefully protected against imitation. Over and over again European travelers and missionaries tried to discover the secret for making the mysterious substance. But the Chinese resisted, their suspicion heightened by the inquisitiveness of the foreigners.

Finally in 1712, a Jesuit father named Francis Xavier d'Entrecolles succeeded in unraveling the secret. He learned the complicated procedures used in the manufacture of porcelain, and obtained specimens of the different earths used in its composition. In a letter worded most cautiously, since he knew it might fall into the hands of persons who would wish to prevent the secret from being transmitted, he conveyed the information to a French friend, who promptly published it. Alas, the description was so abstract, and had been made on the basis of so little practical experience, that it could not be put to immediate use. But it did awaken the interest of scientists, among them an amateur experimenter, René-Antoine Ferchault de Réaumur. He set about a process of trial and error, using earth samples and broken pieces of Chinese porcelain. As he achieved new blends, he published his results. After many trials, the manufacture of porcelain was undertaken at Sèvres, and immediately shrouded in secrecy, for purposes that were now no longer scientific but commercial. The prospect of having sole control over the European manufacture of objects so highly prized was tantalizing.

Meanwhile, a German apothecary and alchemist, Johann Friedrich Böttger, had accidentally produced some porcelain while engaged in secret experiments to find the "philosopher's stone" in order to transmute common substances into gold. He recognized the value of his discovery as soon as he compared it with the Chinese specimens he could find. With this new process, he helped start the Dresden manufacture of porcelain; and in 1710, a factory was founded in nearby Meissen. Secrecy was second nature to Böttger with his alchemist's background; he carried it over with ease to the new trade. The secrecy stimulated the curiosity of outsiders, in turn increasing the need for even stricter measures to protect the secret techniques. A contemporary source describes them as follows:

In order to preserve this art as much as possible a secret, the fabric at Meissen, which is near Dresden, is rendered impenetrable to any but those who are immediately employed about the work; and the secret of mixing and preparing the materials is known to very few of them. They are all confined as prisoners, and subject to be arrested if they go without the walls; and consequently a chapel, and everything necessary is provided within. [3]

Keeping workers thus confined to protect the secrecy of what they are doing may seem extreme, or at least outdated. But the practice is far from unknown even today when it comes to trade secrets as well as military secrets. Both the German and the French porcelain factories became the focus of espionage efforts as soon as their products began to be sold. Clandestine forces fought over the secrets in and around the factories. Surrounding villages were filled with spies and secret agents seeking to ferret out the correct techniques, and to sort out the claims by swindlers and others who hinted that they had secrets to sell. The French process was finally stolen by an English agent who had infiltrated one of the factories, helping England to begin its own manufacture at last.

Industrial espionage and counterespionage grew more common still in the nineteenth century. Companies warred over processes for manufacturing steel, chemicals, machinery of every kind. In order to protect against theft or disclosure of trade secrets, and to quell worker unrest, they employed private detective agencies such as Pinkerton's. By the time of World War I, military development in many countries such as Japan and Russia depended heavily on clandestine purchase or theft of foreign technological information and scarce materials. In the second half of this century, trade secrecy and assaults upon it have come to pervade entire industries and international conglomerates. More sophisticated means are used every year; batteries of lawyers employed by the larger firms take advantage of every subtlety of law and negotiation; and undercover means of both guarding and probing business information are the most fiercely protected trade secrets of all. [4]

If Marx could witness this development, he might take it to be yet one more symptom of the ravages of the "wolfish hunger" for profit in capitalist society. And yet secrecy about industry and invention is often most coercively imposed in the societies farthest from capitalism; and neither socialism nor any other social structure seems to pose obstacles to participation in the international battles over industrial espionage and trade secrecy. Modern industrial societies, of whatever political persuasion, have doubtless brought these battles to their current intensity; but it is often those countries whose leaders see the greatest need to catch up industrially that go to the greatest lengths in industrial espionage—once again, quite independently of their political leanings.

In the United States, a growing number of states now impose criminal liability for the theft of industrial secrets. In 1980, one man was tried and sent to prison for four years, convicted of transferring trade secrets concerning the manufacture of specialized film for computers, satellites, and other uses, estimated as worth over $6 million, from the Celanese Corporation to purchasers in the Japanese Mitsubishi Corporation.[5] And in 1982 an elaborate FBI undercover operation presented evidence that several Japanese firms had bought stolen documents containing IBM trade secrets. If a trade secret has been conveyed in confidence its revelation to others may be seen as a breach not only of trade secrecy but of confidentiality as well. Indeed, the law often punishes such breaches more in the name of respect for promises and contracts of confidentiality than out of concern for the secret itself.*

The tension between secrecy and openness is intensified when economic well-being, at times even survival, seems to be at stake. Incentives are strong to be the sole beneficiary of a process unknown to competitors; so are the forces that press, from within and without, for openness.

A degree of openness is inherent in trade secrecy itself. In contrast to other secret property, hidden away from the world to be enjoyed in seclusion, all the applications resulting from the trade secret are out in the open and indeed pressed upon potential purchasers. Coca-Cola, for instance, aggressively merchandised all over the world, is hardly kept secret; the only thing secret about it is what imitators have failed to uncover for nearly one hundred years—how to reproduce it. Every effort to discover that secret has proved unsuccessful. Even chemical analysis has failed to sort out the sequence of steps used in its manufacture. The trade secret, then, safeguards the process; its products are anything but secret.

More open ways of protecting commercial property are often preferred if they can be counted on to do so. Copyrights, patents, and trademarks

---

*As a result, the best strategy for a company suing a former employee for theft of trade secrets is often to stress the breach of confidentiality rather than the loss of property.

are means of protecting property and of achieving exclusivity without resort to secrecy. With a patent, a process or machine can be used openly, in principle, and treated as property for a set number of years. Many regard the patent system as a way for science and industry to avoid the drawbacks of secrecy. Thus Edwin Land contrasts it with the "horrible, unthinkable alternative,"

a cesspool of secrecy, an industrial environment infiltrated by spies, an industrial environment where a true scientist would be embarrassed to participate because he could not speak freely of what he knew, and where he could not use freely what he had learned.[6]

Yet the patent laws do not always secure protection from competition; when they do, they may be used unfairly by large companies against smaller ones, or by the most unscrupulous against all others. Patents may be sought on minute aspects of a technological process in order to block competition; terms such as "trap patents," "dragnet patents," and "fencing patents" point to the militant use of the patenting process to harm competitors.[7] And large corporations may bring patent-infringement suits against smaller competitors simply to burden them with legal costs.

Moreover, many innovative ideas do not fall into categories that are eligible for patenting or satisfy the requisite criteria of novelty, utility, and nonobviousness. Thus new methods of doing business cannot be patented, nor can customer lists, ideas, or processes injurious to health or to the good of society. Finally, it is much less expensive to maintain trade secrecy than to seek a patent, and if there is litigation, it is more likely to succeed. About half of all lawsuits brought to defend trade secrets are decided in favor of the plaintiffs, but less than 30 percent of patent-infringement suits are decided in favor of the patent owners.[8] As a result, companies are resorting more often to trade secrecy, even when patenting is a possibility.

The debate over trade secrecy is hesitant and conflicted. Articles analyzing it disagree even about what the law should protect: should it be ideas, property, or contracts?[9] Should societies encourage or discourage practices of trade secrecy? These difficulties stem not just from the double function that rationales for secrecy always serve but also from special obstacles in delimiting and justifying trade secrecy itself. They are exacerbated by the growing international tensions and by pressures for increased commercial secrecy on national-security grounds.

Borrowed Finery

More than the rationales examined in other chapters, that of trade secrecy turns out to borrow its justifications from other practices of secrecy, achieving but indirect and at times groping endorsement. Those who argue for trade secrecy usually appeal, at least implicitly, to one or more of five premises: personal autonomy, property, confidentiality, incentives to invest, and national security. How persuasive are these arguments? And what are their limitations?

The appeal to *personal autonomy* is fundamental for the support of individual claims to control over trade secrets. It invokes the individual's legitimate claim to control over secrecy and openness about thoughts, ideas, inventions, and plans. Without such control, I have argued, personal identity might itself be threatened. Someone who cherishes a secret recipe or who is working in secret on a scientific formula or a new design for a machine may see its secrecy as of the highest personal importance, and efforts to discover the secret as invasive in the extreme. The invasiveness of such action is especially blatant when the secret exists in thought only. To try to wrench it loose by force or trickery is then an inroad not only on secrecy but on basic liberty. A society that condoned such inroads in pursuit of trade secrets—as of all others—would be intolerable.

The presumption is therefore strong against overriding such personal autonomy over secrets. But it is not absolute; with trade secrets as with others, concealment may present such dangers that outside pressure to reveal them becomes necessary. If, for instance, someone is known to keep secret the composition of a desperately needed drug that could save the lives of many, the presumption shifts, and the claim to personal autonomy over the secret loses its force.

The claim to personal autonomy over trade secrets, moreover, cannot simply be extrapolated to collective autonomy. Yet the two are often linked in arguments concerning trade secrecy. Thus Warren and Brandeis urged, in their 1890 article on privacy, that "the right to be let alone" should apply to trade secrets as well as to more personal matters.[10] The authors may have been thinking primarily of the individual entrepreneur or inventor, rather than of large firms, and could perhaps not have foreseen trade secrecy on the scale now practiced by the multinational corporations. Other writers have suggested extending privacy law to cover even such conglomerates, but have so far failed to convince the courts to take such a step.[11] Neither the concept of privacy nor that of personal autonomy can, by itself, easily be expanded to fit both the individual entrepreneur and the large corporation.*

Does the second appeal, to *property*, provide the necessary further support for extensive trade secrecy? This argument asserts the right to guard one's property as one sees fit, through secrecy if need be. Many take the right to property to be so fundamental as to need no justification. Yet here again, the legitimacy of extrapolating from individual to collective ownership of trade secrets requires scrutiny. And no matter what one concludes in that regard, the connection of trade secrecy and property raises two further questions: Should secret knowledge necessarily count as property? And does owning something necessarily legitimate keeping it secret? Consider the relationship of secrecy, knowledge, and property in the following two cases, one hypothetical, the other recently decided in an American court:

Suppose that, in a "state of nature," a group of people live near a river and subsist on fish, which they catch by hand, and berries. There is great difficulty in catching fish by hand. Berries are however fairly plentiful. There are bits of metal lying around and I discover how to make one of them into a fishhook. With this invention I quadruple my catch of fish. My neighbours cannot discover the knack and I decline to tell them. They press me to lend them the fishhook or to give them lessons in acquiring the technique. I have however acquired Western notions of property law. . . . I point out that I have a just title to the fishhook. . . .[13]

A chemical company had developed a new process for making methanol, after extensive secret research. Expecting the new product to be highly profitable, company executives decided to build a plant for its manufacture. At one point during the construction, an unfinished roof exposed the interior design of the plant in such a way that a trained eye could detect the nature of the secret process. Spokesmen for the company later brought suit, claiming that a competitor had arranged to photograph the plant from an airplane at the time when the process was discernible. The spokesman alleged wrongful discovery of a trade secret. The court held the competitor culpable, and the company entitled to relief.[14]

If asked, both the inventor of the fishhook and the guardians of the manufacturing process might argue that they are entitled to keep others

*This is not to say that there are no arguments for group autonomy; merely that they cannot be extrapolated from individual autonomy in the context of trade secrecy. To be sure, no firm or government agency could function if every new idea, every tentative plan or draft, were under constant outside scrutiny.[12]

from benefiting from their knowledge; that they have a property right in it, and therefore the right to refuse to hand it over to others or teach them its use, even a right, in the case of the chemical company, to prevent competitors from flying across the plant under construction. These arguments exhibit both the seeming naturalness of the trade secrecy rationale's appeal to property and its weaknesses.

The Western notions of property law mentioned in the first example presuppose a view of property expressed most forcefully by Locke: that individuals have a right to what they have made, joined their labor to, or worked to wrest from nature: "For this *Labour* being the unquestionable Property of the Labourer, no man but he can have a right to what this is once joyned to, at least where there is enough, and as good is left in common for others." [15]

At the most personal level, say of the clothes one has made for oneself or the tools one has fashioned, Locke's theory has intuitive appeal. These can be claimed as belongings by right; and working to make them often creates the sense that one has put part of oneself into them.* [16] Such a personal sense of having invested part of oneself has given rise to a more general argument from desert: that one deserves to own what one has used one's labor to create. [17] But beyond basic personal needs, the intuitive self-evidence of this argument diminishes. As many have pointed out, Locke's theory did not adequately consider what entitlements should ensue when, as is usually the case, one joins one's labor to something already owned or worked on by others, as in farming or industry. And it is especially difficult to stretch his argument so as to justify large-scale corporate ownership. Furthermore, Locke's limiting the right to conditions "where there is enough, and as good is left in common for others" makes his view inapplicable in the conditions of global scarcity we now acknowledge. [18]

If it is difficult to extrapolate from a theory of individual property such as Locke's to one that suits large-scale state or industrial ownership, it is perhaps even harder to move in the opposite direction: to begin with a view justifying collective ownership or some form of communal control over inventions or resources, and to accept, nevertheless, an

---

*Hegel argued that an individual's property is in a sense an extension of himself: that if property is taken from him, he thereby loses a part of himself, and that his own life and his body are his possessions like other things. Such identification between self and possessions risks becoming sentimentalized, however, and can easily lead to a further sentimentalization of both property and work. All forms of work for pay can then be misinterpreted as selling one's self, and all theft, conversely, as physical assault.

individual claim to separate property rights against the collectivity, as in the fishhook example.

Whatever one's view of property, the two examples raise a further question: Should knowledge about how to make fishhooks and how to plan industrial processes count as property in the first place? Is there not a difference, in this respect, between saying, No, you can't use my fishhook, and saying, No, I won't let you find out how to make one to use for yourself? Trade secrets are often odd aspirants to the status of property. They may or may not remain out of reach of the knowledge of others; but one cannot always claim, on grounds of ownership, to have some entitlement to keep them thus unknown. I have argued earlier that the claim to ownership of secrets is often spurious, no matter how legitimate one's actions in guarding them. Certainly company records of trade secrets or machinery embodying them constitute property. To purloin them is theft; but was it theft in the same sense to fly over and photograph the chemical plant?

Still another question remains, even for those who regard all such efforts at discovery as theft and all trade secrets as property: Do the rights that come with property go so far as to justify secrecy? Some have argued that the Lockean view of property establishes a moral right to exclude others from its use or benefit therefrom, that this right is transmissible from one person to another and from one generation to the next. This view of property rights as exclusive, permanent, and transmissible is by no means self-evident. Those who believe such a view ubiquitous or "natural" betray as limited a perspective as that of the many nineteenth-century thinkers who believed that all cultures once exhibited "primitive communism." [19] Few laws concerning property guarantee exclusivity under all circumstances. Someone who turns out to have the only uncontaminated well in an epidemic will not be able to claim the right to exclude others from its use. But even if exclusivity were the rule, it would not automatically entail the right to secrecy for what one owns. For some kinds of property, secrecy would require intolerably high fences, or physical restraints on passers-by, or deceit of various kinds.

Why might secrecy nevertheless be claimed as an extension of exclusivity more often for trade secrets than for other kinds of property? The argument for doing so stems from the peculiar nature of trade secrets. Unlike most forms of property, trade secrets are of an ephemeral nature. They may be lost merely from being photographed or even seen; they may evaporate as the result of someone's facial expression at the moment one guesses at a formula. Controls over exclusivity, permanence, and transmissibility are more fragile for trade secrets than for other property; unusual secrecy is therefore needed to guard them. The special need for secrecy in such cases is clear, but the property argument does not suffice to justify it. This argument cannot easily accommodate both individual and collective trade secrecy; nor does it establish all trade secrets *as* property; nor, finally, does it always legitimate the use of secrecy in the protection of trade secrets.

A third premise, that of *confidentiality*, is often brought in to shore up or even to replace the limited and indirect supports that claims to personal autonomy and property offer. It holds that trade secrets, once shared, should be kept by those who have promised to do so, simply because of the promise itself. The word "confidentiality" in this context can be confusing, for it refers both to promises about trade secrets and to the confidentiality owed employees concerning their personal files. In the first of these two uses, though not in the second, confidentiality has no extra binding force apart from that of promises in general. It is not premised on the personal nature of the information conveyed (except through some vast and sentimentalized identification between persons and their property). One does not confess to trade secrets as one might to personal ones; and the promise of secrecy about a formula or a design is different from that about illness or family rifts.

Confidentiality about trade secrets may bring into play loyalty of a different kind from that in professional relationships: loyalty to the company. Such loyalty may be entirely appropriate; but like all practices of secrecy it becomes morally problematic when it brings individuals into the secret who are thereby hampered, injured, or rendered less free. This can happen when employees, sometimes even without prior knowledge or consent, learn facts that make it more difficult for them to leave their place of employment; or when a condition of employment is that any inventions or innovations by the employee become the property of the employer. The workers held in confinement at the Meissen porcelain factory offer an extreme example; but when any important technological secret is shared, those who share it may thereby be less free. As with the sharing of certain other secrets, they risk bondage, not just bonds, especially since secrets, once learned, cannot easily be unlearned.

Consider, for example, a suit brought by the B. F. Goodrich Company against the former manager of its space-suit division, Donald Wohlgemuth, and heard by the Ohio Court of Appeals in 1963. Mr. Wohlgemuth had left the company to join a rival firm, International Latex, which had recently been awarded the major space-suit subcontract for the Apollo program. As one commentator relates:

At the appeals court level, the Goodrich brief sought an injunction that would prevent Wohlgemuth from working in the space-suit field for *any* other company, prevent his disclosure of *any* information on space-suit technology to *anyone*, prevent his consulting or conferring with *anyone* on Goodrich trade secrets, and finally, prevent *any* future contact he might seek with Goodrich employees.

These four broad measures were rejected by the Ohio Court of Appeals. . . . The court did provide an injunction restraining Wohlgemuth from disclosure of Goodrich trade secrets. In passing, the court noted that in the absence of any Goodrich employment contract restraining his employment with a competitor, Wohlgemuth could commence work with Latex.[20]

A great many companies in Europe and the United States and elsewhere now ask employees to sign some agreement to protect patent and trade-secret rights. Employees may be asked not to accept work with competitors for a specified time after they leave the company, or not to use certain kinds of "know-how" they have acquired in the company, or not to disclose company secrets of a wide variety. And their mobility will be affected from the outset whenever potential employers fear that hiring persons who have signed such a contract may invite a lawsuit.

Confidentiality concerning trade secrets may also conceal dangerous aspects of a product. Under its shield, the side effects of certain drugs have been kept secret, as has the ineffectualness of others. For a number of years the United States Department of the Interior consented to protect as trade secrets all information received from industries about the amount and kinds of pollutants discharged into rivers and lakes from industrial plants.[21] In such cases, trade secrecy is a means of shielding and covering up, much as medical confidentiality can conceal malpractice.

Even when confidentiality regarding trade secrets is not actually dangerous to the public, it may extend far beyond what are ordinarily regarded as trade secrets. Consider the following recommendations by a specialist in trade secrecy. He suggests that a company should post a statement on bulletin boards as part of its "trade-secret program" that should include this provision:

Second, our trade secrets are Company assets. They were developed at great expense and only after long periods of experimentation. . . . if one of the Company's trade secrets is disclosed to a competitor or to the public, an asset of the Company will be destroyed and rendered useless to the Company.
    . . . The following information, although certainly not all-inclusive, is certainly to be considered *at all times* to be confidential:

a. Formulas for all products sold by the Company.
b. Research and development material.
c. Current sales data.
d. Advertising data.
e. Marketing data.
f. Customer information.
g. Purchasing, Pricing, and Profit data.
h. Personnel files.[22]

In such statements—and parallels are to be found in a growing number of companies—vast amounts of information that are not strictly speaking trade secrets are grouped with them for protection. If taken literally, such injunctions would prohibit most work-related conversations. Because they are not taken literally, and because their excesses could never be enforced in court, they are routinely disregarded; as a result, the boundaries surrounding those few trade secrets that companies regard as indispensable grow even more blurred.

Trade secrecy vis-à-vis competitors is, in its strict sense, only one aspect of corporate secrecy, though many other aspects may be brought under its umbrella for protection. In addition, corporations conceal their activities and especially their plans from many others: from shareholders who might question investments and links to other companies; from the government, in order to avoid interference and the publicity that may surround information once it is given over into the government's hands; from consumers, in order not to lose business; and from employees about such matters as hidden dangers at the workplace, imminent relocation plans, and risks of bankruptcy.

In support of such general business secrecy as well as of trade secrecy, we encounter a fourth and fifth argument: the need to preserve incentives to innovate and to invest and the need to guard against foreign competition and industrial espionage. Because these arguments invoke no rights such as autonomy and property, they do not raise the same problems of extrapolation and application as the first three. They concern, rather, the benefits of secrecy to companies and indirectly to society.

The Scope of Corporate Secrecy

The fourth defense of secrecy in business concerns *incentives*. If corporate secrecy did not exist, this argument holds, it would have to be invented. No matter what our views about the inherent right to hold property or to keep secrets, societies need to allow a measure of commercial secrecy in order to preserve the incentive to make changes and to invest resources. Without such incentives, social stability and progress will be endangered.[23] Thus Richard Posner argues that "some measure of privacy is necessary . . . to enable people, by concealing their ideas from other people, to appropriate the social benefits of their discoveries and inventions." [24]

Up to a point, this argument is surely persuasive. To develop new processes and achieve new knowledge in industry takes time and often great resources; to copy them, very little. Why should a company use its stockholders' money and its own manpower and resources to develop, say, a new fertilizer, if other firms can wipe out its future profits by merely copying its final results? Without protection from competing firms, it would have no incentive to make the necessary outlays. In order to avoid the resulting stagnation and failure to innovate, a society must therefore protect some corporate secrecy as a matter of policy.

Arguments pointing to such benefits from secrecy nevertheless have two kinds of limit: the benefits may be overridden by moral considerations, or disputed on empirical grounds. First, the secrecy may concern practices so harmful or invasive that they ought to be revealed, no matter how much secrecy would increase business incentives. Certain kinds of knowledge are owed to the persons who might be adversely affected by what a firm does—to employees, for example, stockholders, customers, or persons living near its factories. Thus newspaper or airline executives may claim the need for secrecy regarding administrative decisions; but such a claim rings hollow when it is used to defend the failure to notify employees of an imminent bankruptcy, so that they find a notice pinned to the entrance door one morning announcing the bankruptcy, effective immediately. Likewise, research processes that present high risks to experimental subjects, or the dumping of toxic chemicals in woods and waterways, might well help firms remain competitive and stimulate investment, but that is hardly a sufficient argument for allowing such secrecy.

Second, even when there is no moral obligation to disclose information, the argument defending corporate secrecy on grounds of incentive has practical bounds. Because it posits benefits of secrecy and costs of openness, it becomes vulnerable as soon as these costs and benefits are in doubt— when secrecy appears counterproductive, so that it not only fails to foster competition and new ideas but helps to stifle them.

A current debate weighs precisely such costs and benefits of corporate secrecy. Some argue that the economy would benefit from greatly reduced secrecy. True, they admit, individual firms might suffer, but society would gain as the market came closer to the "perfect information" that encourages innovation and growth.[25] Others hold, on the contrary, that businesses are now suffering from too much openness and probing into company affairs. They argue that the decline in productivity in the United States is in part traceable to the federal government's first demanding vast quantities of information from firms through innumerable regulations and then failing to keep the data confidential because of the requirements of the Freedom of Information Act. The act, these critics suggest, is increasingly used by businesses as a vehicle for mutual surveillance at the public's expense, to the disadvantage of all.[26]

This debate illustrates the perspectives on secrecy and openness that we have encountered in so many guises. Both sides agree that neither "perfect information," with all that it implies of disclosure and surveillance, nor pervasive corporate secrecy is desirable. Their disagreement stems from differing evaluations of the costs of the various practices of secrecy and openness.

Some of the differences in view stem from the misapprehension that there are *no* costs associated either with secrecy or with openness. I have discussed the drawbacks of secrecy in business, and the disadvantages of full openness. But other costs, sometimes quite specific ones, are often overlooked, such as those of gathering and reproducing the data required for fiscal or other purposes, and the corresponding costs of storing, indexing, protecting, and retrieving the data thus obtained. For an example of the scope and intricacy of the conflicts generated by requirements of openness and secrecy, consider the prolonged controversy over trade secrecy between drug manufacturers and scientists working for the Food and Drug Administration (FDA).

In 1974, fourteen current and former employees of the FDA went before the United States Senate to denounce a number of abuses— among them what they held to be trade secrecy detrimental to the public interest.[27] They charged that their efforts to investigate new drugs met with resistance and harassment, and that the drug industry applied inappropriate pressures to the drug review process. A panel set up to consider the various allegations found little evidence of inappropriate pressures from drug companies; but it held that the secrecy shrouding drug information posed serious problems.[28] The public, kept in ignorance about matters of the highest importance, had no way of knowing about possible mistakes or fraud that might have grave consequences for health. The secret practices forced the public to take the decisions of the FDA on faith. No one other than chosen outsiders could question the data or compare alternative choices.

Equally serious was the danger to human subjects. The secrecy shrouding drug development meant that different companies, working to develop similar drugs, engaged in duplicating experimentation on human beings, placing many more at risk than if the information could have been shared.

Spokesmen for the drug industry replied that trade secrecy was needed in the testing and licensing of new drugs. Competition in the drug industry is fierce. Between two and seven million dollars are expended over several years in the development of the average new drug, and in proving it, to the FDA's satisfaction, sufficiently safe and efficacious to be put on the market. How can the FDA both demand to see the data and refuse the companies confidentiality? How can there be sufficient incentive for the companies to invest in the production of new drugs if "me-too" drugs can quickly be put on the market by competitors that have acquired all the necessary information? Without trade-secrecy protection, these spokesmen argued, there would be no profit in being first, to compensate for the great preliminary investments.

The controversy opposed the drug industry, with its immense investments and resources, to those who fear that secrecy conceals abuses, duplication, and risks to human subjects. To resolve the conflict, and diminish the risks of secrecy while protecting the drug companies' competitive advantage, some have suggested that all files be opened, but that no company be allowed to copy another firm's process for some period of time. In this way, both property and protection would be granted, without need for the secrecy that, in this case, carries so many disadvantages.[29]

Such methods of enforcing disclosure while ensuring incentives to invest and to innovate seem preferable, and may be required increasingly as the effects of corporate secrecy on employees, customers, stockholders, and others come to be better known. It is possible that these solutions, combining accountability and protection, will be aided by the greater difficulty of permanent concealment, in industry as elsewhere; and by the growing realization that much secrecy, unthinkingly applied, is counterproductive. It is also possible, however, that governments will choose to rely more and more on industry-generated information regarding the safety of new drugs or chemicals, rather than on independent sources of evaluation. To the extent that they do, corporate secrecy with all its drawbacks is likely to spread.

While some freedom from scrutiny is obviously necessary to preserve initiative, alternatives to secrecy are preferable whenever they can serve that purpose. For the same reason, patents are thought preferable to trade secrecy. Corporate secrecy differs in this respect from individual secrecy, where the burden of proof is on those who see reason to limit autonomy regarding personal information. Because all collective secrecy magnifies the risk of harm and increases imitation and retaliation, those who advocate more than a minimum must be required to show why additional secrecy is necessary and legitimate. Corporate secrecy differs, too, from those practices of professional confidentiality which concern such personal information (rather than, say, insurance fraud or medical malpractice).

This conclusion, however, is disputed by a last defense of business secrecy—one that is voiced ever more urgently in the 1980s. It is the cost-benefit argument writ large. Translated from national to international terms, it warns of possible catastrophe for societies that do not guard commercial secrecy in the name of *national security*. The costs of industrial openness, or even slackness about security regulation, according to this argument, threaten not only individual firms but entire nations and defense alliances. Thus a spokesman for a company specializing in "security services" argued in 1981 that the United States "has become a soft target for industrial espionage that is costing the nation its technological superiority." The prime weakness, he held, is that the government has no consistent policies "to protect trade secrets and stop the flow of technology out of the country." [30] He proposed tightening up the Freedom of Information Act, placing a total embargo "on information relating to research, technology, manufacturing, and marketing of all American products, military and consumer," and extending security checks to all persons who receive "information of a quasi-classified or highly classified type."

Underlying this argument are two assumptions. The first links economic well-being and strategic security. When societies fall behind economically, they are seen as more vulnerable militarily. According to the second, societies will fall behind unless they protect their industry, commerce, and scientific research from foreign surveillance and theft of secrets; conversely, they must do everything in their power to keep up with technological development abroad.

In evaluating these assumptions, the disadvantages of secrecy are often forgotten. It is easy to think of commercial secrecy in the interests of national security as purely beneficial or at least as inherently neutral—much like a blanket one can put on and remove at will. But a look at nations, such as China and the Soviet Union, where such secrecy is enforced hardly supports this bland view. In addition to the fundamental political dangers of government-sponsored secrecy, it increases the risks of industrial complacency and mismanagement. Heightened commercial secrecy, far from enhancing national security, may therefore have the reverse effect. President Paul E. Gray of the Massachusetts Institute of Technology has warned of such an outcome:

There is growing concern in the Federal Government that the "leaking" of technical material and ideas to other nations imperils national security both by diminishing the ability of the U.S. to compete commercially and by reducing the country's edge in armaments. Yet specific efforts that have been initiated to control technology transfer in the university setting are themselves likely to weaken the U.S. position, and thus do not serve the national interest.[31]

We must ask, finally, just how much information the new practices of secrecy will succeed in safeguarding. Such practices hardly guarantee *actual* secrecy—least of all in a world where the technology of detection and surveillance has been so assiduously pursued. Even from a strictly military point of view, extensive industrial secrecy may therefore be unwise. If implemented, it may offer yet another version of the Maginot Line: a set of fortifications erected at great human and commercial cost that gives a false sense of security even as newer practices of intelligence-gathering continue unabated, and satellites glide across it with ease.

Secrecy and Competition in Science

Rituals of Openness

Denunciation of secrecy is ritualistic in science. Precisely because the conflict that secrecy creates for scientists is so strong, their declarations against it are in part efforts at conjuring away its power. Unlike other professionals such as lawyers or government officials, modern scientists have never staked out a rationale justifying practices of secrecy. They have held free and open communication to be the most essential requirement for their work. Secret practices, though common, have been viewed by outsiders with intense suspicion. What forms has the battle against secrecy in science taken? And is there something special about scientific work that explains, perhaps even justifies, the vehemence of this repudiation?

Modern scientists have directed their disavowals of secrecy, first of all, against the ancient and powerful doctrine of esotericism in science: the view that only the elect can penetrate to the mysteries of science, and that to open up the scientific process would destroy it, along with the hopes of its practitioners. This view is expressed in the Hippocratic Corpus as follows:

Things however that are holy are revealed only to men who are holy. The profane may not learn them until they have been initiated into the mysteries of science.[1]

For a distillation of this creed, and widespread efforts to follow it, one may look to the early alchemists.[2] Not only did they pursue secrets; they did so in the greatest possible secrecy. Theirs was the quest to unfold and to penetrate the deepest mysteries of nature in order to achieve transformations. They hoped to find the secret of eternal youth and to learn to change inert matter into living beings; and they sought to become aware of the universe as macrocosm and microcosm under the rule of the heavenly bodies. The alchemists sought secrecy for their experiments to guard against public disapproval and suspicion. To share the secrets would destroy the quest; at most, hints and guidance for future seekers might be given to selected individuals and inserted into esoteric writings.

In addition to rejecting such an ideal, disclaimers of secrecy in modern science are also meant to assuage the suspicion that scientists might use their knowledge for profiteering and fraud. The public's fear of such abuses of secrecy has been especially strong with respect to medicine. In 1769, Samuel Bard advised physicians:

Do not pretend to Secrets, Panaceas, and Nostrums, they are illiberal, dishonest, and inconsistent with your Characters as Gentlemen and Physicians, and with your Duty as Men—for if you are possessed of any valuable remedy, it is undoubtedly your Duty to divulge it, that as many as possible may reap the Benefit of it; and if not (which is generally the Case) you are propagating a Falsehood and imposing upon Mankind.[3]

And the French *Encyclopédie*, published four years earlier, defined a medical secret as a remedy for which the preparation is kept secret in order to raise its potency and its price. The combination of rapacity among dissembling physicians and gullibility and hope among patients no matter how near death, the authors concluded, will prolong such age-old practices for as long as the world lasts. It will triumph over the strongest and the clearest evidence; to be surprised thereby, one would have to be "bien peu philosophe." [4]

However often denounced, both the pressure for exclusivity and the incentives for profiteering, monopoly, and fraud nevertheless continue in modern science in new guises. In addition, new pressures for secrecy have come to beset scientists, even as scrutiny of their activities is intensified. The impact of government, business, and military policies of secrecy on the nature of scientific work today reaches into most scientific undertakings, and pits demands for secrecy against adherence to the fundamental norms held to govern science.

Foremost among these norms, according to many, is that of open and free sharing of scientific information. It holds that scientists ought not to withhold information but should publish it within a reasonable time, and that their freedom to do so ought not to be limited by any outside institution. While they may keep confidential matters pertaining to privacy (of human subjects in experimentation, for example) or to ongoing research, they should claim no rights of ownership to what they have discovered or invented once it is in the public arena. "Secrecy," according to Robert Merton, "is the antithesis of this norm; full and open communication its enactment." [5] Even in the midst of World War II, as scientists around the world were working under conditions of unaccustomed secrecy, *Nature* published a Declaration of Scientific Principles: according to the seventh principle, the pursuit of scientific inquiry demands complete intellectual freedom and unrestricted international exchange of knowledge. [6]

Another norm held forth to scientists is that which Robert Merton has called disinterestedness. It prescribes that scientists, whatever their personal motives, should have the advancement of scientific knowledge as their primary concern. [7] This norm too supports openness, since it is precisely a lack of disinterestedness that leads to secrecy in the practices envisaged by the Encyclopedists and by others who caution against secret scientific research.

These norms are defended, however, for reasons deeper than the need to combat exclusiveness, profiteering, spurious claims to achievement, and arbitrary government demands. The felt need to take a stand against secrecy also springs from concern for what is most central to the scientific enterprise itself: from a recognition of the damage that secrecy can do to thinking and to creativity, and thus to every form of scientific inquiry. Because secrecy limits feedback and restricts the flow of knowledge, it hampers the scientist's capacity to alter estimates according to new information, to see connections, to take unexpected leaps of thought. And secrecy is costly in that it fosters needless duplication of effort, postpones the discovery of errors, and leaves the mediocre without criticism and peer review. Secrecy, therefore, can cut into the quality of research and slow scientific momentum.

For these reasons, secrecy affects *all* reasoning and creativity, quite apart from its susceptibility to every form of abuse and pathological excess. But the damage is perhaps especially noticeable in science because of its reliance on reasoning and creativity; most noticeable of all among scientists who work in large institutions where secrecy is enforced by surveillance, security clearances, and other methods apt to spread, debilitate participants, and invite abuse.

Modern scientists are now, as never before, pressed from opposite directions: more openness is required of them, not only by peers but by the public; yet some are also being asked to participate in stricter procedures of secrecy in addition to their personal incentives for concealment. Edward Shils described this conflict during the McCarthy era:

Science, which for so long had lived apart and to itself, has increasingly in the present century shown how much it can contribute to technology, welfare, and defense. . . . Under pressure to divulge and not to divulge, science and scientist have fallen into a tormenting cross-fire. Offering the quintessence of the most salvationary secrets, scientists have, at the same time and for the same reason, been drawn into the arena of publicity.[8]

Caught in this cross-fire, some scientists have fought hard against secrecy, especially when it has been imposed from the outside. In the 1950s, a number of American scientists stood up in defense of the freedom to do research and combated the loyalty oaths and security restrictions so arbitrarily imposed, with their distressing effects not only on the lives of individuals accused of disloyalty but also on the conduct of science in its own right. Thus seventeen American Nobel prize-winners, responding in 1959 to a letter from Senator Thomas Henning, agreed (with one exception) that free exchange of information was the lifeblood of scientific progress and that restrictions of this flow were either foolish or destructive.[9] Wartime conditions or extremely sensitive research might require special restrictions, they held, but widespread secrecy was so debilitating that it should be resisted at all costs.

Other scientists were more accommodating. Some made ad hoc responses to the demands for secrecy without trying to sort out the ethical issues. Some entered into the spirit of secrecy without reservation, believing that the threats to national security overshadowed concerns for openness in science. Still others took refuge in the claim that research should be approached in an objective, "value-free" spirit, and thus succeeded in repressing questions of moral choice in their own lives as scientists as well.

Aside from such issues of national security, the debate over secrecy in science has been much less articulate. Two barriers have stood in its way. In the first place, the ritualistic invocation of the norms of openness and disinterestedness in science has served to defuse efforts to analyze the conflict of these norms with secrecy. It is all too easy to slide from the normative to the descriptive in such invocations; to begin to take for granted that what scientists are thought to value must be characteristic of how they act. Such a slide is a form of rationalization that helps to keep potential conflicts over secrecy out of view.

A second form of rationalization, closer to sheer denial, guards a more limited territory. Many argue that, while difficult issues of secrecy do arise for scientists working in private industry or in the development of technology, this is not the case for scientists in the nonprofit sector doing research in government agencies and in the universities. Only in the commercial arena, they hold, are there serious questions of trade or military secrecy. In nonprofit science, on the other hand, openness is still the practice. While such work may at times require temporary protection of ongoing research, it is meant to be published as soon as possible, and thus does not invite the long-term secrecy sometimes imposed on technological research, with all the attendant ethical problems.

The distinction between the nonprofit and the commercial (like that between science and technology and between pure and applied science) is doubtless important; but where ethical problems are concerned, it functions as a smoke-screen, obscuring the perception of how such problems, including those of secrecy, arise for all scientists. I shall suggest, on the contrary, that the claims made for trade and military secrecy come up in somewhat different guise in the nonprofit sector; and that the lines between ethical issues in commercial and nonprofit science are growing more blurred each day, as the same persons participate in both arenas, and as the results of the most theoretical research find swift, often unexpected application. In the temporary secrecy sought for ongoing research, as well as in longer-term secrecy sought for certain lines of inquiry and for the results of some types of research, scientists are encountering perplexing questions of choice and line-drawing.

Temporary Protection of Ongoing Research

Modern scientists work under conditions of heightened competition as compared with their predecessors. On any one frontier of research, many scientists will be at work on very similar projects, often competing for limited resources. The level of specialization is such, moreover, that researchers cannot easily shift gears and turn to a different field. Jerry Gaston, in a study of competition in science, compares it to "a race between runners on the same track and over the same distance at the same time." But such a race differs from track and field events: though many more runners may participate, only winners are rewarded. There are no second- and third-place awards, and "the researcher who presents what is already known to the community may lose all or most of the recognition that would normally accrue to him." [10]

The desire to be first, to have priority, and to achieve recognition by peers can lead to temporary secrecy about ongoing research. This secrecy is not meant to be permanent; on the contrary, the goal is the most rapid possible publication of results. The only question is one of timing. In order to avoid the risk of being anticipated by a competitor who borrows and uses ideas or research data and publishes the results first, investigators may engage in a variety of stratagems. In *The Double Helix*, James Watson describes some of the ways in which he and Francis Crick, in the race to discover the structure of DNA, tried to keep competitors (especially Linus Pauling) selectively ignorant of their progress, and tells how they used publication deadlines and waiting periods to protect and reveal when most needed. [11] And Nicholas Wade recounts, in *The Nobel Duel*, a twenty-one-year-long race for the Nobel Prize between two scientists and former co-workers. The contest between Andrew Schally and Roger Guillemin to complete their discoveries about the peptide hormone of the brain was so intense, involved so many team members on both sides, and absorbed such large funds that secrecy became ever more important. According to Wade, Schally expressly instructed his associates not to talk to the enemy—that is, to anyone working for Dr. Guillemin. [12]

Prizes and personal advancement play a large role in such competitions; for although the knowledge achieved cannot become property in its own right, those who discover it achieve new means *to* property. But recognition by peers and personal gain are far from the only factors. One cannot read Watson's and Wade's accounts without also sensing the excitement of the race itself. Others describe the reverse: an oppressive sense of having to compete, perhaps being able only to hint at progress, while worrying about losing funds for further research if their findings are borrowed. [13] For many scientists, the fate of an entire research project involving a number of collaborators depends on grants for further research—grants that in turn depend on convincing funding agencies of the project's originality and likely success.

The desire for priority undoubtedly speeds innovation, and drives scientists to tolerate frustration, drudgery, and setbacks that might otherwise prove overpowering. But this desire is often concealed, since it conflicts with the norms of disinterestedness and of sharing. Robert Merton, in studying this conflict, worked out a rule of thumb: whenever a scientist claims, in an autobiography or biography, to have little or no interest in priority, there is a reasonably good chance that not many pages later, the reader will find him deeply embroiled in a battle over priority.[14]

Even when research is going badly, scientists may want secrecy, not so much to achieve priority in the near future as to keep others from perceiving their difficulties. Thus one high energy physicist explains that he is reluctant to make known the fact that an experiment is not going well, "because it might get thrown off the accelerator." [15]

Quite apart from the desire for priority and the fear of being anticipated or of having a project terminated, scientists may also keep their unfinished work to themselves out of a sense of reserve. Indeed, the most meticulous and scrupulous scientists may hesitate the longest before making data public, because they want to make certain of their results before announcing them.[16] At issue is the personal claim to control over one's plans and unfinished projects and over deciding when to reveal them. Unlike the desire for priority, which takes a special and possibly extreme form in science, such reserve has close parallels in all creative work. Many processes of research and creation require a chance to mature, to be tested and varied, without publicity. It is in the nature of such efforts to be tentative at first. Creativity requires freedom to do the unexpected, to risk failure, to pursue what to others might seem far-fetched and even pointless.

Whenever people know that their unfinished work will have to be exposed, its nature changes subtly. Just as the diaries writers intend from the outset to publish differ from those meant to be kept secret, so scientists' outlines and drafts and diagrams differ if overseen by others. Not only do they tend to be more elaborate; they are often efforts to legitimize the undertaking and may therefore slip into a certain hypocrisy. It is possible, also, that such documents may take on a special rigidity once they are open to inspection: that other lines of inquiry may seem more sealed off so that the fluidity of the creative process is lost.

Such developments can occur when there is no general public to be considered, but when the work is a team effort. They are even more likely in scientific work that is funded by the government or foundations and thus under supervision by outsiders from the outset. In each case, the disadvantages of this loss must be weighed against the support received.

Neither the desire for priority nor what I have called "reserve" is ethically problematic in its own right. Each is based, in many cases, on legitimate claims to control over secrecy and openness with respect to plans and to property resulting from the investment of resources. To try to wipe out such control would be an intolerable invasion of privacy, and might in addition undercut the incentives for creativity and for the significant personal sacrifices scientists must often undergo.* To the extent that scientists fear theft and anticipation of their ideas, secrecy counteracts these fears and allows leeway for undisturbed research.[17]

Although openness is of special importance in science, therefore, secrecy regarding unfinished work is often justified. But even such preliminary secrecy requires limits. What ought they to be?

First of all, the means used to protect secrets should be limited for scientists as for all others. Fraud in the protection of research is thus problematic from the outset. When clear-cut fraud is uncovered, the scientific community generally deals with it severely. But other forms of misrepresentation are harder to pinpoint. For instance, the current system of financing research may encourage scientists to misrepresentation in order to keep their unfinished work from disclosure. Scientists who seek financial support for their work—and that includes nearly all— are now required to describe in some detail what they plan to do if they receive a grant. Granting agencies must have something to go on if they are not to give out money on the basis of favoritism or past achievement, to the disadvantage of the young or the unknown scientist. But this process exposes research in two ways: it disturbs the privacy of unfinished projects, and it opens research plans to potential competitors on the reviewing boards. Many scientists acknowledge that, as a result, much vagueness and even falsity beset the requests submitted to funding agencies. Some describe portions of their work already finished; others include inaccuracies to throw competitors off the track.

No one should have to resort to deception in order to protect work from premature disclosure or plagiarism. When such motives seem to necessitate fraud, it is often the system itself that must be changed. We might ask, therefore, just how much information funding agencies ought to request from applicants. Without giving up the benefits of peer review, are there alternative ways of making sure that money goes to those who can best use it? Asking for too much information, or the

---

*These arguments concerning secrecy in science bear a strong resemblance to those advanced for trade secrecy. In both cases, claims to plans and to property are invoked. In both, arguments about the social benefits that flow from allowing a measure of secrecy are brought in to buttress these claims. True, the nature of what is thought to be property differs for those who seek protection for unfinished scientific research and those who want long-range control over the products of their research for purposes of profit; and the rewards themselves are often dissimilar. Nevertheless, the underlying arguments are identical in structure, and appeal to the same claims to personal secrecy.

wrong kind of information, merely invites deception in defense of secrecy; and this, in turn, facilitates fraud more generally in order to cut corners and to remain afloat. False and overblown claims create the temptation to live up to these claims at all costs, and encourage imitation and retaliation by those who would otherwise have little incentive to misrepresent their own research or to suspect that of others. The entire scientific community suffers from such opportunistic practices. Its spokesmen have every reason to promote reforms in the allocation of research funds, while stressing more forcefully the importance of the highest standards of accuracy even in preliminary phases of research. With requests for grants as with letters of recommendation, many people are now caught up in a debilitating system of mutual suspicion and misrepresentation that is disadvantageous for all.

Some have argued that no further limitations are needed: that so long as fraudulent means are excluded, scientists ought to be free to decide when to keep ongoing research secret, when to publish the results, and how to weigh the advantages of secrecy and openness. Such an argument sounds simple and clear-cut; and it is consonant with the view that scientific work is the researcher's intellectual property until it is published. But a rule of this kind is inadequate whenever ongoing work affects others or requires outside funding. Further limits on degrees of secrecy *and* openness are then needed.

A blend of openness and secrecy is needed, for example, to protect research that is vulnerable—research that can collapse or lose validity through premature publicity. Such vulnerability is especially common in "double-blind" studies with human subjects, in which neither subjects nor investigators know which subjects are receiving the experimental treatment. Such studies require strict concealment of data. Otherwise it might be impossible to tell whether a subject's responses are attributable to the treatment or to suggestion; investigators might be biased in assigning subjects to groups receiving what they believe to be the most promising treatment, and the results might be interpreted in a biased way. Consequently, the study must also remain sealed off from the public media and others who might desire the information—something not always easy to achieve when the research concerns possible advances in combating such illnesses as cancer.

Ideally, the studies should be allowed to run until the hypothesis under investigation is either confirmed or rejected. But circumstances that justify breaches of secrecy may arise. If it develops, in the course of the study, that one treatment presents greater risks to participants than another or than a placebo treatment, then their safety and their right to know about the risks they run outweigh the benefits of continued concealment. However, it is hard to know just when in the course of the experiment to conclude that such risks exist. For this reason, the so-called "stopping problem" is one of the hardest investigators face. Other pressures may also affect the decision. If investigators lack sufficient training in statistics, they may not understand the length of time and the number of subjects required to arrive at conclusive evidence, and therefore rush into print with temporary results. The outcome of such action can be a premature public interest in new drugs or techniques before they have been shown to be beneficial; or a corresponding loss of confidence in existing therapies that are falsely believed to have been proved useless or harmful.

A second aspect of the vulnerability of ongoing research creates conflicts about secrecy for substantive rather than methodological reasons. What is feared, in such cases, is not that experiments will collapse or lose their validity from premature disclosure; it is, rather, that the research will undergo criticism and perhaps be overhauled or canceled. Such interference must be resisted when based on purely political motives or on dogmatic fears of new knowledge. But as soon as a study places human subjects, laboratory workers, or bystanders at risk, the investigators can no longer claim it as their intellectual property to be revealed or kept secret as they choose. The history of scientific experimentation is burdened with many examples of studies conducted without the knowledge, much less the consent, of those at risk.

Consequently, guidelines and regulations now seek to make quite clear what information must be provided before a study is undertaken, at what stage, and to whom. But the difficulty of regulation is great whenever those at risk cannot be identified or are very numerous. The difficulty is compounded when research is undertaken abroad, as when scientists test contraceptive implants with unknown risks on women in Asia or Latin America, or when a nation tests nuclear devices far from its own shores and its major population centers. The risks may then be very differently understood and assessed on all sides: those who are most endangered may be kept most completely in the dark, or have insufficient power to impose any regulation on the investigators.[18]

Still other aspects of research may require greater secrecy than investigators or sponsoring agencies are prepared to guarantee. Experiments may be conducted on groups of people, such as alcoholics or the mentally ill, for whom confidentiality is especially important. The information gained in such studies is, once again, hardly to be considered the property of the investigators, to reveal or keep back as they choose. The same is true of all investigations in which questions are asked about private matters. At present, there are many obstacles to the careful protection of confidential personal information; yet research subjects are rarely informed about them.

For all these reasons, the simple rule that investigators should decide how much secrecy they desire until the time of publication of results is inadequate. Such a rule assumes that the choice poses risks neither to participants nor to the project that require others to participate in the decision-making. At times such an assumption may be warranted— for instance, in historical or literary research—but in most scientific research, it is not.

Secrecy and the Results of Research

Scientists are also coming under increasing pressure to exercise long-term secrecy over certain research results and over lines of inquiry capable of achieving certain kinds of results. The pressures come primarily from two directions: business and government. What boundaries might scientists want to draw in response to these pressures? Should scientists accommodate to trade or military secrecy less easily than others? Is there something inherent in the role of the scientist that clashes with being used—or with using oneself—as a tool for purposes of commerce or the military?

Trade secrecy, to begin with, envelops not only scientists who work for private business but also many who are based in government and the universities. Companies in many fields are now eager to invest in the services of university researchers by offering them large consulting fees or substantial amounts of stock. In either case scientists acquire a financial stake in the success of the firm and hence may not wish to compromise an important commercial breakthrough by speaking openly about their findings.

As a result, distrust and suspicion spread even among colleagues on the same university faculty. At scientific meetings, disputes have erupted over secrecy, and proposals have been made to censure or expel members who use their business obligations as excuses to avoid taking part in the customary sharing and discussion of new advances. And lawsuits, such as that between the University of California and the pharmaceutical firm Hoffman–La Roche over patent rights to genetic information for the synthesis of interferon, threaten to undercut further the informal exchanges among scientists.*

The distinction between basic and applied science (like the related but not identical boundary between nonprofit and commercial scientific work) may be useful for many purposes, but it cannot serve to draw lines of an ethical nature. It is simply not true that the ethical problems of secrecy somehow come up only in applied or commercial work. Nor can the two be insulated from each other. Many scientists engage in both, sometimes in the course of the same day and in the same laboratories. And work that many regard as basic rather than applied today interests many commercial firms: thus biogenetic companies work closely with scientists performing basic research in biochemistry departments. It is absurd to think that questions about the effects of secrecy on their lives, their treatment of colleagues, their regard for gain, arise only in one of the two contexts. The step from the basic to the applied is often breathtakingly short; considerations of trade secrecy now hover near the most abstract lines of inquiry.

Some ask what is wrong with the role of the scientist as entrepreneur. Why should a biologist, they ask, not use his talents for profit when economists and artists and inventors have long done so? If secrecy is required to derive the fullest benefits from his work, why should he hesitate more than others to impose it?

In answering these questions, it is important to stress, first of all, that every entrepreneur, inside as well as outside the academy, in science as well as in other fields, has reason to be cautious about becoming entangled in trade secrecy. There are justified forms of such secrecy; but they have vast and debilitating excesses and many problematic aspects. When trade secrecy leads to personal bondage of either the entrepreneur or employees; when it tempts the entrepreneur to use fraudulent means; when it damages relations with colleagues; when it conceals discoveries or information needed by society (as would have been the case, for instance, had the discovery of insulin been kept secret); when it covers up illegal acts or the dangers of a product or process, as in the concealment of side effects of drugs; and when it is so extensive that it hampers the free communication about large areas of potential development: then it should be at least as great a cause for concern among scientists as among all others.

If we acknowledge that everyone has reason to be cautious, do we

---

*While patenting by scientists or by universities can help avoid some of the worst excesses of commercial secrecy, it can also contribute to channeling, at times damming up, the free exchange of scientific information.

also want to go further and say that scientists who work in nonprofit institutions have added reason to refrain from practices that require them to participate in trade secrecy? Are scientists different, in this respect, from company-based inventors or free-lance writers?

I believe they are. Having been given special privileges, and possessing, collectively, unprecedented power, these scientists must assume special constraints. When they use university laboratories and draw university salaries, they have special obligations to academic colleagues and to students. When their work draws upon public funds, they have additional obligations toward the public. In all their research, these scientists rely upon the trust and goodwill without which the scientific enterprise would falter, and thus have further reason not to impede the flow of information for private gain.

Scientists working in university settings should therefore not substitute the standards of the marketplace for those of the academy.[19] But to argue that they have added obligations is not to hold that they must never observe trade secrecy. It may be urgently required for speeding the application of research—or be so innocuous as not to matter. Some scientists consult with firms on a part-time basis, much as others consult with government departments of agriculture, energy, or defense. In each case, they may promise silence about what they hear. When such secrecy is not about their own work, few would argue that it damages fundamental aspects of relations with colleagues or students.*

A more difficult problem is increasingly posed for scientists who receive a company's financial support for work in their university laboratories. Firms often ask that these scientists withhold publication and even discussion of important results for a period of months to give the company time to decide whether or not to file a patent claim. The scientists who sign such contracts argue that the secrecy is short-lived; others respond that this may be true for any one set of results, but that as the practice spreads, and as different lines of research interweave, it may be hard to sustain such limitations in time; and they point to the damage to free exchange of views that may result.

Both with consulting and with such time limitations, moreover, it is often hard to know just what topics fall into the category for which one has promised secrecy, and harder still to guess which casual comments might provide clues to an ingenious competitor. The resulting hesitation

---

*A few might argue that *all* consulting by scientists should be abolished, but this argument has little to do with secrecy. Others point out that consulting can come to take over more and more of a scientist's time; in that case, it is obviously more damaging to collegial relationships of all kinds.

about what one can communicate is itself an impediment to full scientific exchange. Even in making exceptions to the general presumption against trade secrecy for academic scientists, therefore, over and above the general caution that trade secrecy should always inspire, special constraints are needed.

A similar redoubling of caution is required with respect to *military secrecy*. Like trade secrecy, it is justified at times. Such secrecy may be required for scientific knowledge vital to national defense or capable of highly destructive use in enemy hands; but it carries immense risks of spreading, of creating bondage, of shielding incompetence and corruption, and of delaying advances in knowledge. Like trade secrecy, it insulates from criticism and feedback, and thus opens the door to abuse; and it is equally capable of inviting imitation and retaliation of every kind. And like trade secrecy, it carries special dangers for science. Here, too, scientists have an added responsibility to exercise restraint.

In the last few years, a controversy has arisen in the field of cryptography that shows how difficult it can be to weigh the arguments for and against scientific involvement in military secrecy—and how hard they are to separate from concerns of trade secrecy.[20] Mathematicians and computer scientists have recently made substantive advances in designing methods of encoding information that are less vulnerable to decoding. Many of the new encryption schemes would require years, perhaps decades, of computer time to decode, and therefore make these codes effectively unbreakable.

As work on such problems began to yield interesting and usable results, the mathematicians came close to the "born secret" region of classified research, in some cases without thinking that their research would prompt government interference.* As they began to publish their results, officials in the National Security Agency (NSA) became concerned, and broke a twenty-five-year tradition of public silence in 1979 in order to indicate the need for discussion of what to do about this form of research. The NSA cautioned the mathematicians and made efforts to take over the funding for some of their projects. Researchers rejected these efforts, fearing that a project funded by the agency could also be censored by it, or classified at its request.

Although the mathematicians have fought these measures in the name

---

*The term "born secret" applies in a strict sense only to information classifiable under the Atomic Energy Act. Research in this category is to be kept secret from the very outset, unlike other research, which is presumed open unless it undergoes classification. The NSA has tried to extend the "born secret" concept to the cryptography area by voluntary agreement rather than by legislative process.

of academic freedom, one group of researchers in cryptography did agree in 1980 to a two-year trial period of voluntary prior restraint, during which they will submit papers on the relevant topics to the NSA for review. But they have not agreed to suppress papers at the request of the agency; nor has the agency explained how it intends to regulate the research—whether through censorship, legal means, or other forms of prohibition.[21]

The official concern about such research is understandable. Without cryptography, modern military strategy would be disabled. Many commentators believe that the Allies were able to shorten World War II by at least a year because their cryptanalysts had broken the Japanese codes, unbeknownst to Japan's military leaders.[22] NSA officials argued that without secrecy for current research on the making and breaking of codes, other nations could learn that their codes are insecure and devise new ones that the NSA could not break.[23]

In the case of cryptography research, military secrecy conflicts with academic immunity from outside restrictions and with the norm of open communication among scientists. But another interest is also in conflict with the proposed restrictions. In both the private and the public sectors, electronic fund transfer and mail systems make the transmission of information highly vulnerable to accidental changes, theft, and destruction. As a result, banks and other organizations have a strong interest in secure means of encoding the data that they transmit. The market for cryptography, long primarily a military interest, has suddenly expanded.

In both the military and the commercial uses, the purposes are triply concerned with secrecy. The conflicts have to do with the degree of secrecy or openness that is legitimate in the transmission of trade secrets or of military secrets, and with the secrecy needed to hide the possibility of such transmission from outsiders and adversaries.

Academics, faced with this interweaving of separate questions of secrecy, find themselves in a double-bind. If, for example, a mathematician is ordinarily in favor of free and open exchanges of information, should he communicate openly the results of his research even though it could allow more complete secrecy in military and business establishments around the world—including the most corrupt or violent ones? He confronts, in unpredictable and paradoxical ways, the tensions associated by Joseph Cade with all secrecy in science, arising from the "simultaneous requirement to promote the flow of thought between some sets of minds yet impede it between others."[24]

The difficulty of predicting the results of opting either for secrecy or for openness in this double-bind is striking. It is partly a matter of strategy: those who foresee specific military risks from disclosing such research often see good reason not to draw attention to them. But in addition, no one can foretell how things would change if unbreakable codes were available, either to the military alone or to all who wished to use them. Although scientists do recognize the danger of pursuing and publicizing certain lines of research (as with cheap, easy-to-assemble means of mass destruction), the risks from publicity about cryptographic research are less direct, and at least in part offset by the advantages sought by commercial firms and banks. The greater the power of a group to inflict harm, the more serious are the risks of its having such codes to shield it from accountability. But if these means were available to many groups, they would thereby provide some protection *against* the most dangerous and invasive groups.

One result of widespread use of unbreakable codes might well be a greater vulnerability of the human beings who initiate or receive the messages. The more secure the process of transmission, the more important senders and receivers of messages become as targets of industrial and military espionage and of bribery, extortion, and other means of probing. One commentator points out that people are much more useful for industrial espionage than any mechanical device, since they "can be bribed, cajoled, blackmailed or, in some cases, merely encouraged to gossip." [25] To the extent that academics do research on such forms of transmission, they could themselves become the targets of and possible participants in these practices.

In considering how mathematicians should respond to pressures to release or keep secret their work on cryptography, one must also ask whether preventing the spread of such knowledge is even possible. Can it be kept secure, especially from those most eager to make use of it? Articles have already been published on this research, thus alerting readers to the possibility of undertaking further research. Scientists also routinely share such knowledge long before publication by means of preprints sent to colleagues around the world. And the voluntary controls now being tried out will work only so long as *all* the researchers agree to participate—an unlikely prospect, as the work is now going on in a number of countries, and as the commercial rewards for the results of such research promise to be high.

This is but one example of how commercial pressures for secrecy intertwine with and sometimes conflict with military pressures. Military secrecy now concerns much more than traditional military matters such as troop movements and defense installations; its focus has become primarily scientific and technological. As research grows more and more indispensable to each country's security, conflicts over whether and how to guard it against surveillance and espionage have intensified.

Since taking office in 1980, members of the Reagan administration have urged greater government control over secrecy in scientific research as in commerce. They have sought to restrict access by certain foreigners to scientific meetings and university campuses, and to stretch export restrictions to cover teaching and research activities. In January 1982, Admiral Inman, deputy director of the CIA, spoke out about the need he perceived for greater control. Arguing that "scientists do not immunize themselves from social responsibility simply because they are engaged in a scientific pursuit," he recommended cooperation between scientists and government officials in determining how to restrict publication of information that could be used by other nations to hurt United States national security interests. He mentioned cryptologic research as an example of a field in need of such restrictions, and added:

There are, in addition, other fields where publication of certain technical information could affect the national security in a harmful way. Examples include computer hardware and software, other electronic gear and techniques, lasers, crop projections, and manufacturing procedures.[26]

Spokesmen for universities and scientific organizations have been quick to protest against the proposed measures.[27] They have expressed doubt that these measures would succeed in blocking the spread of scientific information, while calling attention to the damage that secrecy and censorship would inflict on scientific work as well as on the nation, as universities and individual scientists inevitably turned away from fields of research thus shackled.

This confrontation is of exceptional importance. It takes place in an atmosphere of international tension that can lead to great inroads on freedom and bring about, in turn, a hardening of positions: the quick assumption that more secrecy necessarily brings more security versus the ritualistic invocation of openness in science. What is needed, rather, is a re-examination of the role that secrecy now plays in science in different societies, of the worldwide impact of the combined practices, and of measures that might contain and reduce such secrecy while strengthening it in the narrow regions where it is beneficial.

Such a re-examination would have to consider that secrecy in science has become a vast network of practices enveloping many millions of scientists around the world. In the industrialized nations, over one-third of the budget for research and development is now allocated to military or space or nuclear studies.[28] Policies of secrecy affect much of this work. It is hard even to understand the full scope and impact of the shift in research directions that has taken place in this century. Scientists are now indispensable to the arms buildup throughout the world. They spearhead the development of ever more inhumane forms of chemical and biological weapons. If their collective talents and the vast sums that support them could be redeployed even in part against the problems of hunger, ill-health, overpopulation, environmental deterioration, and energy needs, the world outlook would change dramatically.

The secrecy surrounding much current scientific research makes it difficult for the public to consider such alternative directions for scientific work, and to evaluate the full burden of present research priorities. And secrecy likewise insulates scientists from examining their own role, and from accountability to the public. Many scientists have also testified to the personal and professional costs of working under secrecy restrictions: of having to take part in systems of classification, submit to research delays or outright censorship, and swear loyalty oaths; of fearing espionage; and of being themselves suspected when traveling or conversing with foreigners.

Scientists cannot abdicate the responsibility for confronting these matters, both individually, from the point of view of how they wish to lead their lives, and jointly. Many scientists and scientific organizations have called for inquiries into the questions of responsibility and choice raised by the growing conflicts over secrecy. Collectively, however, scientists have failed to pursue such inquiries and to arrive at careful distinctions with respect to what they are asked to do. In the absence of more forceful efforts to seek a reasoned response to these conflicts, new practices of secrecy may gain such a strong foothold that they affect the momentum, the quality, and the direction of scientific research in ways difficult to reverse.[29]

Secrets of State

Reason of State

"Secrecy, being an instrument of conspiracy," wrote Jeremy Bentham, "ought never to be the system of a regular government." [1] In "On Publicity," he contrasted the advantages of openness with the secretiveness and consequent abuses permitted by the English system of government of his time. Woodrow Wilson spoke out in similar tones against secrecy in his 1912 election campaign, referring again and again to the need for openness, sunshine, and fresh air. Basing his views on a lifelong study of statecraft and politics, he concluded that "government ought to be all outside and no inside," and that "there ought to be no place where anything can be done that everybody does not know about."

Everybody knows that corruption thrives in secret places, and avoids public places, and we believe it a fair presumption that secrecy means impropriety. [2]

Yet once elected to the United States presidency, Wilson fell far short of imposing the ideal of complete openness that he had advocated. After inaugurating biweekly press conferences, he soon gave them up. His cabinet meetings, staff reports, drafts, and personal deliberations were no

more open than those of previous administrations, and in 1917 he introduced wartime censorship through the Committee on Public Information.

Societies differ greatly in the degree of secrecy that characterizes
their governments in any one period; but all who govern, regardless of
their intentions, find themselves guarding some remoteness and separation,
and doing so increasingly the longer they stay in office. Some control
over secrecy and openness is also the rule in courts, legislatures, executive
offices, and diplomatic missions. Under what conditions is such control
justified?

An ancient analogy underlies many defenses of administrative secrecy:
that of the state with an organism. Each needs guarding in similar ways,
according to this analogy; both run risks of ill-health, corruption, and
collapse without the requisite protection. A measure of sacredness is
linked to the secrecy guarding the state as it is to that of individuals. The
rationale defending such secrecy is prior to the administrative and military
rationales that I shall take up later in this chapter and the next: it is
the esoteric claim to secrecy regarding what is set apart in persons and
in governments—both vulnerable and powerful, and off limits to outsiders.

This esoteric rationale for control over government secrecy found its
most articulate expression in the principle of *arcana imperii*: "secrets of
rule," or "mysteries of state." [3] It transferred the aura of sacredness
from the *arcana ecclesiae* of church, ritual, and religious officials to
secular leaders, and was never more strongly invoked than in defense
of seventeenth-century absolutist monarchies. [4] Through the doctrine of
the divine right of monarchs, secret government was given a sanctity
of its own. Thus James I of England spoke to warn intruders: "None
shall presume henceforth to meddle with anything concerning our government or deep matters of state. . . ." [5] And Francis Bacon expressed
the esoteric rationale for government control over secrecy as follows:

Concerning government, it is a part of knowledge secret and retired in both
these respects in which things are deemed secret; for some things are secret
because they are hard to know, and some because they are not fit to utter. We
see all governments as obscure and invisible. [6]

Governments are not only obscure and invisible in themselves, according
to the esoteric rationale, not only unknowable or hard to know for the
uninitiated; they should also be retired, withdrawn from outsiders. Only
then will their secrets be kept from dilution and desecration, and from
injuring those who blunder too near. Government secrecy, according to
such a view, is not less justifiable than individual secrecy but more so;
it does not extrapolate from individual secrecy but rather lends legitimacy

and sacredness to individual rulers, and through them to members of their government.

The esoteric rationale for government secrecy has also drawn on the theory that "reason of state" legitimates action on behalf of a state that would be immoral for private individuals. It holds that the reason of state cannot be reduced to ordinary moral deliberation. Without the state, individuals could not survive to conduct such deliberation; therefore, rulers may be justified when they lie, cheat, break promises, or even torture in order to further their state's welfare. And secrecy regarding such acts was often thought to be of the highest importance in furthering the designs of the state.[7] Indeed, hypocrisy and secrecy even about *holding* such theories has been recommended to rulers seeking to increase their power by questionable means.

Both the esoteric rationale for government secrecy and the more general justification of the reason of state have been invoked to defend the exercise of state power, and at times to ward off criticism of abuses so grave that nothing else could be said in their favor. To the extent that rulers become convinced of their rightful freedom from oversight and from ordinary moral constraints, they grow predictably more corrupt and exploitative. But the two doctrines also respond to the genuine dilemmas so many rulers have faced, in which they have had to choose between two evils in order to ensure the survival of their state.

These doctrines are now rarely defended in their original form, in part because of their obvious invitation to abuse, and in part because of the difficulty of arriving at acceptable new moral standards to replace the ordinary ones. But the question remains whether government gives stronger reasons for secrecy and for transgressing moral norms in the interest of the state.[8] And the primordial sense of government secrecy and power that these doctrines expressed has not diminished. Government leaders still rely on it; and secular state religions draw on it through the veneration of constitutions and of wartime and revolutionary leaders, sharing thereby their aura of distance and sacredness.[9] The more thoroughly government leaders control secrecy and openness, the more they resort to ritual and hierarchy to reinforce such an aura.

In this way, the esoteric rationale for such control may still help subdue and overawe the inhabitants of a state. It rarely has the same effect, however, on outsiders and potential enemies, who do not share the presumption of a regime's special legitimacy or sacredness. Toward them, military secrecy is therefore also invoked. Nor does the esoteric rationale even suffice to legitimate secrecy internally, once the public grows suspicious of secrecy and presses for more open government.

Bentham's plea for publicity, and his claim that "without publicity, no good is permanent; under the auspices of publicity, no evil can continue," is, to my knowledge, the strongest challenge to administrative secrecy in print.[10] It must be seen against the background of a society still as riddled with secret governmental practices as England in the eighteenth century. Yet when phrased so starkly, it cannot do justice to the complexity of the issue. Merely to contrast the benefits of publicity with the evils of secrecy is to oversimplify both.

Publicity, first of all, can be used as a tool of injustice and manipulated to skew public opinion. Administrators who leak personal information about political opponents or publish documents to sabotage peace negotiations use publicity in a way that is far from neutral. The "trial by newspaper" may or may not be manipulative, but it is a form of publicity that can be both unfair and invasive. An extreme example of state manipulation of publicity is the show trial, which combines secret violence and pervasive deceit to produce the desired impression in the full glare of public attention. Such publicity differs from the general openness that Bentham had in mind, and is not only not opposed to secrecy but compatible with all its abuses.[11] As Harold Wilenski pointed out with respect to Orwell's *Nineteen Eighty-four*: "If secret surveillance is one half of that nightmare, the Ministry of Truth is the other half." [12]

Just as publicity is not always beneficial, so government secrecy is not always an evil. Among the many kinds of information that modern governments obtain, store, and generate, there are some that nearly all would agree to protect from full publicity. Why should the personnel files of government employees, for instance, be open to the public? Why should the tentative drafts circulated for discussion within an agency be made public, or sensitive explorations of changes in monetary policy, or the vast amount of private information about individuals that the government gathers for tax, welfare, Medicare, and other purposes? Though one may argue about its limits, government secrecy is at times not only legitimate but indispensable: the call for total publicity would ride roughshod over many just claims to secrecy.

Bentham himself set forth three exceptions to the banning of government secrecy: if publicity favors the projects of an enemy, if it hurts innocent persons, or if it inflicts unduly harsh punishment on guilty persons. These three exceptions interweave and together give leeway for a great deal more secrecy than Bentham seems to allow; it was only by phrasing them so succinctly and letting them remain unanalyzed that he could maintain the sharp evaluative contrast between secrecy and publicity.

What circumstances justify government secrecy? In considering Bentham's last two exceptions and possible other ones, we must go beyond the esoteric rationale for such secrecy and examine what I shall call the administrative rationale.

Administrative Secrecy

Even where no outside enemies threaten, and even where appeals to the esoteric rationale for secrecy have dwindled, a degree of secrecy is needed, not only by governments but by all who seek to further the interests of a group. Businesses, schools, courts, labor unions—all need some shelter in order to be able to arrive at choices and to carry them out. The processes of reasoning, planning, accommodation, and choice are hampered if fully exposed from the outset, no matter how great the corresponding dangers of secrecy.

The administrative rationale for control over secrecy and openness extrapolates from the individual's claims to such control in order to protect plans in the making, their implementation, and confidential relationships. It claims the same legitimacy for collective survival and governance, only expanded in scope. Three arguments are made in its support.

According to the first argument, full transparency would cripple choice and policy-making in any administration. A tentative process of learning, of assimilating information, of considering alternatives and weighing consequences, is required in order to arrive at a coherent position. No one begins with a perfectly thought-out policy; it is shaped gradually, often through conflict and deliberation. If administrators had to do everything in the open, they might be forced to express only safe and uncontroversial views, and thus to bypass creative or still tentative ideas. As a result, they might end by assuming hasty and inadequate positions. Chances to learn might be lost; premature closure with respect to difficult issues would become more likely. In order to create a pattern out of chaos and avoid haphazard choices, administrators must be able to consider and discard a variety of solutions in private before endorsing some of them in public; the process of evolving new policies requires a degree of concealment. For these reasons, unfinished drafts and memoranda and bargaining positions in negotiations are often kept secret, though the final statements are not.

Such an argument, then, asserts that rationality and efficiency are served by a measure of secrecy in administration. As the British Francks Committee wrote in 1972, ministers and administrators must, in order to present clear issues to Parliament and to the electorate, be able, in some instances and at some stages, to "argue out all the possibilities with complete frankness and free from the temptation to strike public attitudes."[13]

A second argument supports secrecy also in the implementation of certain plans, in order to provide the crucial element of surprise. As John Jay wrote in *The Federalist*, the executive might sometimes need "perfect *secrecy* and immediate despatch." [14] Through surprise, officials may forestall resistance and eliminate unfair advantages for special groups. Thus criminal investigations conducted in public would hardly combat crime effectively; nor would decisions to devalue currency have the intended force if announced long before they were to take effect.

The third argument supporting the administrative rationale concerns possible injuries to innocent persons from certain kinds of publicity. Administrators become privy to personal information provided by, for instance, taxpayers, students, or job applicants. If a government agency requests personal information, it assumes obligations of confidentiality toward those who provide it. Likewise, if officials probe into private matters, as in conducting tax audits, they should not release information thus acquired that turns out to be unrelated to the problem under investigation.

Few would quarrel with the need for at least a minimum of administrative secrecy based on these three arguments, invoking the protection of deliberation, surprise, and confidentiality. The differences arise, rather, in actual practice, and in deciding how much secrecy the arguments justify. Regardless of the prevailing laws, tension is incessant in most societies over the legitimacy and extent of government secrecy.

For coercive governments, secrecy is essential to every aspect of the exercise of power. These regimes combine control over secrecy with equal control over what becomes public. But secrecy also becomes the central means of resistance and survival for those who oppose such regimes, whether actively or merely in thought. From childhood on, these citizens surreptitiously learn how to reinterpret propaganda, read between the lines, resist indoctrination, evade the secret police.

In more open societies, some of the same controls over secrecy are at times openly proposed, at times introduced by stealth. But the question of secrecy is at least itself out in the open, and at the center of debate concerning the uses of propaganda, indoctrination, censorship, executive privilege, police practices, and state power more generally. As the state grows more complex, handling more information, reacting with greater immediacy to threats from within and without, having to cope with interlocking problems of finance, foreign policy, and defense, administrators seek ever greater protection from interference. Consequently, they come in increasing conflict with those who argue that, in being deprived of information, they are also effectively deprived of genuine participation.[15]

Every government has an interest in concealment; every public, in greater access to information. In this perennial conflict, the risks of secrecy affect even those administrators least disposed at the outset to exploit it. How many leaders have not come into office determined to work for more open government, only to end by fretting over leaks, seeking new, safer ways to classify documents, questioning the loyalty of outspoken subordinates. Max Weber noted that every bureaucracy tries to increase the superiority of the professionally informed by keeping their knowledge and intentions secret.[16] Concealment insulates administrators from criticism and interference; it allows them to correct mistakes and to reverse direction without costly, often embarrassing explanations; and it permits them to cut corners with no questions being asked.

Because secrecy has these advantages for administrators, it spreads within agencies and executive departments, and in so doing, invites imitation and retaliation. Prying may then become more common, secret groups form in response, and suspicion grow. Leaks from within may be manipulated by high officials or reflect dissent by subordinates. Security measures proliferate; being vulnerable, they often fail; and so the moves and countermoves continue.

Such a tendency for administrative secrecy to spread increases the chances of abuse, especially among officials with a strong sense of mission and of being above ordinary moral considerations. When a government develops secret police powers or control over censorship, the risks are even greater. Secrecy can then become an end in itself, creating subtle changes in those who exercise it, in how they see themselves, and in their willingness to manipulate and coerce in order to uphold the secrecy and thus shield themselves. To the extent that they have used the cover of secrecy to commit crimes, they reach out for ever greater protection.

Some administrators dismiss public concern about government secrecy as overdrawn. They may agree that secrecy carries dangers, but argue that in their own agencies, or even the entire government, openness is the rule. If they are sincere in making such claims, they ignore much that should be obvious to them; more often, they use these claims as a fallback position in defense of existing practices of concealment, meant to defuse attacks on government secrecy by pointing out the exaggerated fears that motivate them. A few even leak secrets or pseudo-secrets in order to demonstrate just how impossible it is to keep anything secret for long in government.

Robert Goodin has made a more general claim to that effect, arguing that secrecy in government should give very little cause for concern.[17] Secrets, he holds, "are likely to leak out fairly promptly," and may be used against holders of power as well as by them; as a result, secrecy does not pose much of a threat in political life. Such an argument is untenable on empirical grounds. The evidence of large-scale administrative secrecy is overwhelming in police investigations, in classified research, and in executive deliberations, as well as in the concealment of political corruption and fraud. In addition, the argument relies on a fallacy: when pointing to the leak of any one secret, or to its discovery, as proof that secrecy in government presents little cause for concern, Goodin slips from single cases to entire practices. But the mere claim that secrets are likely to leak out fairly promptly tells us nothing about the persistence of *practices* of secrecy, nor about their danger. And even those short-lived secrets—say, about a planned government purge or an invasion of a neutral state—may be precisely the kind that publicity could otherwise force into the arena of public deliberation before it is too late.[18]

The belief that government secrecy is either nonexistent or insignificant is as erroneous—and dangerous—as similar notions with respect to science or industry. We should not let it persuade us to dismiss questions about the ethics of practices of secrecy, but weigh, instead, the arguments in favor of these practices against the risks they carry for the administrative process, for administrators, and for all who participate in government secrecy or experience its effects.

In such a weighing, a question of priority arises from the very outset. Should there be a presumption in favor of secrecy or of openness? All regulation of government secrecy must opt for one or the other—declaring secrecy, in effect, guilty until proved innocent, or vice versa.[19]

A small but growing number of countries have opted for a modicum of openness. Their laws require public access to government information, with certain exceptions for matters having to do, for example, with national security or with crime prevention. Among them, Sweden has the longest tradition of government openness: its Freedom of the Press Act of 1766 gives all citizens the right to inspect and to reproduce official documents. In the United States, the Freedom of Information Act was passed by Congress in 1966 and strengthened in 1974, in order to promote disclosure of government information. Neither in Sweden nor in the United States have these acts done away with administrative secrecy; but they have provided access to many documents that would otherwise have remained out of reach, and they have given statutory support to the principle of openness.

The majority of nations have no such laws at all, and many have provisions for extensive government secrecy, with certain limited exceptions. Thus England provides no citizen rights to access to government documents; and its Official Secrets Act of 1911 would, if taken literally, make it possible to accuse officials of a criminal offense who disclose even trivial government information. The act has never been applied so stringently, but it nevertheless has contributed to official caution and to a climate of administrative secretiveness; and it has fostered apprehension on the part of citizens and the press about whether or not to probe into topics the government wishes to shield.[20]

While the laws of different societies show a presumption either for or against government secrecy, they do not always offer guidance with respect to the actual practices of secrecy or openness. The most secretive authoritarian regimes may have impeccably democratic constitutions allowing in principle for perfect openness. And even in societies where laws guaranteeing access to government documents are enforced in an atmosphere of government accountability, many subtle ways can be found to diminish their power. In addition, such laws function alongside a number of influences on the flow of information in courts, legislatures, and investigative bodies, not to mention a variety of claims to executive privilege. The contexts of different traditions of press freedom, of public participation in government, and of government control over information, moreover, all contribute to influencing the effect of laws of public access.

No matter what these side influences, I believe that a guarantee of public access to government information is indispensable in the long run for any democratic society. When such a guarantee is enforced, it changes the public's view of what it has a right to expect and reduces the hesitation that government officials otherwise feel about whether or not to disclose information. It works against the inevitable tendency of government secrecy to spread and to invite abuses; and it provides an avenue for publicity that is more than mere public relations. Otherwise, if officials make public only what they want citizens to know, then publicity becomes a sham and accountability meaningless. As John Stuart Mill asked, how, without publicity, could citizens either "check or encourage what they were not permitted to see?" [21]

All societies that prize citizen access to government decisions ought therefore to reject an official secrets act, or any other law that places the presumption in favor of secrecy. No matter how innocuous such an act may seem, or how little it may be enforced at any particular time, it is inherently undesirable. It can function well only in the rare society that enjoys full and deserved trust in its government's ability to judge wisely what matters ought and ought not to be kept secret. In any other system, legislation resembling the Swedish Freedom of the Press Act or the United States Freedom of Information Act is needed. Such legislation will need tailoring and improvements to function well. It will work best if government *and* citizens reduce the kinds and the amounts of information under dispute: if government agencies request less information of a personal or sensitive nature, and therefore have less to keep secret; and if those who channel information through government agencies—individuals and businesses, for example—reconsider what they think must be kept secret on their behalf.

Above all, such laws can serve the public well only if the exceptions to them are kept to a minimum and are prevented from expanding. Otherwise, the laws may turn out to reinforce government secrecy rather than diminish it. The most common exceptions, even in societies most insistent on public access to government documents, have to do with internal agency memoranda, tax records, crime control, diplomacy, and national defense. But disagreements arise as to how much these exceptions should cover and what limitations, if any, should be placed upon them.

In the United States, this debate focuses on the nine categories of exceptions to the Freedom of Information Act.[22] These exemptions cover, first of all, a vast array of classified national defense and foreign affairs secrets. In addition, purely internal management matters, income tax returns, trade secrets, advice, agency memoranda, medical and personnel files, investigatory files, bank examination records, and certain mineral geology data are covered.

These exceptions are formidable, and allow considerable scope for maneuver. On the one hand, they have hardly removed the need for concern over government secrecy. Critics see the act as still protecting too much. They rightly view with alarm efforts to expand the number and scope of the exempt categories. Others, on the contrary, find the act inadequate in that it safeguards too little. They maintain that criminals, spies, and business pirates use the act to exploit the government's inability to keep records private; and hold that, because requests for information are often of a general nature, the government goes to great expense simply to perform the searches needed to provide all the documents requested. The strongest criticism of the act concerns the threat to national security that some think it poses; these critics hold up the British Official Secrets Act as preferable. The very act that is castigated in Great Britain as outmoded, and as sheltering inefficiency and government manipulation, is sometimes regarded in the United States as a way to return control to the government and thus to reduce its indiscriminate scattering of information to all comers.

For the reasons I have mentioned, a shift back to anything resembling an official secrets act would be unwise and dangerous. And in a climate of polarization and heightened international tensions, the Freedom of Information Act will require increasingly forceful public support if it is to escape piecemeal dismantling.[23] Few tasks are more important than to lend such support. There should be a strong presumption against government control over secrecy because of the abuses it can conceal, the power governments exercise, and their special obligations of accountability. Government secrecy must therefore be even more carefully limited than the other practices that I have discussed. The exceptions providing for secrecy must never be allowed to expand without careful public scrutiny; and every effort must be made to consider possible forms of openness even in practices traditionally veiled in secrecy. Consider the differences, in this respect, between two such practices: the conduct of diplomatic negotiations and the use of disinformation to damage and discredit adversaries.

Negotiations

Open covenants of peace openly arrived at, with no secret international agreements in the future.
PRESIDENT WOODROW WILSON, 1918,
First of *Fourteen Points*

Had we not had secrecy, had we not had secret negotiations with the North Vietnamese, had we not had secret negotiations prior to the Soviet summit, had we not had secret negotiations over a period of time with the Chinese leaders, let me say quite bluntly, there would have been no China initiative, there would have been no limitation of arms for the Soviet Union and no summit, and had we not had that kind of security and that kind of secrecy that allowed for this kind of exchange that is essential, you men would still be in Hanoi rather than Washington today.
PRESIDENT RICHARD NIXON, speaking in May 1973
to prisoners of war returned from Vietnam

These two contradictory positions span the claims for and against secrecy in negotiations. They are ironical, in view of the careers of the two presidents—flung in the face of a world each may have well seen, by the time he spoke, as perversely intent on self-destructive error with respect to secrecy. Woodrow Wilson could not carry out his own promises of openness in government; and his call for openness in international negotiations was made in protest over the secret agreements about how to divide wartime spoils that he knew the Allied Powers had concluded while the war was still in progress. His Fourteen Points were accepted, and yet the negotiations that ensued were conducted with unprecedented secrecy.[24] Richard Nixon's efforts to exert control over both secrecy and publicity (and to record his communications in secret with the aim of later revelation) ended by destroying his presidency.[25] His years in office illustrate the dangers of seeking excessive control over secrecy and publicity in government: dangers that this control will corrupt officials, thwart choice, conceal abuses, elicit imitation and retaliation, and breed fear and suspicion on all sides.

Does some such control nevertheless have a place when it comes to negotiation? Does a degree of secrecy allow negotiation and bargaining a greater chance of success? It is often necessary, first of all, for negotiators to conceal their aims and hopes for the outcome; such secrecy cannot be wiped out, nor is it morally problematic so long as both sides in the negotiation take for granted that all the cards are not on the table from the beginning. Deception in the service of such secrecy is another matter; but the secrecy in its own right, as well as the effort to consider what the other parties to the negotiation might be concealing, is such that no sensible negotiator would give it up. In his essay "Of Negotiating," Francis Bacon recommended that, "in dealing with cunning persons, we must ever consider their ends to interpret their speeches; and it is good to say little to them, and that what they least look for." [26]

A further question of secrecy, and that about which Wilson and Nixon disagreed, has to do with concealment, not so much of one's thoughts from other negotiators, but of the negotiations themselves from the public and the press. Can widely different interests be reconciled if all bargaining has to be done in the full light of publicity at all times? This question arises in all types of negotiation: between the representatives of workers and employers, in bargaining and log-rolling of all kinds, and in the deliberations of states and nations. When their debates are secret, negotiators often reach an accord with one another at the expense of persons or groups absent; such was the case for the European populations whose fates were decided and the boundaries of whose states were redrawn in 1814–1815 at the Congress of Vienna. When entirely open, on the other hand, negotiations can issue in a deadlock, and publicity prevent disputing groups from arriving at any decision whatever.

Consider the debates over the secrecy with which the United States Constitutional Convention of 1787 was conducted. Convened to propose only minor changes in the Articles of Confederation (which allowed the United States no executives, no courts, and no power to tax), the delegates created, instead, a new constitution.[27] Many saw secrecy as a prerequisite for this achievement, given the hostile groups that would have fought any agreement had they known about the proposed changes. Among the first rules the members of the convention adopted were:

That no copy be taken of any entry on the Journal during the sitting of the House without leave of the House.

That members only be permitted to inspect the Journal.

That nothing spoken in the House be printed, or otherwise published, or communicated without leave.[28]

The citizens at large were completely excluded from the deliberations. Neither press nor official communiqués informed them about what was under debate. Without such secrecy, James Madison later argued, no constitution would ever have been adopted. But Thomas Jefferson, unable to attend because he was serving as minister to France, wrote in a letter to John Adams:

I am sorry they began their deliberations by so abominable a precedent as that of tying up the tongues of their members. Nothing can justify this example but the innocence of their intentions, and ignorance of the value of public discussion.[29]

By now, government negotiations, internal and external, have proliferated. In the United States, moreover, different groups are proposing a new constitutional convention, again suggesting that only limited changes be made; and in other societies, conventions are meeting to draw up a new or a revised constitution. It is easy, therefore, to put ourselves in the place of the members meeting in 1787 and to ask, though with the benefit of hindsight, what degree of secrecy we would now choose for our debates.

The arguments for secrecy in such deliberations are of two kinds. In the first place, those who participate may desire confidentiality about their tentative positions, their drafts and explorations with others. Their claim to confidentiality draws on the individual's need for leeway in unfinished projects and for freedom from uninterrupted surveillance.

Similarly, persons whose affairs are taken up in the negotiations may wish to claim confidentiality much as they would in private negotiations. And other parties to the debates, even adversaries, may expect such confidentiality about their own explorations in return for offering it to all participants. Among diplomats and other negotiators, discretion requires the capacity to keep such confidences, not one's own alone, but those of opponents and allies alike.

The second argument derives from the rationale for administrative secrecy. It holds that a group is less likely to reach a coherent internal position unless it has a chance to explore tentative, even unlikely alternatives; that it cannot easily maintain a united position in delicate matters without pressure from special-interest groups and sabotage from opponents unless it has such a chance; and that it cannot easily negotiate with other groups without a process of trial and error, of proposal and counterproposal, of persuasion and bargaining and sometimes threat. Publicity, this argument holds, tempts participants to rigidity and to posturing, increasing the chances either of a stalemate in which no compromise is possible, or alternatively, of a short-circuited and hasty agreement. To pull back from an opening offer, often made for bargaining purposes only, might be interpreted, if done in full public view, as giving in.

These arguments have weight, but only up to a point. Confidentiality is not always appropriate for secrets of negotiation, first of all, any more than for all others, and participants may come to regret the leeway it offers: for this reason, it is not always right to promise or imply confidentiality for the secrets of others, in negotiation as in other relationships. Likewise, the administrative rationale for secrecy is not always persuasive. Many groups succeed in deliberating publicly without the negative consequences conjured up by this rationale. The fear of being watched is often simply irrational; for most it evaporates after a short exposure to public debate. The passage of "sunshine laws" has obliged many groups to negotiate and arrive at decisions in public. They have often been surprised not to encounter the predicted decline in spontaneity and in willingness to speak tentatively, nor have they experienced the short-circuiting or stalemate.

Certain circumstances, however, do make such difficulties likely and increase the need for secrecy. If the negotiators have more to gain from being approved by their own sides than by making a reasoned agreement with competitors or adversaries, then they are inclined to "play to the gallery," with the result that short-circuiting or stalemate is more likely. John Dunlop has pointed out that the harder the issue under negotiation, the greater the temptation becomes for negotiators to please their own constituents at the expense of the public good. He has concluded that negotiations are not fruitfully concluded in public:

Indeed, an indication that negotiators may be serious about reaching a settlement or be willing to explore their problems in earnest is signaled when they exclude the press and refrain from press comment. . . .[30]

If the public exposure is selectively magnified by the media, all the difficulties multiply. Often the media, and especially television, will select a brief, dramatic moment from the debates, which can skew the public's understanding of the ongoing negotiations. The chances of biased public responses are thereby increased, and this in turn can damage the negotiations, most of all in intense and highly publicized debates, such as some of those in the United Nations Security Council.

Dag Hammarskjöld's career as secretary general of the United Nations illustrates the changes that may result from experiencing such pressures. He took his post hoping to uphold Wilsonian ideals of openness; but he came increasingly to defend what he called "quiet diplomacy," believing that it allowed progress where "frozen diplomacy" practiced in public served merely to score propaganda victories.[31] In 1956, Hammarskjöld gave a speech on Woodrow Wilson, asking how he would have reacted to present developments in the United Nations. He concluded that although Wilson had been the spokesman for "open covenants openly arrived at"—for democracy in international negotiation—he would not have approved all of the applications made of that sound principle:

Knowing too well the ways of man to believe in his ability to resist selfish or short-sighted public pressures, he would certainly have found it appropriate to plead for a combination of the new methods of diplomacy of which he was in favor, with such of those time-honored political techniques as would give us the result best serving the interests of peace.[32]

Hammarskjöld himself, however, never made quite clear by what criteria he decided when to use each approach. He repeatedly stressed the importance of allowing public servants to do their work without what he called "back-seat driving" by press and public, pointing out that the driver, after all, sees much more clearly what lies ahead than the passengers in the back seat. It is an understandable view; but the perspective of those being driven about must not be forgotten. The flexibility of quiet diplomacy is needed at times; but the burden of proof should be on those who argue for secrecy. And the secrecy should be limited, even then, in a number of ways.

First, it is generally preferable that there be no secrecy about the *fact* that negotiations are under way. While early hints and signals of a willingness to conduct talks may be too ephemeral or fragile to publicize, the talks themselves, once instituted, should usually be made public. This is important not only for internal consumption but for relations with outsiders. Thus the Nixon-Kissinger secrecy about the overtures to China succeeded in presenting a *fait accompli* at home; but it hurt and surprised the Japanese, who had been kept in the dark in spite of their clear interest in knowing about such a development. True, public emotions on opposite sides of a conflict—in the Middle East, for example— may be so inflamed that any disclosure about ongoing talks risks undercutting the chances of success. Even in such cases, while initial secrecy may be needed, it carries its own risks: it tempts governments to keep up their hostile stance for internal political reasons while they negotiate, and thus renders genuine agreement more difficult.

Second, it is best that there be no secrecy about who the parties to the negotiations are. Whether they be individuals or companies or representatives of states or emissaries of parties, it is important for the public to have knowledge of who they are and what they represent. The Bay of Pigs debacle was caused, in part, by the fact that the government of the United States had entered into negotiations with exiles from Cuba in secret, and had planned the invasion without allowing the American public to participate in the decisions regarding such a venture. The temptation is strong to negotiate in secret with a faction within a foreign country: perhaps a junta that is about to take over or to be toppled, or a political party one hopes will be more friendly than others to one's position. Yet the indignation that follows upon the discovery of such secret talks, both at home and abroad, bespeaks the sense of unfairness that they arouse.

These two conditions are preferable. But are constituents or their representatives legitimately *entitled* to anything more than reviewing the results of negotiations and deciding whether or not to ratify them? If not, why should they not simply wait for the results of negotiations, however secretly undertaken and conducted, and decide for themselves? Such an argument will appeal only to those who have full confidence that those who negotiate on their behalf will not seek to manipulate their ratification and present them belatedly with alternatives leaving them no genuine choice.

No matter what is preferred with respect to the secrecy or openness of ongoing negotiations, however, a third criterion is crucial: there should be no secrecy about the terms of the settlement agreed upon.

While there may have to be seclusion for the talks themselves (given the two qualifications I have listed above), their results must be open to debate and ratification. The temptation here is for governments or other parties to submit to ratification only those aspects of an agreement that they think their constituents will accept, and to make additional deals secretly. Wilson's insistence that there be "no secret international agreements in the future" spoke precisely to this issue.

Without these three limitations on "quiet diplomacy," Hammarskjöld's distinction between the driver and the "back-seat drivers" in the media and among the public is a dangerous one, for it tempts leaders to assume prerogatives the public would not grant them freely. True, full openness would doom many fragile talks. Yet without accountability and public control, secret negotiations like all practices of secrecy in government go against democratic principles. As a result, they call for special safeguards.

Disinformation

In the fall of 1981, reports of a mysterious Libyan "hit squad" began to circulate in the news media. Members of the squad had allegedly been sent to assassinate President Reagan and other top United States officials. The reports were finally confirmed by the State Department, and unusual security precautions were undertaken. But the Libyans accused the United States government of spreading false and defamatory rumors. Later, French officials were quoted as saying that the scare had resulted from an elaborate Soviet disinformation scheme. They claimed it was designed to trap the Reagan administration into attacking Libya, thus drawing world attention away from the military takeover in Poland. Still others wondered if the French reports constituted disinformation in their own right.

"Disinformation" is a neologism that stands for the spreading of false information to hurt adversaries. Common in wartime, and increasingly used by contending secret service networks even in peacetime, it now flourishes in the media, as governments try to influence public opinion against one another and against domestic adversaries. That particular news items are false often goes unnoticed by the reading public and media representatives alike; but when conflicting stories circulate, or accusations of disinformation are voiced, suspicion is natural, however difficult it may be to know just which side is spreading the falsehoods.

Such planted news items differ from the larger accusations governments level at one another—of imperialism, godlessness, or barbarous conduct—in that they concern specific events. The stories could not achieve their effect without secrecy—about their falsity, but above all about their source. Consider the full-page advertisement that major American newspapers published in July 1982, condemning Israel's invasion of Lebanon in forceful language and purportedly signed by six international relief agencies. The following day, these agencies disclaimed the signatures, pointing out that they do not take public positions in conflicts where they attempt to be of service, but offer aid to all who are in need. On checking, the newspaper editors found that the postal address given in the advertisement was false, and that they had no clue as to the originators of the statement. Had it been meant to encourage condemnation of Israel pure and simple? Or to lead, after the expected disclaimers by the relief agencies, to public distrust of the Palestinian sympathizers many concluded were responsible for placing the advertisement? Or, more generally, to confuse the debate over the war, hampering peace negotiations and making potential signers of similar statements, as well as readers, more wary in the future?

The stakes are high in the international and domestic conflicts that give rise to disinformation. Does this fact render such practices more justifiable than "the dust of the evil tongue" that Maimonides deplored in rumor-mongering? [33] Might one argue that there are times of national crisis so threatening that disinformation becomes a legitimate tactic against adversaries? [34] James Q. Wilson has raised this question in considering whether FBI agents should ever be asked to spread malicious gossip or to write anonymous letters to embarrass members of certain groups.

One's immediate instinct is to condemn such acts as contemptible, as indeed they are. But that does not cover the matter. Granted that they are dirty tricks, are they always inappropriate applied to any organization under any circumstances? Against the Soviet secret police? Against an illegal conspiracy bent on terrorist bombings, such as the Weather Underground? . . . But if there are circumstances in which one might reasonably contemplate authorizing such acts, there obviously should be some effort to define, in the most limiting manner, what those circumstances might be. For most of its history, the Bureau did not devote much effort to that issue. [35]

The argument that threatening circumstances might justify limited forms of disinformation to counter either internal or external enemies presupposes, first of all, that there is some advantage to be derived from these acts. Yet it is difficult to find evidence of any real benefit. "Disinformation specialists" may have confidence in the efficacy of such distortion. And their motives for resorting to it are understandable, since they are themselves so often at the receiving end of similar efforts on the part of their adversaries. But studies of rumors show little evidence that they can be guided; once they are planted, they take on a life of their own and reverberate back, as often as not, to embarrass the originators.[36] And the more a government agency or other group is known to generate false information, the more often it will be suspected of having done so, even when it is not responsible for a particular flurry of allegedly false rumors. To the extent that an agency's responsibility can be proved, moreover, its credibility will be impaired.

Furthermore, no matter how sinister the members of a group, they will have a sense of righteous indignation when they learn that they have been maligned in such a way. This will hardly dispose them to improve their own methods; on the contrary, they will retaliate in kind, and accusations and counteraccusations will fly. Therefore, while false rumors may at times secure a short-term advantage over an adversary, the long-run consequences are likely to be self-defeating, and not such as to confer legitimacy upon practices otherwise regarded as "dirty tricks."

But assume that the short-term benefit of such a scheme is tempting, that secrecy renders discovery difficult, and that the adversary is likely to be so hampered as to be unable to retaliate. Might there not then be strong reasons for going ahead? Even so, a larger risk argues against the scheme: the cumulative injury to the system of communication in which all nations, no matter how hostile, have a stake. As Robert Jervis has written, a state that practices deceit does harm to such a general international system; and it may be very hard for a complex system to survive if the level of deception is too high.[37]

The secrecy with which disinformation is manufactured and planted adds to the likelihood that governments will resort to it, and thus contributes to the collective risk.[38] Secrecy allows nations to operate as free riders to the detriment of the communication system on which they must continue to depend. Each year we witness new accusations and suspicions of disinformation. They signal injury to an already defective and vulnerable system of public communication. The deterioration of political discourse and of public trust in official pronouncements is usually not intended, but it could easily have been foreseen.[39] It adds to the difficulty, for governments and citizens alike, of knowing when a message can be trusted. This uncertainty undercuts the chances of peace negotiations and increases the likelihood of further reciprocal resorts to "dirty tricks."

Few government uses of secrecy are so uncontrolled, even in democracies, as the manufacture and dissemination of false reports to hurt adversaries. Compare these practices with diplomatic negotiations, in which the identity of the negotiators is known, the issues are publicly framed, and the agreements, once reached, are open to ratification. One can hardly argue that practices of disinformation require more shelter from accountability because they are more necessary or of greater benefit to nations resorting to them. On the contrary, it is hard to think of any other form of government secrecy of such dubious benefit to individual societies, yet so capable of damaging nations collectively. All states would benefit from a de-escalation of such activities; each has the strongest reasons for submitting its own role in this respect to public oversight.

Chapter XIII

Military Secrecy

Confounding One's Enemies

The contradictions and tensions of secrecy are never stronger than in the military stance of nations. On the one hand, every state requires a measure of secrecy in order to defend itself against enemy forces. The legitimacy of such secrecy in self-defense is clear-cut; and the weaker the state, the more indispensable its reliance on surprise and stratagems. But on the other hand, secrecy is as often a weapon in the hands of the aggressors and an aid in every scheme of oppression. Because it is used, moreover, for takeovers and control within nations as much as between them, it is dangerous for every state that must rely on it for protection. And since military secrets have to be kept from the state's own citizens in order not to reach its enemies, citizens lose ordinary democratic checks on precisely those matters that can affect them most strongly. As Thomas Jefferson pointed out, citizens do assume they have a right to full information about the possibility of a war: "It is their sweat which is to earn all the expenses of the war, and their blood which is to flow in expiation of the causes of it." [1]

Can these contradictions be overcome or even diminished? It is hard to think of a political effort more urgent, given the perils that seem both to call for military secrecy and to increase its power to injure. In order to consider what its proper limits might be, we must first examine the rationale for military secrecy and the reasons for the special ease with which this rationale so often eludes ethical inquiry.

At the root of the rationale for military secrecy is the imperative of self-preservation. Many religious and philosophical traditions take it to be the most fundamental characteristic of living beings. They hold secrecy (and force, if need be) especially natural and legitimate when undertaken to preserve one's life. Without such secrecy, there may be no shelter from assault, no way to guard oneself, one's plans, one's actions or property against aggressors. The rationale for military secrecy, grounded in self-preservation and fundamental to the protection of everything of value in human lives, can be employed to justify both individual and collective secrecy. But it is more commonly used for collective secrecy, since individuals cannot usually defend themselves alone against military attack. And because a degree of military secrecy is so fundamental to survival, it can call on greater sacrifices than all other rationales for secrecy.

The undeniable force of the appeal to military secrecy in promoting national security can make moral questions about its drawbacks and dangers seem inconsequential by comparison. Three factors—psychological avoidance, language, and moral argumentation—help undercut such questions still further.

Strong forces of avoidance, first of all, work to blunt the impact of the reality of war, and especially of war in the nuclear age. Genuine ignorance combines with a pervasive fear of facing the threat of nuclear war to produce psychological numbing, rationalization, and denial: together these shield people against the thought of war, though hardly against war itself.

These forces influence the way we speak about military matters. Indeed, the mere recourse to military metaphors can deflect moral questions, even in circumstances quite devoid of threats to survival. Military metaphors come easily whenever secrecy is at issue; they are perhaps more common than all others.* Thus, in talking of the protection of

---

*It is not surprising that military language comes so easily in all talk of secrecy, since it reflects not only the interpersonal but also the intergroup conflicts over secrecy. Sexual metaphors are almost as common in conveying interpersonal conflicts over secrecy. These metaphors convey the relationships between self and other, between unique and shared experience. They provide much of the force and directness of the language used by mystics, and of all discourse on intimacy sought and withheld, with its capacity not only to create but to consume.

secrets, references are made to defense and fortifications, to camouflage and shields and protective ruses, to sanctuaries sought and strongholds lost, to retreat, surrender, and standing fast. Similarly, in describing assaults on secrecy, the language may be one of strategy and tactics, of diversionary attacks, espionage, and infiltration.

Such metaphors often convey an accurate picture of the hostilities at play, but may also trivialize them from a moral point of view, making them appear as power struggles pure and simple. When social scientists infiltrating religious sects borrow such language to describe their methods, for example, it gives them one more way to avert questions of justification. This is doubly true when military metaphors are used about *military* practices of secrecy and probing—especially in the context of the otherwise oddly indirect and abstract jargon used by defense analysts around the world. The very language that describes questionable practices of secrecy then helps to shield them.

A third factor that aids in deflecting moral questions about military secrecy is its links to the circumstances of war, in which it is difficult, some say impossible, to adhere to moral standards. As a slogan "All's fair in love and war" may be excessive—neither love nor war can legitimate atrocities—and yet it bespeaks the rejection of ordinary notions of fairness at times of intense conflict that Machiavelli and many others have expressed. They have argued that fairness and beneficence and honesty are misplaced concerns when survival is at issue, and that nations must see to their own safety in ways that may well require setting aside moral standards.[2]

While such arguments point persuasively to the special difficulties of living up to moral ideals in wartime, they do not show that moral considerations can be set aside in dealing with enemies. Many military circumstances offer no threat whatsoever to survival, and present diplomatic and military alternatives that can be compared from a moral point of view. And even when survival is at stake, the choices made—of how to treat civilians, for example, or of weapons or of means of concealment—obviously differ from a moral point of view. Even those who refuse to consider the effects of their actions on enemies, and take into account only the strictest national self-interest, would benefit from weighing these differences; for aggression and brutality abroad, whether openly or secretly carried out, have profound effects not only on the personnel asked to participate but on citizens at home. No nation can escape the burden of living with the results of clearly immoral or even questionable choices made in wartime. And with the advent of the nuclear balance of terror, it is less possible than ever for leaders of a state to assume that the destruction planned for their adversaries will not also lay waste their own territory.

The forces of avoidance, the trivializing or brutalizing use of language, and the argument insulating war from moral inquiry serve us poorly. They should not persuade us to stop asking about the justification for what nations do in the name of survival. Many have, indeed, followed Grotius and Kant in pursuing such inquiries. Curiously enough, they have not, in so doing, analyzed the role of military *secrecy* with the same care that they have devoted to the uses of force and deceit. And even those who have written most penetratingly about government secrecy have often pulled back from treating military secrecy. Bentham himself, who spoke so forcefully against the evils of government secrecy, conceded without further analysis that publicity should be suspended when it was calculated "to favor the projects of an enemy." [3]

In speaking thus, Bentham left a large opening in his bulwark against secrecy—one wide enough to permit the re-entry of many of the evils he had been at pains to exclude. The same is true of the United States Freedom of Information Act, which sets forth as its first exemption matters withheld for national security reasons under criteria established by executive order and "properly classified according to an executive order." [4] Measures in most other nations allow equal or greater proportions of secrecy under similar classifications (though of course the nature of the information kept secret varies greatly depending on the size, vulnerability, alliances, and aims of each nation).

There is little that national security cannot come to envelop in secrecy. We have to see the explanation for its extraordinary reach in the self-evidence and sacredness attached to self-defense, achieved by force if need be, but at least with the necessary secrecy; and in the psychological, linguistic, and moral factors that deflect criticism. Yet without criticism, the core of legitimate secrecy cannot be distinguished from its excesses. Under conditions of crisis, when nations feel beleaguered, military secrecy is likely to spread, invite abuse, and undermine the very security it is meant to uphold. The burden of excessive secrecy can be heavy; and the suffering it inflicts, domestically and abroad, may far outweigh even the strict military objectives it was meant to ensure.

Self-Defeating Military Secrecy

Excessive secrecy is often self-defeating even from a strictly military point of view. It can delay, entangle, and undercut military efforts to the detriment of the self-protection governments aim for. For a recent example, consider the helicopter incursion by the United States into Iran in April 1980, the failure of which has been attributed in part to excessive secrecy. A review group established by the Joint Chiefs of Staff studied the rescue mission meant to free American citizens unlawfully imprisoned in Teheran. Surprise was essential to the mission: to ensure it, every security precaution had been taken. The review group concluded:

Many things that, in the opinion of the review group, could have been done to enhance mission success were not done because of OPSEC [Operations Security] considerations. The review group considers that most of these alternatives could have been incorporated without an adverse OPSEC impact had there been a more precise OPSEC plan selectively exercised and more closely integrated with an existing JTF [Joint Task Force] organization.[5]

Secrecy prevented those who planned the mission from seeking sufficient advice during the five-month period that preceded the actual rescue attempt. Likewise, it was in order to maintain the strictest secrecy that members of the task force were each told as little as possible about the mission and that so few helicopters were used. As Zbigniew Brzezinski, President Carter's national security adviser at the time, explained: "The essential element of secrecy and surprise required that the mission be as lean and as closely honed as possible." [6] For the same reason, information was only parceled out to each member according to what he was thought to need to play his particular role. Once the helicopters were under way, flying low across the desert in order to avoid detection by radar, crew members were under such heavy secrecy restrictions that they could not coordinate their activities. According to the official review group:

The helicopter force planned and trained to operate in complete radio silence. Intraflight communication, where possible, was to be done with light signals. The absence of radio communication indicated to the helicopter pilots that all was well and to continue the mission. Subsequently, when helicopter flight became separated in the dust cloud, each separate element lacked vital information. The lead helicopter did not know that #8 had successfully recovered the crew from #6 and continued nor that #6 had been abandoned in the desert. More importantly, after he reversed course in the dust and landed, the lead could not logically deduce either that the other helicopters had continued or that they had turned back to return to the carrier. He did not know when the flight had disintegrated. He could have assumed that they had become separated before he reversed course and unknowingly proceeded. Alternatively, they could have lost sight of him after turning and, mistaking his intentions, continued back to the carrier. Lastly, #5 might have elected to continue had he known that his arrival at Desert One would have allowed the mission to continue and that VMC [visual meteorological conditions] existed at the rendez-vous.[7]

Having to make their way through large dust clouds while coping with engine failures, crew members finally had to abandon the mission on orders from Washington. Had they known more about the project and been able to pool their information, they might have been able to carry on despite the difficult circumstances. While refueling for the return flight, two aircraft collided, causing the death of eight men.

Not mentioned in the official report was secrecy at a different level. Secretary of State Cyrus Vance, known to consider the plan too risky, was kept out of the final decision to proceed with the mission. Secrecy had come to protect the project, not only from disclosure to the Iranians, but from a member of the government critical of it and with the authority to disagree with its execution.

In this way, secrecy directed against military opponents can also come to distort domestic choices. Even from the strictest strategic point of view, considering nothing but national self-defense, secrecy can cause reasoning and planning to go astray. Just as in scientific work secrecy prevents the advancement of knowledge, so in military strategy and tactics it can prevent careful preparation and implementation of projects. In both, it thwarts reasoning: it limits the perception of problems and of alternative ways to approach them, prevents adequate deliberation, and deflects critical feedback, thus restricting choice and decision.

Misapplied or excessive secrecy can be equally dangerous in causing hostile nations to respond inappropriately to one another. This is especially true in situations of approximately equal military strength, as in the current nuclear "balance of terror." If nations overestimate the strength of their adversaries, they may react with an unnecessary and in turn threatening arms buildup; conversely they may, underestimating it, attack.[8]

While all secrecy can thwart reasoning, invite abuse, and spread, military secrecy therefore carries special risks. The need for the security it offers seems so self-evident, and the forces that deflect criticism and efforts to limit it are so strong, that what it conceals and the methods used to ensure it are often taken for granted; yet the combination of these methods with the power that military secrecy now shields can transform individuals and institutions in ways that threaten society more than all other forms of secrecy.

Secrecy, Power, and Transformation

Batter my heart, three-person'd God; for, you
As yet but knock, breathe, shine, and seek to mend;
That I may rise, and stand, o'erthrow me, and bend
Your force, to break, blow, burn, and make me new.
I, like an usurp'd town, to another due,
Labour to admit you, but Oh, to no end,
Reason your viceroy in me, me should defend,
But is captiv'd, and proves weak or untrue.
Yet dearly I love you, and would be loved fain,
But am betroth'd unto your enemy:
Divorce me, untie, or break that knot again,
Take me to you, imprison me, for I
Except you enthral me, never shall be free,
Nor ever chaste, except you ravish me.
JOHN DONNE, *Holy Sonnets*, 14,
cited by Robert Oppenheimer in trying to recall
why he chose the code name "Trinity"
for the test of the first atomic bomb

The means used to guard military secrets may be more elaborate, extensive, and ingenious than most, but they do not differ in kind from those used for other shared secrets. The aims are identical: to limit the number of individuals sharing the secret information; to act upon their loyalty or their fears and thus lessen the chances of betrayal; to store the information safely; to disguise it or transform it by means of special forms of language; to limit it through censorship; to leak false secrets; to provide an overload of information as additional camouflage; and to evade or lie about the secret information if pressed.

Always difficult to maintain, and therefore always prone to deteriorate and spread, such practices are especially vulnerable and problematic in large collectivities. In modern states, the systems of classification, encodement, loyalty tests, and camouflage have grown immensely complex. That they are thereby often self-defeating is hard to deny; but most efforts to cut back on unnecessary or harmful military secrecy meet with the failure of so many assaults on bureaucracy. Mountains of worthless information are stamped Top Secret; levels of secrecy multiply; individuals are scrutinized from the point of view of loyalty even when their work brings them in no contact with secret military information. And still genuine security is out of reach.

These means almost invariably come to be used to conceal ever more, far beyond the original military secrets, especially as more and more kinds of information are perceived as relevant to defense. To insiders, the danger of ill-advised disclosure seems greater than that of ill-advised secrecy. And the appeal to "national security" offers a handy reason to avoid scrutiny of neglect, mistakes, and abuses. As the number of secrets grows, bureaucracies and executives seek the stamp of secrecy to protect themselves, not just the nation. Thus when President Nixon fought to remain in office, he invoked confidentiality and administrative secrecy, but most often and most insistently national security, as reasons for not allowing access to his records and materials.

Military secrecy can therefore expand not only in that it conceals more and more secrets; it can come to be used for purposes of power plays within a society by keeping secrets from additional categories of enemies. The transition from foreign to domestic enemies as persons from whom secrets must be kept is a tempting one for any beleaguered government. In police states this distinction is rarely even made in the first place; internal enemies of the regime are assumed to be conspiring with foreign ones. Personal foes, dissidents, and rivals all fall into this category. And the distinction between keeping secrets *from* enemies and trying to penetrate enemy secrets also blurs at such times; acts, no matter how invasive, may come to seem as legitimate when penetrating secrets as all that is done in defense of them. In all societies there is a danger of such expansion in the category of "enemy" and in the perception of what can rightfully be done to enemies in the name of military secrecy, unless the strictest public control is maintained.

The more secrecy individual states exercise in military matters, the more reason others have to reciprocate. As a result, a cumulative pressure for ever greater secrecy can develop between states, and turn into a "secrecy race" much like an arms race. In such a race, nations are often driven to settle for the lowest common denominator when it comes to restraints on kinds and means of secrecy. In imitation and in retaliation, deceit and coercion on behalf of secrecy may become commonplace, precisely because others are already employing them. Carl Friedrich has argued that secrecy inevitably grows where political systems rival each other; and that police states with their pervasive secrecy have induced other states to respond by ever-growing measures to promote security. As a result, he finds that it has proved exceedingly difficult to keep both secrecy and propaganda within functional limits: "Indeed, they represent at present probably the most serious pathology, at least in free democratic systems." [9]

It is no wonder that military secrecy offers fertile ground for pathological disturbances. The fear of betrayal—seeing enemies everywhere, fearing pervasive conspiracies and hidden designs—flourishes under conditions of external threat between nations. And the secrecy sought in response to such fears begins to seem more and more like a conspiracy in its own right, as it spreads and erodes rationality. Such disturbances are system-wide, as Friedrich noted; but they also affect individuals—most directly those asked to immerse themselves in secrecy in order to carry out the tasks their governments perceive as necesssary for self-protection. As many have testified, the problem is especially severe for those individuals in different societies who work for organizations in which intelligence-gathering encompasses espionage and covert action.[10] To live with secrecy day in and day out, to be aware of a threat both to one's nation and to oneself from a diminution of secrecy, and to be trained to give up ordinary moral restraints in dealing with enemies is an experience that isolates and transforms the participants.

The transformation and isolation that secrecy can lead to are strongest when linked with great power, actual or potential, over others. These forces can be seen working in Robert Oppenheimer and his associates as they struggled to develop the atomic bomb during World War II. The secrecy that surrounded their efforts was at once necessary and debilitating. Isolated in New Mexico, most of the scientists were not told of the scope and aim of the research, though they often guessed. They were asked to disguise the nature of their work in letters to friends and relatives, or to talk in empty terms. Oppenheimer himself wrote in a letter in 1945: "For the last four years I have had only classified thoughts." [11] When looking for a site for the project, he and others used pseudonyms at first; later, townspeople were falsely told that the project had to do with the manufacture of electric missiles.

Without feedback and debate concerning their undertaking, and without day-to-day contact with the rest of the world, the scientists were an easy prey to complete absorption in their task, and to denying or rationalizing away any doubts about their own role. Their isolation, and the power they shared through this most devastating of all secrets, even the sense they describe of having it within their grasp to unleash the most extraordinary physical burst of violence the world had ever seen: these were intoxicating and, for some, utterly corrupting elements.

At the outset, the project was surely in legitimate need of secrecy. The justification for working in secrecy was that of survival—not only of one society, but perhaps of much of civilization. Nazi Germany was threatening destruction and worldwide takeover, and scientists feared that it had begun to develop atomic bombs. The only possible defense appeared to be to do so first, and to threaten Germany, perhaps devastate it, before Hitler could fulfill his intention.

In 1943, however, it became clear that the German effort to develop such bombs had failed. And in May 1945, when Germany finally surrendered, the original justification for continuing with the project had vanished altogether. A number of the scientists who took part in the Los Alamos project have looked back and asked themselves in amazement why they did not at that time reconsider, why they did not leave.[12] Secrecy prevented feedback and criticism from the outside; publicity about the exceptionally important moral decisions affecting the entire world was entirely absent; and the pressures engendered by the moral commitment and the actual circumstances of the war were extraordinarily strong.[13] Secrecy gave the excitement and the sense of uniqueness and power, moreover, that led to the continuation of the project. And it led Oppenheimer, and perhaps others, to the irrational and megalomaniacal belief that by going on to work on the bomb they could make war seem so evil that human beings would reject it forever.[14] The bomb was to save mankind from itself.

In his famous speech to the Los Alamos scientists in November 1945, after their bombs had devastated Hiroshima and Nagasaki, Oppenheimer mentioned the reasons for starting work on such weapons early in the war, and agreed that "these things wore off a little as it became clear that the war would be won in any case." He then listed further reasons for doing the work: curiosity, a sense of adventure, the desire to let the world know about the threat in order to force it to rebel against all war, and a sense that the development of atomic weapons would not have a better a chance anywhere else in the world of leading to a "reasonable solution," nor a smaller chance of leading to disaster, than in the United States. But the fundamental reason, he added, as if in recognition of the disparity between his earlier list and what the bomb had just wrought, was "an organic necessity:"

If you are a scientist you cannot stop such a thing. If you are a scientist you believe that it is good to find out how the world works; that it is good to find out what the realities are; that it is good to turn over to mankind at large the greatest possible power to control the world and to deal with it according to its lights and values.[15]

And then Oppenheimer, himself steeped in secrecy for so many years, argued for openness. It was in the name of openness, and against secrecy, that he claimed the new knowledge had to be revealed. For this reason, he argued, it would be wrong to "attempt to treat science of the future as though it were rather a dangerous thing, a thing that must be watched and managed."

This speech is an extraordinary document of guilt, hopes, and self-defense. Oppenheimer brings in, and mixes together, the various rationales for military and scientific secrecy and openness. But they do not suffice to explain why he went on unquestioningly once the major justification for beginning his work had been removed. Least of all do the noble sentiments in the speech square with Oppenheimer's recommendation that the bombs be used against Japan without warning, thus giving the Japanese no chance to surrender rather than suffer the devastating effects of the bombs.[16] He, who had expended such exceptional care and intelligence on planning, constructing, and testing these weapons, opted for haste in their use—for *not* testing alternatives to having them kill and maim hundreds of thousands of civilians.

Would the outcome have been different if these reasons could have been presented openly before the weapons were used? If their use could have been debated not only by those on one side in the war but by all who would come to live in the shadow of nuclear danger? Perhaps the spread of these weapons could not have been held back long. * But might their actual *use* not have been seen as too inhuman and unprecedented a step for any one nation to take?

The inability to stop for which Oppenheimer adduced so many reasons came in part from the secrecy that he wished to conjure away through the production of his new knowledge, and demonstrates the debilitating effects that secrecy can have on reasoning and moral judgment. The scientists at Los Alamos were in its power, and it had transformed them.

The Role of Public Debate

> One of the most bizarre features of any advanced industrialized society in our time is that the cardinal choices have to be made by a handful of men in secret. . . . men who cannot have a first-hand knowledge of what those choices depend on or what their results may be.

> C.P. SNOW, *Science and Government*

---

*The United States government had chosen to proceed with the development of atomic weapons under conditions of wartime secrecy. But even after the war was over, leaders in the Soviet Union, Britain, France, and China decided to develop such weapons without any public knowledge, much less debate.

By now it is clear that the production of the bomb hardly did away with war; and the proliferation and "improvements" in nuclear weapons make worldwide nuclear war not only possible but likely. Even if no government leader were to initiate an all-out attack, misjudgment or accidental triggering could spark nuclear exchanges that would be difficult, perhaps impossible, to keep from spreading. Under these conditions of unprecedented threat, secrecy regarding plans, research, and military technology is at a premium. How, in that case, is public debate regarding these matters possible?

Many have asked whether the levels of secrecy now thought necessary for national security and the *kinds* of secrets now being kept are compatible with a democratic form of government. Robert Dahl has pointed to the special difficulties that secrecy about atomic energy presents for the democratic process. The destructive potential of what is concealed renders secrecy indispensable; yet elite rule is the inevitable by-product, and irrational policy a likely outcome. The institutionalization of secrecy has resulted, Dahl notes, in the gathering into the hands of a few people "control over decisions of a great magnitude for the values of a larger number of persons than in all probability were ever affected by any old-fashioned authoritarian leader." [17]

How, under such circumstances, can an informed debate and government accountability survive? I find this question the most difficult of all those that secrecy raises. In matters so fundamental to national self-preservation, both secrecy and openness carry risks that may present a genuine impasse. I am not sure that democratic processes *can* persist in the face of current amounts of secrecy, of public ignorance about what should be the public's business above all else, and of the psychological and other forms of avoidance that I have discussed—any more than I have confidence that any society can survive the present arms race with which secrecy has become so inextricably linked.

The difficulty is made greater still by official claims to military secrecy not only for what is kept secret but often also for the reasons justifying the secrecy. The public is asked to take on faith the need for secrecy on the grounds that an open debate of the reasons for such a need might endanger national security. Thus advocates of undercover activities argue that only the failures of such activities come to light, whereas the numerous successes cannot be disclosed without endangering the results obtained. A United States official who recently argued for expanding scientific and commercial secrecy in the interest of national security likewise held that publishing "examples, reasons, and assorted details would certainly damage the nation's interests." He attributed the desire to have the government make its case to a "basic attitude that the government and its public servants cannot be trusted." [18]

But if, as I have argued, there is a strong presumption against government secrecy, such trust should never suffice. Were public debate about the reasons for military secrecy to be silenced by an amalgam of trust on the part of some and avoidance or ineffectual passive distrust on that of others, leaving governments free to operate in secret, then there would be little hope for democracy. But to accept such a development without resistance would be to give up prematurely. Rather, every effort must be made to press public officials to justify their case for secrecy, to produce reasons, and to show why particular practices of concealment are necessary. Neither committees nor legislative groups meeting in secret to oversee clandestine practices offer sufficient guarantees of accountability. Members of the public must be able to question, to bring complaints, and to add information, rather than merely wait to see whether they happen to be called to testify at closed meetings.

In addition, a great deal of information that can serve as a basis for such debates is already in the public domain. There is nothing secret about the links between military secrecy and the arms race, nor about the burdens they impose and the risks they have brought about. Whatever the existing levels of government secrecy, such knowledge calls for response. To point to government secrecy can otherwise be yet another way of shielding against possibilities almost unbearable to contemplate.

The secret practices easiest to combat are those directly harmful even from a military point of view to the nation exercising them. Others are equally injurious indirectly because of their capacity to backfire and to invite abuse. Thus Nicholas Katzenbach has argued that the case against using covert operations to influence political results in foreign countries— such as paying friendly party leaders or trying to damage hostile ones— is so strong that the practice should be abandoned. [19]

Public debate should also examine whether secret government practices are unethical or unlawful or both, and consider whether or not they can be endorsed. To what extent is it right that the secrecy attendant upon the concocting of disinformation, the bribery, or the "destabilization" of other countries form part of the chosen policy of a state? Are its citizens willing to share the responsibility for such a policy? The covert activities a government authorizes bear examining one by one, along with the reasons why they are regarded as necessary.

Among these reasons, the one most frequently voiced is that, while no one would undertake such activities without provocation, they are necessary in order to compensate for similar activities on the part of other states. Such an argument is often exaggerated; but it is undoubtedly true that an atmosphere of competition and retaliation prevents states from giving up otherwise undesirable forms of secrecy.

In such cases, what is needed is a joint dismantling of secrecy among nations: efforts to turn around the secrecy race are as urgent as those to reverse the nuclear arms race.[20] But any "secrecy disarmament talks" will encounter the same problems of mutual mistrust and conflicting interests as nuclear disarmament negotiations. Unilateral abandonment of all military secrecy by any one state is obviously unwise. Is a rejection of secrecy by all nations then the solution? Such a proposal was made for atomic secrecy by Niels Bohr at the end of World War II, as the only workable way to prevent a nuclear arms race and world destruction.[21] Mutual suspicion stood in the way of this proposal; it could work only in the unlikely event that all nations agreed to it. But the goal of shared knowledge can be approached by degrees. Just as with arms limitation talks, the first aim of talks to reduce secrecy should be to stop the efforts to expand military secrecy, followed by detailed provisions for gradual reduction.

In such negotiations, some forms of intelligence-gathering and secrecy will have to be retained as necessary for any nation. Other forms of secrecy will be seen as unavoidable, and possibly beneficial. Thus secrecy concerning the *intentions* of government leaders can never be fully dispelled, unlike secrecy about manpower, weapons, military installations, and research; if it could be, nations would be fully predictable and thus more vulnerable.

Apart from intentions, which can always change and thus never be fully known, much information hitherto cloaked in military secrecy may be easier to share. Recent technological developments have made it possible for nations to know more about one another's troop movements, underground nuclear tests, and similar activities than previously. The capacity for satellite and other surveillance increases year by year, and much that was formerly hidden is today available through open sources.

These new methods may well call forth still more frenzied efforts at secrecy. Nothing guarantees that our societies will cope with the technological advances and political strains. If they mire themselves down in growing secrecy and manipulation of information, there is little hope that they will avert the larger conflicts in which secrecy plays so prominent a part.

But if such efforts are recognized as rear-guard actions doomed to fail in providing genuine security, then it will become possible to consider instead how to derive mutual benefit from reducing secrecy. If so, it will be necessary to sort out the few areas in which openness is either unattainable or injurious. In such a process of evaluation, it is imperative that the costs of secrecy to human beings, to national resources, and to international stability not themselves be concealed.

What can individuals do who arrive at the conclusion that certain military secrets are detrimental to the national interest and should be made public? Should they take it upon themselves to breach secrecy? What factors should they take into account? Such questions confronted Daniel Ellsberg and Anthony Russo as they weighed alternative actions with respect to the Pentagon Papers.*

The Pentagon Papers

Begun in utmost secrecy in 1967 at the request of Robert McNamara, then secretary of defense, the Pentagon Papers were intended to give an account of the United States' involvement in Indochina since before the French fought there in the 1950s.[22] McNamara wanted to provide an accurate history of this involvement. He knew it would expose his own mistakes and his poor judgment in helping to escalate the war; but he wanted the record set straight, and was afraid that crucial documents would no longer be available once the war ended. The study was to be released some time after the end of the war. The task expanded; at the termination of the work on the papers, in June 1969, there were forty-seven volumes.

When Daniel Ellsberg, who had himself worked on the papers in the Defense Department, read them through at the Rand Corporation in 1970, he was shocked. The record of ineptitude, deceit, and concealment was staggering. Successive administrations had misled the American people about the background of the war, and had offered stereotyped explanations for the conflict. American complicity in the plot in 1963 against President Ngo Dinh Diem had been carefully concealed, as had the pervasive duplicity in 1964 preceding and accompanying the buildup of the United States presence in Vietnam: the engineering of the Tonkin

---

*I shall deal primarily with the choice facing Russo and Ellsberg. The Pentagon Papers posed related but by no means identical problems for congressmen and others asked to help make the papers public, for reporters and editors considering whether to publish them, and for the United States Supreme Court weighing a government request for an injunction to prevent the *New York Times* from publishing them.

resolution, the public show of peacefulness during Lyndon Johnson's presidential campaign against Barry Goldwater, and the internal debates concerning massive commitments of American troups and of bombardment. Throughout, as Senator Mike Gravel wrote in the introduction to his 1971 edition of the Pentagon Papers, the documents revealed that "we have created, in the last quarter-century, a new culture, a national security culture, protected from the influences of American life by the shield of secrecy." [23]

Should Ellsberg have attempted to pierce this shield of secrecy? He took for granted that the public had a right to know what had been concealed for so long, but his training as a public servant weighed against revelation. He shared his doubts with Anthony Russo. Together they decided to xerox the documents, carefully covering the Top Secret labels. Then Ellsberg offered copies of the volumes to Senator Fulbright and others, hoping to make them public through these channels. Each time he failed. Finally, he gave copies to Neil Sheehan of the *New York Times*, and their publication began on June 13, 1971.

The debates that ensued brought accusations of treason from some, and praise for self-sacrificing patriotism from others. The critics argued that the two had violated not only administrative secrecy but confidentiality and military secrecy as well, and that they had thereby contributed to the erosion of respect for the processes of government and of law, and to doubts abroad about the solidity of United States foreign policy. Those who supported the move argued, on the contrary, that nothing of military importance had been revealed and that the breach of administrative and military secrecy was necessary in order to expose the evils these had come to cover up and the corrupting growth of secrecy in the country.

The conflict of loyalties Ellsberg describes was sharp; it seemed impossible *not* to betray either his obligations as a civil servant or his conscience and what he believed the public had a right to learn. He knew, first of all, the strong reasons for adhering to the strict secrecy asked of all who had access to the papers. In working on the documents and in borrowing them, Ellsberg had undertaken an obligation not to reveal them. He had not protested at the time the illegitimacy of keeping such matters secret. He knew the importance of loyalty within the government and of standing by his commitments. The doctrine of the "reason of state," moreover, and its contemporary variations, would give reasons to override any personal moral scruples he might have had about what the documents revealed, on the grounds that the moral reasoning involved in governing, and especially in conducting a war, is not reducible to personal morality. Many advocates of realpolitik in and out of government at the time would certainly have downplayed such scruples as naïve and insufficiently hard-headed.

Still another reason might be adduced against the decision to reveal the secrets. Henry Kissinger voices it in explaining why he disapproved of this choice, even though the abuses and errors revealed were not brought about by the Nixon government that he served in 1971 when the papers appeared. Arguing that the purpose of "those who stole the documents" was to "undermine confidence in their government," he saw as the overriding reason for opposing the revelations the fact that "the massive hemorrhage of state secrets was bound to raise doubts about our reliability in the minds of other governments, friend and foe, and indeed about the stability of our political system." [24]

The arguments for breaching secrecy, however, were likewise strong, and it would be simplistic to see in them nothing but a desire to undermine confidence in the government. Against loyalty to the government stood loyalty to the form of government of the United States, and to its foundation of informed choice by the electorate and by their representatives. Ellsberg expressed the need to "find in oneself loyalties long unconsulted, deeper and broader than loyalty to the President: loyalties to America's founding concepts, to our constitutional system, to countrymen, to one's humanity." [25]

The war in Vietnam was already polarizing the country and destroying the prospects of joint efforts to combat poverty and discrimination, disease, and crime. Information about the war could be seen as crucial to the democratic process, and secrecy and deceit about it as injurious to the country and likely to permit further abuse and deterioration—thus, in a larger sense, aiding and abetting the country's enemies and shaking the world's confidence in the values the United States had traditionally stood for.*

Ellsberg intended, further, to assign responsibility for the war: to show that it had resulted from poor choices by particular individuals,

---

*Consider how the same conflicting arguments might have arisen had a French civil servant in the mid-1890s, at the time of the Dreyfus Affair, made a similar choice. What if this civil servant had had access to secret government documents pointing to anti-Semitism at the highest government levels, to deceit and a willingness to convict a citizen of treason on spurious grounds, and to refusals, invoking "reasons of state," to redress the injustice? Had he made the documents public, he too would have been accused of betrayal, and of damaging France in the eyes of the world by raising doubts about the reliability and stability of its government. In response, he too might have argued that greater injury to his country and to its world image would have resulted from continued lies and concealment, and that justice and democracy required that he override loyalty to his administration and concern for his career.

not merely from accident and bad luck. Unless Americans could take
the question of responsibility seriously, he believed they would continue
to subscribe to the myth of the war as a quagmire, as something with
a power of its own that defeated one president after another.[26] Unless
they discarded this erroneous view, they could hardly expect to learn
from the experience and respond less ineptly to future crises. And
without the insight the documents could provide, it would be easier for
adversaries of the United States to stereotype as typically American the
policies adopted by a small number of officials in successive administrations
by means of secrecy and deceit.

Still another reason lent urgency to the effort of making the documents
public: the awareness of the lives being lost, both by Americans and by
Vietnamese, and increasingly by still others, in a war so poorly understood.
If breaching secrecy might reduce the bloodshed, then it could be argued
that one had an obligation to do so: to call attention to how it had come
about and to the failures of policy-making that had led to its continuation
and escalation. This argument differs from the others, however; while
they speak to the question of making knowledge available, this one
presupposes that doing so would actually end the war sooner and reduce
the loss of life. The Nixon government and others argued, on the contrary,
that publishing the papers risked hampering peace negotiations, prolonging
the war, and endangering the lives of soldiers.[27] At the time, both sets
of suppositions were speculative; and even now, there is no consensus
that the Pentagon Papers had any effect in shortening or prolonging the
war.[28]

Aside from this more speculative reason for making the papers public,
I find the others persuasive, especially in conjunction with the documents
themselves. The information about the origins and conduct of the war
in Vietnam should never have been kept secret in the first place. This
information was owed to the people, at home and abroad, who were
bearing the costs and the suffering of the war; keeping them in the dark
about the reasons for fighting the war was an abuse of secrecy. The
extent of the secrecy could be justified neither on military nor on administrative grounds. It demonstrated, rather, the extraordinary danger
to society that endemic secrecy represents.

Are the arguments equally persuasive in justifying the means Ellsberg
and Russo used to make the papers public? The answer to this question
is less clear-cut. It depends in part on whether there would have been
alternative ways of making the knowledge public without violating government secrecy. Would it have been possible, for example, to try to
persuade those in charge of the project of the public's right to the

information? Would there have been legal avenues by which to require its revelation? Unless all such avenues had been explored, and had failed or been judged likely to fail, the means Ellsberg and Russo employed would have been at the very least premature.

What if all such avenues were closed? Even so, other means existed which, while they did violate secrecy, did not involve the taking and publishing of government documents. Ellsberg and Russo could have chosen to leak information anonymously about the documents to journalists or politicians; or they could have spoken out about the papers in public without producing them. It is not clear, however, that such action would have had much effect at the time in the absence of the documents themselves. The two chose instead the elaborate method of xeroxing each volume in secret and then sending copies to persons in a position to make them public. In so doing, they knew that they were violating government procedure most explicitly.

Some violate rules of secrecy surreptitiously, with few compunctions. Ellsberg and Russo, on the other hand, did so openly; they were willing to take responsibility for their acts and to accept the possibility of a criminal conviction. In justifying their choice of civil disobedience, they could invoke a principle similar to the one applied by the Nuremberg Tribunal, holding that individuals are at times obligated to disobey government orders that violate international law. True, this principle has hardly prevailed in courts since the Nuremberg trials. From a moral point of view, however, a similar principle applies. To the extent that a government violates the law and fundamental moral principles, men and women of conscience may consider themselves morally obliged to refuse any part in these activities. And to the extent that a government betrays its citizens by keeping such activities secret, the obligation may extend to combating these activities by exposing them in public.[29]

Such an open declaration has dangers for all who speak out about abuses, whether or not they violate existing laws or rules—indeed, even if, in speaking out, they obey their professional code of conduct. Retribution is often swift; suspicion, even of those whose breach of secrecy is seen as justified, lingers on. The following chapter will take up more general issues of dissent and whistleblowing, and assess institutional arrangements that could improve the access to information while reducing the need for individuals to run the high risks associated with revelations from within.

Whistleblowing and Leaks

Revelation from Within

*All that pollution up at Mølledal—all that reeking waste from
the mill—it's seeped into the pipes feeding from the pump-room;
and the same damn poisonous slop's been draining out on the
beach as well. . . . I've investigated the facts as scrupulously
as possible. . . . There's irrefutable proof of the presence of
decayed organic matter in the water—millions of bacteria. It's
positively injurious to health, for either internal or external
use. Ah, what a blessing it is to feel that you've done some
service for your home town and your fellow citizens.*
Dr. Thomas Stockman, in HENRIK IBSEN,
An Enemy of the People, Act 1

Such was Dr. Stockman's elation, in Ibsen's play, after having written
a report on the contamination of the town's newly installed mineral
baths. As the spa's medical director, he took it for granted that everyone
would be eager to learn why so many who had come to the baths for
health purposes the previous summer had been taken ill; and he assumed

that the board of directors and the taxpayers would gladly pay for the extensive repairs that he recommended. By the fifth act of the play, he had been labeled an "enemy of the people" at a public meeting, lost his position as the spa's medical director, and suffered through the stoning of his house by an angry crowd. But he held his ground: "Should I let myself be whipped from the field by public opinion and the solid majority and other such barbarities? No thank you!" [1]

"Whistleblower" is a recent label for those who, like Dr. Stockman, make revelations meant to call attention to negligence, abuses, or dangers that threaten the public interest. They sound an alarm based on their expertise or inside knowledge, often from within the very organization in which they work. With as much resonance as they can muster, they strive to breach secrecy, or else arouse an apathetic public to dangers everyone knows about but does not fully acknowledge. [2]

Few whistleblowers, however, share Dr. Stockman's initial belief that it will be enough to make their message public, and that people who learn of the danger will hasten to counter it. Most know, rather, that their alarms pose a threat to anyone who benefits from the ongoing practice and that their own careers and livelihood may be at risk. The lawyer who breaches confidentiality in reporting bribery by corporate clients knows the risk, as does the nurse who reports on slovenly patient care in a hospital, the engineer who discloses safety defects in the braking systems of a fleet of new rapid-transit vehicles, or the industrial worker who speaks out about hazardous chemicals seeping into a playground near the factory dump.

For each of the rationales of shared secrecy that I have discussed—confidentiality, trade secrecy, secrecy for research, and administrative and military secrecy—concealment of negligence and abuses creates strong tensions for insiders. They must confront questions of loyalty, conscience, and truthfulness, and personal concerns about careers and peace of mind. What should they consider revealing? And which secrets must they at all costs bring to public attention?

Would-be whistleblowers also face conflicting pressures from without. In many professions, the prevailing ethic requires above all else loyalty to colleagues and to clients; yet the formal codes of professional ethics stress responsibility to the public in cases of conflict with such loyalties. Thus the largest professional engineering society asks members to speak out against abuses threatening the safety, health, and welfare of the public. [3] A number of business firms have codes making similar requirements; and the United States Code of Ethics for government servants asks them to "expose corruption wherever uncovered" and to "put loyalty to the highest moral principles and to country above loyalty to persons, party, or Government department." [4] Regardless of such exhortations, would-be whistleblowers have reason to fear the results of carrying out the duty to reveal corruption and neglect. However strong this duty may seem in principle, they know that in practice, retaliation is likely. They fear for their careers and for their ability to support themselves and their families.

Government service in the United States offers insight into the variety of forms that retaliation can take. A handbook issued during the Nixon era recommends reassigning "undesirables" to places so remote that they would prefer to resign. Whistleblowers may also be downgraded or given work without responsibility or work for which they are not qualified; or else they may be given more tasks than they can possibly perform.

Another risk to outspoken civil servants—devastating to their careers— is that they may be ordered to undergo a psychiatric "fitness for duty" examination. Congressional hearings in 1978 uncovered a growing tendency to resort to such mandatory examinations, and found that it frequently results from conflicts between supervisors and employees. A person declared unfit for service can then be "separated" and his assertions discredited. The chairman of the investigating subcommittee, Senator Edward Kennedy, concluded that "there was general agreement . . . that involuntary psychiatric examinations were not helpful to the Government, unfair to employees, and that the agencies placed psychiatrists in an impossible situation." [5]

Outright firing, finally, is the most direct institutional response to whistleblowers. Those who bring suit incur heavy legal expenses and have little assurance of prevailing in court. One civil servant, reflecting on her experience and on that of others, stated that their reactions, after speaking out about the agency in which they worked, had "ranged from humiliation, frustration, and helpless rage to complete despair about our democratic process." [6]

The plight of whistleblowers has been documented in the last decade by the press and by a growing number of books and scholarly articles. [7] Evidence of the hardships imposed on those who chose to act in the public interest has combined with a heightened awareness of professional malfeasance and corruption to produce a shift toward greater public support of whistleblowers. Public-service law firms and consumer groups have taken up their cause; institutional reforms and legislation have been enacted to combat illegitimate reprisals. Some would encourage ever greater numbers of employees to ferret out and publicize improprieties in the agencies and organizations where they work.

Given the indispensable services performed by so many whistleblowers—

as during the Watergate period and after—strong public support is often merited. But the new climate of acceptance makes it easy to overlook the dangers of whistleblowing: of work and reputations unjustly lost for those falsely accused, of privacy invaded and trust undermined. There comes a level of internal prying and mutual suspicion at which no institution can function. And it is a fact that the disappointed, the incompetent, the malicious, and the paranoid all too often make groundless accusations. Worst of all, ideological persecution throughout the world traditionally relies on insiders willing to inform on their colleagues or even on their family members, often through staged public denunciations or press campaigns.

The very societies that encourage such revelation from within of political or religious deviation are often least tolerant of whistleblowing concerning abuse or neglect in ruling circles. Such messages require some larger context where secrecy, corruption, and coercion are less solidly entrenched, some forum where an appeal to justice can still be made. They also require an avenue of concerted public response; for if the audience is not free to receive or to act on the information—as when censorship or fear of retribution stifles response—then the message only rebounds to injure the whistleblower. If protest within a nation is thus blocked, international appeals may be the only remaining possibility. Depending on the severity of the repression, only the most striking injustices may then filter through with sufficient strength to alert ordinarily indifferent foreigners. Alarms, like ripples in the water, weaken as they move away from their point of origin; if forced to go below the surface, they may be further attenuated.

No society can count itself immune from the risk that individuals or groups in power might use whistleblowing for their own purposes, and crush it when they see fit. A society that fails to protect the right to speak out even on the part of those whose warnings turn out to be spurious obviously opens the door to political repression. Given such protection, however, we still need to weigh the uses and the costs of whistleblowing, and to try to distinguish between its more and its less justifiable forms. From the moral point of view, there are important differences between the aims, messages, and methods of dissenters from within.

Blowing the Whistle

The alarm of the whistleblower is meant to disrupt the status quo: to pierce the background noise, perhaps the false harmony, or the imposed silence of "business as usual." Three elements, each jarring, and triply jarring when conjoined, lend acts of whistleblowing special urgency and bitterness: dissent, breach of loyalty, and accusation.*

Like all *dissent*, first of all, whistleblowing makes public a disagreement with an authority or a majority view. But whereas dissent can arise from all forms of disagreement with, say, religious dogma or government policy or court decisions, whistleblowing has the narrower aim of casting light on negligence or abuse, of alerting the public to a risk and of assigning responsibility for that risk.

It is important, in this respect, to see the shadings between the revelations of neglect and abuse which are central to whistleblowing, and dissent on grounds of policy. In practice, however, the two often come together. Coercive regimes or employers may regard dissent of any form as evidence of abuse or of corruption that calls for public exposure. And in all societies, persons may blow the whistle on abuses in order to signal policy dissent. Thus Daniel Ellsberg, in making his revelations about government deceit and manipulation in the Pentagon Papers, obviously aimed not only to expose misconduct and assign responsibility but also to influence the nation's policy toward Southeast Asia.

In the second place, the message of the whistleblower is seen as a *breach of loyalty* because it comes from within. The whistleblower, though he is neither referee nor coach, blows the whistle on his own team. His insider's position carries with it certain obligations to colleagues and clients. He may have signed a promise of confidentiality or a loyalty oath. When he steps out of routine channels to level accusations, he is going against these obligations. Loyalty to colleagues and to clients comes to be pitted against concern for the public interest and for those who may be injured unless someone speaks out. Because the whistleblower criticizes from within, his act differs from muckraking and other forms of exposure by outsiders. Their acts may arouse anger, but not the sense of betrayal that whistleblowers so often encounter.

---

*Consider the differences and the overlap between whistleblowing and civil disobedience with respect to these three elements. First, whistleblowing resembles civil disobedience in its openness and its intent to act in the public interest. But the dissent in whistleblowing, unlike that in civil disobedience, usually does not represent a breach of law; it is, on the contrary, protected by the right of free speech and often encouraged in codes of ethics and other statements of principle. Second, whistleblowing violates loyalty, since it dissents from within and breaches secrecy, whereas civil disobedience need not and can as easily challenge from without. Whistleblowing, finally, accuses specific individuals, whereas civil disobedience need not. A combination of the two occurs, for instance, when former CIA agents publish books to alert the public about what they regard as unlawful and dangerous practices, and in so doing openly violate, and thereby test, the oath of secrecy that they have sworn.

The conflict is strongest for those who take their responsibilities to the public seriously, yet have close bonds of collegiality and of duty to clients as well. They know the price of betrayal. They know, too, how organizations protect and enlarge the area of what is concealed, as failures multiply and vested interests encroach. And they are aware that they violate, by speaking out, not only loyalty but usually hierarchy as well.

It is the third element of *accusation*, of calling a "foul" from within, that arouses the strongest reactions on the part of the hierarchy. The charge may be one of unethical or unlawful conduct on the part of colleagues or superiors. Explicitly or implicitly, it singles out specific groups or persons as responsible: as those who knew or should have known what was wrong and what the dangers were, and who had the capacity to make different choices. If no one could be held thus responsible—as in the case of an impending avalanche or a volcanic eruption—the warning would not constitute whistleblowing. At times the whistleblower's greatest effort is expended on trying to show that someone *is* responsible for danger or suffering: that the collapse of a building, the derailment of a train, or a famine that the public may have attributed to bad luck or natural causes was in reality brought about by specific individuals, and that they can be held responsible, perhaps made to repair the damage or at least to avoid compounding it.

The whistleblower's accusation, moreover, concerns a present or an imminent threat. Past errors or misdeeds occasion such an alarm only if they still affect current practices. And risks far in the future usually lack the immediacy needed to render the alarm compelling, as well as the close connection to particular individuals that would justify accusations. Thus an alarm can be sounded about safety defects in a rapid-transit system that threaten or will shortly threaten passengers; but the revelation of safety defects in a system no longer in use, while of historical interest, would not constitute whistleblowing. Nor would the disclosure of potential problems in a system not yet fully designed and far from being implemented.

Not only immediacy but also specificity is needed for the whistleblower to assign responsibility. A concrete risk must be at issue rather than a vague foreboding or a somber prediction. The act of whistleblowing differs in this respect from the lamentation or the dire prophecy.

Such immediate and specific threats would normally be acted upon by those at risk. But the whistleblower asssumes that his message will alert listeners to a threat of which they are ignorant, or whose significance they have not grasped. It may have been kept secret by members within the organization, or by all who are familiar with it. Or it may be an "open secret," seemingly in need only of being pointed out in order to have its effect. In either case, because of the elements of dissent, breach of loyalty, and accusation, the tension between concealing and revealing is great. It may be intensified by an urge to throw off the sense of complicity that comes from sharing secrets one believes to be unjustly concealed, and to achieve peace of mind by setting the record straight at last. Sometimes a desire for publicity enters in, or a hope for revenge for past slights or injustices. Colleagues of the whistleblower often suspect just such motives; they may regard him as a crank, publicity-hungry, eager for scandal and discord, or driven to indiscretion by his personal biases and shortcomings.[8]

On the continuum of more or less justifiable acts of whistleblowing, the whistleblower tends to see more such acts as justified and even necesssary than his colleagues. Bias can affect each side in drawing the line, so that each takes only some of the factors into account—the more so if the action comes at the end of a long buildup of acrimony and suspicion.

The Leak

When Otto Otepka sent classified documents and names of persons he considered security risks to "Red-hunter" Julian Sourwine of the Senate Internal Subcommittee in the early 1960s, or when "Deep Throat" revealed facts about Watergate in deepest secrecy, each was engaged in a practice that has come to be called "leaking." [9] Each meant to disclose information from within but to do so covertly, unlike the whistleblower or the official who resigns in protest.*

Any kind of information can be leaked; but the word "leak" is most often used in connection with administrative secrets, such as the anonymous revelations in 1980 from within the Department of Justice concerning the ABSCAM investigations of members of Congress, or with classified military secrets.[10] The originator of a leak is usually unknown to the public and sometimes even to the journalist or other intermediary. Anonymous messages may be sent by mail, dropped at doorsteps, transmitted in coded form on computers.

*The two cases differ in that Otepka's actions come much closer to informing than most efforts to leak. Leaks are generally directed to the public via an intermediary, whereas informing is meant for the authorities. But Otepka considered those in charge of federal appointments to be overly lenient, and so chose a different outlet for his revelations.

Leaking has a symbiotic relationship with secrecy. Without secrecy there would be no need to leak information. As government secrecy grows and comes to involve more people, the opportunities to leak from within expand; and with increased leaking, governments intensify their efforts to shore up secrecy.

At the same time as they combat leaking, however, executives use it selectively to further their own policies. With modern governments guarding vast amounts of information, much of it inaccessible to the public or actively kept secret, and with the media eager to circulate newsworthy revelations to vast audiences, the leak, unlike acts of whistleblowing, has become an important tool of governing.* Administrators may leak stories as trial balloons, to deflect attention from recent failures, or to smear political opponents. And civil servants who want to combat policies or particular decisions may leak selected compromising facts. If a secret plan is sufficiently sensitive, those who learn about it may, in this way, exercise a veto power over its execution. Thus the members of congressional committees overseeing CIA activities know that they need only leak details concerning any one of them to destroy its effectiveness.

Press and television reporters cooperate in bringing many of these leaks to public attention. They may discard pieces of information that cannot be verified or that seem of little interest; but at times they publish the flimsiest of rumors. Whether knowingly or not, they are also often the conduits for leaked disinformation. Because of their eagerness for news and "scoops," reporters become, as Francis Rourke has pointed out, "willing if not enthusiastic collaborators" with those who engage in leaking to influence public opinion.[11]

Unlike whistleblowing, leaking need not concern danger, negligence, or abuse, though both bring something that is secret or unnoticed into the open from within an organization. Thus a civil servant may leak secret documents in his agency's possession concerning another nation's military preparedness, or specifying steps in fragile diplomatic talks. But when a leak from within does concern misconduct, it is a variant of whistleblowing, undertaken surreptitiously because the revealer cannot or does not want to be known as its source.

Whether as a surreptitious form of whistleblowing, a tool for news management by administrators, or a means of bureaucratic maneuvering,

---

*Leaks are often seen as related to national, state, or local government affairs. But there is no reason not to use the word for analogous revelations from international government bodies such as UN agencies or OPEC circles, or from nongovernmental ones such as IBM or Nestlé.

leaking has become one of the main forms of communication about matters of public interest. But it is far from ideal from the point of view of the media or the public. For while it is preferable to complete secrecy, and offers one of the few ways of learning about risky policies and mismanagement otherwise shrouded in secrecy, it does so haphazardly and is ceaselessly used to manipulate public opinion.

Both leaking and whistleblowing can be used to challenge corrupt or cumbersome systems of secrecy—in government as in the professions, the sciences, and business. Both may convey urgently needed warnings, but they may also peddle false information and vicious personal attacks. How, then, can one distinguish the many acts of revelation from within that are genuinely in the public interest from all the petty, biased, or lurid tales that pervade our querulous and gossip-ridden societies? Can we draw distinctions between different messages, different methods and motivations?

We clearly can, in a number of cases. Whistleblowing and leaks may be starkly inappropriate when used in malice or in error, or when they lay bare legitimately private matters such as those having to do with political belief or sexual life. They may, just as clearly, offer the only way to shed light on an ongoing practice such as fraudulent scientific research or intimidation of political adversaries; and they may be the last resort for alerting the public to a possible disaster. Consider, for example, the action taken by three engineers to alert the public to defects in the braking mechanisms of the Bay Area Rapid Transit System (BART):

The San Francisco Bay Area Rapid Transit System opened in 1972. It was heralded as the first major breakthrough toward a safe, reliable, and sophisticated method of mass transportation. A public agency had been set up in 1952 to plan and carry out the project; and the task of developing its major new component, a fully automatic train control system, was allocated to Westinghouse.

In 1969, three of the engineers who worked on this system became increasingly concerned over its safety. They spotted problems independently, and spoke to their supervisors, but to no avail. They later said they might well have given up their effort to go farther had they not found out about one another. They made numerous efforts to speak to BART's management. But those in charge were already troubled by costs that had exceeded all projections, and by numerous unforseen delays. They were not disposed to investigate the charges that the control system might be unsafe. Each appeal by the three engineers failed.

Finally, the engineers interested a member of BART's board of trustees, who brought the matter up at a board meeting. Once again, the effort failed. But in March 1973, the three were fired once the complaint had been traced to them. When they wrote to ask why they had been dismissed, they received no answer.

Meanwhile, the BART system had begun to roll. The control system worked erratically, and at times dangerously. A month after the opening, one train overshot the last station and crashed into a parking lot for commuters. Claiming that some bugs still had to be worked out, BART began to use old-fashioned flagmen in order to avoid collisions.

The three engineers had turned, in 1972, to the California Society of Professional Engineers for support. The society, after investigating the complaint, agreed with their views, and reported to the California State legislature. It too had launched an investigation, and arrived at conclusions quite critical of BART's management.

The engineers filed a damage suit against BART in 1974, but settled out of court in 1975. They had difficulties finding new employment, and suffered considerable financial and emotional hardship in spite of their public vindication.[12]

The three engineers were acting in accordance with the law and with engineering codes of ethics in calling attention to the defects in the train control system. Because of their expertise, they had a special responsibility to alert the company, and if need be its board of directors and the public, to the risks that concerned them. If we take such a clear-cut case of legitimate whistleblowing as a benchmark, and reflect on what it is about it that weighs so heavily in favor of disclosure, we can then examine more complex cases in which speaking out in public is not so clearly the right choice or the only choice.

Individual Moral Choice

What questions might individuals consider, as they wonder whether to sound an alarm? How might they articulate the problem they see, and weigh its seriousness before deciding whether or not to reveal it? Can they make sure that their choice is the right one? And what about the choices confronting journalists or others asked to serve as intermediaries?

In thinking about these questions, it helps to keep in mind the three elements mentioned earlier: dissent, breach of loyalty, and accusation. They impose certain requirements: of judgment and accuracy in dissent, of exploring alternative ways to cope with improprieties that minimize the breach of loyalty, and of fairness in accusation. The judgment expressed by whistleblowers concerns a problem that should matter to the public. Certain outrages are so blatant, and certain dangers so great, that all who are in a position to warn of them have a *prima facie* obligation to do so. Conversely, other problems are so minor that to blow the whistle would be a disproportionate response. And still others are so hard to pin down that whistleblowing is premature. In between lie a great many of the problems troubling whistleblowers. Consider, for example, the following situation:

An attorney for a large company manufacturing medical supplies begins to suspect that some of the machinery sold by the company to hospitals for use in kidney dialysis is unsafe, and that management has made attempts to influence federal regulatory personnel to overlook these deficiencies.

The attorney brings these matters up with a junior executive, who assures her that he will look into the matter, and convey them to the chief executive if necessary. When she questions him a few weeks later, however, he tells her that all the problems have been taken care of, but offers no evidence, and seems irritated at her desire to learn exactly where the issues stand. She does not know how much further she can press her concern without jeopardizing her position in the firm.

The lawyer in this case has reason to be troubled, but does not yet possess sufficient evidence to blow the whistle. She is far from being as sure of her case as was Ibsen's Dr. Stockman, who had received laboratory analyses of the water used in the town spa, or as the engineers in the BART case, whose professional expertise allowed them to evaluate the risks of the faulty braking system. Dr. Stockman and the engineers would be justified in assuming that they had an obligation to draw attention to the dangers they saw, and that anyone who shared their knowledge would be wrong to remain silent or to suppress evidence of the danger. But if the attorney blew the whistle about her company's sales of machinery to hospitals merely on the basis of her suspicions, she would be doing so prematurely. At the same time, the risks to hospital patients from the machinery, should she prove correct in her suspicions, are sufficiently great so that she has good reason to seek help in looking into the problem, to feel complicitous if she chooses to do nothing, and to take action if she verifies her suspicions.

Her difficulty is shared by many who suspect, without being sure, that their companies are concealing the defective or dangerous nature of their products—automobiles that are firetraps, for instance, or canned foods with carcinogenic additives. They may sense that merely to acknowledge that they don't know for sure is too often a weak excuse for inaction, but recognize also that the destructive power of adverse publicity can be great. If the warning turns out to have been inaccurate, it may take a long time to undo the damage to individuals and organizations. As a result, potential whistleblowers must first try to specify the degree to which there is genuine impropriety, and consider how imminent and how serious the threat is which they perceive.

If the facts turn out to warrant disclosure, and if the would-be whistleblower has decided to act upon them in spite of the possibilities of
reprisal, then how can the second element—breach of loyalty—be overcome
or minimized? Here, as in the Pentagon Papers case, the problem is
one of which set of loyalties to uphold. Several professional codes of
ethics, such as those of engineers and public servants, facilitate such
a choice at least in theory, by requiring that loyalty to the public interest
should override allegiance to colleagues, employers, or clients whenever
there is a genuine conflict. Accordingly, those who have assumed a
professional responsibility to serve the public interest—as had both Dr.
Stockman in Ibsen's play and the engineers in the BART case—have a
special obligation not to remain silent about dangers to the public.

Before deciding whether to speak out publicly, however, it is important
for them to consider whether the existing avenues for change within
the organization have been sufficiently explored. By turning first to
insiders for help, one can often uphold both sets of loyalties and settle
the problem without going outside the organization. The engineers in
the BART case clearly tried to resolve the problem they saw in this
manner, and only reluctantly allowed it to come to public attention as
a last resort. Dr. Stockman, on the other hand, acted much more im-
petuously and with little concern for discretion. Before the directors of
the mineral baths had even received his report, he talked freely about
it, and welcomed a journalist's request to publicize the matter. While
he had every reason to try to remedy the danger he had discovered, he
was not justified in the methods he chose; on the contrary, they were
singularly unlikely to bring about corrective action.

It *is* disloyal to colleagues and employers, as well as a waste of time
for the public, to sound the loudest alarm first. Whistleblowing has to
remain a last alternative because of its destructive side effects. It must
be chosen only when other alternatives have been considered and rejected.
They may be rejected if they simply do not apply to the problem at hand,
or when there is not time to go through routine channels, or when the
institution is so corrupt or coercive that steps will be taken to silence
the whistleblower should he try the regular channels first.

What weight should an oath or a promise of silence have in the conflict
of loyalties? There is no doubt that one sworn to silence is under a
stronger obligation because of the oath he has taken, unless it was
obtained under duress or through deceit, or else binds him to something
in itself wrong or unlawful. In taking an oath, one assumes specific
obligations beyond those assumed in accepting employment. But even
such an oath can be overridden when the public interest at issue is

sufficiently strong. The fact that one has promised silence is no excuse for complicity in covering up a crime or violating the public trust.

The third element in whistleblowing—accusation—is strongest whenever efforts to correct a problem without going outside the organization have failed, or seem likely to fail. Such an outcome is especially likely whenever those in charge take part in the questionable practices, or have too much at stake in maintaining them. The following story relates the difficulties one government employee experienced in trying to decide whether to go public with accusations against superiors in his agency:

As a construction inspector for a federal agency, John Samuels (not his real name) had personal knowledge of shoddy and deficient construction practices by private contractors. He knew his superiors received free vacations and entertainment, had their homes remodeled, found jobs for their relatives—all courtesy of a private contractor. These superiors later approved a multimillion no-bid contract with the same "generous" firm.

Samuels also had evidence that other firms were hiring nonunion laborers at a low wage while receiving substantially higher payments from the government for labor costs. A former superior, unaware of an office dictaphone, had incautiously instructed Samuels on how to accept bribes for overlooking sub-par performance.

As he prepared to volunteer this information to various members of Congress, he became tense and uneasy. His family was scared and the fears were valid. It might cost Samuels thousands of dollars to protect his job. Those who had freely provided him with information would probably recant or withdraw their friendship. A number of people might object to his using a disctaphone to gather information. His agency would start covering up and vent its collective wrath upon him. As for reporters and writers, they would gather for a few days, then move on to the next story. He would be left without a job, with fewer friends, with massive battles looming, and without the financial means of fighting them. Samuels decided to remain silent.[13]

Samuels could be sure of his facts, and fairly sure that it would not help to explore avenues within the agency in trying to remedy the situation. But was the method he envisaged—of volunteering his information to members of Congress and to the press—the one most likely to do so, and to provide a fair hearing for those he was charging with corruption and crime? Could he have gone first to the police? If he had been concerned to proceed in the fairest possible manner, he should at least have considered alternative methods of investigating and reporting the abuses he had witnessed.

These abuses were clearly such as to warrant attention. At other times, potential whistleblowers must also ask themselves whether their message, however accurate, is one to which the public is entitled in the first place or whether it infringes on personal and private matters that no one should invade. Here, the very notion of what is in the public interest is at issue: allegations regarding an official's unusual sexual or religious practices may well appeal to the public's interest without therefore being relevant to "the public interest." Those who regard such private matters as threats to the public voice their own religious and political prejudices in the language of accusation. Such a danger is never stronger than when the accusation is delivered surreptitiously; the anonymous allegations made during the McCarthy period regarding political beliefs and associations often injured persons who did not even know their accusers or the exact nature of the charges.

In fairness to those criticized, openly accepted responsibility for blowing the whistle should therefore be preferred to the secret denunciation or the leaked rumor—the more so, the more derogatory and accusatory the information. What is openly stated can be more easily checked, its source's motives challenged, and the underlying information examined. Those under attack may otherwise be hard put to it to defend themselves against nameless adversaries. Often they do not even know that they are threatened until it is too late to respond.

The choice between open and surreptitious revelation from within is admittedly less easy for the persons who intend to make them. Leaking information anonymously is safer, and can be kept up indefinitely; the whistleblower, on the contrary, shoots his bolt by going public. At the same time, those who leak know that their message may be taken less seriously, precisely because its source remains concealed. And because these messages go through several intermediaries before they appear in print, they may undergo changes along the way. At times, they are so adulterated that they lose their point altogether.

Journalists and other intermediaries must make choices of their own with respect to a leaked message. Should they use it at all, even if they doubt its accuracy? Should they pass it on verbatim or interpret it? Or should they seek to "plug" the leak? Newspaper and television bureaus receive innumerable leaks but act on only some of them. Unless the information is accompanied by indications of how the evidence can be checked, the source's anonymity, however safe, diminishes the value of the message.

In order to assure transmission of their message, yet be safe from retaliation, leakers often resort to a compromise: by making themselves known to a journalist or other intermediary, they make it possible to verify their credibility; by asking that their identity be concealed, they still protect themselves from the consequences they fear.

If anonymous sources can point to independent evidence of genuine risk or wrongdoing, the need for them to step forward is reduced and their motives are less important. For this reason, the toll-free numbers that citizens can use to report on government fraud, tax evasion, or police abuse serve an important purpose in protecting critics both from inside and from outside an organization. Without such evidence, accusations openly made by identifiable persons are preferable. The open charge is fairer to the accused, and allows listeners to weigh the motives and the trustworthiness of the whistleblowers.

Must the whistleblower who speaks out openly also resign? Only if staying on means being forced to participate in the objectionable activity, and thus to take on partial responsibility for its consequences. Otherwise, there should be no burden on whistleblowers to resign in voicing their alarm. In principle, at least, it is often their duty to speak out, and their positions ought not thereby to be at issue. In practice, however, they know that retaliation, forced departure, perhaps blacklisting, may be sufficient risks at times so that it may be wise to resign before sounding the alarm: to resign in protest, or to leave quietly, secure another post, and only then blow the whistle.[14] In each case, those who speak out can then do so with the authority and knowledge of insiders, but without their vulnerability.

It is not easy to weigh all these factors, nor to compensate for the degree of bias, rationalization, and denial that inevitably influences one's judgment. By speaking out, whistleblowers may spark a re-examination of these forces among colleagues and others who had ignored or learned to live with shoddy or corrupt practices. Because they have this power to dramatize moral conflict, would-be whistleblowers have a special responsibility to ask themselves about biases in deciding whether or not to speak out: a desire for self-defense in a difficult bureaucratic situation, perhaps, or unrealistic expectations regarding the likely effects of speaking out.*

As they weigh the reasons for sounding the alarm, or on the contrary for remaining silent, they may find it helpful to ask about the legitimacy

---

*If, for example, a government employee stands to make large profits from a book exposing the iniquities in his agency, there is danger that he might slant his report in order to cause more of a sensation. Sometimes a warning is so clearly justifiable and substantiated that it carries weight no matter what the motives of the speaker. But scandal can pay; and the whistleblower's motives ought ideally to be above suspicion, for his own sake as well as for the sake of the respect he desires for his warning. Personal gain from speaking out increases the need to check the accuracy of the speaker.

of the rationale for collective secrecy in the particular problem they face. If they are wondering whether or not to blow the whistle on the unnecessary surgery they have witnessed, for example, or on the manufacture of unsafe machinery, what weight should they place on claims to professional confidentiality or corporate secrecy?

Reducing bias and error in moral choice often requires consultation, even open debate; such methods force us to articulate the arguments at stake and to challenge privately held assumptions. But choices about whether or not to blow the whistle present special problems for such consultation. On the one hand, once whistleblowers sound their alarm publicly, their judgment *will* be subjected to open scrutiny; they will have to articulate their reasons for speaking out and substantiate their charges. On the other hand, it will then be too late to retract their charges should they turn out to have been unfounded.

For those who are concerned about a situation within their organization, it is therefore preferable to seek advice *before* deciding either to go public or to remain silent. But the more corrupt the circumstances, the more dangerous it may be to consult colleagues, and the more likely it is that those responsible for the abuse or neglect will destroy the evidence linking them to it. And yet, with no one to consult, the would-be whistleblowers themselves may have a biased view of the state of affairs; they may see corruption and conspiracy where none exists, and choose not to consult others when in fact it would have been not only safe but advantageous to do so.

Given these difficulties, it is especially important to seek more general means of weighing the arguments for and against whistleblowing; to take them up in public debate and in teaching; and to consider changes in organizations, law, and work practices that could reduce the need for individuals to choose between blowing and "swallowing" the whistle.[15]

Organizational Change and Social Policy

What changes inside and outside organizations might protect the rights of dissenters and critics, and assure the public of needed information, while cutting down on undue breaches of loyalty and on false accusations?

An organization can reduce the need to resort to whistleblowing by providing mechanisms for evaluating criticism before it reaches the press or the courtroom. These mechanisms must work to counteract the blockages of information within an organization and the perennial pressures to filter out negative information before it reaches those who make decisions.[16] The filtering process may be simple or intricate, well-intentioned or malevolent, more or less consciously manipulated. Some abuses are covered up at the source; others are sidelined en route to department heads; still others are kept from reaching review boards or trustees.

Surveying the damage from such failures of communication, David Ewing has argued that managers have much to gain by not discouraging internal criticism.[17] In a recent survey, he found that over 60 per cent of the business firms responding to a questionnaire claimed that a senior executive's door is always open to anyone with a grievance.[18] A number of managers have other ways of encouraging the views of dissenters, and promise that no one will be unfairly dismissed or disciplined.

Such an "open-door" policy may suffice at times. When the policy is taken seriously by management, and its results are publicized, employees learn that they have nothing to lose from speaking out. But such policies are frequently inadequate. In the first place, the promises of protection given by top management cannot always be fulfilled. Though employees may keep their jobs, there are countless ways of making their position difficult, to the point where they may be brought to resign of their own volition or to stay while bitterly regretting that they had spoken out. Second, it would be naïve to think that abuses in industry or in government are always unknown to top management and perpetrated against their will by subordinates. If those in charge knowingly manufacture unsafe products or engage in corporate bribery, then the open-door policy is but a trap for the outspoken; even when employees suffer no reprisal for having voiced a criticism to management, they will usually find that it has simply been ignored.

For these reasons, proposals have been made to ensure independent internal consideration of the criticisms, while protecting those who voice them more formally. Internal review boards, ombudsmen, consumer or citizen representatives on boards of trustees, bills of rights for employees: these methods of protection spring up and die away with great rapidity. When they work, their usefulness is undeniable. They allow for criticism with much less need for heroism; give a way to deflect the crank or the witch-hunter *before* his message gains publicity, and a process of checking its accuracy; make it easier to distinguish between urgent alarms and long-range worries; and provide an arena for debating the moral questions of motive, loyalty, and responsibility to the public.

The methods fail when they are but window-dressing from the outset, meant only to please or exhaust dissenters; or when they change, no matter how independent at the start, into management tools. Such is the fate of many a patient representative in hospitals: their growing loyalty to co-workers and to the management and their distance from the patients they are meant to represent once again leave critics little choice between submission and open revolt. Still another reason for the failure of such intermediaries is that they often lack credibility. No matter how well-meaning, they will not be sought out if they cannot protect from retaliation those who turn to them for help. Even if they can give such protection, but cannot inspire confidence in their independence, their role will be largely ceremonial. Finally, they may protect the outspoken but not succeed in correcting the problem brought up; once again, they will quickly lose credence.

In the last decade, a growing number of laws have been enacted to protect employees against reprisals. First to be passed were laws covering federal and state employees; these, however, still work slowly and unevenly. In April 1981, Michigan became the first state to enact a "Whistleblowers Protection Act" covering corporate employees.[19] It allow courts to grant back pay, reinstatement in the job, and costs of litigation to employees who can demonstrate improper treatment.

Alan Westin points out that citizens of Michigan had special reason to support such legislation.[20] In the mid-1970s, a chemical company mistakenly shipped PBBs (polybrominated biphenyls) to state feed-grain cooperatives instead of their regular nutritional supplement. As a result, the health of residents was seriously injured, and a great many cattle died. The sponsor of the law stated that an official inquiry was begun when the farm animals began to die in large numbers. But it was seriously hampered by the reluctance of employees of the chemical company to come forth with information that might have given a clue to the link between the deaths of the animals and the accidental delivery of PBBs. Employees later testified that they had been threatened with dismissal if they told investigators that the PBB accident might have been the cause.

It is too early to tell whether laws such as that enacted in Michigan will become the rule rather than the exception, and whether they will succeed in protecting whistleblowers. The problem with such laws is that there are so many other ways to penalize employees without detection; and that it is not always easy for courts to tell the difference between legitimate and spurious complaints.* Nevertheless, such laws will continue

---

*In watching the evolution of such laws, their broader effect must also be kept in mind. To what extent might they contribute to making institutions more litigious? And to what extent will protection in one place put increased pressure on another? Is it not possible, for example, that the increasing difficulty in firing incompetent federal employees led to the growing resort to psychiatric fitness-for-duty examinations, and that these, in turn, have become a new weapon with which to fight outspoken critics within a bureaucracy?

to be needed to protect whistleblowers against the most egregious reprisals, and to encourage firms to set up more workable internal mechanisms for complaint.[21]

A different method for reducing the tension and risk of whistleblowing can complement laws that protect those who voice criticism. It is to state clear conditions under which those who learn about a certain kind of danger *must* report it. If such requirements to report are properly limited and if they succeed in deflecting reprisals, they can lessen the conflict of loyalties felt by would-be whistleblowers and strengthen their resolve. Such laws already exist in a number of places. One is the Toxic Substances Control Act, enacted in 1977, which requires companies to instruct employees that any person must report information about a chemical they take to present "a substantial risk of injury to health or to the environment." [22]

This type of law, like that protecting whistleblowers, can be undercut and circumvented in a number of ways; it is nevertheless useful insofar as it facilitates reporting of serious and documented dangers. Such laws must, however, be limited to clear-cut improprieties; and the lines must be firmly drawn against requiring reporting on political dissent or on purely personal matters. In many societies, citizens are asked to report "deviations," fellow workers encouraged to spy on one another, and students asked to expose the subversive views of their teachers and vice versa. No matter how great the need to eradicate unlawfulness and corruption, such parallels should not be ignored.

The alarms of whistleblowers would be unnecessary were it not for the many threats to the public interest shielded by practices of secrecy in such domains as law, medicine, commerce, industry, science, and government. Given these practices, whistleblowers perform an indispensable public service; but they do so at great human cost, and without any asssurance that they uncover most, or even the worst, abuses. While they deserve strong support in their endeavors, every effort should therefore be made to combat the problems they signal by other means.

The most important task is to reduce the various practices of collective secrecy in order to permit the normal channels of public inquiry to take the place of whistleblowing and of leaking. The more encrusted a society becomes with unnecessary secrecy, confidential procedures, systems of classification, and means of corporate, professional, and administrative self-protection, the harder it is for the public to learn in time about risks and wrongdoing.

As I have argued, all secrecy cannot and should not be discarded. But even where limited secrecy fulfills an important function, as in pro-

tecting certain military secrets, controls are needed in order to reduce the dangers that arise when power and secrecy combine. And
whatever the assumed benefits of secrecy, its role in damming up the
usual alternatives to whistleblowing is a cost all too often forgotten.

Instrusive Social Science Research

A Prophecy for Social Science

Triumphant, brooking no opposition—such was the future that Emile Durkheim envisaged for the social sciences at the beginning of this century. Science, he predicted in his massive study, *The Elementary Forms of Religious Life*, would come to take over the subjects that religion and philosophy had traditionally sought to explain: nature, man, and society.[1]

Science, according to Durkheim's prophecy, was going to dispel the mystery that seemed to surround these topics. It would "set aside the veil with which mythological imagination has covered them for them to appear as they really are." Religion would have to retire before science. Durkheim claimed that science was better equipped for the study of these topics because of its spirit of criticism and its efforts to hold aside all "passions, prejudices, and all subjective influences." Not only would science take over the subject matter of these earlier, speculative approaches: it would focus its scrutiny on the psychic life itself, and on religious and moral "phenomena" in their own right. It was here that Durkheim foresaw the fiercest resistance against scientific probing: "The great majority of men continue to believe that there is an order of things which the mind cannot penetrate except by very special ways." [2] Durkheim saw his own study of religious life as pathbreaking in the scientific effort to penetrate the prevailing "wholly superficial" mystery. In this effort, he believed that science was bound to win out and that it would forever after submit religion to "its criticism and control."

Innumerable social scientists have followed his lead. They have sought to probe and to describe the most intimate and secret practices. They have studied the sacred in its manifestations across the earth, not only from the outside but from the perspective of an insider as well. By taking part in the activities of a tribe or a secret society or a religious sect, they have carried out "participant observation," collecting data and publishing their results. Few still share Durkheim's faith in the capacity of social science to allow nature, man, and society to "appear as they really are." Yet the hope lingers on in the elaborate schemes for surreptitious observation, aimed at catching human behavior unawares. As Florence Kluckhohn, an early advocate of what she called "hypocritical" participant observation, pointed out:

There are in all groups certain kinds of data which are guarded more closely than other types. Direct questions regarding such information may be met with evasions if not outright misrepresentations. Indirect questions may also fail. Simulation of behavior made possible by participation may, however, open the door to this guarded realm. [3]

The attraction of "this guarded realm" for many researchers is not rooted in their desire for knowledge alone, nor only in their hope that it might bring insight and possible benefits. They are also drawn to it by the allure of secrecy, of boundaries, and of the forbidden. Some take pleasure in dispelling the mystery, in showing it to be "wholly superficial," in Durkheim's words. Others, on the contrary, want to get to the heart of the secret in order to partake of it, relish its intimacy. Trespassing on what is taboo attracts still others. The extraordinary amount of research into every minute aspect of sexuality or religious belief is simply not explicable on other, strictly scientific grounds.

In exploring the reasons given for probing this guarded realm—especially its most closely kept secrets—it is important to consider the legitimacy of the methods used, in particular the most surreptitious ones. The following example will convey the high interest of some such studies, and illustrate some of the methods used to carry out invasive probes without the knowledge of the individuals under investigation.

Sharing the Wait for the End of the World

Few religious phenomena have intrigued outsiders more than messianic
or millenarian beliefs that some cataclysmic event—the coming of a
savior or the destruction of the world—would take place on a specific
date in the near future, at a specific location. A group of European
Anabaptists believed that the millennium would come in 1534 and that
Muenster would be the New Jerusalem. And in the seventeenth century,
a large proportion of Jews throughout the world were convinced that a
young rabbi from Smyrna named Sabbatai Sevi was the Messiah and
that the messianic kingdom was to come at a specified, imminent date.
In these movements, as in the many millenarian sects in the United
States, people sold their homes, gave up their jobs, and brought their
families to the appointed place, only to find their prayers unanswered
and their expectations unfulfilled.

What happens to faith at such times of disappointment? What happens
to belief in the signs that had seemed to foretell the cataclysmic event?
What do members of such groups do with their lives, having previously
given up all ties to ordinary existence? And how do they respond to the
pity and the taunting that they encounter?

These questions could hardly fail to interest social scientists. One
sociologist, Leon Festinger, directed a study of the discrepancy—the
"cognitive dissonance"—between the original beliefs about what was to
happen and the later understanding of what actually did happen.[4]
He predicted that given a firm enough conviction and strong group
support, members would respond to disconfirmation in an unexpected
way. Rather than giving up their original belief, he argued, they would
turn to proselytizing in order to buttress it. Signs would be re-examined,
dates computed anew. Gaining new adherents would serve to confirm
their own belief, and thus to counteract the dissonance with which they
were struggling. Not until beset by further discouraging news would
their own faith begin to waver, and the group gradually dissolve.

Festinger pointed out, however, the difficulties of proving or disproving
his hypothesis by looking merely at historical records; for the factor of
greatest interest to him—the proselytizing after disconfirmation—might
not have seemed of sufficient interest at the time to have been noticed
and recorded. And then, quite by accident, he came across a newspaper
report indicating that the process was about to repeat itself not far away.

The reader can then imagine the enthusiasm with which we seized the opportunity
to collect direct observational data about a group who appeared to believe in a
prediction of catastrophe to occur in the near future.

. . . One day in late September the Lake City *Herald* carried a two-column story, on a back page, headlined: PROPHECY FROM PLANET. CLARION CALL TO CITY: FLEE THAT FLOOD. IT'LL SWAMP US ON DEC. 21, OUTER SPACE TELLS SUBURBANITES. The body of the story expanded somewhat on these bare facts:

> Lake City will be destroyed by a flood from Great Lake just before dawn, Dec. 21, according to a suburban housewife. Mrs. Marion Keech, of 847 West School Street, says the prophecy is not her own. It is the purport of many messages she has received by automatic writing, she says . . . sent to her by superior beings from a planet called Clarion. These beings have been visiting the earth, she says, in what we call flying saucers. During their visits, she says, they have observed fault lines in the earth's crust that foretoken the deluge.[5]

Festinger and his colleagues decided to study the group not only in the remaining months before the expected calamities but on the appointed day and for a period afterwards. A first visit with Mrs. Keech led them to opt for a surreptitious approach.

In our very first contact with the central members of the group, their secrecy and general attitude toward non-believers made it clear that the study could not be conducted openly.[6]

Having made such a choice, the investigators adopted a complex strategy. They made contact with the believers by means of elaborate cover stories designed to "obtain a quick but firm entrée into the movement." They made false personal claims, and acted as if they were genuinely persuaded by the evidence from outer space and interested to learn how to avoid the flood. But still they were not allowed entry into the innermost circle of the "advanced seekers." At that point, they explain, "we decided to equip our representative with an 'experience' with the supernatural," borrowed from a Mexican folk tale. Similarly, another observer told the group that she had had a dream that fitted in with their prophecies:

I was standing on the side of a hill. . . . There was a man standing on top of the hill with a light all around him. There were torrents of water, raging water all around, and the man reached down and lifted me up out of the water. I felt safe.[7]

The group greeted this story and the earlier one with enthusiasm. The second investigator was taken to bring a message from outer space, and was asked to record the dream on tape so that others could hear it. It came to count as corroborating evidence—a fact that, not surprisingly, caused the investigators some concern about their role.

As the time foreseen for the cataclysm—December 21—approached, the investigators kept continuous watch over the group without letting on that they were doing so. They saw its members grow increasingly agitated, maintaining strict secrecy toward the curious and the reporters who had gathered to cover the outcome. But as the day came and went, and nothing unusual happened, the group members gave up their secrecy. They made frantic efforts to convince outsiders, telephoning the reporters they had so recently scorned, pressing information on every visitor. They took to proselytizing, just as the investigators had expected them to, and at the same time were anxiously on the lookout for signals and instructions from outer space.

Over the next few weeks, bewildered and dejected, reaching for every straw and disappointed anew each time, the group finally began to fall apart. No new converts had been made; no new signals seemed forthcoming. It became increasingly difficult to uphold the faith. Gradually, the group scattered. The investigators left, satisfied that their hypothesis had been confirmed. In their book about these events—*When Prophecy Fails*—they concluded that their work had been "as much detective work as observation." [8]

Through such means, they had gained entry to what members of the sect strove to keep secret. Intending to make their findings public, they had deceived the members into revealing their innermost hopes and fears as they never would have to strangers and least of all to researchers. The investigators' behavior and cover stories had led group members to become even more confident in the signals from outer space. By every definition of privacy, the investigators had invaded that of their unwitting subjects; and they had done so, not out of any desire to help these men and women, but strictly for purposes of research.

What is it about research that is thought to outweigh, at times, the respect for human boundaries? Why do for its sake what one might otherwise repudiate—pry, manipulate, and lie to invade private and closely guarded realms? Do the purposes for which social scientists pursue their studies lend special legitimacy to such methods? [9]

To See Through and to Unmask

The rationale for social science research serves, like those discussed in earlier chapters, partly to answer, partly to deflect such questions. Four arguments—invoking the pursuit of knowledge, the benefits of research, the freedom of inquiry, and "value-free" research—defend research in general, and are extended by some to justify intrusive studies. A supportive argument concerns such studies more specifically, claiming that they are not truly invasive.

The *pursuit of knowledge* can surely justify probing that would ordinarily be indiscreet or even degrading, so long as it is undertaken with the consent of those subjected to the probing, as when individuals agree to examinations by physicians, psychiatrists, and others which they would reject from other quarters. When social scientists invoke the pursuit of knowledge to justify research such as that conducted by Festinger, they likewise take it to outweigh common moral considerations. Fewer now believe in the possibility of attaining "true knowledge" than in Durkheim's time; yet research may at least push back the boundaries of ignorance and felt chaos. Perhaps it may also achieve greater insight into all that is private, exclusive, even sacred.

But how should one go about such research when people are so reluctant to have these aspects of their existence studied, or else so unable to respond spontaneously in experimental situations? The physical world lends itself at least in part to experimental manipulation in the search for knowledge; human beings can be much more grudging. As a result, researchers have worked out ways to take people by surprise before they have a chance to resist revealing themselves, and have developed means of deceiving them in such ways that they do not know what is being studied. Under such circumstances, people may betray their "true" responses as they would not if they had been forewarned.

Yet the pursuit of knowledge cannot by itself justify deceit and intrusiveness that bypass consent. Might not Festinger justly have protested if his neighbors or local journalists had trespassed upon his most closely guarded intimacy for purposes of greater knowledge? But if that is so, what makes the difference when social scientists do so in the course of their research?

Does the difference lie in the possible *benefits of research*—benefits great enough to override such protests about intrusive probing? Might researchers claim that it is one thing to pry into the religious practices of neighbors out of mere curiosity and quite another to undertake *research* into such practices? Could Festinger have argued that his study sought knowledge about conduct that seemed irrational at first glance, and that this knowledge could help individuals as well as society to cope more wisely with cognitive dissonance?

The hope to provide such benefits has undoubtedly motivated many investigators. C. Wright Mills has pointed to the frequency with which social scientists state their aims as "prediction and control." [10] Through research, they seek knowledge that could help individuals and influence social policies—the treatment of welfare recipients, for example, or of schoolchildren, or the prevention of crime. But when they undertake intrusive, perhaps deceptive studies (as in all other research), social scientists have widely diverging views about the kind of influence they hope to exert. They may conduct such studies in order to predict and to influence consumer choice on behalf of companies, or apply similar techniques to voting behavior in order to swing support to the political candidates who employ them. Or they may want to shock the public into acknowledging misery and injustice. Thus social commentators have sought to penetrate and then to expose mental hospitals or camps for migrant workers, hoping to pierce the wall of public indifference even at the risk of breaching individual boundaries of reserve—as when films are made of inmates against their wishes.

Anthropologists, likewise, have sought to exercise leverage of widely different and sometimes conflicting kinds. Some have studied groups and cultures that are threatened in order to speak on their behalf. [11] Any intrusiveness on their part, they argue, is minimal compared to the impact of the outside world, as one culture after another becomes extinct or is annihilated by commercial or military means. [12] Other social scientists, on the contrary, have worked to help outside groups to penetrate where overt military or commercial efforts might encounter resistance. Like missionaries, they have at times been used for propaganda or infiltration, and at times in order to learn how to stifle social protest: some eager to place themselves at the service of a cause they admire, others as unwitting tools, perhaps shielding themselves from asking hard questions about the impact of their work.

With so many different aims for the "prediction and control" of social science research, and with such unspecified, often disputed, benefits from this research, intrusive studies can hardly be justified merely by invoking possible benefits. [13] Those who conduct intrusive studies have not shown the links between their research and such benefits, nor explained why they think the hypothetical gains from their research should override the desires of those being studied.

The ill-starred Project Camelot served as an eye-opener for social scientists in these respects, and drew explicit attention to the traps and risks of doing research without careful consent procedures. [14] Begun in 1964 by the United States Army, the project involved the largest single set of grants ever directed to a social science study. Its purpose was stated as follows, in a paper sent to potential participants:

To determine the feasibility of developing a general social systems model which would make it possible to predict and influence politically significant aspects of social change in the developing nations of the world.

If researchers could learn to predict the preconditions for social conflict and "insurgency," then, the planners hoped, it might be possible to control such unrest more effectively, or even to prevent it. Latin American countries were, unbeknownst to their governments, citizens, or public media, to be at the center of the research. Social scientists from a number of nations agreed to participate; but the project was canceled less than a year after it had begun, after rumors about it had aroused a storm of protest in Chile and elsewhere.

Such projects illustrate the pitfalls of putting intrusive research to the task of prediction and control. The hoped-for benefits of research are as insufficient to justify intrusive studies as are references to the pursuit of knowledge. Such arguments are important when accepted by volunteers who agree, for instance, to take part in studies that might give clues to ways of stopping smoking or combating fatigue; but they cannot justify research conducted on people against their wishes—expressed or putative.

The rationale for social science research may draw on an additional argument that presupposes neither the value of particular studies nor the benefits to be derived from them: the claim to *freedom for scientific inquiry* no matter how inconsequential or even unpopular some lines of research may be in the eyes of critics. Such a requirement is indispensable for the protection of freedom of thought that is central to scientific inquiry; science, without such protection, is vulnerable to the many who would impose censorship, blacklists, or limitations on the study of selected topics. Scientific freedom threatens every hierarchy purporting to have access to the full truth, or to truth more important than that sought by science.

Because scientific research must be protected against such attacks, many scientists have been reluctant to accept any outside criticism or restraints whatsoever. But in describing the freedom of scientific inquiry, the words "freedom" and "inquiry" can be stretched far beyond the freedom of thought. Their placid connotations can then help to ward off concern about what scientists do, and about limits to invasive or dangerous research. The concept of "inquiry" in science evokes the solitary seeker for knowledge. Freedom of such inquiry is freedom of limitless thought and unfettered speech. Steven Weinberg conveys a splendid image of the world of such a scientist:

In the Science Museum in Kensington there is an old picture of the Octagon Room of the Greenwich Observatory, which seems to me beautifully to express the mood of science at its best: the room laid out in a cool, uncluttered, early eighteenth-century style, the few instruments standing ready for use, clocks of various sorts ticking on the walls, and from the many windows, filling the room, the clear light of day.[15]

These solitary, reflective, almost passive connotations of "scientific inquiry" do not in fact correspond with many of the activities of today's scientists. These men and women are hardly solitary in their interaction with others. They are far from passive in their use of vast public funds, or in their resort to manipulative techniques for human studies. Some use electronic and chemical means to act upon human beings in ways hitherto inconceivable. Others intrude upon, and help to alter, the most fundamental beliefs individuals may hold. The freedom to do such studies is not the freedom of thought and speech that must be defended for all people, but freedom of action. The latter cannot be limitless, for scientists any more than for others, and least of all when it places unsuspecting individuals at risk.

The passive connotations of such terms as "inquiry" and "freedom" may also help explain the unquestioning faith with which some social scientists have held to the notion that the conduct of their research could be "value-free."[16] Through the 1960s, a number of researchers subscribed to a misinterpretation of Max Weber's call for *wertfrei*, or "value-free," social science. Instead of seeing it as a warning not to let values influence the interpretation of results, they came to regard any concern with ethical questions as unscientific, and to confuse the scientific ideals of disinterestedness and objectivity with a denial of the role that values play in all thinking and all work, including their own. Weber himself would have been the last to deny this role—the last, too, to refuse to acknowledge the moral dimension of research that affects human beings as research subjects or otherwise.[17]

The concept of "value-free research" is broad; but even those who subscribe to it make an illegitimate leap if they deduce from it some notion of completely value-free *conduct* of research, or conjure up the specter of a value-free social scientist. Most researchers would themselves condemn egregious abuses in research, and use moral criteria in so doing; but the confused concept of "value-free research" has blunted the application of the same criteria to less egregious but nevertheless troubling cases.

Neither the shield of freedom of inquiry nor that of value-free research suffices to ward off all questions about intrusive research. An additional argument is occasionally brought to its defense—one we have already encountered in the context of military secrecy. This argument holds that there is no need to be concerned about secrecy or about probing, since there is very little that people succeed in keeping secret in the first place. Restraints on probing by social scientists would be like locking the barn door after the cows have run away. Modern life, according to this argument, necessitates so much openness and revelation that discretion on the part of social scientists would be prudish and unnecessary. Why should social scientists be prevented from observing what everyone else is at liberty to see?

Insofar as information is thus open, the argument is surely persuasive. It would be absurd to argue, for instance, that the observation of traffic patterns or of horse-racing audiences poses a problem, and that it should proceed only with the consent of all who are being observed. It would be equally uncalled-for to forbid research on what some people are willing to expose, just because others guard it closely. Rather, what is at issue is research on the private behavior of individuals without their knowledge or against their will. Of such intrusions, one can hardly claim that what is being studied is open for all to see. If it were, why would investigators regard it as necessary to employ surprise and pressure and deceit in order to penetrate what for them is so readily apparent?

Such intrusive research is not always conducted in secret. It can proceed openly by taking subjects by surprise and thus wrenching from them responses they might have guarded against had they been forewarned. It can also rely on pressure. Students taking courses in sociology or social psychology may have no choice but to take part as subjects of intrusive research. Such participation may be the prerequisite for taking a course, or for belonging to a department. Preadolescents in school often find it hard to refuse to answer probing questionnaires about family life or sexual matters. And welfare clients have difficulty distinguishing between the studies to which they are subjected and the many other procedures they must go through.

More often, however, intrusive research is surreptitious. Infiltration, cover stories, hidden cameras, and one-way mirrors—few methods known to the world of detection and espionage are foreign to social science. The means for such covert observation grow more ingenious each year; and in some fields such methods are thought especially likely to allow examination of subjects behaving "naturally."

Consider, for example, the investigator who simulated a "lookout" meant to warn homosexuals in men's rooms. He not only observed their activities covertly, but also traced the participants, took notes on their homes and their neighborhoods, and finally interviewed them, giving a false reason for doing so, without revealing to them his earlier monitoring of their actions.[18]

Or take the innumerable questionnaires and psychological tests ostensibly given for one purpose while in reality used to try to penetrate much more intimate attitudes, perhaps even ones causing the subjects great anxiety, such as sexual problems or feelings of self-hatred.

Or consider the following letter to Ruth Benedict from Jaime de Angelo, whom she had asked for help in finding an Indian informant willing to reveal sacred ceremonials:

Ruth, you have no idea how much that has hurt me. . . . Do you realize that it is just that sort of thing that kills the Indians. I mean it seriously. It kills them spiritually first, and as in their life the spiritual and the physical element are much more interdependent than our own, they soon die of it physically. . . . Don't you understand the psychological value of secrecy at a certain level of culture? . . . there are things that must not be brought to the light of day, otherwise they wither and die like uprooted plants.[19]

Whether or not the author of this letter was right in his surmise about the particular case in question, his concern points to a pattern of neglect by many early anthropologists. Because they were so interested in the knowledge they might gain, they sometimes failed to take into account the responses of those whom they studied, especially among cultures very different from their own. Some looked at the peoples they were studying much as they would have looked at exotic specimens in their laboratories.[20] Others felt closer to them, but never imagined that the rituals and secrets they exposed in print might find their way back to the tribes they had probed to cause them embarrassment and a sense of shamed exposure.

None of the arguments I have examined can be stretched to justify invasive studies of the unwilling or the secretive; nor do they give such justification in the aggregate. Research lends no special legitimacy to actions otherwise disrespectful of human beings, unless they have expressly consented thereto. In that case, what conclusions should we draw with respect to research such as that of Festinger? Should social scientists leave untouched those regions of privacy and sacredness that Durkheim had singled out for future study?

Restraints

Asking social scientists to leave certain regions of privacy untouched would, as Herbert Kelman has argued, severely hamper research:

A blanket prohibition of research that might conceivably touch on such areas [ones that would violate private space]—which would include, among others, the topics of sex, personal health, death, religion, ethnicity, politics, money, and parent-child relations—would destroy or trivialize social research.[21]

Such a blanket prohibition of entire areas would not only decimate research; it would also be quite unnecessary from the point of view of privacy. Much research concerning these areas is retrospective or statistical or otherwise nonintrusive. And the research that some see as intrusive is acceptable to others, even welcomed by a few. What one person wishes to shield, another discusses freely. For instance, research on sexuality with consenting mature subjects is not intrusive, whatever one may think about its validity or taste.

Rather than foreclose entire areas of research, therefore, it is preferable to seek restraints on methods of research. Standards are needed, rather, for making sure that the subjects for sensitive research have consented to be studied; that those who are unable to consent, being, perhaps, too young or too ill, not be exposed to anything that might then or later violate their sense of privacy and self-respect; and that no one ever be *asked* to consent to research so invasive or degrading that most people would reject it out of hand.

Social scientists are increasingly aware of the need for some constraints. Their codes of ethics now proclaim in general terms that privacy should be respected and harm to subjects avoided. But most of these codes fail to mention, much less prohibit, the use of secrecy or deception in research.[22] The most recent set of ethical principles for psychologists does mention such practices, only to leave the determination of whether to engage in them up to the investigators themselves:

Methodological requirements of a study may make the use of concealment or deception necessary. Before conducting such a study, the investigator has a special responsibility to (i) determine whether the use of such techniques is justified by the study's prospective scientific, educational, or applied value; (ii) determine whether alternative procedures are available that do not use concealment or deception; and (iii) ensure that the participants are provided with sufficient explanation as soon as possible.[23]

The obstacles to moral inquiry that I have discussed go far to explain the blandness or permissiveness of such codes. These documents caution against harming human subjects but do not take seriously the risks from invasive research or deception in any study, whether the aim is invasive or not. The determination of what is invasive and what is not obviously differs from person to person, and should therefore be left up to each subject, not to the investigators. No amount of explaining the study design and its aims after it is over can justify the failure to offer subjects such a choice beforehand.

Social scientists would take it for granted that such a requirement should be imposed were they themselves to be the main targets of infiltration and intrusive probing. But their subjects are often people they do not know, or with whom they are in a relationship of authority, as with students or children, or from whom they feel a distance of some other kind. Edward Shils has traced the beginnings of direct research on human beings in the social sciences. He has shown how frequently the earliest studies were done on aborigines or members of social classes, races, or groups with whom researchers felt they had little in common— "people regarded as not possessing the sensibilities which demand privacy or the moral dignity which requires its respect." [24] Because the ethical problems inherent in such approaches were not clearly seen from the outset, it was harder to formulate them later, when research came to be conducted on more varied groups. And the poor, the unemployed, the mentally ill, and children continued to be studied in ways that researchers might have found troubling if applied to their own families or to themselves.

Consider a study, carried out on "120 children attending an elementary school in a lower-class neighborhood in Pittsburgh," to measure the relationship between stealing and "temporal orientation." The children, selected from grades 2 to 8, were first presented with an "opportunity for stealing."

An opportunity for stealing was devised in the following fashion. The experimenter, officially present in the school with facilities to conduct hearing examinations, sent a message to the teacher of the subject with a note explaining that the subject was needed by the experimenter. Upon entering the room, the subject saw the experimenter standing beside her desk, in an apparently flustered fashion. Beside the experimenter and near the desk on the floor was a woman's handbag, overturned, with its contents spilled out. Cards, a comb, assorted papers, and $.65 (2 dimes, 2 nickles, and 35 pennies) were scattered about and nearby was an opened small change purse. The experimenter said:

> Look at this mess. I spilled my purse and everything fell out. I have to go up to the kindergarten now [the room most remote from the experimental room] and I don't have time to clean this up. Would you mind getting these things together? I don't care about the change. I don't know how much it is but I think it is only pennies. Most of it rolled away, I guess. Just try to get the papers together. I'll be back in about five minutes. [25]

Forty-nine children took some of the money. The investigators speculate whether "for the present lower-class subjects, proficiency in stealing was a 'realistic' mode of adjustment." But nowhere do they evince the slightest questioning of their own procedure, much less make any effort to put a class label on their own attitude to the children. Their study illustrates a willingness to manipulate others for research purposes that underlines both the temptations and the dangers when investigators feel free to bypass the consent of the individuals they plan to involve in an experimental study.

Quite apart from the effects on those subjected, like these children, to manipulative and intrusive research, investigators should consider the risks of self-injury. What happens to someone who lies to 120 children, one after another, in order to tempt each one to steal? However cleverly she manipulates and deceives, however expert she becomes at keeping her scheme secret from the children, she knows that their confidence in her is unwarranted. I argued in earlier chapters that learning to handle secrecy calls for coming to see oneself and others as capable of moral choice and as owed respect; and that impairments of this understanding—of discretion—are reflected in moral judgment generally. Investigators have every reason, therefore, to consider how they will change as a result of subjecting others to experiments requiring manipulative uses of secrecy. The harm may be greater to the psychologist who resorts repeatedly to such tactics than to the experimental subjects— who may, after all, never run into another intrusive experiment again.[26]

Social scientists have responsibilities, as well, to those whom they employ to carry out their research. Most deceptive and intrusive studies, while directed by senior investigators and faculty members, are actually carried out by graduate students, who may be torn between a desire to move ahead in their chosen fields and distaste for what they are asked to do. Thomas Murray has described this conflict among young researchers. Some retire from the field rather than take part in such research, whereas others engage in compromises and rationalizations in order to continue.[27] Both the distaste and the rationalization are self-protective responses, signaling the felt risks to discretion and to integrity from subjecting others to manipulative and intrusive research. As for the many social scientists who do no such research, they still have to reckon with suspicion and with studies damaged by false or mocking responses by persons who imagine that they are being duped and who retaliate in kind.

Another problem with invasive research methods is that they might alter the outcome of the experiments themselves (in addittion to the very fact of observation that affects all research).* Few researchers are such perfect actors as not to have their deceit change other aspects of their behavior. And since deceptive studies such as those of Festinger are conducted without any control groups, the effects are hard to measure. Festinger's results were clearly skewed when the investigators gave the group members spurious evidence of such a kind as to reinforce the very beliefs under the study. Add to that the fact that the researchers had a high stake in the study's turning out to confirm their hypothesis, and one may well conclude that, whatever else their book *When Prophecy Fails* may have been, it was quite likely also a self-fulfilling prophecy that succeeded.

When secretly intrusive research proceeds on the assumption that the subjects suspect nothing, its validity may be further impaired. Students, who serve as subjects in most studies, are often suspicious from the very beginning. Some pride themselves on deceiving the investigators in return, or on responding in ways that simulate feeble-mindedness or psychosis.[28] Others alter their answers to reflect what they believe is expected of them. The validity of such studies is shaky, to say the least.

Given the risks to all involved and to the validity of the intrusive studies, much more thought should be given to alternative ways of gaining knowledge. Consider, once again, Leon Festinger's study of the millenarian sect. One reason he thought it important to infiltrate the sect was its secretiveness, combined with the scant and unverifiable evidence concerning past groups. But while he and his colleagues were writing up the results of their study, Gerschom Scholem was completing *Sabbatai Sevi*, a monumental study of a seventeenth-century millenarian movement.[29] Scholem had recourse neither to intrusion nor to cover stories for his work; yet he illuminates the processes and persons he describes and conveys the spirit of messianism as few others have. He focuses, moreover, on precisely the question that was of such interest to Festinger and his colleagues: how individuals react to the failure of the prophecies for which they have sacrificed everything.

The search for alternatives to intrusive studies should therefore not be limited to one's own profession, nor consider only one particular point in time. If the millenarian group in 1954 or 1955 was secretive, another one, a few years later, might not be. Indeed, several such groups since

---

*Unlike natural scientists, social scientists have not yet paid sufficient attention to the effects of manipulation and intrusion on the very validity of their studies. But if such methods render the studies invalid, then even the slightest risk for participants, imposed upon them without their knowledge, is unwarranted even apart from other moral considerations.

that time have been more than willing to give detailed interviews concerning their expectations and responses to disappointment.[30] It would accordingly be premature to conclude that one must intrude on secretive groups merely because one cannot discern or foresee that the knowledge could be gained in other ways, perhaps by individuals in entirely different disciplines.

Let us postulate, however, that there appear to be no alternatives to invasive research regarding a particular hypothesis—for example, that of the relationship between stealing and temporal orientation among children. In that case, it would generally be preferable to let the hypothesis remain untested. There may be exceptional circumstances, in social science work as elsewhere, that justify recourse to intrusive probing. But the mere absence of alternatives to any one study that an investigator believes to have "prospective scientific, educational, or applied value" (to use the words of the American Psychological Association's 1981 Ethical Principles) in no way suffices to justify such probing.

Other social scientists—among them Edward Shils, Kai Erikson, and Margaret Mead—have set higher, and to my mind more appropriate, standards for research.[31] They have rejected intrusive and covert experimental designs out of concern for the integrity of research as much as for the persons whose life it touches. Thus Margaret Mead spoke out against covert methods of investigation as follows:

When a human being is introduced who is consciously distorting his position, the material of the research is inevitably jeopardized, and the results always are put in question as the "participant"—introduced as a "psychotic" into a mental ward, or a "fanatic" into a flying-saucer cult group—gives his subjects false clues of a nonverbal nature and produces distortions which cannot be traced in his results. . . . The deception violates the conventions of privacy and human dignity and casts scientists in the role of spies, intelligence agents, Peeping Toms and versions of Big Brother. Furthermore, it damages science by cutting short attempts to construct methods of research that would responsibly enhance, rather that destroy, human trust.[32]

Combating Corruption Through Research

Should social scientists exercise similar restraint with respect to persons or groups who abuse secrecy? Even those investigators who agree to ask members of religious sects, children, students, and others for consent before probing their private and hidden concerns might question the need to treat persons suspected of crime (police corruption, say, insurance fraud, or abuses by government officials) with similar respect.

The Watergate scandal brought about a realization among researchers that official secrecy can conceal illegal activities that mere observation from the outside cannot penetrate. Some held that social scientists had let the United States down in not being more alert to how secret systems work against the public interest in bureaucracies. As official secrecy spreads, they suggested, more aggressive methods of probing are needed in turn.[33]

This proposal deserves serious consideration. Government and business and other affairs—and certainly criminal activities wherever they occur—are clearly different from strictly individual privacy. Those who act unjustly or in breach of the law or against the public interest cannot as easily complain of intrusive interference. Their secrets are illegitimate, and their claims to privacy concerning them or to executive privilege are often transparent defenses against fulfilling their obligations of accountability.

It is not clear, however, that all social scientists would reserve such intrusive methods of investigation for cases of suspected serious wrongdoing. On the contrary, some among them work with such an expansive view of corruption that nearly all practices qualify for aggressive investigations. They argue that in order to expose the truth about such social ills as racism or corruption, social scientists must adopt an adversary and secretive stance toward the people they study. Without such a stance, they fear being co-opted, and thus biased. Thus one researcher, Jack D. Douglas, proposes that

we must expect to do our study by getting *inside* the group or groups to be studied, in order to observe carefully and systematically how they manage their everyday lives. Only in this way can we be sure of penetrating the misinformations, evasions, lies and fronts that groups use to screen out enemies in conflict situations.[34]

Invasive probing, for Douglas, is a necessary response to the pervasive secrecy, the lies, and the hypocrisy in society. Those who raise ethical questions are self-deceivers, blind to the deception that he takes both to require and to justify surreptitious probing in return by social scientists.

Such claims use moral language to dismiss moral inquiry. But the notion that one is justified in lying to someone so long as one has convinced oneself he is a liar is open to two challenges. In the first place, one's assessment may well be in error—especially when one expands it, as here, to include entire groups and societies. Second, even if one is correct, one's judgment that someone is a liar does not in itself justify lying to him any more than knowing him to be a thief justifies stealing from him.[35]

Finally, Douglas relies on two of the arguments that I have already discussed as insufficient to justify treating others for the purposes of research as one could never defend treating them otherwise: the argument that research legitimates such methods because it is undertaken in pursuit of knowledge or truth; and the claim to high hopes for benefits from research which will outweigh any inroads on the privacy of individuals or groups: "I feel a bit more in a good cause, that of trying to reveal truths about us all which may in the long run be of vital help to us all, is not too much to bear." [36]

Such exalted views of the "truth" available to researchers and of the social benefits of their studies may become more tempting the less justification their work seems to command on its own. Margaret Mead has suggested that the experimenter who needs to justify demeaning other human beings may compensate by a belief in "becoming someone who benefits mankind on a large scale." [37] But say that a research team has strong evidence of genuine wrongdoing. Even so, nondeceptive methods of probing should have priority. A great deal of evidence about abuses can be gathered without probing from outside, or be exposed by knowledgeable insiders. Indeed, such wrongdoing is often—like blighted city blocks or starving refugee populations—in clear view yet never fully acknowledged. Even if probing from without is needed, a great many nonclandestine methods are available. The more skilled the observers, the less duplicity they will need in order to secure such evidence.

Certain forms of secret abuse are nevertheless so ingeniously concealed that only disguised probing may be capable of detecting them. For such a task, the training, the qualifications, and the public accountability of those who propose to do the investigating become important factors. How does social science research into government corruption or criminal practices compare, from these points of view, with other investigative approaches? In order to answer, we must take into account the growth and the scope of organized prying in modern societies: the widespread investigations by credit bureaus to winnow out persons who conceal debts or liabilities that increase the risk of lending them money, or by insurance companies to detect fraudulent claims for reimbursement; the undercover exploration by employers and "head-hunters" of the personal and occupational backgrounds of prospective employees; the sports espionage and the gathering of business intelligence throughout the world; the undercover investigations by reporters and private detectives; and most of all, the probing by government agencies and police forces in different nations.

A comparison of the various forms of surreptitious probing arouses little enthusiasm for the current proliferation of investigative practices, in which innumerable operatives from different professions feel free to lie, set traps, and invade private life in pursuit of some goal they regard as overriding normal constraints. It should be a matter of public concern to set standards for these practices and for who should take part in them, with what training, what guidelines, and what safeguards. It is not clear that social scientists would end up high on such a list. They are neither trained for investigative tasks of such a nature nor subject to the standards of accountability, evidence, or protection of witnesses that are desirable for the investigation of crime or official wrongdoing. Nor do most social scientists see such investigation as a task for which their methods are appropriate or likely to be useful. Finally, there is hardly a dearth of social ills in need of study and so glaringly evident that they can be approached without recourse to underhanded means of probing.

Durkheim's prophecy for the social sciences—that they will displace religious and philosophical thought about human problems, and at long last show nature, man, and society "as they really are"—can never be fulfilled. It expresses the perennial drive to dispel mystery and to achieve complete transparency without which scientific inquiry might well slacken. But it leads too easily to a lack of concern for the limitations and biases that hamper even the most exacting research, and to a sense of legitimacy in overriding ordinary moral restraints for the sake of science. Paradoxically, the prophecy then becomes self-defeating: the more one strains by such means to approach a greater understanding of nature, man, and society, the more it scatters and recedes into the distance.

Investigative Journalism

Limits to Probing?

The press is the most important counterbalance we possess against each of the rationales for secrecy discussed in earlier chapters. Without reporters free to probe and motivated to do so, government and commercial and other forms of secrecy would have much less to challenge and restrain them (witness those societies where the media are most subject to control and censorship by the government). The press, along with the other media of communication, has, therefore, a much clearer *public* mandate to probe and to expose than do, for instance, social scientists or private detectives.

This mandate affects the way in which journalists experience the conflicts felt by all who inquire into what is concealed. It adds legitimacy to their probing of secrets and enhances the allure of the unknown. But reporters invariably encounter claims that much of what they wish to investigate is confidential, be it state secrets or medical or corporate ones. They experience, too, efforts at co-optation, at including them within a chosen circle of persons in the know who cannot reveal all that they know. At other times, reporters have reason to fear reprisals from those whose secrets they have exposed.

Should journalists recognize limits to what they can legitimately probe and to the means for doing so? Or would such restraints inevitably threaten independent reporting and the freedom of expression? I shall discuss these questions first with respect to prying into personal secrets and private lives, and then in the larger context of the public's right to know; finally, I shall take up the issue of secretive and deceptive means of investigation. These problems have been dealt with at length in the law, though not always conclusively. As the following example shows, however, the legal and the moral issues are not identical.

Exposing Private Lives

In 1937, James Thurber unwittingly set in motion what he later described as the most important legal case in the history of the *New Yorker* magazine and its only conflict ever to reach the Supreme Court.[1] Using the pseudonym Jared L. Manley, he published an essay entitled "April Fool!" about a man once famous as a child prodigy who now shunned every mention of his former feats.[2] The essay brought out the contrast between the brilliant but exploited childhood of William James Sidis and what seemed an undistinguished, indeed shabby and ludicrous, later life.

Almost from birth, the boy was subjected to training sessions, hypnosis, and psychological experimentation by his father, Boris Sidis, a psychologist bent on producing a genius. William learned to read and write both English and French in his earliest years. At five, he had written a treatise on anatomy, and at eight he proposed a new table of logarithms. Boris Sidis reported on each new feat to the press. He wrote a book entitled *Philistine and Genius* to promote his methods of education.[3] Conventional education, he insisted, turns children into uncritical philistines and willing cannon fodder. By stimulating early development, on the other hand, one will "not only prevent vice, crime, and disease, but will strengthen the individual along all lines, physical, mental, and moral." He claimed to be able to speak with authority, "from my own experience with child-life."

When William was nine, his parents began taking him to nearby Tufts College. At eleven, having transferred to Harvard, the boy gave a stunning lecture before students and faculty on "four-dimensional bodies." The national press gave front-page coverage to this event, and editorialists gave favorable notice to the educational theories of Boris Sidis.[4] But in the ensuing years, William refused to cater to his father's hopes. Although he completed his college studies, he rejected the future his father had mapped out for him. Finding publicity offensive and mathematical work increasingly distasteful, William turned down all further requests that he display his powers in public. He left graduate school without a degree.

After a brief stint at college teaching, he abandoned academic life for good, severed relations with his family, and took up one menial job after another, only to leave it each time someone discovered he was the same William Sidis who had been so famous as a child prodigy. His childhood feats could not be kept secret or wiped out. They were public knowledge. But his *connection* to those feats—this he could try to conceal.

The *New Yorker* article cornered him. Drawing on the account of an unnamed woman who "recently succeeded in interviewing him," its author exposed Sidis at age thirty-nine, living alone in an untidy "hall bedroom of Boston's shabby south end." After recounting once again Sidis's childhood exploits, the article focused with ruthless detail on his quest for anonymity and his incongruous present behavior. "He seems to have difficulty in finding the right words to express himself," the author noted, "but when he does, he speaks rapidly, nodding his head jerkily to emphasize his points, gesturing with his left hand, uttering occasionally a curious, gasping laugh." [5]

Writing the piece may have had its pleasures of accurate depiction and condescending humor. Reading it may have served for many as a reminder of the downfall of the famous and as a warning against pressing children too far. But for Sidis himself, the article came as a blow where he was most vulnerable. His fragile defenses were penetrated. Not only did the essay shine a hated spotlight once more on the life he wanted to live in obscurity; it also held him up, he felt, to ridicule and shame. His response was to sue for invasion of privacy, claiming that the article

tended to expose, and did expose, the private life of the plaintiff to unwarranted and undesired publicity of a nature unfamiliar and harmful to the plaintiff, and tended to and did hold up the plaintiff to public scorn, ridicule, and contempt causing him grievous mental anguish, humiliation, and loss of reputation. [6]

After the case had gone to court, Thurber explained that he had wanted to "help curb the great American thrusting of talented children into the glare of fame and notoriety" by showing how these children suffer in later life. [7] This aim is not evident in the essay itself, the less so as its author did more than anyone else to renew the glare of notoriety for Sidis. What comes across, rather, is a distant and amused contempt for those judged to be doing less than they might, and living boring lives in one-room apartments.

Sidis lost his suit and lost again on appeal. Judge Clark, though characterizing the *New Yorker* article as "merciless," held that it did not constitute punishable invasion of privacy.[8] In the first place, much of what the article had revealed about Sidis's childhood was already public knowledge. People have no legal claim to erase their childhood fame, nor to remain unconnected with it in later life. In addition, courts have held that, once a public figure, one has fewer lawful claims to privacy than other persons. The health of public officials, for example, or their children's peccadilloes cannot legally be kept out of the press in the same way that such information about private individuals might be.

When the Supreme Court refused to hear the case, Sidis had no further recourse. The courts may well have been right to rule as they did. To have acceded to Sidis's claims could have endangered much reporting about matters of public importance; every shady venture could then try to hide behind similar claims to invasion of privacy.

Nevertheless, Sidis felt violated—and *was* violated. What for many might have seemed a tolerable exposure touched, for him, on aspects of his identity that he ached to veil in secrecy. Wishing above all to be forgotten, he was condemned to being remembered.[9] Much abused as a child, he had developed an exaggerated sense of vulnerability; he now had higher but also more fragile defenses than most. When they were broken down, he felt more injured than most. In 1944, Sidis—unemployed and destitute—was found unconscious in his apartment and died without regaining consciousness.[10]

Though unusually hurt by his exposure, Sidis is far from alone in being drawn into publicity against his wishes. Yet it would be wrong to conclude that journalists ought to write only about persons who have given their consent. As I have indicated in earlier chapters, those who use secrecy to cover up for abuses often resort to spurious claims of privacy, confidentiality, or national security. It is important for reporters not to take those claims at face value.

There is no clear line surrounding private life that can demarcate regions journalists ought not to explore. The serious illness of a political candidate or the paranoia of a government leader are surely matters for legitimate public concern. Health professionals should not conceal them, much less lie about them as has so often been done, nor should reporters help keep the public in the dark through misguided discretion. Such concealment helped disguise from the public the mental deterioration suffered by Winston Churchill in his last years, and Hubert Humphrey's worsening cancer at the time when he announced he would campaign to be the Democratic candidate in the 1976 presidential election.

Those who take public positions cannot always complain if they receive scrutiny of a kind that would be intrusive for completely private citizens. Thus a reporter who wrote a story proving that a prominent member of the American Nazi Party was half Jewish was not overstepping the bounds of legitimate privacy. True, the information was of a kind that the Nazi wanted kept secret; but having taken a strong public stance of anti-Semitism, he could hardly hold the information irrelevant to the public's evaluation of his views. Nor did his death, in what seemed to be suicide, the day after the story appeared render it more invasive.[11]

The children of those who have sought public attention, on the other hand, often have a stronger claim to be left in peace. Some are pursued relentlessly, the victims of a system of probing and reporting that draws few lines with respect to the invasion of privacy.[12] The Sidis case is marginal from this point of view. On the one hand it was Sidis, and not only his parents, who had been in the public eye. On the other hand, Sidis might have argued that he could not, as a child, have put up sufficient resistance to his father's efforts to publicize his precocity, nor even have known how they would affect him. Should he have to acquiesce in continued scrutiny because his parents had sought to make him famous? The judge in the Sidis case thought so. He held that public interest in Sidis was legitimate because of his earlier brilliance and fame.

The public doubtless had an interest in Sidis; and its interest was legitimate, not only in the sense of attaching to someone already in the public eye but also more generally. It is not wrong to be interested in another person's life, no matter whether that person is famous or not. However, the public's interest in Sidis was not based on any *need* to know what had befallen him—unlike, for instance, the need to know the whereabouts and employment record of someone running for political office. This difference in need engenders a difference in the degree to which reporters should respect requests for anonymity and privacy. Though readers might well have had a legitimate interest, based on curiosity, to know more about Sidis, they could hardly claim a right to acquire such knowledge against his wishes.

The confusing expression "the public's right to know" is often used to justify all that reporters do to cater to both need and interest on the part of the public, of whatever degree of legitimacy. Thus the 1973 Code of Ethics for journalists holds that "the public's right to know of events of public importance and interest is the overriding mission of the mass media," and states that "journalists must be free of obligations to any interest other than the public's right to know." [13]

To question what is done to satisfy such an all-inclusive right to know is to risk being accused of making dangerous inroads on the constitutionally guaranteed freedom of the press. We see here once again a rationale serving the double function of offering reasons and of warding off legitimate criticism. Yet questioning is surely needed.

The Public's Right to Know

Taken by itself, the notion that the public has a "right to know" is as quixotic from an epistemological as from a moral point of view, and the idea of the public's "right to know the truth" even more so. It would be hard to find a more fitting analogue to Jeremy Bentham's characterization of talk about natural and imprescriptible rights as "rhetorical nonsense— nonsense upon stilts." [14] How can one lay claims to a right to *know the truth* when even partial knowledge is out of reach concerning most human affairs, and when bias and rationalization and denial skew and limit knowledge still further? And how can one claim a *right* even to all the limited insights that it might be possible to acquire? Even such limited knowledge can rarely be viewed as a matter of right; indeed, there are realms about which we recognize that we must claim no rights to knowledge: the personal letters others wish to keep private, for example, or their intimate relationships.

So patently inadequate is the rationale of the public's right to know as a justification for all that reporters probe and expose, that although some still intone it ritualistically at the slightest provocation, most now refer to it with tired irony. Yet at the same time the slogan is not given up, for in spite of its inadequacy it is linked to vital public interests and entitlements. I shall examine these links, therefore, in the hope of drawing from the rationale the factors that affect moral choice.

In the United States, the notion of a public "right to know" is closely linked with the First Amendment and its guarantee that "Congress shall make no law . . . abridging the freedom of speech, or of the press." [15] This guarantee lends dignity and even sacredness to the function of the press; for many reporters, it suffices to justify almost all they do. But exactly how does the link function? How does the First Amendment connect with the public's right to know?

Some argue that the First Amendment presupposes the existence of the public's right to know. Were there no such right, they hold, there would be no need for the amendment. This view, however, merely states a conclusion without arguing for it. No evidence is offered for the link; and it is not clear why, even in the absence of an underlying right to know, the freedom of speech and of the press would not be thought indispensable. Others argue that the link is so close that it is one of mirroring: we cannot have freedom of the press without having it reflected in a public right to knowledge. Since we recognize the former, we must recognize the latter as well. Each presupposes the other, and justifies it in turn. Thus Laurence Tribe has held that at times the right to know "means nothing more than a mirror of such a right to speak, a listener's right that government not interfere with a willing speaker's liberty." [16]

Ronald Dworkin has argued, on the contrary, that the right to speak does not entail or mirror the right to know; at most, he holds, it may support a right to *listen*, and thus not to have the government interpose obstacles to that right between willing speakers and willing listeners. But such a right to listen is "very different from the right to know, because the latter, unlike the former, supposes that those who have the information have a duty and not simply a right to publish it. The Supreme Court has not recognized a right to know as a constitutional right. No one could sue the *New York Times* for *not* publishing the Pentagon Papers." [17]

Dworkin's distinction is persuasive. We cannot legitimately argue from someone's right to disseminate a story to the public's right to the information it contains, much less to any obligation to disseminate it. The entailment by the First Amendment of the public's right to know, therefore, is not tenable, and cannot provide the justification for all that is done in the name of catering to such a right.

If we give up this foundation for the public's right to know, might it not be possible to say that the freedom of the press can, in itself, provide the needed justification for all that reporters do? This is certainly the assumption of many who have begun to doubt the solidity of the right to know. Whatever the errors and abuses by reporters, they argue, the freedom of the press and of speech more generally must be protected against every inroad. Yet this assumption is too hasty. Even in the law, certain excesses are prohibited. And a *legal* right to free expression cannot do away with the need for *moral* scruples in choosing what to publish. Consider a derisive and condescending newspaper article about rape victims, complete with photographs and addresses acquired against their will. A reporter might not go to jail for publishing it, but he should nevertheless consider the moral reasons against publication before going ahead. He could not reasonably argue that the public has a right to such information; nor could he legitimately ignore the effects of his story on those already violated.

Some see another kind of link, of a dialectical nature, between the

claim to the public's right to know and the countervailing claims to
rights of privacy over experiences that the public arguably has no right
whatsoever to learn about.[18] In the perennial tensions between concealment
and probing, reciprocal strategies often arise. In recent decades, each
side has turned to the language of rights. I have previously discussed
the spreading use and the frequent abuse of claims to privacy by individuals
and organizations. As reporters find growing barriers erected against
their probing in the name of such a right to privacy, they have come to
turn more often for legitimacy to arguments equally vague in the name
of the right to know. (Interestingly, the 1973 Code of Ethics for journalists,
quoted on p. 253, made no references to this right in its earlier 1923
version.)

Reciprocal bombast, however, does not make for clarity. Both claims—
to privacy and to knowledge—serve increasingly as rationalizations. The
more diffusely they come to be applied, the more they blur and delay
moral inquiry. The undoubted dialectical relationship between the claims
to these rights does not, any more than the First Amendment, provide
justification for excesses of reportorial probing.

A third link comes closer to justifying zealous, even otherwise intrusive
reporting—but only for a circumscribed category of information. Here
we no longer speak of some indiscriminate and vague public right to
know, but of a clear legal right. It is the statutory right of the public
to know about its government, expressed by the United States Congress
in establishing the Freedom of Information Act (discussed in Chapter
XIII). For the great majority of government records, Congress held,
"the public as a whole has a right to know what its government is
doing." [19]

Long before such a law was enacted, this right was advocated as a
means of limiting executive and legislative secrecy. In 1747, at a time
of complete legislative secrecy in England, the *London Magazine* stated:
"Every subject not only has the right, but is duty bound, to inquire into
the public measures pursued." [20] And in the American Colonies, where
equal secretiveness prevailed, the issue was similarly joined as one of
whether the people did or did not have a right to know about government.

Such a right to know does correspond to a duty to reveal: the government
has the duty to reveal that which the public has a right to know. In
the same way, doctors have the duty not to withhold the information
to which their patients have a right. Just as it is wrong to keep certain
secrets from individuals, so it is wrong to keep some information from
the public—about the misconduct of a war, for example, or the use of

taxpayers' money for an official's private gain. But neither physicians nor governments have a duty to provide indiscriminate disclosure of all possible information.

Unlike the patient's right to information, the public's right to know about government activities can rarely be satisfied directly. To be sure, some can have direct access to certain information, or request it in person; but most people must rely on the media as indispensable intermediaries. As a result, the public's right to know about government does require a free press and access by the press to congressional and other deliberations.

But the public clearly has an equally legitimate interest in matters far beyond the domain of government. Unsafe private housing developments are of public concern fully as much as unsafe public housing; and the marketing of automobiles that are firetraps matters as much to the public as if the government were responsible for them. Indeed, it has become increasingly hard to draw a clear line between government information and information about the private sector. Commercial secrecy and scientific secrecy now blend with military secrecy in ways hardly imaginable by the early advocates of the public's right to know about government. And administrative secrecy now covers agencies and categories of persons and information to an extent equally difficult to foretell.

In addition, many countries have no statutorily guaranteed *right* of knowledge about government affairs; yet the public in those countries clearly has as great, and as legitimate, an *interest* in government action as elsewhere, and the press, therefore, as strong a mandate to inform the public. Indeed, quite apart from one's country of residence, societies are now so dependent upon one another's fortunes that the public in each has a legitimate interest in the affairs of all the others. Thus the publics in the many countries without nuclear weapons can hardly be said to have less to lose from the production of such weapons in other states than the inhabitants of these states themselves. When the governments of the United States, the Soviet Union, England, France, and China chose in secret to develop such weapons, not only were citizens in their countries deprived of their right to debate the choices that were to affect their future so profoundly; people the world over were equally deprived of an opportunity to influence their own fate.

For these reasons, it would be wrong merely to cling to a legalistic notion of a statutory right to know about the affairs of one's government. Rather, the role of the press should be to satisfy in the first place the public's legitimate interest in learning about matters—governmental or not—that affect its welfare. The reporting concerning such matters should be forceful; and it should not accede to all the claims we have examined: to privacy, confidentiality, or trade, scientific, administrative, and military secrecy. At times these shields are legitimate; but their legitimacy cannot be taken for granted. The inherent secretiveness of governments and all other institutions calls for the greatest vigilance on the part of the media.

Some hold that the vigilance must be of an adversary nature—that there can be no truce between politicians and the press.[21] This goes too far, since adversary relations engender so many biases of their own. They lead too easily, as I have shown, to the adoption of quasi-military rationales that blur moral choice. And the adversary posture of one side only intensifies that of the other. Rather than celebrate such a posture as a model, the media might strive for one of vigilant objectivity with respect both to government rationales and to their own. The co-optation that is an ever-present danger can come not only from establishment groups but from opposition groups, even from the journalistic fraternity itself.

To sum up: The public's right to know, even where protected by statute, cannot be a right to knowledge or truth, but at best to access to information; and not to all information, but only to some. The public has a legitimate interest, however, in all information about matters that might affect its welfare, quite apart from whether a right to this information can be established. If the press is to fulfill its public mandate, it should provide the greatest possible public access to this broad range of information. In addition, journalists also report on much that is of interest to the public, not because of any need for information, but rather to satisfy curiosity. Such reporting is equally legitimate, but it requires special attention to individual privacy. It is in this respect that the story about Sidis went too far; and though its publication did not violate any law, no public right or need gave moral warrant to carry it through without securing William Sidis's consent.

We cannot know whether Sidis was interviewed without being informed that there would be a *New Yorker* article about him. Perhaps he did not even know that the young woman from whose interview Thurber drew his details *was* interviewing him for publication. If so, Sidis had reason to complain, not just about having been made the subject of an article against his will, but about the underhanded means used to acquire the information about him. It is to questions about the means of journalistic investigation that I want to turn next.

Reporters in Disguise

The reporter's role, like all others, masks the individual within and signals caution to outsiders. Reporters know that their very presence at a meeting, if known, alters that meeting. Participants are on their guard; many play to the gallery, and consider how the public will respond to the interpretation of what they do or say. And all who have something to hide are doubly cautious when they talk to journalists. The desire is therefore strong for reporters not to appear as reporters in order to catch those they study off guard, to unmask them or see beneath the appearances, to reach to "real" individuals, plans, and activities.

One way for reporters to disguise their intentions is to appear merely as anonymous participants. Another is to assume a new and different role. This can be done through a quick lie, as when a reporter gives a false name to secure entry to a gathering of celebrities or to the signing of a peace treaty. It can also be done by means of the most elaborate webs of deceit. Thus a group of reporters for the *Chicago Sun-Times* bought and operated a bar—the Mirage—in 1977, in order to try to expose some of the payoffs, tax fraud, bribery, and illegal gun and liquor sales plaguing Chicago. With reporters working as bartenders, and others listening in and taking photographs from a hidden room, they gathered so much evidence that the authorities could hardly cope with all the indictments and investigations that ensued.[22] The scandal helped to unseat city officials and brought out countless reports of similar pressures for kickbacks and bribes by police, vending-machine operators, fire inspectors, and others. In this scheme, reporters assumed the investigative role of the police and indeed worked closely with certain police officials. In justification, those who sponsored the project held that the police could not cope with the pervasive corruption in the city, that the public was injured by not knowing enough to try to stop it, and that the persons who were profiting unfairly from the corrupt practices should be brought to trial.

Perhaps the best-known and most versatile master of disguise and infiltration for purposes of exposure is the German publicist Günter Wallraff. He has used every means of deceit and concealment in order to enter and explore secret domains. He has tricked the police into employing him as an informer infiltrating radical student groups, impersonated a guard in an insurance company in Cologne, and acted the part of a right-wing emissary of Franz-Joseph Strauss offering to arm and finance General Spinola's plot for a coup in Portugal. His books documenting these and other probes have sold throughout the world.[23]

Born in Cologne during World War II, Wallraff approaches his tasks
with military precision and carefully mapped strategy. The enemy, for
him, is the German state, and the press and bureaucracies and corporations
that support it and feed on it. He has, therefore, a much more extensive
mission of battle against corruption and coercion than the reporters who
manned the Mirage bar in Chicago. He could never, as they did, let
police officials know from the beginning about his plans. And to a much
greater extent than they, he presupposes plots by the establishment to
bring him down and to silence him.

Wallraff's most celebrated foray was the infiltration of the German
tabloid *Bild-Zeitung*. Having exchanged his glasses for contact lenses,
changed his way of combing his hair, bought an expensive suit, and
changed his body language to give the impression of an ingratiating but
ruthless careerist, he presented himself as "Hans Esser" for an interview
with the local editor in Hanover. Hired as a free-lance editor, he saw
from within how stories were forced out of unwilling witnesses, exaggerated, given the right political slant, sometimes made up from whole
cloth. The macabre, the monstrous, and the titillating were extracted
from everyday occurrences; and neither employees nor those interviewed
were spared in the pressure for sensational stories. Social criticism was
edited out of his articles, sexual innuendo brought in. Wallraff entered
so wholly into his role that he made rapid progress. In his diary, he
wrote of his constant fear of discovery and expressed his anxiety that
he might be turning into the kind of person he portrayed.

What is it really that changes? One goes through something, and there is
always a residue, one cannot act as though one escaped completely unharmed. . . .
it is as with smoking: one needs at least as long a time of not smoking to return
to normal. Here one is also infected in some manner. One needs a long time.
But what is it that has changed? Perhaps one is somewhat more coldblooded
from now on, more hardboiled, colder toward many, and can feel aloof from
things more easily. Much that earlier would have caused horror does not touch
one anymore. One says: I don't see the story.[24]

As if to set his books apart from all his dissembling toward others
and from the falsified stories he wrote while working for the *Bild-Zeitung*,
Wallraff has gone to unusual lengths to insist on the truthfulness of
his reporting. "Of course," he wrote in the preface to the book describing
that experience, "nothing is either invented or fabricated." [25]

Such assurances are not unusual among journalists who undertake
infiltrative reporting; the stealthier their methods of probing, the more
forcefully they proclaim honesty and accuracy in reporting. It is as if

they asked to be judged solely by what they say in print, not by what they do to investigate. But when a reporter infiltrates a newspaper, as Wallraff did, and writes misleading stories in order to maintain his disguise, the difficulty is compounded. He can no longer draw the distinction between honest writing and deceptive action. And, as his diary excerpt shows, he feared being changed by the false role he lived. Just as one looks at others differently once one knows them to be smooth and experienced liars, so one's view of oneself may alter. For purposes of self-respect, it may then become especially important to set aside some aspect of one's work or some relationships in which one holds oneself to the highest standards.

To escape from the pressure of impersonating Hans Esser, Wallraff would take a few days off now and then, and spend time with friends in whom he confided and with whom he could be himself. He knew, he wrote, that many of them conveyed the secret to still others in spite of promises of confidentiality, and was pleased that, "during four months, nothing came out to the other side, that no one betrayed me for money or advancement." [26]

Abruptly, his cover was broken. A friend warned him that a small left-wing magazine was about to publish the news that Günter Wallraff was working for the *Bild-Zeitung* under the name of Hans Esser. Wallraff failed to show up for work the next day, and the newspaper chain, accusing him of a warped personality and "crypto-Communism," brought suit for "false impersonation and unauthorized use of title." The suit was lost, but the debate over Wallraff's methods continued in the media. Were they justified? And did the justification depend in part on one's view of what Wallraff meant to expose?

Wallraff goes to unusual lengths in answering such questions in his book. To begin with, he dismisses criticism from his opponents, arguing that they have forfeited all credibility in complaining about his deceptive methods. They are themselves so steeped in deceit and coercion, he holds, that they can hardly object to his dissimulation without the most contemptible hypocrisy. But by itself, this argument does nothing to justify his methods; certain critics may have ruled themselves out as credible judges by their own behavior; but Wallraff must, if he is to justify his methods, confront also the standards of persons he would recognize as more objective.

A second argument is meant to do so; it points to the disparity between his own small deceits and the vast conspiracies of coercion and manipulation they are mustered to combat. "I decided to conspire in order to take a look over the wall of camouflage, denials, and lies. The method I adopted was only slightly illegal by comparison with the illegal deceptions and maneuvers that I unmasked," Wallraff argues.[27] His job was "to deceive in order not to be deceived—to break the rules of the game in order to disclose the secret rules of power." [28]

By itself, this argument is also insufficient. No matter how deceitful or lawless the powers that Wallraff hoped to unmask, he might well agree that ordinary reportorial means should be preferred whenever possible. A third argument comes to the support of the preceding two: it claims necessity. Because his opponents are so powerful and so closely linked in a vast conspiracy with state, industry, and the military, no alternative method, according to this argument, can succeed. Anyone who is serious about the mission of unmasking must therefore use disguise and deceit. A sense of urgency comes to underline the need for such methods. The social crisis requires rapid action, by whatever means.

This argument resembles those made for deceit in war. Ordinary channels of correction and control have broken down; law and morality cannot be counted upon; more primitive principles come into operation, justifying actions with claims such as "All is fair in love and war." Such an argument requires for its effectiveness a sure belief in the hostility of those one combats and in the depth of their evil. And it explains the constant use of military language even in schemes that are not otherwise of a military nature.

Arguments of this kind are sometimes to the point, but they are peculiarly likely to function as rationalization. They obscure reasoning and invite bias of every kind. They often exaggerate the crisis at hand and the conspiratorial nature of opponents, and they underestimate the adequacy of other methods of investigation. Wallraff could not, in effect, demonstrate either conspiracy or crisis in the newspaper he was investigating, nor show why the many shabby practices that he uncovered could be exposed only by means of infiltration. For journalists as for social scientists and other probers, the infiltrator is often seeking a shortcut for which the more experienced have no need.

There are nevertheless cases of abuse so serious, and kept so secret, that few methods short of deceptive ones would be capable of the exposure that is clearly needed. Exploitative migrant-labor camps or substandard homes for the aged may exclude all investigators save those who gain entry under false colors. Can reporters claim to be justified, at such times, in presenting false papers of employment and identity in order to witness the abuses from within?

Even in such cases, while it may be true that reporters have no

open means of investigation, public authorities do. Because journalists lack means such as subpoenas or search warrants, they may be
tempted more often to resort to deceit. As a *Los Angeles Times* reporter
is said to have remarked after posing as an animal keeper in a zoo, an
employee in a juvenile detention facility, an oil pipeline worker in Alaska,
and a doctor in a hospital emergency room:

I'm a great believer in the reporter as observer. First-hand observation is the
ultimate documentation. A reporter doesn't have a badge or subpoena power
or . . . wiretap authority. He has to use his . . . wits. That's what I try to
do. . . . Almost every big story I've done, I've had to impersonate someone.[29]

So long as the police or other public authorities are coping with the
problem, it is not enough for journalists merely to show that *they* do not
have methods of entry as satisfactory as infiltration. If the police can
investigate openly what journalists must ferret out in disguise, the former
have to be preferred. And even police undercover agents—though their
methods are dangerous in their own right—are subject to more stringent
regulation than the swarms of other investigators engaged in similar
pursuits.

At times, however, the police either cannot or will not take part in
the investigation. The government itself may be corrupt, or the police
inefficient or overworked, sometimes even prevented from investigating
a problem. In the Watergate affair, for instance, it would have been
useless for journalists to seek police cooperation. When the government
itself is at fault, or high officials within it, the justification earlier
inferred from the public's right to know comes into play once again; the
press's role as intermediary must then give way to a degree of probing
and of suspicion ordinarily excessive.

If a group of editors and reporters have concluded that they see no
alternative means and no alternative agencies of investigation to whom
the probing of a particular problem can safely be left, they must still
weigh the moral arguments for and against deceptive infiltration or other
surreptitious methods. Knowing that such means are morally questionable,
they must then ask whether their goal warrants the use of such methods.
This would not be the case with respect to minor infractions. But once
again, in the case of the Watergate investigation by the *Washington Post*,
the issue was obviously of the highest importance. The reporters in that
case did not use infiltrative means, and it is doubtful whether these
would have worked, but they did resort to deception at times. Their
book reveals no soul-searching on this score, and we cannot know whether
the deception was necessary to uncovering the story.[30] If such a necessity

could be shown, then the case would offer persuasive grounds for using limited deception.

Another consideration that newspaper or television editors should take seriously before going ahead even with clandestine investigations they consider important has to do with the effect on their own credibility and that of the media in general. They know that public confidence in media reliability is already low, and they recognize the existing pressure for rushed stories, forever incomplete, all too often exaggerated or mis-interpreted. If the public learns about an elaborate undercover operation such as that of the Mirage bar, many may ask why they should have confidence in the published stories based on information acquired through such an elaborate hoax. The press can hardly afford to saddle itself with more grounds for mistrust; and this consideration should form part of editorial decision-making, even if it leads to the curtailment of an otherwise dramatic cover story.

The press and other news media rightly stand for openness in public discourse. But until they give equally firm support to openness in their own practices, their stance will be inconsistent and lend credence to charges of unfairness. It is now a stance that challenges every collective rationale for secrecy save the media's own. Yet the media serve commercial and partisan interests in addition to public ones; and media practices of secrecy, selective disclosure, and probing should not be exempt from scrutiny.

Without such scrutiny, the routine invocation of the public's right to know will combine with the fierce competition in news reporting to deflect questions about limits to what reporters and editors can do in pursuing their professional goals. And without such scrutiny, we shall see perpetuated the media's uneasy alliance with other forms of institutional secrecy—the dependency by certain insiders on favors granted by corporate and government executives, the over-reliance on leaks and on secret sources, and the silence about politically or commercially "sensitive" topics. Because the task of reporting the news is both an indispensable public resource and big business, and because of the great power now wielded by the media, a commitment to openness and to accountability is more necessary than ever.

Undercover Police Operations

Secrecy in Police Work

Secret police—the very words bring to mind in concentrated form all the dangers of state power when it combines with secrecy. No democratic society freely chooses to submit to such policing; it is either inherited or imposed by duplicity or force. The secret police networks that grew so powerful in Europe in the eighteenth and nineteenth centuries were the prime targets of those who fought to make government less despotic. And Americans at the time viewed such "Continental" systems with intense suspicion. The majority of the peoples in the world still live in the shadow of secret police systems; even when the regimes that employ such methods are overthrown, they are too often succeeded by rulers who simply continue the same police practices under new names and against new adversaries.

Given their entirely reasonable suspicion of any drift toward a secret police system and their distaste for government secrecy of any kind, democratic societies usually have laws requiring the police to operate with considerable openness. Uniformed police, open patrolling, openly recorded arrests, charges, and trials, clear rules of evidence, and thorough protection of the rights of those suspected or accused of crimes: such are the safeguards held forth. Where they are breached in practice, it is not out of disregard in principle. Nor were such laws intended to accommodate police provocation of crimes, roving secret agents, and other methods characteristic of secret police systems.

Most people nevertheless accept certain forms of secrecy as necessary to any police system. The planning and execution of criminal investigation cannot be entirely open without giving up every chance of success from the outset. The police cannot very well announce openly every suspicion or tip-off they receive. The records of those suspected of crimes but not charged or convicted must be kept confidential out of respect for individual rights and for the reputation of those who turn out to be innocent. And the identity of informers must often be concealed, or no one would accept such a role.

Such limited secrecy is indispensable, but the difficulties of containing it are great. Governments may extend surveillance to broader categories of suspects, including political adversaries. And police can slip into more extensive and dangerous practices of concealment no matter how dedicated to openness a society may be. Studies show that police secrecy is almost inevitable as the police see themselves at risk and develop loyalties that can be maintained only by means of concealment.[1]

Between the forms of secrecy that most people regard as legitimate for the police and forms that, however common throughout the world, would be rejected by all who were free to choose, lies a murky cluster of practices. Thus police officers often maintain secrecy about mistakes in arrest, excesses in interrogation, and illegal actions by fellow officers. Indeed, rookie officers are often told that one of the most fundamental rules for police officers is that they must never betray other officers, least of all by testifying against them in court.

I cannot examine all these practices of concealment, nor is it my aim to do so. I shall take up, rather, one set of secret police investigations that may shed some light on the rationales for secrecy in police work more generally, and especially on the arguments for and against the most troubling practices. The investigations are those known as ABSCAM, short for "Arab Scam," that came to public knowledge early in 1980.

With ABSCAM as a starting point, I would then like to consider what degree of police secrecy a democratic state might wish to authorize in view of the current pressures on law enforcement. Having given the state a mandate to use coercion and force if need be to protect citizens from one another and from external enemies, must we not also grant the state powers to act secretly in pursuit of these purposes when necessary? Yet if secrecy is allowed, can it succeed without deception? And if both are allowed for the police within limits, may they be used not only for investigating crimes but for generating them? Can a democratic society tolerate the tools of secret police networks—secrecy, deceit, and provocation—and still be confident that it possesses safeguards that will prevent these practices from corrupting agents and officials, spreading beyond the original limited usages, and giving governments too free a hand?

The ABSCAM Investigations

"Operation ABSCAM" was the code name for the most extensive investigation of legislative corruption in the history of the United States, and the first that deployed undercover strategies against public servants on a vast scale. Twenty-three months in the making, it took up the time of over one hundred FBI agents and cost over $800,000. Secrecy was at issue on all sides. Officials in one branch of government decided in secret to launch an undercover investigation of individuals in other branches. The latter, suspected of participating in secret crimes, were induced in what they took to be secrecy to offer their services in return for money or stocks. The transactions were secretly recorded and videotaped, and used as evidence for the indictments that ensued.

Thanks to the videotaping, the public could see what most had never encountered except in fiction and imagination: the actual offering and taking of bribes. They saw agents posing as wealthy Arabs meeting United States congressmen and other officials on a yacht—the *Corsair*—specially outfitted for the purpose, or in a similarly outfitted Washington house, opulently furnished to give an impression of exotic luxury. Each was equipped with devices for recording the exchanges and conversations. Many takers were attracted—more, according to the FBI, than could be accommodated—since word had spread, with the help of informers and early recipients, that money was to be had in return for promises of favors.

All came of their own free will. While they later complained of the elaborate deceit that had been practiced upon them, no one could point to any threat or coercion. Nor had constitutional rights been breached through unauthorized tapping of personal telephones, surreptitious entries and searches, or physical coercion of any kind. No one had been forced or urged to confess criminal intentions; all had, rather, incriminated themselves unwittingly. No one, finally, could claim that he did not know that accepting such large sums of money without reporting them was illegal.*

Neither critics nor supporters of the government's undercover methods in the ABSCAM investigations deny that similar methods have long been used to combat street crime. For instance, agents disguised as vulnerable elderly persons walk the streets at night, duping muggers. In parks, other agents can occasionally be found lying seemingly intoxicated on the ground with money sticking out of their pockets to attract thieves who can then be caught in the act. Sales of drugs and stolen goods are similarly invited by still other unacknowledged police.

While undercover methods are of ancient lineage, a shift took place in the United States in the 1970s toward greater reliance on such methods than in the past, and toward using them against white-collar crime as well as street crime. Specialized anticrime units were formed in police departments, beginning with that of New York City; and the FBI budget for undercover operations rose from under $1 million in 1977 to $7.7 million in 1981.[2] The shift was spurred in part by criticism from congressional committees and others to the effect that the FBI seemed "soft on establishment crimes."[3] In part, too, it was facilitated by improved techniques of recording and videotaping the transactions that eliminated the need to rely on the dubious testimony of informers.

The public response to news of the ABSCAM probe has been divided. Many accepted it as necessary in the battle against corruption, and were fascinated by the evidence brought to light. Others disapproved of the methods used, and deplored the extent and the planned nature of the deceit, as well as the government's role in not only taking part in crimes but actually setting the stage for them. Still others were troubled not so much by the methods themselves as by the FBI's effort to incriminate public officials. They saw methods that were tolerable for catching drug dealers, spies, and extortionists as much less permissible when it came to congressmen and city officials.

To some extent the latter response was undoubtedly motivated by class feeling—a sense that certain kinds of persons are more worthy of respect than others, so that, even when they are suspected of crime, they should not be treated as others are. But there was more to the response. Some held that bribery is simply a less serious crime than the drug trafficking and crime-syndicate "contracts" with which they associated undercover methods (ignoring the common recourse to such methods against prostitution and to infiltrate dissident political groups).

---

*It is at times difficult to tell the difference between bribes and campaign contributions or personal gifts, but no one argued that there had been such difficulty in the case of the offers made in the ABSCAM investigation.

Even among those who recognized the seriousness of the offenses brought to light by ABSCAM, many recoiled at the use of undercover methods to investigate such practices. They could easily envisage being the victims of such a hoax, and may have wondered whether they would be strong enough to resist the temptations offered. While they might be sure they would never engage in extortion or in drug dealing, or even solicit a bribe, they could not be equally sure they would resist all financial temptations offered in fraudulent ways. Suddenly it seemed to them possible that they might be drawn into criminality merely through weakness, and not as a result of having chosen to break the law and risk the consequences.

The Rationale for Undercover Investigation of White-Collar Crime

Equal treatment of criminals from different social backgrounds was a central aim of those who decided to go ahead with the ABSCAM investigation. As one of them asked, "Did we have the courage to treat congressmen and other public officials exactly as we treat others?" [4] The undercover methods used by the FBI were far from new and had never been struck down or even cut back by the courts. Indeed, there was very little law connected with the planting of informers and with police undercover action—much less than with wiretapping and electronic eavesdropping. So long as undercover methods were marshaled against street crime, why hold back from using them against white-collar crime?

The sense of the unfairness of such restraint was increased by the knowledge that corrupt public servants and other white-collar criminals were costing the nation far more than street criminals. [5] The burden of white-collar crime is immense; through the corruption of a few, it weighs on all citizens. White-collar or economic crime encompasses such activities as tax fraud, bribery, labor racketeering, arson-for-profit, insurance fraud, and toxic-waste violations. It has been estimated to cost the nation ten times as much as all the street crimes such as bank robberies and burglaries put together—a staggering $44 billion in 1977. [6] For example, whereas the average robbery involves a loss of under $400, most of the bribes offered and accepted in ABSCAM were as high as $50,000.

The social harm from corruption, however, is not only financial. Taking bribes, misappropriating funds, or exercising nepotism for private gain at public expense impairs government programs and injures the public in turn. When officials take bribes in connection with Medicare or Medicaid fraud, for example, countless individuals are exposed to inadequate, sometimes life-threatening care. When money allocated to welfare or housing is pocketed by corrupt officials, members of the public are again the victims. To be sure, such activities beset all societies. They may even, as Carl Friedrich has argued, allow for flexibility in societies that are too rigid or bureaucratized to function well; but they are profoundly destructive of the sense of community and fairness.[7] Corruption transforms not only the individuals who take part in it but also many around them, as well as the social institutions it feeds on.

But there was more to the sense of unfairness in shielding public servants from means of investigation used against others: the commonly shared view that their position calls on officials to be more resistant to criminal temptation than the average citizen. Congressmen can hardly claim ignorance or poverty as mitigating circumstances. They have received advantages not open to many and assumed offices of public trust, sealing them with their oaths of office. If they resort to secrecy and deceit in defrauding the public, and renege on their responsibilities by accepting bribes and selling the public interest short, why should they be spared methods that use secrecy and deceit to expose them?* Have they anyone but themselves to blame if they do not say No to a bribe that they clearly ought not to accept?

These arguments are persuasive. The difference between street crime and white-collar crime gives no reason to disqualify investigative methods in the former from being used in the latter. Holders of public office have no special claim to be exempt from scrutiny; on the contrary, since they have been entrusted with unusual power, and are subjected to uncommon pressures, they should recognize a special obligation of accountability. But this conclusion does not suffice to legitimate the methods employed in the ABSCAM investigation. We still have to ask whether these methods should be used at all, no matter what the type of crime or criminal.

The main argument for using such methods derives from the rationale for police work in general: that the state has the right to use force, trickery, and coercion when necessary in order to protect citizens against those who would injure them or interfere with their personal control over their lives and property. When the government authorizes the use

---

*The more so since it appears that corrupt officials, like other white-collar criminals, are much more likely than other offenders to be deterred from repeated crimes, once exposed. Many genuinely fear bad publicity; even when they do not, the institution in which they work usually does. A convicted accountant or physician or politician has much greater difficulty in returning to former criminal practices than, say, a convicted burglar. And only rarely are their crimes of the passionate or habitual kind that withstand calculation about effects.

of force—in collecting taxes, for example, or in waging war or in incarcerating prisoners—it establishes an office with rules and safeguards that distinguish such acts from similar ones by citizens. If force can be thus insulated and seen as different when employed by the government, so that tax collectors are distinguished from thieves and executioners from murderers, why should limited secrecy and deception not receive similar official sanction? And if official status can be given to police deception undertaken for the public safety, then why not also grant it to police participation in crime for purposes of detection, and even to creating opportunities for wrongdoing?

The analogy is appropriate, even though far from sufficient to justify every form of police manipulation and guile. Clearly some secrecy in addition to the confidentiality of records is legitimate in dealing with a state's internal and external enemies, and at times just as necessary as force. The same is true of deception;[8] and even the participation in crime may be called for to provide evidence of ongoing violations, as when police agents purchase stolen goods or smuggled weapons. But the analogy provides no blanket justification for these practices, any more than it condones indiscriminate use of force by the state. On the contrary, state exercises of force have to be carefully circumscribed. Tax collectors and executioners are subject to strict standards of openness and accountability for this reason. The peculiar fact is that undercover activities, which, according to this analogy, should be similarly regulated, have received so little outside attention, either from legislatures or courts.

Such regulation is clearly needed. By itself, the rationale for police secrecy, while it justifies limited concealment, hardly suffices to justify its widespread and unregulated use in undercover work, nor the staging of elaborate deceits as in ABSCAM. What additional arguments might provide stronger justification for such schemes?

An advocate of undercover operations would point out, first of all, that in a certain respect they cut down on police reliance on dissimulation and deceit by reducing the need for informers. Among police activities, the use of informers is notoriously fraught with problems. Informers vary greatly as to motive and reliability; they are constantly at risk of discovery; they are known to be unreliable, and may encourage crime or help corrupt police agents.[9] Because undercover operations such as those of ABSCAM minimize the reliance on informers and allow careful supervision of police agents, one can argue that the likelihood of deceit and abuse is lessened.

It is certainly true that undercover operations are not alone in relying on secret and deceptive methods of investigation, and that they may

limit the reliance on informers, with all their drawbacks. But the amount
of deception and the reliance on it are nevertheless greatly increased in
undercover investigations. A shift has taken place in recent years toward
ever more elaborate deception through schemes such as ABSCAM. Their
budgets have risen sharply (in spite of reduced allocation of resources
to police work in general), and much more planning and manpower go
into them. Where at first they were aimed primarily at vice and at
political radicals, they are now used for a broad variety of crimes, including
white-collar crime, violent crime, and property crime.[10] In addition, the
deception and secrecy in ABSCAM were meant to set the stage for
crimes not yet committed, unlike traditional methods of detection that
focus on solving past or ongoing crimes.

Advocates of undercover investigation argue further that even such
departures from accepted practice are justified, given their advantages
for society. Two arguments specify these social benefits. One holds that
the police, by setting up "sting" operations, can use new techniques of
recording and videotaping to depict crimes in the process of being committed, and thus obtain more reliable evidence of guilt than the scattered
and biased reports of witnesses, victims, or investigators. A videotaped
encounter between givers and takers of bribes, for example, can offer
evidence difficult to contradict. It can show, as well, the extent to
which the undercover agents stayed within the bounds of legitimate
investigation.

As a result, it is argued, such operations are not only less likely to
be abused but also more accurate than methods relying primarily on
informers or on unsupervised police agents. And the evidence gained
reduces the need to rely on less satisfactory testimony, such as confessions
with all their drawbacks, or eyewitness accounts with their well-known
biases and contradictions. Because the evidence on videotape is voluntarily
self-incriminatory, finally, it is free of the taint of coerced statements.
For all these reasons, the likelihood of convicting the guilty on the basis
of such evidence is higher; the possibility of deterrence is therefore
arguably higher as well.

The second and most important argument supporting undercover
methods holds that they are indispensable for combating a large category
of crimes that would otherwise go undetected. These are secret crimes,
and secrecy alone is thought capable of uncovering them. These so-
called invisible crimes are those for which no complaint is filed. Unlike
muggings, bank robbery, or murder, such crimes offer no evidence that
there have been victims, and no witnesses step forward to testify.[11]
There may be no victims ready to come forward or visibly injured because

no one in effect feels victimized—as in bribery, where the participants may act voluntarily and regard themselves as having benefited. In toxic-waste disposal or embezzlement, on the other hand, there are persons who would feel victimized if they knew about the crime, but who file no complaint since they are unaware of it. Crimes may be invisible to law enforcers, in addition, whenever people feel victimized but know of no legal remedy, or are too frightened to seek one out, as in some cases of extortion or child abuse.*

Most white-collar crimes are invisible in one of these senses. Official corruption, computer crimes, the illegal disposal of toxic substances, fraudulent medical billing, and the exploitation of privately owned old-age homes: such practices are hard to detect so long as no one brings a complaint. Ordinary police methods, according to the rationale for undercover work, do not serve well against such crimes. Physical search, arrest and interrogation, and the intervening of witnesses can hardly succeed so long as no crime or planned crime is in evidence. Only through secret operations and reliance on informers can the veil of invisibility be torn from these offenses. If this method is the only workable alternative for investigation, then the choice is between using it to fight invisible crimes or allowing them to continue, which is what using traditional methods amounts to.

These two arguments, when added to the rationale for police work in general, serve to strengthen that for undercover police operations such as those of ABSCAM. The force of this rationale is considerable, and speaks to the actual practices of policing rather than to some idealized notion of crime control. Police officials know the growing concern over crime; but they have to contend with higher standards for admissible evidence, stricter regulation of police conduct, and diminishing allocation of funds to their work. Through sting operations, they try to investigate crime in a cost-effective manner that provides clear evidence of guilt without a trace of police brutality or any violation of constitutional rights. What more, they ask, can the public demand?

In reply, we must consider, first, how indispensable a scheme such as ABSCAM really is in combating corruption among public officials. After all, the last decades have seen a strengthened assault in the United States on official corruption, resulting in many more criminal convictions than in previous periods. Most of these convictions were obtained without

---

*Some include in the category of invisible crimes those not yet committed. This vastly expands the category, and the invisibility here must be recognized as of a very different nature. Unless the two kinds of invisibility are carefully distinguished, it becomes impossible to limit practices of preventive detention, infiltration, and surveillance.

recourse to undercover operations or heavy reliance on paid informers. Rather, they usually resulted from inside information by witnesses or former participants willing to testify in court. In addition, it has not been conclusively shown that undercover investigation does anything to reduce the level of crime. The figures are hard to pin down, but insofar as they have been determined, in several studies having to do with antirobbery units and fencing stings, the amount of crime does not appear to decrease for more than a brief period even after highly successful sting operations.[12] Nevertheless, fencing stings often succeed in returning stolen goods to owners. The same cannot be said of operations such as ABSCAM. There is insufficient evidence, in fact, that such an operation succeeds in anything except in *documenting those crimes that it generates.*

It is clearly unwise to devote scarce public resources to schemes such as ABSCAM without evidence that they reduce corruption among public officials. And because these investigations require extensive deceit on the part of the government, there is further reason to proceed with caution. Even if the evidence were in hand, however, crucial moral questions would remain, questions that the rationale for undercover operations leaves out: of possible harm, unfairness, and undermining of trust.

Harm and unfairness to whom? In the first place, to at least some of the persons tricked and lied to. I have argued earlier that limited secrecy and deception can be legitimate in police work, in the absence of countervailing considerations and subject to strict regulation. But are they legitimate when aimed at persons who may not be guilty of any crime or even thinking of committing one? Might these persons not be unfairly drawn into crime by the police? And is this not contrary to all that the government and the police should aim for?

If an undercover scheme induces someone to break the law who might otherwise have gone through life without ever committing a crime, he will surely have been harmed; but can he also claim to have been treated unfairly? There are matters of degree to be taken into account in answering this question. No one can reasonably argue that it is unfair of the police to send out vulnerable-looking people to impersonate persons whom muggers might mistake for easy victims. To acknowledge that one is tempted to such acts by the seeming weakness of passers-by is already to forfeit claims of being unfairly treated by those who look, but turn out not to be, weak enough to be assaulted and robbed. Nor can one reasonably argue that it is unfair of police agents to fail to disclose their identity in patrolling the highways for drivers who endanger public safety, or in making purchases of illegal or stolen goods to acquire evidence, so long as these practices are common knowledge and do not set up unusual temptations to crime. But the police agent who impersonates someone asleep on a park bench with money clearly in sight might well tempt some otherwise innocent persons to theft; the more so, the larger the sum of money.

Similarly, sting operations in which stolen goods are accepted with no questions asked may encourage further theft and bring in clients who might otherwise have refrained from theft but are lured by the easy money. And undercover agents who offer drinks to a person they know to be a problem drinker and then suggest a criminal project to him may draw him into breaches of the law that he would otherwise have ignored or avoided. Police methods are unfair to the extent that they lead someone—whether through excessive temptation, exploiting weakness, affecting judgment, or threats—to take part in crimes he would probably never have committed otherwise.

Might one argue that such unfairness is a price society has to pay for an investigatory technique that also spots the guilty and deters the marginally criminal? Such an argument would be no more legitimate as a yardstick for criminal investigation than that of punishing innocent persons in court in order to deter would-be criminals. Imagine an undercover team that lowered the crime rate in a large city by means that also turned a dozen law-abiding persons into lawbreakers each year. If we do not allow innocent persons to be sacrificed for such purposes in court, why should we do so indirectly by luring them into crime before we punish them?

The difficulties arise, of course, in deciding just who is and is not clearly innocent. Some advocates of undercover methods attempt to resolve these difficulties by claiming that people, on the whole, are either criminal or law-abiding, and that the issue of enticing the latter into crime would therefore rarely arise in practice. Right-thinking persons would refuse to have anything to do with the shady deals; others must take their chances. Even in ordinary circumstances, such a distinction is too rigid, the more so as the number of laws has multiplied. Traffic laws, tax laws, and regulations for financial disclosure have created innumerable possibilities for breaches. It is hard to know at all times what is needed to be law-abiding. And under the conditions of temptation, persuasion, and pressure that undercover agents can create, the distinction may blur still further.

Yet it is the distinction between being and not being predisposed to commit a crime that is central to the current legal doctrine of what constitutes "entrapment" by the state. Chief Justice Warren expressed it as follows: "[To] determine whether entrapment has been established, a line must be drawn between the trap for the unwary innocent and the trap for the unwary criminal." [13] A minority view on the United States Supreme Court (represented, among others, by Justices Brandeis, Douglas, and Stewart) has held, on the contrary, that certain forms of conduct fall below the standards for government conduct—and that one is the actual instigation of crime by the government. When the government stoops to such methods, it hardly matters whether those encouraged to break the law are "unwary innocents" or "unwary criminals." The dangers to the public and to the government itself from such conduct override any benefit it may ensure. [14]

Quite apart from the strictly legal question whether or not the inducements offered in the ABSCAM investigation qualify as entrapment, government officials should take the minority view seriously in planning investigations. Any policy that presupposes an unnaturally clear line between innocent and guilty persons risks unfairness to individuals and injury to the state. Yet even with respect to persons independently *known* to be engaged in unlawful conduct, a question remains: Are some methods of tricking them into self-incriminating acts illegitimate? What if the police could surreptitiously administer a drug to such persons that would make them re-enact their past crimes before hidden cameras? Would we not be disturbed by such uses of police power even if we knew they would be directed only against lawbreakers? The courts have set rigorous boundaries to the amount of deceit and trickery that police agents can use in extracting confessions even from persons accused of serious crimes; must we not recognize similar boundaries for using deceit to induce criminality and thus provoke unwitting self-incrimination? If so, we must evaluate undercover investigations from the point of view of whether they exceed those boundaries.

A strong argument can nevertheless be made that methods unfair to most people would be less so when directed at public officials such as judges, mayors, and congressmen. They, more than others, should be circumspect; and quite apart from whether or not they go to jail, the public must be grateful if an investigation removes from public power officials who could so easily be tempted to break the law and to abuse the power entrusted to them. If their personal problems with alcohol or finances weaken their judgment to the point that they risk betraying their public responsibilities, then they owe it to the public to seek help, perhaps to resign, and to take special care that their weakness is not exploited. Most would agree that public servants should hold themselves to high standards, and that they have little cause to complain if tricked into exposure. And of all crimes, accepting bribes is one of the most serious. Along with treason, as John Noonan points out, it is "one of two crimes for which the United States Constitution specifically prescribes impeachment for the president, vice-president, and 'all civil officers of the United States.'" [15]

The public and the many honest officials hurt by the suspicion of widespread corruption might therefore welcome unusually stringent scrutiny of official wrongdoing. Even so, undercover investigations such as ABSCAM would still present problems. For the harm and the unfairness of undercover operations, whatever one decides about their seriousness in any one case, are not limited to those who are shown to be guilty via hidden cameras and microphones. The police agents themselves, and those who oversee their work and plan it, run risks as well. No more than Günter Wallraff, whose forays were discussed in the previous chapter, can they be sure of emerging unscathed from their undercover existence. Agents have described their feelings of stress and sense of treachery as they come to know those whom they are investigating and deceiving. And the possibility that agents will themselves become unable to draw the line between impersonating and becoming lawbreakers is not negligible, as many who have written on undercover investigations of street crime have pointed out. [16]

A more subtle risk from undercover methods such as those used in ABSCAM is that the respect for and trust in the administration of justice may be diminished. The loss of trust is likely to be greater when the government knowingly bypasses normal restraints than when it is unable to prevent breaches of the law. Certain methods may simply be too disreputable to be useful to the government and its agencies, no matter how attractive they seem in the short run. The resort to such methods may erase the difference the public sees between the police and the lawbreakers they are supposed to be combating. If the government legitimates the instigation of crime, it may lose the trust that is already such a vulnerable public commodity. This may be especially true for deception so extensive, so planned, and so manipulative as that in ABSCAM.

Unless constantly held back, moreover, secret police practices have a tendency to spread. If undercover methods become commonplace, the offenses for which they are used will become more numerous. All would acknowledge that the government would go to dangerous extremes if it undertook elaborate undercover operations to test, for instance, the capacity of shoppers to resist opportunities for theft, or the fraudulent reporting of scientific results among researchers. Yet such operations, on a smaller scale, have traditionally been deployed against even small-time gambling and prostitution, and against activities not criminal at all, such as political dissent.[17] Most countries, including our own, have experienced the periodic blurring of lines between investigating crime and investigating political beliefs, and between instigating crimes and provocation to political self-indictment. There is every reason to be cautious about methods that facilitate such abuses.

As we consider the reasons for and against investigative practices such as those used in ABSCAM, however, we are placing ourselves outside the situation faced by those who had to decide whether or not to go ahead with that project. They had to choose whether to make an exception for public officials suspected of corruption in using methods that were common for others. They believed these methods fully lawful and were under pressure from Congress to combat secret white-collar crime more vigorously. It would be hard to expect them to reject ABSCAM on their own, without a more general review of undercover methods.

From the public's point of view, on the other hand, such a review is indispensable. The shift to large-scale undercover operations has come quickly. Even the effectiveness of these operations is in doubt; and their potential for harm, for unfairness, and for abuse is considerable. In weighing such methods against possible alternatives, what are some of the factors that should be taken into account, and what standards might be appropriate?

Limits and Alternatives

Because police undercover tactics are so far from neutral from a moral point of view, they should be limited whenever possible, and not used when other methods of investigation suffice, nor deployed against activities that are only marginally or not at all criminal. They can nevertheless not be ruled out altogether. Sometimes, as in international drug traffic stings, they represent standard investigative procedure for clear-cut lawbreaking of an ongoing nature by persons well known to be involved and fully aware of the possibility of police undercover efforts. Sometimes the methods are employed against threats so immediate or so great as to call for every possible form of resistance. If a city such as Paris or Athens is beset by warring foreign groups, acting in secret to exterminate one another's members and thereby also threatening innocent bystanders, police infiltration may be needed in order to prevent bloodshed.

Even in such cases, safeguards must still be observed because of the dangers I have enumerated. Care must be taken not to set up a scheme in which an innocent person might be trapped into criminal activities; all methods of seducing, coercing, or tricking people into committing offenses should therefore be avoided. The deception and participation in crime that agents undertake must be as limited as possible in time and scope, involve as few persons as possible, and entail a minimum of make-believe and manipulation. And intrusion into the private lives even of "unwary criminals" should be avoided. Finally, to ensure that such bounds are not exceeded, the supervision of undercover operations must be meticulous. It is not enough, for such purposes, that police agents be answerable only to their superiors. I see no reason why the government's recourse to undercover operations in all their variety should be so much less strictly regulated than the government's use of electronic eavesdropping; no reason why warrants should be required for the latter but not for the former. In both cases, such independent oversight is needed to guard against abuses of police power.[18]

Merely adding restrictions is not enough; the public debate over methods of investigation requires attention to how they affect one another. The restrictions placed on so many forms of police work have contributed to the greater allure of undercover methods. Each restriction has had its own genesis in considerations of fairness or social benefit; but they do not fit harmoniously with one another and cannot all be accommodated without great pressure for less orthodox methods.

The funding for police work, to begin with, is crucial. Whenever funds for law enforcement are cut and police training and recruitment are reduced, while the clamor for energetic action against crime grows stronger, the temptation to resort to shortcuts and dramatic demonstrations of results will increase. The same is true of the many measures that make it ever harder for the police to acquire evidence solid enough to satisfy the courts. The more difficult it becomes to have access to the bank accounts of persons suspected of crime, for instance, the more tempting it will be for police officers to try to trick these suspects into enacting their otherwise secret deals in front of hidden cameras in order to obtain incontrovertible evidence of wrongdoing. Similarly, the greater the obstacles that society places in the way of granting search warrants, or of the giving of evidence by suspects and by witnesses, the stronger the pressure to set the stage for tricking suspects into unwitting self-incrimination.

There are good reasons for all these legal safeguards. My point is not that some should automatically be weakened in order to decrease the resort to police instigation of crime, but rather that they have to be examined together, since restricting some of the methods of acquiring evidence inevitably increases the pressure to resort to others.

Adding to this pressure is the growing awareness of the scope of large-scale "invisible" crime, and of the harm it inflicts on society. Most legal systems are better prepared to deal with individual than with organized crime, especially when the latter is surrounded by the protections granted business firms, government agencies, labor unions, even police departments in their own right. The protection of privacy and confidentiality that we rightly see as fundamental for individuals is often invoked, as I have indicated throughout this book, as a shield for collective practices of wrongdoing. The undercover investigation of such abuse is often an effort to place personal responsibility on the shoulders of scattered individuals for much more widespread practices that injure the public. Secret surveillance, the instigation of crime, and manipulation by the police are in part an outcome of the frustration engendered by a growing understanding of the burden society must carry as a result of such extensive but secret lawbreaking.

Joint action to lessen the professional, administrative, corporate, and other forms of secrecy would therefore also lessen the need for undercover investigation. But if the police strive to counter the damage wrought by excessive secrecy through secretive and deceptive operations that create opportunities for crime and temptations to participate, and if governments and courts encourage this development, then it will become increasingly difficult to distinguish those whose task it is to uphold the law from those who aim to violate it. The efforts to combat the social ills that thrive under secrecy will not only run the risk of being piecemeal and ineffective; the remedy they prescribe will be living proof of the extent and tenacity of the disorder.

Conclusion

Though you travel every road, you will not discover the limits of the soul, so deep is its logos.

HERACLITUS, *Fragments*

Through the study of secrecy, we encounter what human beings want above all to protect: the sacred, the intimate, the fragile, the dangerous, and the forbidden. I have sought to convey the depth and the scope of the conflicts that such secrecy inevitably generates. But it is hard to grasp the full meaning of these conflicts, so imbedded are they in all that we do. They are rooted in the most basic experience of what it is to live as one human being among others, needing both to hide and to share, both to explore and to beware of the unknown.

In studying this experience of the conflicts of secrecy, I have drawn on accounts in myth and in literature, and in personal documents, research, and reporting of many kinds. Together, they may shed light on what often seems too familiar to merit much attention—a child's efforts to keep from revealing family quarrels to outsiders, a student's passing hesitation about whether to read a roommate's diary, an artist's silence about unfinished work, or the meanderings of office gossip. We may then recognize the day-to-day experience of secrecy and its conflicts even in situations that for most of us are genuinely unfamiliar, such as the initiation rites of secret societies, the operations of corporate espionage in competing for the most advanced technology, and undercover police investigations.

Control over secrecy and openness gives power: it influences what others know, and thus what they choose to do. Power, in turn, often helps increase such control; a child has less of it than an adult, citizens less than their government. With no capacity for keeping secrets and for choosing when to reveal them, human beings would lose their sense of identity and every shred of autonomy. Their plans would be endangered and their creativity stifled; they could not count on retaining even the most fundamental belongings. And yet this capacity too often serves to thwart the very same human needs, since it risks damaging the judgment and character of those who exercise it, and conceals wrongdoing of every kind. These risks are great when control over secrecy is combined with personal unscrupulousness; greater still when it is joined to unusual political or other power and to special privileges of secrecy such as those granted to professionals; and greatest of all when it is in the hands of government leaders.

To the extent that we harbor unexamined views of secrecy in our personal and working lives, we are ill-equipped to keep these views from carrying over to collective secrecy. They will then blur and distort our understanding of the vast practices of trade, professional, and government secrecy, and of their correlatives of whistleblowing and espionage, and, by keeping us from seeing how these practices are linked, will make it impossible for us to evaluate them in more than a piecemeal, too often ineffective fashion.

I see no need to repeat, in the pages that remain, the various conclusions I have set forth on these matters throughout this book. Rather, I would like to express two more general convictions that I have reached in the course of my inquiry. The first concerns the sheer extent of all we do not know about many aspects of secrecy, and the need for careful comparative and interdisciplinary studies devoted to them. Whether I was examining the experience of secrecy in childhood, the importance of concealment for political and religious practices of initiation, the roles of different practices of trade secrecy, or the function of confidentiality in different types of work, I was struck by the scope and the significance of all that still awaits exploration. At times, the resulting ignorance is costly.

Why, for instance, has there been—to my knowledge—no broad-gauged study of secrecy in police work in different societies, of the role it plays in different forms of government, and of the political and other factors that influence it? Why no studies comparing even a few politically similar societies from the point of view of their reliance on undercover investigations? Many Western nations resort rarely, if at all, to such methods. Has this hampered them in dealing with crime? With white-collar crime? If so, what have they done to compensate? And in the United States, where such probing is more common, why have there been so few attempts to analyze its effectiveness as compared with alternative ways of combating crime?

Cutting across police and many other practices of secrecy are larger questions having to do with the transformation secrecy can assist. I have discussed the influence that forms of secrecy and openness can exert on judgment and character. But we have much to learn about the nature of this influence. What effect does prolonged secrecy have on people? How do these effects differ, if at all, from those of intense secrecy of shorter duration? What difference does it make that what is kept secret is something others want to know, sometimes need to know? What personal traits affect the responses to secrecy? And how are all these factors affected by whether the experience is voluntarily undertaken or results from coercion? True, these questions are illuminated in literature (as in Joseph Conrad's extraordinary novel of secrecy and betrayal, *Under Western Eyes*) and through theoretical discussions such as Georg Simmel's;[1] anecdotal and intuitive reporting are also of great interest. But many answers are still missing, and all require more analysis than they have received.

To illustrate this need, consider C. P. Snow's attribution of a loss in judgment to secrecy: his account of how F. A. Lindemann, Winston Churchill's all-powerful adviser during World War II, responded to the wartime "euphoria of secrecy" by miscalculating and giving poor advice, and in particular, by persuading Churchill to launch the policy of strategic bombardment of civilians in German cities. According to Snow, the policy was not only inhumane; it diverted bombers from pressing needs in the Atlantic, and thus endangered the outcome of the war. "The euphoria of secrecy," he wrote, "goes to the head very much like the euphoria of gadgets. . . . It takes a very strong head to keep secrets for years and not go slightly mad. It isn't wise to be advised by anyone slightly mad."[2]

Even those who disagree with Snow's judgment in this case may offer their own examples of someone "slightly mad" in his sense. It would obviously be important to clarify exactly what characterizes such a state, while taking into account all the pitfalls in attributing poor judgment.

One would then want to study the degree to which prolonged or intense secrecy can distort judgment, and to examine the social, psychological, and neurological aspects of the change. Would it then be possible to specify what traits or circumstances predispose people to such a change, and to know what, on the contrary, makes it unlikely—what constitutes, in Snow's words, "a very strong head"? Surely the results of such studies would be useful to all those who undertake work of a secret nature, or who consider joining organizations that require oaths of secrecy; useful, too, in determining who should be entrusted with, say, diplomatic or military responsibility requiring discretion. About these and so many questions concerning secrecy and openness, there is room for research of unusual importance.

My second conviction, far stronger at the end than at the beginning of my work on this subject, is one of urgency. The conflicts over secrecy may be perennial, but the accelerating pace of technological innovation and the present worldwide political tensions are now unsettling the already precarious standards for keeping, probing, and revealing secrets. New techniques, from ever more sophisticated devices for eavesdropping to computerized data banks, have vastly enlarged the amount of information at the disposal of those with the know-how and the resources to acquire it. This poses extensive threats to individual privacy. It has also made governments and other organizations feel more vulnerable, and increased the felt need for added security. In the last few years, heightened international tensions have added to the sense of vulnerability—to fears that plans will be exposed and national security threatened as military, commercial, and scientific secrets are stolen.[*]

Some governments, such as those of the Soviet Union and China, have long exercised pervasive control over secrecy; others are urging greater secrecy in self-defense, responding to what they perceive as a dangerous imbalance between such control and the openness of their own societies, given the greater availability of information. Thus the last year has seen "spy trials" in both Norway and Sweden, in which peace researchers have been indicted for assembling information from openly available sources that the authorities judged dangerous for military security.[3] The accused men worked for no foreign nation and did nothing

---

[*]The very proliferation of methods of probing, trained investigators, and instruments belies the widespread notion that we now have less secrecy because everything is so much more out in the open than before. It is in part all that is done to seek out information that has expanded the practices of secrecy—both because the probing itself is so often secretive and because it generates renewed efforts at concealment on the part of those who wish to avoid exposure.

that remotely resembled spying in any ordinary sense of the word; they used, rather, government publications, telephone books, and other sources to put together their data concerning activities at certain military installations. *

In the United States, the Reagan government is moving to institute sweeping changes that offer an insight into its assessment of the seriousness of the technological and political pressures. I have discussed these proposals in Chapters X to XIII: they concern not only cutbacks in the scope of the Freedom of Information Act, greater power to classify information as secret on grounds of national security, and diminished regulation of undercover activities abroad, but also closer regulation of scientific research and publication, stricter control over the access of foreign students to university courses and libraries and of scientists to symposia, and greater restrictions on commerce and exports. Together, these proposals signal an intention to reverse sharply the last two decades' movement toward greater public access to government information and to impose upon United States citizens government controls unprecedented in peacetime.

While such a response to the growing international tensions and to the greater sense of vulnerability is to some extent understandable, it risks weakening, not strengthening, any nation that adopts it, for it rests on two illusions. The first is that of the efficacy of secrecy given the present level of technological development and of worldwide communication—the notion that, short of turning an open society into a garrison state, it will be possible to shut down trade, travel, exchange of scientific information, and media and other investigations enough to achieve the desired security. The second illusion is the belief that such secrecy and controls are neutral, that they carry no risks of their own, no danger of damaging creativity, innovation, and research, no barriers to commerce, no dangers to judgment and to character, and no risks of encouraging official negligence and corruption.

But why accept this course as inevitable? We need not hasten to give up hard-earned freedoms through indifference or panic. The very hostilities and technological advances that threaten security also challenge us to reassess the complex role of secrecy in containing or escalating their danger. Suc a re-examination can spur collective uses of information for genuine security, and help avert spreading government controls over secrecy and openness that prove injurious to nations and stifling to the free choice of individuals in their own lives.

*The Scandinavian indictments struck many as excessive reactions in light of the relative innocuousness of what the researchers exposed, the obvious fact that adversaries must long since have acquired the same information, and the serious implications of restrictions on research using open sources.

Notes

Chapter I. **Approaches to Secrecy**

1. Hesiod, *Works and Days*, in *Hesiod: The Homeric Hymns and Homerica*, trans. Hugh G. Evelyn-White (Cambridge, Mass.: Harvard University Press, 1914), pp. 5–9.

2. See Georg Wissowa et al., eds., *Paulys Realencyclopädie der Classischen Altertumswissenschaft* (Stuttgart: Alfred Druckenmüller Verlag, 1962), cols. 1716–18; Walter Porzig, "Das Rätsel der Sphinx," in Rüdiger Schmitt, ed., *Indogermanische Dichtersprache* (Darmstadt: Wissenschaftliche Buchgesellschaft, 1968), pp. 172–76. Porzig suggests that the original riddle may have been more succinct: "There is on earth something two-footed and four-footed that has but one voice." He points to links between such riddles and the many to which the answer is "a pregnant woman" or "a pregnant horse," as well as to formulaic prayers for all the two-footed and four-footed creatures on earth.

3. See Arthur Darby Nock, *Conversion* (London: Oxford University Press, 1933); René Guénon, *Aperçus sur l'initiation* (Paris: Editions Traditionelles, 1953). See also my discussion in Chapter IV of the role of initiation in secret societies.

4. Christopher Marlowe, *Doctor Faustus*, ed. Sylvan Barnet (New York: Signet Books, 1969), pp. 101–2.

5. Claude Lévi-Strauss has argued, in "Structural Study of Myth," *Journal of American Folklore* 68 (1955):428–44, that the purpose of myth is to provide a logical model for overcoming contradictions such as those of life and death. Myth surely serves other purposes than this; and the logical models that Lévi-Strauss ferrets out of myths are not always plausible. Yet myths do illustrate such ways of overcoming, and rarely more compellingly than with respect to the contradictions of secrecy and openness in all their variations.

6. The Indo-European root is **skeri-*, from which we derive not only words that have to do with separating, cutting, and sifting but also words such as "riddle," "crime," "crisis," "discernment," "discrimination," and "critic." The meaning of something hidden is prominent, as well, in such words as the Greek *kruptos*, the Sanskrit *gupta*, the Latin *occultus*, and the German *verborgen*.

7. The concepts of "discernment" and "secret," however different, are closely related etymologically. Both *discernere*, from which we have "discernment," and *secernere*, from which "secret" derives, have the same meaning of separating out. "Discernment" (as well as "discretion") comes from the active form of the first; "secret," from the passive form of the second. Discerning, correspondingly, is the activity of separating out; the secret, something that has been thus set apart.

8. *Arcanum* derives from the Indo-European root **arek-*, meaning to hold, contain, or guard; from it we have words such as "ark," "coerce," and "autarky."

Rudolph Otto, *Das Heilige* (1917), trans. John W. Harvey as *The Idea of the Holy* (London: Oxford University Press, 1928), p. 31. See also Roger Caillois, *L'Homme et le sacré* (Paris: Gallimard, 1950); Mary Douglas, *Purity and Danger* (London: Routledge & Kegan Paul, 1966); Emile Durkheim, *The Elementary Forms of the Religious Life*, trans. Joseph Ward Swain (London: George Allen & Unwin, 1915); Mircea Eliade, *The Sacred and the Profane*, trans. Willard R. Trask (New York: Harcourt, Brace & World, 1959).

10. The Indo-European root of *heimlich* is **kei-*, meaning to lie; bed, night's lodging, home; beloved, dear. We derive from it words such as "hide," "home," and "cemetery." For Freud's views on the meanings of *heimlich*, see his paper "The Uncanny," 1919, in *The Complete Psychological Works of Sigmund Freud*, ed. and trans. James Strachey (London: Hogarth Press, 1955), 17:219–52.

11. See *Encyclopédie; ou, Dictionnaire raisonné des sciences, des arts et des métiers* (Neufchatel: Samuel Faulché & Co., 1765), 14:562–63. The second entry concerns medical remedies kept secret—a practice condemned in severe terms. For other definitions of a secret as something one has a right to conceal, see Robert E. Regan, *Professional Secrecy in the Light of Moral Principles: With an Application to Several Important Professions* (Washington, D. C.: Augustinian Press, 1943), pp. 1–3; Austin Fagothey, *Right and Reason*, 5th ed. (Saint Louis, Mo.: C. V. Mosby Co., 1972), p. 238.

For a view of secrets as neutral rather than negative or positive in their own right, see Rudolf Eckstein and Elaine Caruth, "Keeping Secrets," in Peter L. Giovacchini, ed., *Tactics and Techniques in Psychoanalytic Therapy* (London: Hogarth House, 1972), pp. 200–15; Russell Meares, "The Secret," *Psychiatry* 39 (1976):258–65; Stanton K. Tefft, "Secrecy as a Social and Political Process," in Tefft, ed., *Secrecy: A Cross-Cultural Perspective* (New York: Human Sciences Press, 1980), pp. 319–41; Richard Wilsnack, "Information Control: A Conceptual Framework for Sociological Analysis," in *Urban Life* 8 (1980):467–99.

12. Woodrow Wilson, *The New Freedom* (New York: Doubleday, Page, & Co., 1913), p. 114.

13. Robert Norton et al., "Risk Parameters Across Types of Secrets," *Journal of Counseling Psychology* 21 (1974):450–54. David Bakan, in "A Reconsideration of the Problems of Introspection," *Psychological Bulletin* 51 (1954):105–18, claims that "a secret is a secret by virtue of the anticipation of negative reactions by other people." And Carol Warren and Barbara Laslett define secrecy as the concealment of something negatively valued by the excluded audience, in "Privacy and Secrecy: A Conceptual Comparison," in Tefft, ed., *Secrecy*, p. 26.

14. Carl Gustav Jung, *Modern Man in Search of a Soul* (New York: Harcourt, Brace & Co., 1933). Later, Jung qualified this view of secrecy: see, for example, *Memories, Dreams, Reflections*, ed. Aniela Jaffé, trans. Richard and Clara Winston (New York: Pantheon Books, 1961), pp. 342–44.

15. Henri F. Ellenberger, *The Discovery of the Unconscious* (New York: Basic Books, 1970), pp. 44–48.

16. Origen was commenting on Luke 2:35: "That the thoughts of many hearts may be revealed"; see *Homiliae in Lucam*, in *The Early Christian Fathers*, ed. and trans. Henry Bettenson (Oxford: Oxford University Press, 1956), p. 253.

17. Samuel Johnson, *A Dictionary of the English Language*, 1755 (London: Henry G. Bohn, 1852).

18. The word "private" comes from the Latin *privatus*, meaning withdrawn from public life, and in turn from *privare*, meaning to bereave and deprive. The Greek word *idiotes*, which means a private person but also an ignorant, ill-formed, awkward person, indicates the limitations and inadequacies the Greeks associated with the exclusively private, as distinguished from that which allows for a public life. Compare the English

word "homely" and the Swedish word *hemsk*, which now means horrible or frightful, but comes from the root *hem*, meaning home and relating to all that has to do with kinship and privacy. The person who remained always in the home was thought simple-minded, frightened, and strange, and was characterized as *hemsk*, a meaning that has now been transferred to what inspires such fear. For a history of the word "private" in English, see Raymond Williams, *Keywords* (New York: Oxford University Press, 1976), pp. 203–4.

19. The work on privacy in the social sciences, drawing on that of Georg Simmel and William James among others, has been pursued by many, including Irwin Altman, Erving Goffman, Herbert Kelman, Morris Rosenberg, Edward Shils, and Alan Westin. For a thorough discussion, see Alan Westin, *Privacy and Freedom* (New York: Atheneum Publishers, 1967). For a collection of recent articles and bibliographies, see Stephen T. Margoulis, ed., "Privacy as a Behavioral Phenomenon," *Journal of Social Issues* 33 (1977):5–21. For a discussion of the treatment of privacy in philosophy and law, see J. Roland Pennock and John W. Chapman, eds., *Privacy* (New York: Atherton Press, 1971); the articles by Richard A. Posner, Charles Fried, Edward J. Bloustein, et al., in *Georgia Law Review* 12 (1978):393–551; H. J. McCloskey, "Privacy and the Right to Privacy," *Philosophy* 55 (1980):17–38; Ruth Gavison, "Privacy and the Limits of the Law," *Yale Law Journal* 89 (1980):421–71; and Robert Ellis Smith, *Privacy: How to Protect What's Left of It* (Garden City, N.Y.: Doubleday & Co., Anchor Books, 1979).

20. Those who have compared secrecy and privacy have held widely divergent views: that the two may be used interchangeably; that secrecy is part of privacy, the part which is impenetrable; that secrecy differs from privacy in that revelation about it is forbidden by law; that secrecy concerns private matters which are discreditable. See Richard Posner, *The Economics of Justice* (Cambridge, Mass.: Harvard University Press, 1981), chap. 9; Edward A. Shils, *The Torment of Secrecy* (Glencoe, Ill.: Free Press, 1956), pp. 22–26; Westin, *Privacy and Freedom*, p. 26; McCloskey, "Privacy," p. 24; Stanley Cavell, *The Claim of Reason* (New York: Oxford University Press, 1979), p. 330; Gavison, "Privacy," pp. 424–28; Warren and Laslett, "Privacy and Secrecy," in Tefft, ed., *Secrecy*, pp. 25–34; Charles Fried, *An Anatomy of Values* (Cambridge, Mass.: Harvard University Press, 1970), p. 140. For a searching and provocative analysis of preconceptions about privacy, see Cavell, *The Claim of Reason*, pt. 4.

21. Irwin Altman, *The Environment and Social Behavior* (Monterey, Calif.: Brooks/Cole Publishing Co., 1975), chap. 1.

22. Locke, Kant, and Hegel described a personal sphere in spatial terms, arguing for the moral right to property as an extension, in this sense, of human beings. Gaston Bachelard, in *La Poétique de l'espace* (Paris: Presses Universitaires de France, 1957), discusses internal and external spaces. Robert Nozick has based his theory of individual rights on a conception of boundaries marking "an area in moral space around an individual"; see *Anarchy, State and Utopia* (New York: Basic Books, 1974), p. 57. See also Frederick A. Hayek, *The Constitution of Liberty* (Chicago: University of Chicago Press, 1960), p. 21, and Erving Goffman, *Relations in Public* (New York: Harper & Row, 1972) pp. 28–61.

23. See Edward T. Hall, *The Hidden Dimension* (Garden City, N. Y.: Doubleday & Co., 1966); Westin, *Privacy and Freedom*, p. 9; Edward O. Wilson, *Sociobiology* (Cambridge, Mass.: Harvard University Press, 1980), chap. 12.

24. See Robert F. Murphy, "Social Distance and the Veil," *American Anthropologist* 66 (1964):1257–74. For discussions of the cultural context of privacy, see Westin, *Privacy and Freedom*, chap. 1, and Irwin Altman, "Privacy Regulation: Culturally Universal or Culturally Specific?" *Journal of Social Issues* 33 (1977):66–84.

25. Erving Goffman, *Asylums: Essays on the Social Situation of Mental Patients and Other Inmates* (Chicago: Aldine Publishing Co., 1961), p. 23.

26. Robert L. Laufer and Maxine Wolfe, "Privacy as a Concept and a Social Issue: A Multidimensional Developmental Theory," *Journal of Social Issues* 33 (1977):29.

27. See Robert K. Merton, *Social Theory and Social Structure* (Glencoe, Ill.: Free Press, 1949), p. 343. See also Edward Shils, *Center and Periphery* (Chicago: University of Chicago Press, 1975), pp. 317–344.

28. See Mary Midgley, "Brutality and Sentimentality," *Philosophy* 54 (1979):385–89.

29. See Richard Sennett, *The Fall of Public Man* (New York: Vintage Books, 1978), for a discussion of privacy and public life. In the United States the impetus for the development of the law of privacy came in an impassioned and influential article published in 1890, in which Samuel Warren and Louis Brandeis affirmed that the time had come to recognize a separate legal right to privacy: "The Right to Privacy," *Harvard Law Review* 4 (1890):193–220. They argued that the previously separate offenses of eaves-dropping, publishing private matters, breaches of confidentiality, copying private letters, and illegal search and seizure are fundamentally similar: they are all violations of the right to privacy—"the right to be let alone"—and not merely discrete offenses against trust, property, or bodily integrity. Thus were the doors opened, in the United States, to litigations claiming invasion of privacy. The authors could perhaps not have foreseen how far their principle would be carried; but the seeds of the present confusion are discernible in their basing this right on an intuitive and undeveloped view of the nature of privacy. "Privacy" has turned into a code word for many, often difficult to distinguish from "liberty." See Gavison, "Privacy," for a critical examination of this development; also Edward J. Bloustein, *Individual and Group Privacy* (New Brunswick, N. J.: Transaction Books, 1978).

Chapter 11. *Secrecy and Moral Choice*

1. Robert K. Holz. ed., *The Surveillant Science: Remote Sensing of the Environment* (Boston: Houghton Mifflin Co. 1973), p. 361.

2. Meister Eckhart, "Like a morning star, God shines," *Sermons*, in *Meister Eckhart*, trans. Raymond B. Blakney (New York: Harper & Row, 1941), p. 220.

3. Jean-Paul Sartre, "Ce que je suis," interview conducted by Michel Contat, *Le Nouvel Observateur*, June 23, 1975, p. 72.

4. George Orwell, *Nineteen Eighty-four* (1949; New York: New American Library, Library Edition, 1961), p. 19.

5. Robert Merton, in *Social Theory and Social Structure*, pp. 341–357, discusses the need of all who exercise authority to be informed about the norms and the behavior of those in the groups they wish to control, and the conflict of this need with the resistance to full visibility he presupposes in all groups.

6. Paul Federn, cited in Leston Havens, *Approaches to the Mind* (Boston: Little, Brown & Co., 1973), p.194.

7. Friedrich Nietzsche, *On the Genealogy of Morals; Ecce Homo*, ed. Walter Kaufmann (New York: Vintage Books, 1969), p. 343.

8. "Sacred" is derived from the Latin *sacer*, meaning set apart, unique. See, for discussions, Emile Durkheim, *Sociology and Philosophy*, trans. D. F. Pocock (Glencoe, Ill.: Free Press, 1953), p. 58; Durkheim, *Elementary Forms of the Religious Life*, pp. 52–62; Erving Goffman, "The Nature of Deference and Demeanor," *American Anthropologist* 58 (1956):473–502; Edward A. Shils, "Social Inquiry and the Autonomy of the Individual," in Daniel Lerner, ed., *The Human Meaning of the Social Sciences* (New York: Meridian Books, 1959), pp. 116–57.

9. *The Confessions of Lady Nijō*, trans. Karen Brazell (New York: Doubleday & Co.,

Anchor Books, 1973). See Sigrid Undset, *Kristin Lavransdatter*, trans. Charles Archer and J. S. Scott (New York: Alfred A. Knopf, 1921), for a novel dealing, with equal insight, with a woman's experience of pregnancy—this time in fourteenth-century Norway.

10. August Strindberg, *Fadren*, trans. Arvid Paulsen as *The Father*, in *Seven Plays* (New York: Bantam Books, 1960), pp. 54–55.

11. Thomas Carlyle, *Sartus Resartus* (London: Kegan Paul, Trench & Co., 1889), p. 204.

12. "Proper," "propriety," and "property" relate to *pro privo* in Latin, and thus to "privacy."

13. H. L. A. Hart, *The Concept of Law* (Oxford: Clarendon Press, 1961), p. 192.

14. Lord Acton, in Abbot Gasquet, ed., *Lord Acton and His Circle* (London: Burns & Oates, 1906), p. 166.

Chapter III. *Coming to Experience Secrecy and Openness*

1. Ruth Benedict, *Patterns of Culture* (Cambridge, Mass.: Riverside Press, 1959), chaps. 5, 6.

2. Elizabeth A. Brandt, "On Secrecy and the Control of Knowledge: Taos Pueblo," in Tefft, ed., *Secrecy*, pp. 123–144.

3. Mary Douglas, *Cultural Bias*, Royal Anthropological Institute of Great Britain and Ireland, Occasional Paper no. 34, p. 2.

4. Jean Piaget, *The Language and Thought of the Child* (1929; paperback ed., London: Routledge & Kegan Paul, 1959), p. 38. For a different view of the role of secrecy in childhood, see Paul Tournier, *Le Secret* (Geneva: Editions Labor et Fides, 1964).

5. See Jerome S. Bruner, "The Ontogenesis of Speech Acts," *Journal of Child Language* 2 (1975):1–19; Jerome S. Bruner and Alison Garton, eds., *Human Growth and Development* (New York: Oxford University Press, 1978), pp.62–84.

6. Margaret A. Boden, *Jean Piaget* (New York: Viking Press, 1980), pp. 56–60; Margaret Donaldson, *Children's Minds* (London: Fontana Books, 1978), chap. 2.

7. See Sigmund Freud, "The Uncanny" and "Character and Anal Erotism," *Collected Papers*, trans. under supervision of Joan Riviere (London: Hogarth Press, 1949), 2:45–50; Selma Fraiberg, "Tales of the Discovery of the Secret Treasure," *Psychoanalytic Study of the Child* 9 (1954): 218–41; Alfred Gross, "The Secret," *Bulletin of the Menninger Clinic* 15 (1951):37–44.

8. See V. Propp, *Morphology of the Folktale* (1928), trans. Laurence Scott, Publications of the Indiana University Research Center in Anthropology, Folkore, and Linguistics, no. 10 (Bloomington, 1958). Propp, in a study of the structure of Slavic folktales, stresses the role that prohibitions play in them. He points out that many folktales begin with parents leaving their abode after telling their children not to do something—not to unlock a certain door, eat a certain fruit, or go into the forest. Invariably, the prohibition is violated and misfortune brought near.

9. See Jon Elster, *Ulysses and the Sirens: Studies in Rationality and Irrationality* (Cambridge: Cambridge University Press, 1979), pp. 50–51.

10. John Calvin, *Institutes of the Christian Religion*, trans. Ford Lewis Battles (Philadelphia: Westminster Press, 1980), 2:931–32. For the mingling of awe and dread, see Lucan's description of the sacred grove near Massilia that Caesar ordered his soldiers to cut down, in Lucan, *The Civil War*, trans. J. D. Duff (Cambridge, Mass.: Harvard University Press, 1962), pp. 143–47.

11. Apuleius, *The Metamorphoses* (ca. A.D. 180), trans. Robert Graves as *The Golden Ass* (New York: Farrar, Straus & Giroux, 1951).

12. Leon Trotsky, *My Life* (New York: Pathfinder Press, 1970), pp. 103–4.

13. Virginia Woolf, *To the Lighthouse* (1927; New York: Harcourt, Brace & World, Harvest Edition, 1949), p. 79.

14. Stanley Cavell, *The Claim of Reason* (New York: Oxford University Press, 1979), pp. 354, 378.

15. Ibid., p. 459.

16. Georg Simmel, *The Sociology of Georg Simmel*, ed. Kurt H. Wolff (New York: Free Press, 1950), pp. 333–34.

17. Jung, *Memories, Dreams, Reflections*, p. 21. Jung held a full-blown view of secrecy as pathogenic. In *Modern Man in Search of a Soul*, p. 35, he wrote: "The maintenance of secrets acts like a psychic poison, which alienates their possessor from the community. In small doses, this poison may actually be a priceless remedy, an essential preliminary to the differentiation of the individual." It was in its latter form that secrecy, Jung felt, had helped him as a child.

18. See Betty Jean Lifton, *Lost and Found: The Adoption Experience* (New York: Dial Press, 1979); Anselm Strauss, *Mirrors and Masks* (Glencoe, Ill.: Free Press, 1959), chap. 4.

19. Edmund Gosse, *Father and Son* (New York: Charles Scribner's Sons, 1907), pp. 37–39.

20. Adapted from Thomas J. Cottle, "Willie Fryer," *Children's Secrets* (Garden City, N.Y.: Doubleday & Co., Anchor Books, 1980), pp. 33–40. For a discussion of family secrets, see Lily Pincus and Christopher Dare, *Secrets in the Family* (New York: Pantheon Books, 1978).

21. As I indicated in Chapter I, note 6, "discretion", "discernment", and "secrecy" are closely related etymologically, the first two deriving from the active form of *discernere*, meaning to separate out, and the last from the passive form of *secernere*, with the same meaning.

22. The term "age of discretion" is used to denote the time of life when a particular stage of judgment has been reached; but because of the different meanings of "discretion," quite different ages are indicated by it. Thus in English law, the age of discretion has long been fourteen years; in eighteenth-century United States discourse, it was sixteen. In popular French illustrations of the "stages of life," on the other hand, a person does not reach the years of discretion until age forty.

23. See Valerian J. Derlega and Alan L. Chaikin, "Privacy and Self-Disclosure in Social Relationships," *Journal of Social Issues* 33 (1977):102–15. For research on self-disclosure, see Sidney M. Jourard, *The Transparent Self* (Princeton, N.J.: D. Van Nostrand Co., 1964); Shirley J. Gilbert and Gale G. Whiteneck, "Toward a Multi-Dimensional Approach to the Study of Self-Disclosure," *Human Communications Research* 2 (1976):347–55; Paul C. Cozby, "Self-Disclosure: A Literature Review," *Psychological Bulletin* 79 (1973):73–91.

24. Plutarch, "Concerning Talkativeness," *Moralia*, trans. W. C. Helmbold (Cambridge, Mass.: Harvard University Press, 1939), 6:407. The emblems for silence have been numerous. Thus Cesare Ripa, in his *Iconologia* of 1630, shows a "grave lady in black garments" who is locking her mouth with a key as the emblem for secrecy or silence. Jean Seznec, in *The Survival of the Pagan Gods* (New York: Pantheon Books, 1953), pp. 120, 142, discusses an emblem for silence that is also that for prudence: "a being with three male heads, representing Memoria, Intellegentia, and Praevidentia, whose respective functions are to conserve the past, to know the present, and to foresee the future."

25. Chester C. Bennett, "What Price Privacy?" *American Psychologist* 22 (1967): 371–76.

26. See, for example, William C. Schutz, *Joy: Expanding Human Awareness* (New York: Grove Press, 1967).

27. See Morton A. Lieberman, Irving D. Yalom, and Matthew B. Miles, *Encounter*

Groups: First Facts (New York: Basic Books, 1973), p. 174. For a comparative study that cites figures from less than 1% to 48%, see Dianne Hartley, Howard B. Reback, and Stephen Abramowitz, "Deterioration Effects in Encounter Groups," *American Psychologist* 31 (March 1976):247–55.

Chapter IV. *Secret Societies*

1. See, for discussion of secret societies: Jean Chesneaux, *Secret Societies in China* (London: William Heinemann, 1971); Arkon Daraul, *Secret Societies Yesterday and Today* (London: Frederick Muller, 1961); Ben Zion Goldberg, *The Sacred Fire* (New York: Horace Liveright, 1930); P. Gordon, *L'Initiation sexuelle et l'évolution religieuse* (Paris: Presses Universitaires de France, 1946); René Guénon, *Aperçus sur l'initiation*, chap. 12; Charles William Heckethorn, *The Secret Societies of All Ages and Countries* (London: James Hogg, 1875), 2 vols.; Serge Hutin, *Les Sociétés secrètes* (Paris: Presses Universitaires de France, 1970); John Heron Lepper, *Famous Secret Societies* (London: Sampson Low, Marston & Co., 1932); Norman MacKenzie, ed., *Secret Societies* (New York: Holt, Rinehart & Winston, 1967); Marianne Monestier, *Les Sociétés secrètes féminines* (Paris: Les Productions de Paris, 1963). Jean-Charles Pichon, *Histoire universelle des sectes et des sociétés secrètes* (Paris: Robert Laffont, 1969), 2 vols.; Georg Simmel, "Secret Societies," *Sociology*, pp. 345–76; Hutton Webster, *Primitive Secret Societies* (New York: Macmillan Co. 1908); Camilla H. Wedgwood, "The Nature and Function of Secret Societies," *Oceania* 1 (1930):129–41.

2. See Chesneaux, *Secret Societies in China*, chaps. 4–7; Jack Belden, *China Shakes the World* (New York: Harper & Brothers, 1949), pp. 162–64; Jonathan Unger, "The Making and Breaking of the Chinese Secret Societies," *Journal of Contemporary Asia* 5 (1975):89–98.

3. See Louis Dumont, *Homo Hierarchicus*, ed. Julian Pitt-Rivers and Ernest Gellner (Chicago: University of Chicago Press, 1970), for a discussion of the role of hierarchy and caste.

4. Chesneaux, *Secret Societies in China*, p. 173.

5. See the libretto of Mozart's *Magic Flute* for an expression of the desire for growth and self-transformation that secret societies can inspire.

6. See L. S. Vygotsky, *Mind in Society*, ed. Michael Cole et al. (Cambridge, Mass.: Harvard University Press, 1978); Donald Woods Winnicott, *Playing and Reality* (London: Tavistock Publications, 1971).

7. Jung, *Memories, Dreams, Reflections*, pp. 342–43.

8. Karl Menninger, *Man Against Himself* (New York: Harcourt, Brace & Co., 1938), pp. 251–53.

9. Quoted and paraphrased from Heckethorn, *Secret Societies*, 1:42–45.

10. Daraul, *Secret Societies Yesterday and Today*, p. 238. See also Chesneaux, *Secret Societies in China*, pp. 40–41, 115–25.

11. R. Swinburne Chymer, *The Fraternitatis Rosae Crucis* (Quakertown, Penn.: Philosophical Publishing Co., 1929), p. 147.

12. See Elliot Aronson and Judson Mills, "The Effect of Severity of Initiation on Liking for a Group," *Journal of Abnormal and Social Psychology* 59 (1951):177–81.

13. For a discussion of initiation, see the works of Mircea Eliade; Mary Douglas, *Purity and Danger*; René Guénon, *Aperçus sur l'initiation*; Arthur Darby Knock, *Conversion*.

14. John Lawson, *History of North Carolina* (1714; reprint ed., Richmond, Va.: Garrett & Massie, 1952), pp. 253–54.

15. Albert Hopkins, ed., *Opinions of Distinguished Men on the Influence of Secret Societies*, pamphlet, ca. 1858 (no publisher or publication date listed).

16. Heckethorn, *Secret Societies*, 2:101–2.

17. Franco Venturi, *Roots of Revolution* (New York: Alfred A. Knopf, 1960), pp. 365–66.

Chapter V. *Secrecy and Self-Deception*

1. *Petrarch's Secret, or the Soul's Conflict With Passion* (ca. 1350), trans. William H. Draper (London: Chatto & Windus, 1911), p. 8.
2. See Paul Ricoeur, *Freud and Philosophy* (New Haven, Conn.: Yale University Press, 1970), pp. 32–33, for a discussion of the role of interpretation, and for his description of Marx, Nietzsche, and Freud as the "three masters of suspicion" because of their stress on false consciousness and on "truth as lying."
3. For discussion of self-deception, see, apart from works cited in this chapter and Chapters VI and VII, Raphael Demos, "Lying to Oneself," *Journal of Philosophy* 57 (1960):588–95; Herbert Fingarette, *Self-Deception* (London: Routledge & Kegan Paul, 1969); M. R. Haight, *A Study of Self-Deception* (Sussex: Harvester Press, 1980); Amélie Rorty, "Belief and Self-Deception," *Inquiry* 15 (1972):387–410; Amélie Rorty, "Self-Deception, Akrasia, and Irrationality," *Social Science Information* 19 (Summer 1980):905–22; and my comment on this last article in the same journal, "The Self Deceived," pp. 923–35. I draw on this comment in the present chapter.
4. Heinz Hartmann, *Ego Psychology and Adaptation* (1937), trans. David Rapaport (New York: International Universities Press, 1958), p. 64. See also Anna Freud, *The Ego and the Mechanisms of Defense* (New York: International Universities Press, 1946); George E. Vaillant, *Adaptation to Life* (Boston: Little, Brown & Co., 1977).
5. See, for instance, Carl Fullerton Sulzberger, "Why It Is Hard To Keep Secrets," *Psychoanalysis* 2 (Fall 1953):37–43; Russell Meares, "The Secret," *Psychiatry* 39 (1976):258–65; and Rudolf Eckstein and Elaine Caruth, "Keeping Secrets," in Giovacchini, ed. *Tactics and Techniques in Psychoanalytic Therapy*, pp. 200–15.
6. Jean-Paul Sartre, *L'Etre et le néant* [Being and Nothingness] (Paris: Gallimard, 1943), p. 88. For Sartre's reference to "magic unity," see p. 92.
7. Ibid., p. 87.
8. Ibid. For a discussion of "bad faith" in Sartre's philosophy and of his stance toward moral philosophy, see Peter Caws, *Sartre* (London: Routledge & Kegan Paul, 1979); Francis Jeanson, *Le Problème moral et la pensée de Sartre* (Paris: Editions du Myrte, 1947); Thomas C. Anderson, *The Foundation and Structure of Sartrian Ethics* (Lawrence: Regents Press of Kansas, 1979); John King-Farlow, "Self-Deceivers and Sartrian Seducers," *Analysis* 23 (1963):131–36; Mary Warnock, *The Philosophy of Sartre* (London: Hutchinson & Co., 1965), pp. 50–60.
9. Sigmund Freud, "Splitting of the Ego in the Defensive Process," *Collected Papers*, ed. and trans. James Strachey (London: Hogarth Press, 1957), 5:372–75. See, for a discussion of the concept of "splitting," Paul W. Pruyser, "What Splits in Splitting?" *Bulletin of the Menninger Clinic* 39 (1975):1–46.
10. See, for example, the works by Fingarette and Rorty and the references in my article "The Self Deceived," all cited in note 3.
11. Ivor A. Richards, *Principles of Literary Criticism* (London: Kegan Paul, Trench, Trubner & Co., 1925), p. 40.
12. Jean Bodin, *De la démonamanie des sorciers* (Paris, 1582), preface. See also the discussion of this work in R. Trevor Davies, *Four Centuries of Witch Beliefs* (London: Methuen & Co., 1947), pp. 25–27; and in Hugh R. Trevor-Roper, *The European Witch-Craze of the 16th and 17th Centuries* (New York: Penguin Books, 1969), pp. 49 and 61.
13. Albert Speer, *Inside the Third Reich* (New York: Avon Books, 1970). For commentaries on the self-deception in Speer's life, see David Burrell and Stanley Hauerwas, "Self-Deception and Autobiography: Theological and Ethical Reflections on Speer's

Inside the Third Reich," *Journal of Religious Ethics* 2 (1974):99–117; Yrsa Stenius, *Jag älskar mig: gåtan Albert Speer* (Helsinki: Söderströms Förlag, 1980).

14. Speer, *Inside the Third Reich*, p. 376.

15. See Dennis Thompson, "Moral Responsibility of Public Officials: The Problem of Many Hands," *American Political Science Review* 74 (1980):906–16, for a discussion of the grounds for attributing responsibility to public officials.

16. Kent Bach, in "An Analysis of Self-Deception," *Philosophical and Phenomenological Research* 41 (1981):351–70, argues, more generally, that "even though the self-deceiver is not fully aware of what he is doing, we do hold him responsible for it" (p.368), and that all self-deception is negligent.

17. Bishop Butler, *Sermon X*, "Upon Self-Deceit," *Works*, ed. W. E. Gladstone (Oxford: Clarendon Press, 1896), 2:168–184. Passage quoted, p. 176.

18. According to one set of estimates, a person receives 10,000 sensory impressions per second. See Paul Watzlawick, Janet H. Beavin, and Don D. Jackson, *Pragmatics of Human Communication* (New York: W. W. Norton & Co., 1967), p. 95.

19. Fingarette, in *Self-Deception*, sees this failure to spell out some feature of the world or of one's engagement in it as underlying self-deception. See also Bach, "Analysis of Self-Deception," for a discussion of the elements of self-deception. See also the works of Harry Stack Sullivan for his account of "selective inattention," especially *The Interpersonal Theory of Psychiatry*, ed. Helen Swick Parry and Mary Ladd Gave (New York: W. W. Norton & Co., 1953). Irving L. Janis and Leon Mann discuss the elements of "defensive avoidance" in *Decision Making* (New York: Free Press, 1977); and Robert J. Lifton considers "psychic numbing" in *The Life of the Self* (New York: Simon & Schuster, 1976).

20. For discussions of processes of denial in dying patients, see Loma Feigenberg, *Terminal Care* (New York: Brunner/Mazel, 1980); Richard S. Lazarus, interviewed by David Goleman, "Positive Denial: The Case for Not Facing Reality," *Psychology Today* November 1979, pp. 44–60; A. D. Weisman, *On Dying and Denying* (New York: Behavioral Publications, 1972).

21. Arnold R. Beisser, "Denial and Affirmation in Illness and Health," *American Journal of Psychiatry* 136 (1979):1029.

22. For a discussion of the value of ignorance, see Wilbert E. Moore and Melvin M. Tumin, "Some Social Functions of Ignorance," *American Sociological Review* 14 (1949):787–95; Robert E. Goodin, *Manipulatory Politics* (New Haven, Conn.: Yale University Press, 1980), pp. 37–40; and Harold L. Wilenski, *Organizational Intelligence* (New York: Basic Books, 1967).

23. *Petrarch's Secret*, pp. 190–92.

24. Simmel, *Sociology*, p. 466.

Chapter VI. Confessions

1. Jean-Jacques Rousseau, *Les Confessions* (1782; Paris: Editions Garnier Frères, 1964), pp. 3–4.

2. Albert Camus, *La Chute* [The Fall], in *Théâtre, Récits, Nouvelles* (Paris: Bibliothèque de la Pléiade, 1962), pp. 1537–38. Compare *Notebooks*, vol. 1, *1935–1942* (New York: Alfred A. Knopf, 1963), p.4: "A guilty conscience needs to confess. A work of art is a confession, and I must bear witness."

3. "Relation de ce qui s'est passé . . . en la Nouvelle France ès années 1653 et 1654," in *The Jesuit Relations and Allied Documents*, ed. R. G. Thwaites (Chicago: Loyola University Press, 1959), 41:188, cited in Raffaele Pettazoni, *La confessione dei peccati*, 3rd ed. (Bologna: Forni Editore, 1968), 1:25–26. See also Pettazoni's "Confession of Sins and the Classics," *Harvard Theological Review* 30 (1937):1–14.

4. For confessions to the police, see Yale Kamisar, *Police Interrogation and Confession* (Ann Arbor: University of Michigan Press, 1980).

5. Thomas Aquinas, *Summa Theologiae*, I–II, 71.6, in Anton C. Pegis, ed., *Basic Writings of Saint Thomas Aquinas*, 2:568. For a recent discussion of Catholic writings on confession, see Richard A. McCormick, *Notes on Moral Theology 1965 through 1980* (Washington, D.C.: University Press of America, 1981), pp. 63–67, 137–44.

6. Augustine, *Confessions*; John Bunyan, *Grace Abounding to the Chief of Sinners* (1666), ed. John Brown (Boston: Houghton Mifflin Co., 1880), p. 10; Leo Tolstoy, *A Confession* (1888), trans. Aylmer Maude (London: Oxford University Press, 1940).

7. Sir Wallis Budge, ed., *The Book of the Dead* (New York: Bell Publishing Co., 1960), pp. 586–87.

8. Dietrich Bonhoeffer, *Life Together*, trans. John W. Doberstein (New York: Harper & Row, 1954), p. 112.

9. Origen, *Homiliae in Lucam*, in Bettenson, ed., *Early Christian Fathers*, p. 253.

10. In the early Christian penitentials, after the sixth century A.D., penances were often prescribed for offenses, such as murder, that were also against the law. In the ensuing centuries, priests continued to exercise a quasi-judicial function that allowed them to prescribe penalties according to the offense. See Ludwig Bieler, ed., *The Irish Penitentials* (Dublin: Institute for Advanced Studies, 1963); John McNeill and Helena M. Gamer, eds., *Medieval Handbooks of Penance* (New York: Columbia University Press, 1938).

11. See Tertullian, *De Poenitentia*, 7, in Bettenson, ed. *Early Christian Fathers*.

12. Lateran IV, cited in James F. McCue, "*Simul iustus et peccator* in Augustine, Aquinas, and Luther: Toward Putting the Debate in Context," *Journal of the American Academy of Religion* 48 (March 1980):86.

13. Aquinas, *Summa Theologiae*, I-II, 74.8, in Pegis, ed., *Basic Writings*, 2: 610–13.

14. Elliot P. Currie reports that estimates of the numbers of witches executed in Western Europe varies but that half a million is an average count. See his "Crimes Without Criminals: Witchcraft and Its Control in Renaissance Europe," *Law and Society Review* 3 (1968):7–32. See also Mary Douglas, "Introduction Thirty Years After *Witchcraft, Oracles and Magic*," in Douglas, ed., *Witchcraft, Confessions and Accusations* (London: Tavistock Publications, 1970), p. xxvii.

15. Martin Luther, letter to a follower in Frankfurt: "The Pagan Servitude of the Church," in John Dillenberger, ed., *Martin Luther: Selections from His Writings* (New York: Doubleday & Co., 1961), pp. 345, 321. See also Erik Erikson, *Young Man Luther* (New York: W. W. Norton & Co., 1958), pp. 130–35.

16. Michel Foucault, *The History of Sexuality*, trans. Robert Hurley (New York: Pantheon Books, 1978), Part III, and *Power/Knowledge*, ed. Colin Gordon (New York: Pantheon Books, 1980). For a study of confession in different cultures, see Pettazoni's three volumes on confessional practices throughout history, *La confessione dei peccati*, and his article cited in note 3 above.

17. Theodor Reik, *The Compulsion to Confess* (New York: Farrar, Straus & Cudahy, 1959). See also Andreas Shoeck, *Confession and Psychoanalysis* (Westminster, Md.: Newman Press, 1964). Sigmund Freud rejected the notion that psychoanalysts aim at "the post of a secular father confessor," in *An Outline of Psychoanalysis*, ed. and trans. James Strachey (New York: W. W. Norton Co., 1949), p. 64. Freud argued that analysts, unlike confessors, probe not only what the patient knowingly conceals "but what he does *not* know."

18. Nancy M. Henley, "Power, Sex and Nonverbal Communication," *Berkeley Journal of Sociology* 18 (1973):1–26. See also Valerian J. Derlega and Alan L. Chaikin, "Privacy and Self-Disclosure in Social Relationships," *Journal of Social Issues* 33 (1977):102–15; Paul Cozby, "Self-Disclosure: A Literature Review," *Psychological Bulletin* 79 (1973): 73–91.

19. Sigmund Freud, "Recommendations to Physicians Practicing Psychoanalysis" (1912), in Strachey, ed., *Complete Psychological Works*, 12:111–20.

20. *The Diary of Anaïs Nin*, vol. 1, *1931–1934*, ed. Gunther Stuhlman (New York: Harcourt Brace Jovanovich, 1966), p. 108.

21. Choderlos de Laclos, *Les Liaisons dangereuses* (1782), trans. P. W. K. Stone (New York: Penguin Books, 1961), p. 187. Compare Søren Kierkegaard's views on the role of manipulation in seduction, in "Immediate Stages of the Erotic," and "Diary of a Seducer," in *Either/Or*, trans. David F. Swenson and Lilian M. Swenson (Princeton, N.J.: Princeton University Press, 1944; paperback ed., 1967), 1:43–134, 297–440.

22. *Diary of Anaïs Nin*, 1:161.

23. Camus, *La Chute*, in *Théâtre, Récits, Nouvelles*, p. 1546.

24. See, for example, George A. Huber and Loren Roth, "Preserving the Confidentiality of Medical Record Information Regarding Non-patients," *Virginia Law Review* 66 (1980):583–96.

25. An example of this attitude is the reaction of Tsar Nicholas I of Russia to Bakunin's confession written from prison, stating that he would only confess to his own sins, not reveal those of others. The tsar wrote in the margin: "By that, he already destroys my entire confidence; if he felt the whole seriousness of his sins, only a full and unconditional confession could be considered a true confession." See Mikhail Bakunin, *Confession*, trans. Paulette Brupbacher (Paris: Les Editions Rieder, 1932).

26. Siegfried Bernfeld, "The Facts of Observation in Psychoanalysis," *Journal of Psychology* 12 (1941):289–305; quotation on p. 294.

Chapter VII. Gossip

1. Leo Tolstoy, *Anna Karenina*, trans. Constance Garnett (New York: Random House, Modern Library, 1950), p. 158.

2. *The American Heritage Dictionary* (Boston: Houghton Mifflin & Co., 1969).

3. Aristotle, *Nicomachean Ethics*, bk. 4, chap. 3, 31. Aristotle contrasted the "great-souled man" with the "small-souled man," on the one hand, who claims less than he deserves, and with the "vain man" on the other, who claims more than he deserves. I have used the traditional translation of Aristotle's *anthropos megalopsuchos*, as "great-souled man"; it must, needless to say, not be thought to refer to males only.

4. Thomas Aquinas, *Summa Theologica* II–II. Ques. 73–74, trans. Fathers of the English Dominican Province (New York: Benziger Brothers, 1918), pp. 290–303.

5. Søren Kierkegaard, *Two Ages* (1846), trans. Howard V. and Edna H. Hong (Princeton, N.J.: Princeton University Press, 1978). See esp. pp. 97–102.

6. Martin Heidegger, *Being and Time* (New York: Harper & Row, 1962), p. 213. See p. 212 for Heidegger's view of the role of gossip and "scribbling" in "idle talk."

7. Warren and Brandeis, "The Right to Privacy," pp. 193–220. For a discussion of this article and of the authors' distaste for gossip, see Dorothy J. Glancy, "The Invention of the Right to Privacy," *Arizona Law Review* 21 (1979): 1–39.

8. For the central role of gossip for information storage and retrieval in a society, see John M. Roberts, "The Self-Management of Cultures," in Ward H. Goodenough, *Explorations in Cultural Anthropology* (New York: McGraw-Hill Book Co., 1964), p. 441. And for an economic interpretation of information management through secrecy and gossip, see Richard A. Posner, "The Right to Privacy," *Georgia Law Review* 12 (Spring 1978):398–422.

9. See, among others, Max Gluckman, "Gossip and Scandal," *Current Anthropology* 4 (1963):307–16; Don Handelman, "Gossip in Encounters: The Transmission of Information in a Bounded Social Setting," *Man*, n.s. 8 (1973):210–27; Robert Paine, "What is Gossip About? An Alternative Hypothesis," *Man*, n.s. 2 (1967):278–85; Ralph

L. Rosnow and Gary A. Fine, *Rumor and Gossip: The Social Psychology of Hearsay* (New York: Elsevier, 1976); John Beard Haviland, *Gossip, Reputation, and Knowledge in Zinacantan* (Chicago: University of Chicago Press, 1977).

10. We need not go back to Aesop, Plutarch, or the eighteenth-century moralists for vivid examples of such distinctions based on sex. Carl Fullerton Sulzberger permitted himself the following tortuous speculation, put forth as self-evident fact, in "Why It Is Hard to Keep Secrets," p. 42: "As we all know, most women habitually indulge in acquiring secrets only to give them away with celerity and obvious enjoyment. . . . When I once asked a patient why she was so eager to acquire and then spread secret rumors, her first associaton was, 'it is like adorning myself with borrowed feathers.' . . . the greater readiness of women to disseminate secrets entrusted to them is directly related to the working of the castration complex."

11. Michael McGiffert, ed., *God's Plot: The Paradoxes of Puritan Piety, Being the Autobiography and Journal of Thomas Shepard* (Amherst: University of Massachusetts Press, 1972); Jonathan Edwards, *Religious Affections* (Edinburgh: W. Laing & J. Matthews, 1789). See also Perry Miller, *The New England Mind: The Seventeenth Century* (New York: Macmillan Co., 1939).

12. Gluckman, "Gossip and Scandal," p. 315.

13. See Gordon W. Allport and Leo Postman, *The Psychology of Rumor* (New York: Henry Holt & Co., 1947), and articles cited in note 9 above.

14. Luigi Pirandello, *Right You Are! (If You Think So)*, in Montrose J. Moses, ed., *Dramas of Modernism and their Forerunners* (Boston: Little, Brown & Co., 1931), pp. 239–75.

15. "FBI Admits It Spread Lies About Actress Jean Seberg," *Los Angeles Times*, September 15, 1979, p. 1, and editorial, September 19.

16. The Babylonian Talmud, cited in Francine Klagsbrun, *Voices of Wisdom: Jewish Ideals and Ethics for Everday Living* (New York: Pantheon Books, 1980), p. 74.

17. La Rochefoucauld, *Maximes et réflexions diverses* (1664; Paris: Gallimard, 1976), p. 143.

18. Jane Austen, *Pride and Prejudice* (New York: E. P. Dutton & Co., 1976), p. 384.

19. Maimonides, *Code*, "Laws Concerning Moral Dispositions and Ethical Conduct," chap. 7, secs. 1–4, quoted in Klagsbrun, *Voices of Wisdom*, p. 75.

20. Haviland, *Gossip, Reputation, and Knowledge in Zinacantan*, p. 15.

21. George Eliot, *Daniel Deronda*, Standard Edition, *The Works of George Eliot* (Edinburgh & London: William Blackwood & Sons, 1897), 1:207.

22. Plutarch, "Concerning Talkativeness," *Moralia*, 6:399.

23. Heidegger, *Being and Time*, p. 213.

24. See Elizabeth Drew, *The Literature of Gossip: Nine English Letter-Writers* (New York: W. W. Norton & Co., 1964), p. 26, for examples of gossipers who can "inspire the commonplace with an uncommon flavor, and transform trivialities by some original grace or sympathy or humor or affection."

25. See, for example, Kierkegaard, *Two Ages*, p. 100, and Heidegger, *Being and Time*, p. 212.

Chapter VIII. **Secrecy, Power, and Accountability**

1. Empedocles, *The Purifications*, in *The Fragments of Empedocles*, trans. William Ellery Leonard (La Salle, Ill.: Open Court Publishing Co., 1908), pp. 50–58.

2. See G. J. Warnock, *The Object of Morality* (London: Metheun & Co., 1971), pp. 12–26. See also John Rawls, *A Theory of Justice* (Cambridge, Mass.: Harvard University Press, 1971), pp. 126–30; H. L. A. Hart, *The Concept of Law*, pp. 189–95; J. R. Lucas, *The Principles of Politics* (Oxford: Clarendon Press, 1966) pp. 1–10.

3. Hume noted, in *An Enquiry Concerning the Principles of Morals* (1751), sec. 3, pt. 1, that justice would not be needed if scarcity and failures of benevolence were not so prevalent. But abundance and benevolence do not in fact eliminate moral conflict or preclude the need for justice, because of the second element of the predicament and the third, which requires far more than universal benevolence in order to be overcome. See Henry D. Aiken, ed., *Hume's Moral and Political Philosophy* (New York: Hafner Publishing Co., 1948, pp. 185–92.

4. Gasquet, ed., *Lord Acton and His Circle*, p. 166; John E. E. Dalberg Acton, *Essays on Freedom and Power*, ed. G. Himmelfont (Boston: Beacon Press, 1948), letter to Mandell Creighton, p. 364.

5. Immanuel Kant, "Perpetual Peace," in Hans Reiss, ed., *Kant's Political Writings* (Cambridge: Cambridge University Press, 1970), pp. 112–13.

6. See Jacob R. Marcus, *The Jew in the Medieval World* (Cincinnati, Ohio: Sinai Press, 1938), pp. 364–65.

7. Benjamin Franklin, *Poor Richard: The Almanacks for the Years 1733–1758*, ed. Van Wyck Brooks (New York: Heritage Press, 1964), July 1735, p. 30.

8. Robert E. Goodin, *The Politics of Rational Man* (New York: John Wiley & Sons, 1976); Mancur Olson, *The Logic of Collective Action* (Cambridge, Mass.: Harvard University Press, 1965).

9. See Wayne Lee, *Decision Theory and Human Behavior* (New York: John Wiley & Sons, 1971), pp. 117–18.

10. Irving L. Janis, *Victims of Groupthink* (Boston: Houghton Mifflin Co., 1972); Janis and Mann, *Decision Making*.

11. See Guido Calabresi and Philip Babbitt, *Tragic Choices* (New York: W. W. Norton & Co., 1978).

12. See Daraul, *Secret Societies*, pp. 202–11; Theodor Linder, *Die Veme* (Münster: Ferdinard Schoningh, 1888). A number of secret societies conducted secret trials. For a development resembling that of the Holy Vehm, see the discussion of the Triad in Chesneaux, *Secret Societies in China*, pp. 13–35.

13. Jeremy Bentham, "On Publicity," *Essay on Political Tactics* in *The Works of Jeremy Bentham*, ed. John Bowring (Edinburgh: W. Tait, 1843), 2:310–17; John Stuart Mill, *Considerations on Representative Government* (South Bend, Ind.: Gateway Editions, 1962), pp. 213–16. See also Maure L. Goldschmidt, "Publicity, Privacy, and Secrecy," *Western Political Quarterly* 7 (1954):401–16.

14. Henry Sidgwick, *The Methods of Ethics* (1907; New York: Dover Publications, 1966), p. 490. On p. 492, however, in discussing group practices that diverge from ordinary moral rules, Sidgwick argues that an enlightened utilitarian might try to remove the conflict, either by open arguments in favor of relaxing the ordinary rule or by trying to enforce acceptance of that rule. See also Bernard Williams, *Morality* (New York: Harper & Row, 1972), pp. 101–7; Adrian M. S. Piper, "Utility, Publicity, and Manipulation," *Ethics* 88 (1978):189–206.

15. Sidgwick, *Methods of Ethics*, p. 490.

16. Sissela Bok, *Lying: Moral Choice in Public and Private Life* (New York: Pantheon Books, 1978), chap. 7, "Justification," pp. 103–5. See, also, references in that chapter to others who have argued for the necessity of publicity.

17. The word for "deliberation" used by Aristotle is *bouleusis*: it is related to *boule*, meaning council, and thus again suggests an open debate. See John M. Cooper, *Reason and Human Good in Aristotle* (Cambridge, Mass.: Harvard University Press, 1975), chap. 1.

18. Mill, *Representative Government*, p. 214.

19. Reiss, ed., *Kant's Political Writings*, p. 125. In addition to seeing publicity as a thought-experiment, it is possible to bracket the vicissitudes and biases accompanying human choice that permeate such experiments even in the most abstract thought processes.

This may be done by using societal models from which such difficulties have been removed. Thus John Rawls, in *A Theory of Justice*, postulates a "well-ordered society" which has already attained a "large measure of justice" and in which physical needs and psychological capacities are all "within the normal range."

Chapter IX. **The Limits of Confidentiality**

1. See Robert E. Regan, *Professional Secrecy in the Light of Moral Principles* (Washington, D. C.: Augustinian Press, 1943); Alan H. Goldman, *The Moral Foundations of Professional Ethics* (Totowa, N.J.: Rowman & Littlefield, 1980); LeRoy Walters, "Ethical Aspects of Medical Confidentiality," in Tom L. Beauchamp and LeRoy Walters, eds., *Comtemporary Issues in Bioethics* (Encino, Calif.: Dickenson Publishing Co., 1978), pp. 169–75; Susanna J. Wilson, *Confidentiality in Social Work* (New York: Free Press, 1978); William Harold Tiemann, *The Right to Silence: Privileged Communication and the Pastor* (Richmond, Va.: John Knox Press, 1964); William W. Meissner, "Threats to Confidentiality," *Psychiatric Annals* 2 (1979):54–71.

2. From the newsletter *Hard Choices*, of the Office for Radio and Television for Learning (Boston, 1980), p. 9.

3. For a discussion of whether this partial autonomy over personal information should be defended in terms of property, see Arthur R. Miller, *The Assault on Privacy* (Ann Arbor: University of Michigan Press, 1971), pp. 211–16.

4. For the marital privilege, see Sanford Levinson, *The State and Structures of Intimacy* (New York: Basic Books, forthcoming). For the Chinese tradition, see Derk Bodde and Clarence Morris, *Law in Imperial China* (Cambridge, Mass.: Harvard University Press, 1967), p. 40.

5. Hugo Grotius, *The Law of War and Peace*, trans. Francis Kelsey (Indianapolis: Bobbs-Merrill Co., 1925), bk. 2, chap. 11, p. 331.

6. I discussed the question of lying to protect confidences in *Lying*, chap. 11.

7. For different views on the binding force of promises, see William Godwin, *Enquiry Concerning Political Justice* (1793; 3rd ed. 1798), bk. 3, chap. 3; Richard Price, *A Review of the Principal Questions in Morals* (1758; 3rd ed. 1787), chap. 7 (both in D. H. Munro, ed., *A Guide to the British Moralists* [London: William Collins, Sons & Co., 1972], pp. 187–97, 180–86). For more general treatments of promising, see Grotius, *Law of War and Peace*, bk. 2, chap. 11, pp. 328–42; John Searle, *Speech Acts* (Cambridge: Cambridge University Press, 1969); Charles Fried, *Contract as Promise* (Cambridge, Mass.: Harvard University Press, 1981).

8. Nietzsche, in *Ecce Homo*, trans. Kaufmann, p. 64, relates such pledges to the bond between debtor and creditor; he argues that the memory necessary for people to keep promises only developed through such painful, often cruel experiences.

9. For discussions of whether some or all of these premises should be accepted, and whether they are grounded on utilitarian or deontological considerations, see Goldman, *Moral Foundations of Professional Ethics*; Leo J. Cass and William J. Curran, "Rights of Privacy in Medical Practice," partially reprinted in Samuel Gorovitz et al., *Moral Problems in Medicine* (Englewood Cliffs, N.J.: Prentice-Hall, 1976), pp. 82–85; Benjamin Freedman, "A Meta-Ethics for Professional Morality," *Ethics* 89 (1978):1–79; Benjamin Freedman, "What Really Makes Professional Morality Different: Response to Martin," *Ethics* 91 (1981):626–30; Mike W. Martin, "Rights and the Meta-Ethics of Professional Morality," *Ethics* 91 (1981):619–25.

10. Henry E. Sigerist, *A History of Medicine*, vol. 1, *Primitive and Archaic Medicine* (New York: Oxford University Press, 1951), p. 433.

11. Jeremy Bentham, otherwise opposed to testimonial privileges for professionals, argues in favor of "excluding the evidence of a Catholic priest respecting the confessions

intrusted to him," holding that freedom of religion outweighs the social costs of such practices. See *Works of Jeremy Bentham*, 7:366–68.

12. Code of Ethics, 1949 World Medical Association, in *Encyclopedia of Bioethics* (New York: Free Press, 1978), pp. 1749–50.

13. I have discussed abortion in "Ethical Problems of Abortion," *Hastings Center Studies* 2 (1974):33–52.

14. Lawrence Weed, *Your Health Care and How to Manage it* (Arlington, Vt.: Essex Publishing Co., 1978), p. 79.

15. See Judge Tobriner, *Tarasoff* v. *Regents of the University of California*, Opinion #551, 1. 2d 334, 131 Cal. Rptr. 14 (1976).

16. See, for example, Harvey L. Ruben and Diana D. Ruben, "Confidentiality and Priviledged Communication: The Psychotherapeutic Relationship Revisited," *Medical Annals of the District of Columbia* 41 (1972):365: "The patient in analysis must learn to free associate and to break down resistances to deal with unconscious threatening thoughts and feelings. To revoke secrecy after encouraging such risk-taking is to threaten all further interaction."

17. Alan A. Stone, "The Tarasoff Decisions: Suing Psychotherapists to Safeguard Society," *Harvard Law Review* 90 (1976):358–78.

18. David Wechsler, in "Patients, Therapists, and Third Parties: The Victimological Virtues of Tarasoff," *International Journal of Law and Psychiatry* 2 (1979):1–28, argues that, as a practical matter, most threats by patients concern family members or close associates, who usually know about the hostility aimed at them. Requiring psychotherapists to disclose such dangers, Wechsler argues, may force them to give up their counter-productive focus on the patient alone and to consider much more carefully, as well, his relationship with others.

19. See Regan, *Professional Secrecy*, pp. 104–13.

20. For diverging views of the lawyer's responsibility of confidentiality, see American Bar Association, Proposed Final Draft, Model Rules of Professional Conduct, 1981, pp. 37–47; and the Roscoe Pound–American Trial Lawyers Foundation, Discussion Draft, The American Lawyer's Code of Conduct, June 1980, pp. 101–10.

21. For accounts of the story of Anneliese Michel and of the trial after her death, I have relied on *Die Zeit*, July 30, 1976, and April 7, 1978; *Der Spiegel*, July 2, 1976, and April 3, 1978; and *Süddeutsche Zeitung*, which had stories almost daily during the period of the trial, March 30–April 24, 1978.

22. See Paul Brodeur, *Expendable Americans* (New York: Viking Press, 1973).

23. Ethics Advisory Board, Department of Health and Human Services, The Request of the Center for Disease Control for a Limited Exemption from the Freedom of Information Act. 1980.

Chapter X. *Trade and Corporate Secrecy*

1. American Law Institute, *Restatement of Torts*, 1939, §757, comment b. See further, for works on trade secrecy: Michael Barclay, "Trade Secrets: How Long Shall an Injunction Last?" *UCLA Law Review* 26 (October 1978):203–33; Rudolf Callman, *Unfair Competition, Trademarks, and Monopolies*, 3rd ed. (Wilmette, Ill.: Callaghan & Co., 1976), pars. 51–54; William J. French, Comment, "The Scott Amendment to the Patent Revision Act: Should Trade Secrets Receive Federal Protection?" *Wisconsin Law Review*, 1971, no. 3, pp. 900–21; R. M. Cummings, "Some Aspects of Trade Secrets and Their Protection," *Kentucky Law Journal* 54 (1966):190–205; Gordon L. Doerfer, "The Limits of Trade Secret Law Imposed by Federal Patent and Antitrust Supremacy," *Harvard Law Review* 80 (1967):1432–62; Ridsale Ellis, *Trade Secrets* (New York: Baker, Voorhis & Co., 1953); Roger M. Milgrim, *Trade Secrets* (1967; New York: Matthew Bender,

1978); Roger M. Milgrim, *Protecting and Profiting from Trade Secrets* (New York: Practicing Law Institute, 1979); Note, "Protection and Use of Trade Secrets," *Harvard Law Review* 64 (1951):976–86; Brian J. O'Connell, "Secrecy in Business: A Sociological View," in Tefft, ed., *Secrecy*, pp. 229–44. John C. Stedman, "Trade Secrets," *Ohio State Law Journal* 23 (1962):4–34.

2. See "Porcelaine de la Chine," *Encyclopédie; ou dictionnaire raisonné des sciences, des arts et des métiers*, 13:106–22; George Richardson Porter, *A Treatise on the Origin, Progressive Improvement, and Present State of the Manufacture of Porcelain and Glass* (Philadelphia: Carey, Lea & Blanchard, 1834), pp. 20–26; Gottfried Christian Bohns, *Waarenlager oder Wörterbuch der Produkten und Waarenkunde* (Hamburg: Carl Ernst Bohn, 1789–1806), 2:384.

3. *The Universal Dictionary of Trade and Commerce* (London: John Knapton, 1757), 2:497–505; quotation on p. 505.

4. See Jacques Bergier, *Secret Armies: The Growth of Corporate and Industrial Espionage*, trans. Harold J. Samuelson (Indianapolis: Bobbs-Merrill Co., 1975); Paul I. Slee Smith, *Industrial Intelligence and Espionage* (London: Business Books, 1970). For a discussion of industrial secrecy and travel restrictions on British skilled artisans in the nineteenth century, see David Landes, *The Unbound Prometheus* (Cambridge: Cambridge University Press, 1969), pp. 148–52.

5. Dorothy Glancy, "The U.S. Crime of Trade Secret Theft," *European Intellectual Property Review* 1 (July 1979):179–82.

6. Edwin Land, "Thinking Ahead: Patents and New Enterprises," *Harvard Business Review* 37 (September–October 1959):7–10.

7. See Walton Hamilton, *The Politics of Industry* (New York: Alfred A. Knopf, 1957), chap. 3.

8. See Russell B. Stevenson, Jr., *Corporations and Information—Secrecy, Access, and Disclosure* (Baltimore: Johns Hopkins University Press, 1980), p. 21.

9. See, for example, Note, "Nature of Trade Secrets and Their Protection," *Harvard Law Review* 42 (1928):254–58; John P. Sutton, "Trade Secret Legislation," *Idea* 9 (1965–66):587–607; Doerfer, "The Limits of Trade Secrets Law"; Ellis, *Trade Secrets*; Stedman, "Trade Secrets."

10. Warren and Brandeis, "The Right to Privacy," p. 212.

11. Cym H. Lowell, "Corporate Privacy: A Remedy for the Victim of Industrial Espionage," *Patent Law Review* (renamed *Intellectual Property Law Review*) 4 (1972): 407–49.

12. For a discussion of the role of administrative secrecy in business, see Mark V. Nadel, "Corporate Secrecy and Political Accountability," *Public Administration Review* 35 (1975):14–23; Brian J. O'Connell, "Secrecy in Business," pp. 229–44.

13. A. M. Honoré, "Property, Title, and Redistribution," in Virginia Held, ed., *Property, Profit, and Economic Justice* (Belmont, Calif.: Wadsworth Publishing Co., 1980), pp. 84–92; case on p. 88.

14. Stevenson, *Corporations and Information*, p. 16; case referred to is *E. I. duPont de Nemours & Co., Inc. v. Christopher*, 431 F.2d 1012 (5th Cir. 1970).

15. John Locke, *The Second Treatise of Government* (1690), ed. Thomas P. Peardon (Indianapolis: Bobbs-Merrill Co., 1952), p. 17. See also Robert Nozick, *Anarchy, State, and Utopia*.

16. *Hegel's Philosophy of Right*, trans. T. M. Knox (Oxford: Clarendon Press, 1942), pp. 40–57.

17. See Lawrence C. Becker's discussion in *Property Rights: Philosophic Foundations* (London: Routledge & Kegan Paul, 1977).

18. For discussions of Locke's and Hegel's theories, see Becker, *Property Rights*, and Christopher J. Berry, "Property and Possession: Two Replies to Locke—Hume and

Hegel," in Pennock and Chapman, eds., *Property*, pp. 89–100, as well as other articles in the same volume.

19. See Melville J. Herskovits, *Economic Anthropology* (New York: Alfred A. Knopf, 1952), chap. 14.

20. See Michael S. Baram, "Trade Secrets: What Price Loyalty?" *Harvard Business Review* 46 (November–December 1968): 66–74. See also Rolande Cuvillier, "No-competition and Non-disclosure Obligations: Bond or Bondage for the Employee?" *International Labour Review* 115 (1977):193–209; Stanley H. Lieberstein, *Who Owns What Is in Your Head? Trade Secrets and the Mobile Employed* (New York: Hawthorn Books, 1979).

21. Ralph Nader, Peter Petkas, Kate Blackwell, *Whistle Blowing*, (New York: Grossman Publishers, 1972) p. 211.

22. Milgrim, *Protecting and Profiting*, pp. 303–64; quoted passage on p. 308. See also Lawrence Stressin and Ira Wit, *The Disloyal Employee* (New York: Man & Manager, 1967), p. 20.

23. Compare Hume's view, dismissing claims that property exists in a state of nature, that it is a right emanating from men's joining their labor to objects or to nature, and that men have property in their own persons. Property, according to Hume, is a convention established by men to "bestow stability on the possession of those external goods, and leave every one in the peaceable enjoyment of what he may acquire by his fortune and industry"; David Hume, *A Treatise of Human Nature*, ed. L. A. Selby-Bigge (Oxford: Clarendon Press, 1978), bk. 3, sec. 2.

24. Posner, *Economics of Justice*, p. 148.

25. See Stevenson, *Corporations and Information*, chaps. 1, 4. Compare R. H. Tawney, *The Acquisitive Society* (New York: Harcourt, Brace, & World, 1920), chap. 8.

26. See, for example, John E. Marthinsen and Laurence S. Moss, "Business Move to Get Low-Cost Government Information About Competitors," *Collegiate Forum*, Fall 1980, p. 3.

27. U.S., Department of Health, Education, and Welfare, *Review Panel on New Drug Regulation, Final Report*, May 1976.

28. Norman Dorsen and Jeffrey M. Miller, "The Drug Regulation Process and the Challenge of Regulatory Reform," *Annals of Internal Medicine* 91 (December 1979): 908–13.

29. See Thomas O. McGarity and Sidney A. Shapiro, "The Trade Secret Status of Health and Safety Testing Information: Reforming Agency Disclosure Policies," *Harvard Law Review* 93 (1980): 837–88.

30. Herschell Britton, "The Industrial-Spy Peril," *New York Times*, June 30, 1981, p. 15.

31. Paul E. Gray, "Technology Transfer at Issue: The Academic Viewpoint," *IEEE Spectrum*, 19 (May 1982): 64.

Chapter XI. *Secrecy and Competition in Science*

1. Hippocrates, *Law*, trans. William Henry Samuel Jones (Cambridge, Mass.: Harvard University Press, 1923), p. 265. For the role of secrecy in early medicine, see also Sigerist, *History of Medicine*, vol. 1, *Primitive and Archaic Medicine*.

2. See J. Edward Mercer, *Alchemy: Its Science and Romance* (London: Macmillan Co., 1921); John Read, *Prelude to Chemistry; And An Outline of Alchemy* (New York: Macmillan Co., 1937); Sherwood Taylor, *The Alchemists* (Woodstock, N. Y.: Beckman Publishers, 1977).

3. Samuel Bard, *Discourse upon the Duties of a Physician*, excerpted in Stanley Reiser, Arthur Dyck, and William Curran, eds., *Ethics in Medicine* (Cambridge, Mass.: MIT Press, 1977), p. 17.

4. *Encyclopédie; ou dictionnaire raisonné des sciences, des arts et des métiers*, 14:562–63.

5. See Robert Merton, "The Normative Structure of Science," *The Sociology of Science* (Chicago: University of Chicago Press, 1973), pp. 267–78. See also Robert Merton, "Priorities in Scientific Discovery: A Chapter in the Sociology of Science," in Bernard Barber and Walter Hirsch, eds., *The Sociology of Science* (New York: Free Press, 1962), pp. 447–85; John T. Edsall, *Scientific Freedom and Responsibility* (Washington, D.C.: American Association for the Advancement of Science, 1975); Ward Pigman and Emmett B. Carmichael, "An Ethical Code for Scientists," *Science* 111 (June 16, 1950):643–47; André Cournand, "The Code of The Scientist and Its Relation to Ethics," *Science* 198 (November 18, 1977):699–705; and *Principles of Scientific Freedom and Responsibility* (Washington, D.C.: AAAS, 1980).

6. "The Commonwealth of Science," *Nature*, 148 (October 4, 1941):393. The Declaration of Principles was presented by Sir Richard Gregory, Bart, F.R.S., at the end of the Conference on Science and World Order in 1941.

7. Robert Merton, articles cited in note 5 above. Ian I. Mitroff has argued, however, that the norms set forth by Merton have counternorms in scientific work; see *The Subjective Side of Science* (New York: Elsevier, 1974). And Michael J. Mulkay sees such norms as part of the ideology through which scientists present themselves to the public; see "Norms and Ideology in Science," *Social Sciences Information* 15 (April 1976): 637–56.

8. Shils, *Torment of Secrecy*, pp. 46–47. See also Joseph A. Cade, "Aspects of Secrecy in Science," *Impact of Science on Society* 21 (November 2, 1971):181–90; Don K. Price, "Security and Publicity Risks," in *Government and Science* (New York: Oxford University Press, 1962), chap. 4.

9. "Views in Secrecy by American Nobel Prize-Winners," *Science* 130 (July 10, 1959):85–86; see also Shils, *Torment of Secrecy*; Francis E. Rourke, *Secrecy and Publicity* (Baltimore: Johns Hopkins University Press, 1961); AAAS Committee Report, "Civil Liberties of Scientists," *Science* 110 (August 19, 1949):177–79; Lloyd V. Berkner, "Secrecy and Scientific Progress," *Science* 123 (May 4, 1956):783–86; Edward U. Condon, "Science, Secrecy, Security," *Harper's Magazine*, February 1950, pp. 58–63; Isidor Isaac Rabi, "The Costs of Secrecy," *Science: The Center of Culture* (New York: World Publishing Co., 1970), pp. 101–10.

10. Jerry Gaston, *Originality and Competition in Science* (Chicago: University of Chicago Press, 1973), p. 74. See also John Ziman, *Public Knowledge* (Cambridge: Cambridge University Press, 1968), pp. 96–98 and chap. 6; Warren O. Hagstrom, *The Scientific Community* (New York: Basic Books, 1965).

11. James D. Watson, *The Double Helix* (New York: Atheneum Publishers, 1968). See also Horace F. Judson, *The Eighth Day of Creation* (New York: Simon & Schuster, 1979), p. 177.

12. Nicholas Wade, *The Nobel Duel* (Garden City, N.Y.: Doubleday & Co., Anchor Books, 1981).

13. See, for instance, June Goodfield, *An Imagined World: A Story of Scientific Discovery* (New York: Harper & Row, 1981); Irving Louis Horowitz, "Socialization into Secrecy," in Horowitz, ed., *The Rise and Fall of Project Camelot* (Cambridge, Mass.: MIT Press, 1967), pp. 347–60; John D. Bernal, *The Social Function of Science* (New York: Macmillan Co., 1939), pp. 107–08.

14. Robert Merton, "The Ambivalence of Scientists," in Norman Kaplan, ed., *Science and Society* (Chicago: Rand McNally & Co., 1965), p. 116.

15. Gaston, *Originality and Competition*, p. 124.

16. Ibid., p. 123. See also Spencer R. Weart, "Scientists with a Secret," *Physics Today* 29 (1976):23–30; Ziman, *Public Knowledge*, p. 97.

17. Ian I. Mitroff argues that secrecy can thereby further the progress of science (*Subjective Side of Science*, p. 76). For a study of motivations and pressures among

scientists, see Bruno Latour and Steve Woolgar, *Laboratory Life* (Beverly Hills, Calif.: Sage Publications, 1979).

18. I have discussed the question whether some research should be not only kept secret but actually declared out of bounds, prohibited, in "Freedom and Risk," in Gerald Holton and Robert Morison, eds., *Limits of Scientific Inquiry* (New York: W. W. Norton & Co., 1979), pp. 115–28.

19. See Derek Bok, *Beyond the Ivory Tower: Social Responsibilities of the Modern University* (Cambridge, Mass.: Harvard University Press, 1982), chap. 6.

20. Deborah Shapley, "Intelligence Agency Chief Seeks Dialogue With Academics," *Science* 202 (October 27, 1978):407–10; Gina Bari Kolata, "Cryptography: A New Clash Between Academic Freedom and National Security," *Science* 209 (August 29, 1980):995–96. For a study of the history and forms of cryptology, see David Kahn, *The Code-Breakers: The Story of Secret Writing* (New York: Macmillan Co., 1967).

21. Gina Bari Kolata, "Prior Restraints Recommended," *Science* 211 (February 20, 1981):797; "MIT Committee Seeks Cryptography Policy," *Science* 211 (March 13, 1981):1139–40.

22. Kahn, *Code-Breakers*, chap. 17.

23. Gina Bari Kolata, "Prior Restraints on Cryptography Considered," *Science* 208 (June 27, 1980):1442–43.

24. Cade, "Aspects of Secrecy in Science," p. 182, n. 8.

25. Smith, *Industrial Intelligence and Espionage.* p. 10.

26. Adm. Bobby R. Inman, "National Security and Technical Information," reprinted in *Aviation Week & Space Technology* 82 (February 8, 1982):10–11.

27. Reply to Inman by William D. Carey, in ibid., pp. 10–11; see also Stephen H. Unger, "The Growing Threat of Government Secrecy," *Technology Review* 85 (February–March 1982):31–39, 84–85; Paul E. Gray, "Technology Transfer at Issue," pp. 64–68.

28. *North-South: A Program for Survival* (Cambridge, Mass.: MIT Press, 1980), authored under the chairmanship of Willy Brandt, p. 14; Colin Norman, *The God That Limps: Science and Technology in the Eighties* (New York: W. W. Norton & Co., 1981), pp. 71–78.

29. An earlier version of this chapter appeared in *Science, Technology, and Human Values* 7 (Winter 1982):32–41.

Chapter XII. *Secrets of State*

1. Bentham, "On Publicity," *Works of Jeremy Bentham*, 2:310–17.

2. Wilson, *The New Freedom*, pp. 113–14. See also his *Congressional Government* (Boston: Houghton Mifflin Co., 1885), pp. 72–83, for a discussion of legislative secrecy.

3. See note 8, Chapter I, for the derivation of *arcanum*.

4. See Carl J. Friedrich, *The Pathology of Politics: Violence, Betrayal, Corruption, Secrecy, and Propaganda* (New York: Harper & Row, 1972), pp. 177 ff.; Ernst H. Kantorowicz, "Mysteries of State: An Absolutist Concept and Its Late Mediaeval Origins," *Harvard Theological Review* 48 (1955):65–91; Wolfgang H. Kraus, "The Democratic Community and the Problem of Publicity," in Carl J. Friedrich, ed., *Nomos*, vol. 4, *Community* (New York: Liberal Arts Press, 1959), pp. 225–55.

5. James I to the Speaker of the House of Commons, quoted in Kraus, "The Democratic Community and the Problem of Publicity," p. 235.

6. Francis Bacon, *The Advancement of Learning* (1605), bk. 2, par. 47, in *The Advancement of Learning and New Atlantis*, ed. Thomas Case (London: Oxford University Press, 1951), p. 235.

7. Friedrich Meinecke, *Die Idee der Staatsräson in der neueren Geschichte* (Munich and Berlin: Druck und Verlag von R. Oldenburg, 1925). See also works listed above

in note 4; Quentin Skinner, *The Foundation of Modern Political Thought* (Cambridge: Cambridge University Press, 1978), 1:248–62; Giovanni Botero, "Of Secrecy," *The Reason of State* (1589), trans. P. J. and D. P. Waley (London: Routledge & Kegan Paul, 1956), pp. 47–48.

8. For recent discussions, see Stuart Hampshire, ed., *Public and Private Morality* (Cambridge: Cambridge University Press, 1978).

9. See Robert Goodin's discussion of manipulation through "magico-religious rituals" in *Manipulatory Politics* (New Haven, Conn.: Yale University Press, 1980), pp. 157–94.

10. Bentham, "Of Publicity," *Works of Jeremy Bentham*, 2:314.

11. See my discussion of the senses of "publicity" in Chapter VIII. See also the discussions of publicity in Goldschmidt, "Publicity, Privacy, and Secrecy," pp. 401–16; Rourke, *Secrecy and Publicity*; Shils, *Torment of Secrecy*.

12. Harold L. Wilenski, *Organizational Intelligence: Knowledge and Policy in Government and Industry* (New York: Basic Books, 1967), p. 73.

13. Report of Departmental Committee on Section 2 of the Official Secrets Act of 1911, Cmnd. 5104 (1972), par. 11. Quoted in James Christoph, "A Comparative View. Administrative Secrecy in Britain," in Francis E. Rourke, ed., "Administrative Secrecy: A Comparative Perspective," *Public Administration Review* 35 (Jan.–Feb. 1975):23–32.

14. John Jay, Federalist Paper no. 64, in Alexander Hamilton et al., *The Federalist*, ed. Edward Mead Earle (Washington D.C.: Robert B. Luce, 1976), p. 419.

15. I can therefore not agree with Georg Simmel's view that there is a historical development according to which "general affairs become ever more public, and individual affairs ever more secret" (Simmel, *Sociology*, p. 336).

16. H. H. Gerth and C. Wright Mills, trans. and ed., *From Max Weber: Essays in Sociology* (New York: Oxford University Press, 1946), p. 233. See Wilenski, *Organizational Intelligence*, for a discussion of the role of secrecy in bureaucracies.

17. Goodin, *Manipulatory Politics*, pp. 63–64, 233.

18. Carl J. Friedrich, in *The Pathology of Politics*, views secrecy differently. He sees it as functional in a society up to a point, after which it becomes pathological and "disfunctional," causing injury to the system much as disease may to an individual. He offers no criteria, however, for distinguishing between forms and degrees of secrecy, on moral or system-preserving grounds. See chs. 1, 11.

19. For comparative studies of government secrecy, see Itzhak Galnoor, ed., *Government Secrecy in Democracies* (New York: Harper & Row, 1977); Donald C. Rowat, ed., *Administrative Secrecy in Developed Countries* (New York: Columbia University Press, 1979); Thomas M. Franck and Edward Weisband, eds., *Secrecy and Foreign Policy* (New York: Oxford University Press, 1974).

20. See Kenneth G. Robertson, *Public Secrets: A Study of the Development of Government Secrecy* (New York: St. Martin's Press, 1982), chaps. 3, 4, 5, for an account of the British system and of debates concerning it.

21. Mill, *Considerations on Representative Government*, p. 34.

22. Freedom of Information Act, 5 U. S. C. S 552, enacted in 1966, codified in 1967, amended in 1974. See "Freedom of Information Case List," U. S. Office of Information, Law, and Policy, March 1979.

23. For a discussion, see Norman Dorsen and Stephen Gillers, *None of Your Business: Government Secrecy in America* (New York: Viking Press, 1974); Morton H. Halperin and Daniel N. Hoffman, *Top Secret: National Security and the Right to Know* (Washington, D.C.: New Republic Books, 1977); Rourke, ed., "Administrative Secrecy"; Arthur Macy Cox, *The Myths of National Security: The Perils of Secret Government* (Boston: Beacon Press, 1975).

24. Harold Nicolson, *Peacemaking 1919* (Boston: Houghton Mifflin Co., 1933), p. 43.

25. For President Nixon's remarks on secrecy, see "Remarks at a Reception for Returned Prisoners of War," May 24, 1973, *Public Papers of the Presidents: Richard*

Nixon, 1973 (Washington, D.C.: Government Printing Office, 1975), p. 560. See also Francis E. Rourke, "Watergate and the Presidency," *Administration and Society* 6 (1974):174–75; Norman Dorsen and John H. F. Shattuck, "Executive Privilege, The Congress, and the Courts," *Ohio State Law Journal* 35 (1974):1–40.

26. Francis Bacon, "Of Negotiating," *Essays* (1625; London: Oxford University Press, 1975), p. 197.

27. See Clinton Rossiter, *1787, The Grand Convention* (New York: Macmillan Co., 1966); Fred Rodell, *Fifty-Five Men* (New York: Telegraph Press, 1936).

28. See James Madison, *Journal of the Federal Convention*, ed, E. H. Scott (Chicago: Albert Scott & Co., 1894), p. 58.

29. Thomas Jefferson to John Adams, August 30, 1787, in Lester J. Cooper, ed., *The Adams-Jefferson Letters* (Chapel Hill: University of North Carolina Press, 1959), 1:196.

30. John Dunlop, "The Negotiations Alternative to Markets and Regulation," unpublished manuscript, August 1979.

31. Wilder Foote, ed., *The Servant of Peace: A Selection of the Speeches and Statements of Dag Hammarskjöld* (London: Bodley Head, 1962), pp. 53–54 and 113. See also Brian Urquhart, *Hammarskjöld* (New York: Alfred A. Knopf, 1972).

32. Foote, *Servant of Peace*, p. 113.

33. See Chapter VII, p. 99.

34. I have discussed the question of lying to enemies in *Lying*, Chap. 10.

35. James Q. Wilson, *The Investigators* (New York: Basic Books, 1978), pp. 84–85.

36. For a report on such studies, see Tamotsu Shibutani, *Improved News: A Sociological Study of Rumor* (Indianapolis: Bobbs-Merrill Co., 1966), pp. 191–200.

37. Robert Jervis, *The Logic of Images in International Relations* (Princeton, N.J.: Princeton University Press, 1970), p. 71.

38. Compare Phillip Bonacich, "Secrecy and Solidarity," *Sociometry* 39 (1976): 200–8.

39. Robert Goodin, in *Manipulatory Politics* (New Haven, Conn.: Yale University Press, 1980), discusses the deterioration of political discourse through manipulation.

Chapter XIII. Military Secrecy

1. Thomas Jefferson to Elbridge Gerry, January 26, 1799, in Albert Ellery Bergh, ed., *The Writings of Thomas Jefferson* (Washington, D.C.: Thomas Jefferson Memorial Association, 1907), 10:83.

2. Stanley Hoffman, in *Duties Beyond Borders* (Syracuse, N.Y.: Syracuse University Press, 1981), discusses the moral questions arising between nations, and the limitations on moral choice in international relations, as does Michael Walzer in *Just and Unjust Wars* (New York: Basic Books, 1977).

3. Bentham, "On Publicity," *Works of Jeremy Bentham* 2:310–15.

4. Freedom of Information Act, 5 U.S.C., § 552.

5. U.S., Department of Defense, Joints Chiefs of Staff, *Rescue Mission Report*, August 1980.

6. Zbigniew Brzezinski, "The Failed Mission," *New York Times Magazine*, April 18, 1982, pp. 30–31.

7. *Rescue Mission Report*, p. 48.

8. See Martin C. McGuire, *Secrecy and the Arms Race* (Cambridge, Mass.: Harvard University Press, 1965), for an economic model of the role of secrecy and information in an arms race between two world powers. The author cautions readers, however, that his model is stylized, and that it gives scant attention to irrationality in the arms race (p. 232).

9. Friedrich, *Pathology of Politics*, p. 231.

10. For a personal account, see Joseph Burkholder Smith, *Portrait of a Cold Warrior* (New York: G. P. Putnam's Sons, 1976). For a review of many of the recent books on the subject, see Harry Howe Ransom, "Being Intelligent About Secret Intelligence Agencies," *American Political Science Review* 74 (1980):141–48. See also Thomas Powers, *The Man Who Kept the Secrets: Richard Helms and the CIA* (New York: Alfred A. Knopf, 1979).

11. Alice Kimball Smith and Charles Weiner, eds., *Robert Oppenheimer: Letters and Recollections* (Cambridge, Mass.: Harvard University Press, 1980), p. 289.

12. See R. W. Reid, *Tongues of Conscience: War and the Scientist's Dilemma* (London: Constable & Co., 1969), pp. 181–85, for a discussion of the controversy among scientists apprised of the project, especially at Chicago, about whether or not to drop the bombs on cities such as Hiroshima and Nagasaki (an early possibility had been Kyoto), or to demonstrate the weapon's power in a desert or on an island far from population centers. See also Morton Grodzins and Eugene Rabinowitch, eds., *The Atomic Age: Scientists in National and World Affairs* (New York: Basic Books, 1963); Bertrand Goldschmidt, *Les Rivalités atomiques 1939–1966* (Paris: Fayard, 1967).

13. See General Leslie Groves, *Now It Can Be Told: The Story of the Manhattan Project* (New York: Harper & Row, 1962).

14. Oppenheimer was not the first scientist working on lethal weapons to express such hopes. Alfred Nobel stated, four years before his death, that "on the day that two army corps can mutually annihilate each other in a second, all civilized nations will surely recoil with horror and disband their troops." See Reid, *Tongues of Conscience*, p. 19.

15. Oppenheimer, *Letters and Recollections*, p. 317.

16. Ibid., pp. 291–92. See also works cited in note 12 above, and Martin J. Sherwin, *A World Destroyed: The Atomic Bomb and the Grand Alliance* (New York: Alfred A, Knopf, 1975).

17. Robert A. Dahl, "Atomic Energy and the Democratic Process," in "The Impact of Atomic Energy," *Annals of the American Academy of Political and Social Science* 290 (November 1953):1–6; passage quoted on pp. 2–3. See also Harry Howe Ransom, *Can American Democracy Survive Cold War?* (Garden City, N.Y.: Doubleday & Co., 1963).

18. Adm. Bobby R. Inman, "Speech to the American Association for the Advancement of Science," *Aviation Week and Space Technology* 116 (February 8, 1982):10–11. See also sources quoted in Harry Howe Ransom, "The Uses (and Abuses) of Secret Power," *Worldview* 18 (May 1975):11–15.

19. Nicholas de B. Katzenbach, "Foreign Policy, Public Opinion, and Secrecy," *Foreign Affairs* 52 (October 1973):1–19.

20. See Alva Myrdal, *The Game of Disarmament* (New York: Pantheon Books, 1976), pp. 302–4; Edward Teller, "The Feasibility of Arms Control and the Principle of Openness," *Daedalus* 89 (1960):781–99.

21. Teller, "Feasibility of Arms Control," pp. 795–97.

22. See *The Senator Gravel Edition: The Pentagon Papers* (Boston: Beacon Press, 1971), four vols. See also Hannah Arendt, "Lying in Politics," *Crises of the Republic* (New York: Harcourt Brace Jovanovich, 1972), pp. 3–47; Leonard B. Boudin, "The Ellsberg Case: Citizen Disclosure," in Franck and Weisband, eds., *Secrecy and Foreign Policy*, pp. 290–311; Daniel Ellsberg, *Papers on the War* (New York: Simon & Schuster, 1972); Halperin and Hoffman, *Top Secret*; Peter Schrag, *Test of Loyalty: Daniel Ellsberg and the Rituals of Secret Government* (New York: Simon & Schuster, 1974); Sanford Ungar, *The Papers and the Papers* (New York: E. P. Dutton & Co. 1972).

23. *Pentagon Papers*, Introduction, 1: xi.

24. Henry Kissinger, *The White House Years* (Boston: Little, Brown & Co., 1979),

p. 730. Kissinger also argued that the documents, when published, unfairly injured reputations and were selective and one-sided.

25. Quoted in Schrag, *Test of Loyalty*, p. 41.

26. See Daniel Ellsberg, "The Quagmire Myth and the Stalemate Machine," *Public Policy*, 19 (Spring 1971):262–63.

27. *New York Times Co. v. United States*, 403 U.S. 713 (1971) at 762–63.

28. See Floyd Abrams, "The Pentagon Papers a Decade Later," *New York Times Magazine*, June 7, 1981, pp. 22–25, 72–95.

29. It was lawlessness on the part of the government that brought to a halt its suit accusing Ellsberg and Russo of espionage, conspiracy, and theft of government property. President Nixon had ordered the office of Ellsberg's physician to be burglarized, his and Russo's telephones to be surreptitiously tapped, and a number of other invasions of their legal rights. Consequently, the suit was dismissed in June 1973, before a determination had been made with respect to the allegations. See Melville B. Nimmer, "National Security Secrets v. Free Speech: The Issues Left Undecided in the Ellsberg Case," *Stanford Law Review* 26 (1974):311–33.

Chapter XIV. **Whistleblowing and Leaking**

1. Henrik Ibsen, *An Enemy of the People*, (1882), in *Henrik Ibsen: The Complete Major Prose Plays*, trans, and ed. Rolf Fjelde (New York: New American Library, 1965), pp. 281–386; passage quoted on p. 384.

2. I draw, for this chapter, on my earlier essays on whistleblowing: "Whistleblowing and Professional Responsibilities," in Daniel Callahan and Sissela Bok, eds., *Ethics Teaching in Higher Education* (New York: Plenum Press, 1980), pp. 277–95 (reprinted, slightly altered, in *New York University Education Quarterly* 11 (Summer 1980):2–10; "Blowing the Whistle," in Joel Fleishman, Lance Liebman, and Mark Moore, eds., *Public Duties: The Moral Obligations of Officials* (Cambridge, Mass.: Harvard University Press, 1981), pp. 204–21.

3. Institute of Electrical and Electronics Engineers, Code of Ethics for Engineers, art. 4, *IEEE Spectrum* 12 (February 1975):65.

4. Code of Ethics for Government Service, passed by the U.S. House of Representatives in the 85th Congress, 1958, and applying to all government employees and office holders.

5. U.S., Congress, House of Representatives, Committee on Post Office and Civil Service, Subcommittee on Compensation and Employee Benefits, *Forced Retirement/ Psychiatric Fitness of Duty Exams*, 95th Cong, 2d sess., November 3, 1978, pp. 2–4. See also Subcommittee Hearings, February 28, 1978. Psychiatric referral for whistleblowers has become institutionalized in government service, but it is not uncommon in private employment. Even persons who make accusations without being employed in the organization they accuse, moreover, have been classified as unstable and thus as unreliable witnesses. See, for example, Jonas Robitscher, "Stigmatization and Stone-walling: The Ordeal of Martha Mitchell," *Journal of Psychohistory* 6 (Winter 1979):393–407.

6. Carol S. Kennedy, "Whistle-blowing: Contribution or Catastrophe?" Address to the American Association for the Advancement of Science, February 15, 1978, p. 8.

7. For analyses and descriptions of whistleblowing, see: Rosemary Chalk and Frank von Hippel, "Due Process for Dissembling 'Whistle-Blowers,'" *Technology Review* 81 (June–July 1979):49–55; Louis Clark, "The Sound of Professional Suicide," *The Barrister* 5 (Summer 1978):10–19; Helen Dudar, "The Price of Blowing the Whistle," *New York Times Magazine*, October 30, 1977, pp. 41–54; John Edsall, *Scientific Freedom and Responsibility*; David W. Ewing, *Freedom Inside the Organization* (New York: E. P. Dutton & Co., 1977); Nader, Petkas, and Blackwell, *Whistle Blowing*; Charles Peters and Taylor Branch, *Blowing the Whistle* (New York: Praeger Publishers, 1972); Alan F. Westin

and Stephan Salisbury, eds., *Individual Rights in the Corporation* (New York: Pantheon Books, 1980); Alan F. Westin, *Whistle Blowing! Loyalty and Dissent in the Corporation* (New York: McGraw-Hill Book Co., 1980).

8. Judith P. Swazey and Stephen R. Scheer suggest that when whistleblowers expose fraud in clinical research, colleagues respond *more* negatively to the whistleblowers who report the fraudulent research than to the person whose conduct has been reported. See "The Whistleblower as a Deviant Professional: Professional Norms and Responses to Fraud in Clinical Research," Workshop on Whistleblowing in Biomedical Research, Washington, D.C., September 1981, to be published.

9. See Peters and Branch, *Blowing the Whistle*; Carl Bernstein and Robert Woodward, *All the President's Men* (New York: Simon & Schuster, 1974).

10. On leaking, see Bernstein and Woodward, *All the President's Men*; Douglass Cater, *The Fourth Branch of Government* (Boston: Houghton Mifflin Co., 1959); Rourke, *Secrecy and Publicity*; David Wise, "The President Leaks a Document," *The Politics of Lying* (New York: Random House, 1973), pp. 117–33; Halperin and Hoffman, *Top Secret*; and the works cited above on whistleblowing and in note 14 on resignation in protest.

11. Rourke, *Secrecy and Publicity*, p. 198.

12. See Robert J. Baum and Albert Flores, ed., *Ethical Problems in Engineering* (Troy, N.Y.: Center for the Study of the Human Dimensions of Science and Technology, 1978), pp. 227–47; Chalk and von Hippel, "Due Process for Dissenting 'Whistle-Blowers,'" pp. 4–55.

13. This case is adapted from Clark, "The Sound of Professional Suicide."

14. On resignation in protest, see Albert Hirschman, *Exit, Voice, and Loyalty* (Cambridge, Mass.: Harvard University Press, 1970); Brian Barry, in a review of Hirschman's book in *British Journal of Political Science* 4 (1974):79–104, has pointed out that "exit" and "voice" are not alternatives but independent variations that may occur separately or together. Both leaking and whistleblowing represent "voice." They can be undertaken while staying on at work, or before one's voluntary exit, or simultaneously with it, or after it; they can also have the consequence of involuntary or forced "exit" through dismissal or being "frozen out" even though retained at work. See also Edward Weisband and Thomas M. Franck, *Resignation in Protest* (New York: Viking Press, 1975); James Thomson, "Getting Out and Speaking Out," *Foreign Policy*, no. 13 (Winter 1973–1974), pp. 49–69; Joel L. Fleishman and Bruce L. Payne, *Ethical Dilemmas and the Education of Policymakers* (Hastings-on-Hudson, N.Y.: Hastings Center, 1980).

15. Alan Westin discusses "swallowing" the whistle in *Whistle Blowing!*, pp. 10–13. For a discussion of debate concerning whistleblowing, see Rosemary Chalk, "The Miner's Canary," *Bulletin of the Atomic Scientists* 38 (February 1982): pp. 16–22.

16. John C. Coffee, in "Beyond the Shut-eyed Sentry: Toward a Theoretical View of Corporate Misconduct and an Effective Legal Response," *Virginia Law Review* 63 (1977):1099–1278, gives an informed and closely reasoned account of such "information blockages," such "filtering out," and of possible remedies. See also Christopher Stone, *Where the Law Ends: The Social Control of Corporate Behavior* (New York: Harper & Row, 1975), pp. 201–16.

17. David W. Ewing, "The Employee's Right to Speak Out: The Managment Perspective," *Civil Liberties Review* 5 (September–October 1978):10–15.

18. David W. Ewing, "What Business Thinks About Employee Rights," *Harvard Business Review* 55 (September–October 1977):81–94.

19. Alan Westin, "Michigan's Law to Protect the Whistle Blowers," *Wall Street Journal*, April 31, 1981, p. 18.

20. Ibid.

21. For a discussion of legal approaches, see Alfred G. Feliu, "Discharge of Professional

Employees: Protecting Against Dismissal for Acts Within a Professional Code of Ethics," *Columbia Human Rights Law Review* 11 (1979–1980):149–87; Westin, *Whistle Blowing!*

22. Environmental Protection Agency, "Toxic Substances Control Act," *Federal Register*, Thursday, March 16, 1978, pt. 5.

Chapter XV. *Intrusive Social Science Research*

1. Durkheim, *Elementary Forms of Religious Life*, p. 429. When Durkheim and others use the word "science" with respect to such studies, they voice an aspiration and a value judgment as to what should and should not count as scientific inquiry that are coming under increasing debate.

2. Ibid. p. 430.

3. Florence Kluckhohn, "The Participant-Observer Technique in Small Communities," *American Journal of Sociology* 46 (1940): p. 338.

4. Leon Festinger, Henry W. Riecken, and Stanley Schachter, *When Prophecy Fails* (Minneapolis: University of Minnesota Press, 1956), chap. 1. For discussions of millenarian societies, see Ernest Lee Tuveson, *Millennium and Utopia* (New York: Harper & Row, 1964); Sylvia Thrupp, ed., *Millennial Dreams in Action* (The Hague: Mouton & Co., 1962); Norman Cohn, *The Pursuit of the Millennium* (New York: Oxford University Press, 1970).

5. Festinger, *When Prophecy Fails*, pp. 30–31.

6. Ibid., p. 237.

7. Ibid., p. 240.

8. Ibid., p. 252.

9. For discussion of research methods and of the purposes for which they are used, see Carl B. Klockars and Finbarr W. O'Connor, eds., *Deviance and Decency: The Ethics of Research with Human Subjects* (Beverly Hills, Calif.: Sage Publications, 1979); Edward Diener and Rick Crandall, *Ethics in Social and Behavioral Research* (Chicago: University of Chicago Press, 1978); Martin Bulmer, ed., *Social Research Ethics* (New York: Holmes & Meier Publishers, 1982); Kai T. Erikson, "A Comment on Disguised Observation in Sociology," *Social Problems* 14 (1967):366–73; Stuart W. Cook, "Ethical Issues in the Conduct of Research in the Social Sciences," in Stuart W. Cook, Claire Selltiz, and Lawrence S. Wrightsman, eds., *Research Methods in Social Relations* (New York: Holt, Rinehart, & Winston, 1976), pp. 200–49; Herbert Kelman, "Privacy and Research with Human Beings," *Journal of Social Issues* 33 (1977):169–95; Julius Roth, "Comments on Secret Observation," *Social Problems* 9 (1962):283–84; Oscar Ruebhausen and Orville G. Brim, "Privacy and Behavioral Research," *American Psychologist* 21 (1966):423–44; Donald P. Warwick, *The Teaching of Ethics in the Social Sciences* (Hastings-on-Hudson, N.Y.: Hastings Center, 1980); Joan Cassell and Murray L. Wax, eds., "Ethical Problems of Fieldwork," *Social Problems* 27 (1980):259–377; Shils, "Social Inquiry and the Autonomy of the Individual," in Lerner, ed., *Human Meaning of the Social Sciences*.

10. C. Wright Mills, "The Bureaucratic Ethics," in Maurice Stein and Arthur Vidich, eds., *Sociology on Trial* (Englewood Cliffs, N.J.: Prentice-Hall, 1963), pp. 12–25; passage quoted on p. 22.

11. See David Maybury-Lewis, "Don't Put the Blame on Anthropologists," *New York Times*, March 15, 1974.

12. Sometimes anthropologists are even expressly requested to study materials formerly kept secret, by cultures fearing to lose their traditions. Thus the people of Telefolmin, in New Guinea, recently called in a Canadian anthropologist to collect the sacred lore from a cult center about to be sacrificed to the construction of copper mines. They had decided to do away with the site, but feared the loss of sacred lore. In that case there

was, of course, no intrusiveness or deception in the research. See "Prompt Assistance for Telefolmin," Newsletter, *Cultural Survival* 3 (Spring 1979).

13. For a discussion of the uses of social science research, see Charles E. Lindbloom and David K. Cohen, *Usable Knowledge: Social Science and Social Problem Solving* (New Haven, Conn.: Yale University Press, 1979).

14. Warwick, *Teaching of Ethics*, p. 34; Michael T. Klare, *War Without End* (New York: Alfred A. Knopf, 1972), pp. 88–116; Horowitz, ed., *Rise and Fall of Project Camelot*; Ralph L. Beals, *Politics of Social Research* (Chicago: Aldine Publishing Co., 1969).

15. Steven Weinberg, "Reflection of a Working Scientist," *Daedalus* 103 (1974):45.

16. See Warwick, *Teaching of Ethics*; Alvin W. Gouldner, "Anti-Minotaur: The Myth of a Value Free Sociology," in Stein and Vidich, eds., *Sociology on Trial*, pp. 35–52; Gunnar Myrdal, *Value in Social Theory* (London: Routledge & Kegan Paul, 1958); Gunnar Myrdal, *Objectivity in Social Research* (New York: Pantheon Books, 1969).

17. Max Weber, *The Methodology of the Social Sciences*, trans. and ed. Edward A. Shils and Henry A. Finch (Glencoe, Ill.: Free Press, 1949).

18. Laud Humphreys, *Tearoom Trade* (Chicago: Aldine Publishing Co., 1970).

19. Jaime de Angelo, "Letter to Ruth Benedict," reprinted in Margaret Mead, *An Anthropologist at Work: Writings of Ruth Benedict* (Boston: Houghton Mifflin Co., 1959), p. 296. See also Gerald Berreman, *Behind Many Masks*, Society for Applied Anthropology, Monograph no. 4 (Ithaca, N.Y.:1962); Joseph J. Jorgenson, "On Ethics and Anthropology," *Current Anthropology* 12 (1971):321–34.

20. See J. A. Barnes, "Some Ethical Problems in Modern Fieldwork," *British Journal of Sociology* 14 (1970):118–54; Shils, "Social Inquiry." For a recent discussion of the ethics of fieldwork, see William F. May, "Doing Ethics: The Bearing of Ethical Theories on Fieldwork," *Social Problems* 27 (February 1980):358–70.

21. Herbert Kelman, "Research, Behavioral," *Encyclopedia of Bioethics* (New York: Macmillan Co., 1978), 4:1470–81.

22. See, for example, American Political Science Association, Ethical Problems of Academic Political Scientists, 1968; American Anthropological Association, Professional Ethics, 1973; American Sociological Association, Ethical Code, 1971.

23. American Psychological Association, Ethical Principles of Psychologists, *American Psychologist* 36 (1981):633–38; passage quoted on p. 638.

24. Shils, "Social Inquiry," pp. 116–17.

25. Timothy C. Brock and Carolyn del Giudice, "Stealing and Temporal Orientation," *Journal of Abnormal and Social Psychology* 66 (1963):91–94.

26. See Roger Homan and Martin Bulmer, "On the Merits of Covert Methods: A Dialogue," in Bulmer, ed., *Social Research Ethics*, pp. 105–21.

27. Thomas H. Murray, "Learning to Deceive," *Hastings Center Report* 10 (April 1980):11–14. See also Jorgenson, "On Ethics and Anthropology."

28. See Sidney M. Jourard, *Disclosing Man to Himself* (Princeton, N.J.: D. Van Nostrand Co., 1968); Murray, "Learning to Deceive"; Donald P. Warwick, "Deceptive Research: Social Scientists Ought to Stop Lying," *Psychology Today*, February 1975, pp. 38–40.

29. Gershom Scholem, *Sabbatai Sevi; The Mystical Messiah* (1957), trans. R. J. Zwi Werblowsky (Princeton, N.J.: Princeton University Press, 1973).

30. See, for example, Marilyn Evans, "Awaiting Heaven's Call: Rapturists Are Certain They'll Ascend by Saturday," *Boston Globe*, August 6, 1981, p. 24.

31. See Shils, "Social Inquiry"; Erikson, "Disguised Inquiry."

32. Margaret Mead, "The Human Study of Human Beings," *Science* 133 (January 20, 1961):163.

33. Gideon Sjoberg, "Ethics, the 'Hidden Side' of Bureaucracy, and Social Research," in Paul Nejelski, ed., *Social Research in Conflict with Law and Ethics* (Cambridge, Mass.: Ballinger Publishing Co., 1976), pp. 35–50.

34. Jack D. Douglas, *Investigative Social Research* (London: Sage Publications, 1976), p. 28.

35. See *Lying*, chap. 9, "Lying to Liars," pp. 123–33.

36. Douglas, *Investigative Social Research*, p. xv.

37. Mead, "Research with Human Beings," p. 376.

Chapter XVI. **Investigative Journalism**

1. James Thurber, *The Years with Ross* (Boston: Little, Brown & Co., 1957), pp. 28, 210–12.

2. Jared L. Manley, "April Fool!" *The New Yorker*, August 14, 1937, pp. 22–26.

3. Boris Sidis, *Philistine and Genius* (Boston: R. G. Badger, 1917), p. 113. Sidis also wrote *The Source and Aim of Human Progress* (Boston: R. G. Badger, 1919), as well as experimental studies of sleep, of "nervous ills," and of the psychology of suggestion.

4. For a discussion of the role of publicity in William Sidis's life, and of the education he received, see Kathleen Montour, "William Sidis, the Broken Twig," *American Psychologist* 32 (April 1977):265–79.

5. Manley, "April Fool!" p. 25. (The title refers to Sidis's April 1 birthdate.) The reader is not told by what stratagem the unnamed young woman managed to interview Sidis; it cannot have been by requesting an interview for the magazine in the normal manner, since his lawsuit would have had to be differently framed if he had consented to such a request.

6. 34 F. Supp. 19, 20 (S.D.N.Y. 1938). Sidis also sued for libel on account of a small inaccuracy and was actually awarded a small sum in compensation for libel, even though he lost his suit for invasion of privacy. For a discussion of the cases and their background, see Emile Karafiol, "The Right to Privacy and the Sidis Case," *Georgia Law Review* 12 (1978):513–38.

7. Thurber, *The Years with Ross*, p. 212.

8. *Sidis* v. *F-R Publishing Corp.*, 113 F.2d 806 (2d Cir. 1940).

9. Emile Karafiol suggested this formulation in a personal communication.

10. Obituary, *New York Times*, July 18, 1944, p. 21. Some have asserted that Sidis took his own life, but there is no clear evidence for such an assertion.

11. *New York Times*, October 31, 1965, p. 1, and November 1, 1965, p. 1.

12. See Dennis F. Thompson, "The Private Lives of Public Officials," in Joel Fleishman, Lance Liebman, and Mark Moore, eds., *Public Duties: The Moral Obligations of Government Officials* (Cambridge, Mass.: Harvard University Press, 1981), pp. 221–48.

13. Society of Professional Journalists, Sigma Delta Chi, Code of Ethics, adopted 1926 and revised 1973. For an account of the teaching of journalistic ethics, see Clifford G. Christians and Catherine L. Covert, *Teaching Ethics in Journalism Education* (Hastings-on-Hudson, N.Y.: Hastings Center, 1980).

14. Jeremy Bentham, "Anarchical Fallacies," *Works of Jeremy Bentham*, 2:501.

15. U.S., *Constitution*, Amend. 1. See also Thomas I. Emerson, "Legal Foundations of the Right to Know," *Washington University Law Quarterly*, 1976, no. 1, pp. 1–25; Harold Cross, *The People's Right to Know* (New York: Columbia University Press, 1953).

16. Laurence Tribe, "Accommodating Rights to Know, Rights Not to Know, Open Minds, and Closed Communities," *American Constitutional Law* (Mineola, N.Y.: Foundation Press, 1978), p. 675. See also Louis Henkin, "The Right to Know and the Duty to Withhold: The Case of the Pentagon Papers," *University of Pennsylvania Law Review* 120 (1971):271–80.

17. Ronald Dworkin, "Does the Public Have a Right to Know?" in U.S., Department of Health and Human Services, Ethics Advisory Board, *Appendix: The Request of the*

National Institutes of Health for a Limited Exemption from the Freedom of Information Act, 1979.

18. I am grateful to Joel Feinberg for the suggestion that such a compensatory relationship might exist between the two sets of claims. For a discussion of the hortatory and dynamic uses of the language of rights, see Ruth Macklin, "Moral Concerns and Appeals to Rights and Duties," *Hastings Center Report* 6 (1976):31–8.

19. U.S., Congress, Senate, 89th Cong., 1st sess., 1965, S. Rept. 813, p. 5.

20. Cited in James Russell Wiggins, *Freedom of Secrecy* (New York: Oxford University Press, 1964), p. 7.

21. See William L. Rivers, *The Adversaries: Politics and the Press* (Boston: Beacon Press, 1970).

22. Zay N. Smith and Pamela Zekman, *The Mirage* (New York: Random House, 1979).

23. Günter Wallraff, *Wallraff the Undesirable Journalist*, trans. Steve Gooch and Paul Knight (London: Pluto Press, 1978); *"Wir Brauchen Dich"* (Munich: Rütten & Loening Verlag, 1966); *Von einem der auszog und das Fürchten lernte* (Munich: Willi Weisman Verlag, 1970); *Neue Reportagen, Untersuchungen und Lehrbeispiele,* 1972; *Die Reportagen,* 1976; *Aufdeckung einer Verschwoerung,* 1976; and *Der Aufmacher: Der Mann, der bei Bild Hans Esser war,* 1977 (the last four published at Cologne: Verlag Kiepenheuer & Witsch).

24. Wallraff, *Der Aufmacher.* p. 223 (my translation).

25. Ibid., p. 10.

26. Ibid., p. 224.

27. Quoted in *Wallraff the Undesirable Journalist,* p. 8 (from his testimony at an earlier trial).

28. Ibid. pp. 2–3. It is not clear whether the author of this statement is Wallraff speaking in the third person about himself, or an unidentified other.

29. David Shaw, "Deception—Honest Tool of Reporting," *Los Angeles Times,* September 20, 1979, p. 29.

30. Bernstein and Woodward, *All the President's Men.* See also David Anderson and Peter Benjaminson, *Investigative Reporting* (Bloomington: Indiana University Press, 1976), chap. 2; John L. Hulteng, *The Messenger's Motives: Ethical Problems of the News Media* (Englewood Cliffs, N.J.: Prentice-Hall, 1976); Paul N. Williams, *Investigative Reporting and Editing* (Englewood Cliffs, N.J.: Prentice-Hall, 1978), chap. 5.

Chapter XVII. *Undercover Police Operations*

1. Peter K. Manning, *Police Work: The Social Organization of Policing* (Cambridge, Mass.: MIT Press, 1977); William K. Muir, *Police: Street Corner Politicians* (Chicago: University of Chicago Press, 1977); Jonathan Rubinstein, *City Police* (New York: Farrar, Straus & Giroux, 1973); Lawrence W. Sherman, *Scandal and Reform* (Berkeley: University of California Press, 1978); William A. Westley, "Secrecy and the Police," *Social Forces* 34 (1956):254–57; William A. Westley, *Violence in the Police: A Sociological Study of Law, Custom, and Morality* (Cambridge, Mass.: MIT Press, 1970), chap. 4.

2. See Roger S. Young, assistant director of the FBI, quoted by Leslie Maitland in "At the Heart of the Abscam Debate," *New York Times Magazine,* July 25, 1982, p. 22.

3. James Q. Wilson, "The Changing FBI—The Road to Abscam," *Public Interest,* no. 58 (1980), pp. 3–14.

4. The quotation is taken from the address at the Hastings Center Conference on Undercover Activities, 1981, by Philip Heymann, who was assistant attorney general in charge of the Criminal Division during the period of the ABSCAM investigation.

5. Gilbert Geis, ed., *White Collar Criminal: The Offender in Business and the Professions*

(New York: Atherton Press, 1968); U.S., Department of Justice, *National Priorities for the Investigation and Prosecution of White Collar Crime*, Report of the Attorney General, 1980.

6. American Management Association, *Crimes Against Business Project—Background, Findings, and Recommendations* (New York, 1977). While these figures are regarded as the best estimates currently available, they are still only estimates. Moreover, the AMA did not include offenses such as tax fraud, toxic-waste disposal, or other forms of fraud which, if added, could easily double the estimate.

7. Carl J. Friedrich, "Corruption," *Pathology of Politics*, pp. 127–71. See, on corruption, Arnold J. Heidenheimer, ed., *Political Corruption: Readings in Comparative Analysis* (New York: Holt, Rinehart & Winston, 1970).

8. I have discussed this question in *Lying*, chap. 10, "Lying to Enemies," pp. 134–45.

9. Paul Chevigny, *Cops and Rebels: A Study of Provocation* (New York: Pantheon Books, 1972); Gary T. Marx, "Thoughts on a Neglected Category of Social Movement Participant: Agents Provocateurs and Informants," *American Journal of Sociology* 80 (1974):402–42; Geoffrey R. Stone, "The Scope of the Fourth Amendment: Privacy and the Police Use of Spies, Secret Agents, and Informers," *American Bar Foundation Research Journal*, 1976, pp. 1193–1271; James Q. Wilson, *The Investigators* (New York: Basic Books, 1978).

10. Gary T. Marx, "The New Police Undercover Work," *Urban Life* 8 (January 1980):399–446.

11. Mark H. Moore, "Invisible Offenses: A Challenge to Minimally Intrusive Enforcement," forthcoming in Gerald Caplan, ed., *ABSCAM Ethics: Moral and Ethical Issues in Deceptive Investigations* (Washington, D.C.: The Police Foundation, 1982).

12. See Carl Klockars, "Jonathan Wild and the Modern Sting," in James A. Inciardi and Charles E. Faupel, eds., *History and Crime: Implications for the Contemporary Criminal Justice* (Beverly Hills, Calif.: Sage Publications, 1980), pp. 225–60; Gary To Marx, "Who Really Gets Stung? Some Issues Raised by the New Police Undercover Work," *Crime and Delinquency*, 13 (April 1982):165–67, 185–89.

13. Chief Justice Warren, *Sherman* v. *United States* 356 U.S. 369 (1932), at 372.

14. See, for a discussion of these views, *United States* v. *Russell*, 411 U.S. 423 (1973), at 423–49.

15. John C. Noonan, "Bribery," *Encyclopedia of Crime and Justice* (New York: Free Press, forthcoming).

16. See, for accounts of this experience, Muir, *Police*; Marx, "The New Police Undercover Work," pp. 426–28.

17. See Frank J. Donner, *The Age of Surveillance: The Aims and Methods of America's Political Intelligence System* (New York: Alfred A. Knopf, 1980).

18. For a discussion of these questions, see Sanford Levinson, "Infiltration and Betrayal: A Legal and Theoretical Analysis," *The State and Structure of Intimacy*, (New York: Basic Books, forthcoming); Posner, *Economics of Justice*, pp. 321–22; Stone, "The Scope of the Fourth Amendment."

Chapter XVIII. Conclusion

1. Joseph Conrad, *Under Western Eyes* (1911; New York: Penguin Books, 1957); Simmel, *Sociology*.

2. Charles Percy Snow, *Science and Government* (Cambridge, Mass.: Harvard University Press, 1961), p. 73. See also his *Appendix to Science and Government* (Cambridge, Mass.: Harvard University Press, 1962), pp. 24–30.

3. A few years earlier, in 1979, a case in the United States had troubled even many

who would ordinarily reject any interference with research from open sources. The magazine *The Progressive* planned to publish an article, based on information acquired entirely lawfully, concerning details of the construction of hydrogen bombs. The government obtained a temporary injunction against publication of the article. The injunction was appealed, but the case was declared moot when a Wisconsin newspaper published a similar article.

Subject Index

Index of Names

ABOUT THE AUTHOR

Sissela Bok was born in Sweden and educated in Switzerland, France, and the United States. She has taught courses in ethics and decision-making at Harvard Medical School and the John F. Kennedy School of Government, and is a lecturer on the Core Curriculum at Harvard University. She is the author of *Lying: Moral Choice in Public and Private Life* (Pantheon, 1978).